George Eliot and Blackmail

Alexander Welsh

Harvard University Press
Cambridge, Massachusetts
London, England
1985

Printed in the United States of America

10 9 8 7 6 5 4 3 2 1

Publication of this book has been aided by a grant
from the Hyder Edward Rollins Fund.

This book is printed on acid-free paper,
and its binding materials have been chosen for
strength and durability.

Library of Congress Cataloging in Publication Data

Welsh, Alexander.
George Eliot and blackmail.

Includes index.
1. Eliot, George, 1819–1880—Political and social
views.   2. Extortion in literature.   3. Secrecy in
literature.   4. Privacy in literature.   5. Social ethics
in literature.   6. Knowledge, Sociology of—History—
19th century.   I. Title.
PR4692.E92W4   1985   823'.8   85-773
ISBN 0-674-34872-9

For Tom Welsh

2271174

Preface

After writing *The Mill on the Floss* in 1859–1860, George Eliot turned to an aspect of society that must have been evident to her for some time but now forcibly drew her attention: a relation between knowledge and accountability that is still without a name but may easily be recognized in the criminal form blackmail. Beginning with *Silas Marner*, stories of blackmail appeared in her novels, and she was by no means the only novelist to employ such stories at this time. This book attempts to answer the question of why blackmail took hold of the modern imagination. Essentially it is a book about the later novels of George Eliot and the culture of information.

In 1859 another Victorian, a brilliant student of his times who did not write novels, addressed the danger to individual freedom from public opinion. The original inspiration of Mill's *On Liberty* was his reading of De Tocqueville twenty-five years before, but now it seemed imperative to warn against an encroachment of society upon the individual that was destined "to grow more and more formidable." Mill was very clear that the threat to liberty was more from public opinion than from legislation, more social than political. He was aware that it was a modern and still latent development of society that threatened to become "the vital question of the future." I do not suppose that he could be fully aware of the irony that he himself, like most Victorians who gave thought to such matters, believed very strongly in public opinion as a force for progress in the first place, and preferred it to legislation. Public opinion was the socially efficacious side of knowledge, the cultivation of which is the premise of the strong utilitarian arguments of *On Liberty*. Mill understood, when he wrote that "every one lives under the eye of a hostile and dreaded censorship" (his metaphor for myriad forms of social pressure), that we are in some degree constrained by the knowledge that is a general condition of social advancement. But it was the novelists of the following decade who explored the felt sensation of the forms of knowledge and accountability by inventing a great many blackmail plots—plots that very likely exceeded the actual practice of reputational blackmail and certainly preceded the modern use of the word in the sense of threatening to reveal secrets. Their fictions tell us more nearly what we need to know on such a subject than either social theory or the "facts" of history as usually presented, for it is the possibility of blackmail, the fear of blackmail, and even the pleasure of imagined blackmail that help explain how a society founded on information begins to feel to the individuals who constitute it. Because of increased awareness of the burden of information in the twentieth century, moreover, we are better able to appreciate George Eliot's and Mill's contribution in this area than were their contemporaries.

The experience of the Victorians has led to our own, and their fictions to our fictions. To illustrate the imagined role of blackmail, therefore, I have described in the introductory part of the book a popular film produced about halfway in years between the time of George Eliot's death and this writing, and then compared the film with a popular novel of the 1860s in order to make a few points about typical Victorian concerns. The second part of the book surveys the growth of knowledge and communications in England and some of the problems of a society increasingly dependent upon information. These chapters make almost no use of George Eliot; they are about the general conditions of blackmail. The rise of publicity over the last two hundred years has changed the significance of privacy and created a real or imagined need for secrecy. A number of students of the period, mainly influenced by Michel Foucault, have now begun to take seriously the strains of mystery and watchfulness in the Victorian novel; and my own understanding of the relation of knowledge to secrecy has been influenced by the sociology of Georg Simmel. There is a case for arguing that secrets have a history, which is also the history of information.

In the third part I take up two specific conditions of George Eliot's writing, her pseudonymity and her relation to George Henry Lewes. The so-called pastoral novels concern me chiefly as they deliberately distance but also reflect these conditions, especially in their treatment of reputation. Though *The Mill on the Floss,* the last of the early novels, is generally autobiographical, its heroine's life differs most conspicuously from the novelist's life in being all of one piece. Maggie Tulliver's death ensures that she will not lead a second life divorced from the first, as Marian Evans did in London and as many other persons did in the nineteenth century. During the writing of this novel, George Eliot's identity became known. This eventuality, which might have been foreseen, played a part in moving her to describe lives that had been broken off and resumed, and made her more sensitive to the conditions of living in the modern world associated with the prevalence of information and a peculiarly abstract sense of accountability. It is at this time, in writing to her publisher about *Silas Marner,* that George Eliot characterized her novels as belonging to "successive mental phases," and it is at this time that reputational blackmail makes its appearance in her work.

The fourth and longest part of the book is devoted to the major novels of the later period, each one of which was a remarkable experiment having to do with the management of discontinuous lives and the bearing of information upon them. Above all, I have tried to show what these novels teach us about the culture of information. I do not mean to suggest that this is the only way to read them, but simply what seems to me, and perhaps to others, most important at this time. Still, *Romola, Middlemarch,* and *Daniel Deronda* demand quite different approaches, and the previous kinds of criticism devoted to these novels, particularly *Middlemarch,* has also been a factor in determining how to treat each one. I have tried to respect the integrity of each work as a narrative, and I have also treated them sequentially as part of George Eliot's canon, since one of my purposes has been to complement U. C. Knoepflmacher's and Henry Auster's books on the early novels. *Silas Marner* has here been subordinated to *Romola,* and *Felix Holt* to *Middlemarch;* and as the culmination of so much that is modern in George Eliot, *Daniel Deronda* has been studied in the fullest detail. Neither as individual texts nor as a canon do I regard these works of literature as especially privileged. George Eliot's novels are superior to most, but to regard them as other than acts of communication from author to reader would be to ignore the general assumptions of this book. To express this position, I might borrow the concluding words of Jerome Beaty's study of the compo-

sition of the novel that most people agree is George Eliot's greatest—
"What, in 1869–1872, George Eliot had to say is *Middlemarch.*"

It is because George Eliot had so much to say to us in two decades
of her life that we continue to read her work. Her achievement was in
some ways representative of its time and in other ways predictive of
the future. The moral temper of Victorian fiction has always been
evident, but whereas Lord Acton, in a review of J. W. Cross's *Life,*
called George Eliot "a consummate expert in the pathology of conscience," we may be prepared to think of her as expert in the pathology of consciousness. In the Freudian model of the mind, the
threatened revelation of repressed memories is like blackmail, and in
the last part of the book I suggest that the psychoanalytic movement
follows naturally from the first century of the age of information. The
social relations described in nineteenth-century novels, especially,
point the way to Freud. But some radical selection needed to be made
even among novels of blackmail: to lift some of the burden of proof
from George Eliot and bring the argument to a close, I have reverted
briefly to an American classic that impressed the English novelist
nearly as much as it did Henry James.

One cannot pursue any question about George Eliot very far without realizing that she was in touch with the best thinking of her time
and acknowledging that she has her following today among the best
students of Victorian literature. Long before I thought of writing
about her work, I was fortunate to become friends with Gordon S.
Haight, Barbara Hardy, U. C. Knoepflmacher, and George Levine,
and I need hardly say how important their example has been to me in
the present undertaking. While editing *Nineteenth-Century Fiction*
from 1975 to 1981, I was repeatedly exposed to new work on George
Eliot; and in 1980 I was very kindly invited to conferences commem-
orating the novelist at the University of Leicester and Rutgers University, where I met or renewed acquaintance with many more
scholars in the field. These experiences, rewarding in themselves,
have helped me greatly with this book, and I wish to express my gratitude to all who are associated with them. I also wish to thank the
members of three seminars on George Eliot's novels, and particularly
Bonnie Lisle, who has often shared her knowledge with me. Joan
Maltese expertly retyped each chapter after it was revised and sometimes revised again. I have hectored too many friends about blackmail, and nearly all have responded with stimulating thoughts on the

subject. To Ruth Bernard Yeazell I owe more than I can say, for her arguing of many points, her constructive reading of the manuscript, and her companionship. The book is dedicated to a son whose persistence at work and play has convinced me that long projects like this one must be pleasurable.

A book about information, even the perverse results of information, enlists the services of very many writers, editors, publishers, printers, and others. The Law, Biomedical, and Research Libraries and the English Reading Room of the University of California, Los Angeles, have preserved the requisite information and made it freely available. I am especially grateful to the University for a term of sabbatical leave and to the UCLA Research Committee for financing a visit to the British Library. There, within the precincts of the British Museum, it is still possible—at least for the present—to study in the vast Reading Room that was opened to the public in the year in which George Eliot published her first story.

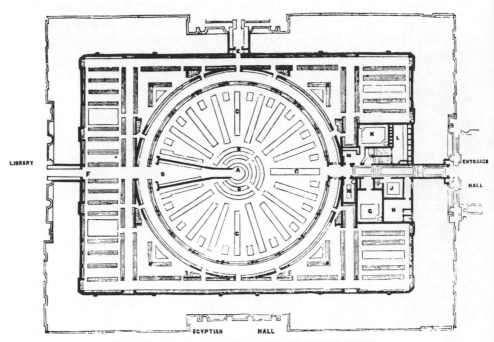

LIBRARY

ENTRANCE

HALL

EGYPTIAN   HALL

GROUND-PLAN OF THE NEW READING-ROOM, ETC., BRITISH MUSEUM.

Contents

Texts and Abbreviations

Quotations from George Eliot's fiction and poetry are from *The Works of George Eliot*, Illustrated Cabinet Edition, 24 vols. (New York: Merrill and Baker, n.d.). In order to facilitate reference to later editions, however, I have identified quotations by standard chapter numbers in parentheses; and a similar practice is followed for other novelists, once the text has been given in a footnote. When it has seemed advisable to do so, I have consulted the two available volumes in the Clarendon Edition of the novels of George Eliot—now in progress under the general editorship of Gordon S. Haight—and other editions.

The following frequently cited works are identified by abbreviations in the footnotes. It goes without saying that I am more indebted to the editors and publishers of these works, and of many other works, than citation alone can suggest.

C.W.   *Collected Works of John Stuart Mill*, ed. J. M. Robson et al. (Toronto: University of Toronto Press, and London: Routledge, 1963–)

G.E.L.   *The George Eliot Letters*, ed. Gordon S. Haight, 9 vols. (New Haven: Yale University Press, 1954–1978)

S.E.   *The Standard Edition of the Complete Psychological Works of Sigmund Freud*, ed. and trans. James Strachey et al., 24 vols. (London: Hogarth Press and Institute of Psycho-Analysis, 1953–1974)

Carroll   *George Eliot: The Critical Heritage*, ed. David Carroll (New York: Barnes and Noble, and London: Routledge, 1971)

Pinney   *Essays of George Eliot*, ed. Thomas Pinney (New York: Columbia University Press, 1962, and London: Routledge, 1963)

I

The Art of Blackmail

A flight of steps leads up to the principal entrance. Go on. Do not fear any surly looks or impertinent glances from any person in attendance. You are upon safe ground here. . . .

You are now in the great Hall—a lofty room, with a fine staircase. In an adjoining room a book is presented to you, in which one of a party has to write his name and address, with the number of persons accompanying him. That is the only form you have to go through; and it is a necessary form, if it were only to preserve a record of the number of persons admitted. In each year this number amounts to about seventy thousand; so you see that the British Museum has afforded pleasure and improvement to a great many people. We hope the number of visitors will be doubled and trebled; for exhibitions such as these do a very great deal for the advance of a people in knowledge and virtue.

—*Penny Magazine*, 7 April 1832

I

A Talking Film

Blackmail in the modern sense—that is, payment exacted by threatening to reveal a secret—became a popular theme in English fiction in the second half of the nineteenth century. One can almost date the theme precisely by reference to the publication in 1860 of Anthony Trollope's *Castle Richmond*, in which Sir Thomas Fitzgerald is painfully paying off his wife's first husband, and Wilkie Collins's *The Woman in White*, in which Walter Hartright employs blackmail to checkmate Sir Percival Glyde and Count Fosco. The so-called sensation novels that followed in the eighteen-sixties afford many more examples. But we are concerned not merely with the spate of novels that the *Quarterly Review* characterized as written for "excitement, and excitement alone."[1] Each novel written by George Eliot subsequent to *The Mill on the Floss* contains blackmail or a related action. In *Silas Marner* Godfrey Cass is being blackmailed by his brother Dunstan, while the hero of the novel is himself trying to bury a secret past. In *Felix Holt* at least three blackmailers, Jermyn, Christian, and Johnson, are working in various ways the secrets of Harold Transome's and Esther Lyon's pasts. In *Middlemarch*, most notoriously, a scurrilous character named Raffles appears from the past to blackmail Nicholas Bulstrode, whose secrets have strange bearing on the fortunes of Will Ladislaw and Dorothea Casaubon. And *Romola*, in the action of Baldassare against Tito Melema, and *Daniel Deronda*, in several curious actions, have plots that resemble blackmail.

1 *Quarterly Review*, 113 (1863), 482. An ample account of this fiction and its reception is available in Winifred Hughes, *The Maniac in the Cellar: Sensation Novels of the 1860s* (Princeton: Princeton University Press, 1980).

It is of course possible to dismiss such actions as the erudite novelist's lapses or awkward bids for popularity. George Eliot's novels have rewarded study in so many ways that it is easy to forgive her a little blackmail, or to look aside. But then she is in quite remarkable company in this respect. It is by no means clear that merely popular novelists began the blackmail fashion. Dickens had a hand in it, most importantly in *Bleak House* but tangentially in his novels from *Oliver Twist* to *Our Mutual Friend*—and in *Pickwick*, though Mrs. Bardle may have been sincere in her misapprehension of the hero's intentions, the lawyers Dodson and Fogg operate more like blackmailers. In the decade preceding 1860, Hawthorne's Chillingworth in *The Scarlet Letter* and Westervelt in *The Blithedale Romance* are agents from the past who resemble blackmailers. Even the authorial Coverdale and Holgrave hover about like prospective blackmailers, while the mysterious monk in *The Marble Faun* apparently possesses the secret of Miriam's past. In 1861 Thackeray employed a blackmail plot for *The Adventures of Philip*, and in that decade Trollope continued to take up the theme. The ambiguous threat to the hero from Mrs. Hurtle in *The Way We Live Now* becomes an explicit blackmail threat on similar grounds in *John Caldigate*. At the end of his career Trollope turned increasingly to stories of the management or exploitation of secrets, most notably in the main occasion for the action of *Dr. Wortle's School.*[2] One of the questions we have to ask is whether the art of blackmail was merely a literary fashion, or—to put the question more broadly—whether a literary fashion is ever merely literary. That so many thoughtful novelists took up this theme presumes a wider interest, suggests in fact that we have before us a phenomenon of general historical significance. George Eliot's erudition, the unlikelihood of blackmail in her pages coupled with its undeniable presence, are precisely what make inquiry worthwhile.

Blackmail is a nineteenth-century theme with striking resonances for our own lives. There is every indication that the novelists anticipated, rather than reacted to, the widespread practice of reputational blackmail.[3] Even the word "blackmail," in the sense in which it is

2 See Robert Tracy, *Trollope's Later Novels* (Berkeley: University of California Press, 1978), pp. 252–283.

3 No significant quantitative data are available. Because of the nature of the crime, increased prosecutions for blackmail may actually reflect a decline in effective threats to reputation. The cases described by Mike Hepworth, *Blackmail: Publicity and Secrecy in Everyday Life* (London: Routledge, 1975), create the impression that the

used here, is very recent. For though George Eliot and her contemporaries employed blackmail plots and helped make their readers conscious of blackmail, they did not use the word as such. Nor was the word used in the modern sense in the courts or criminal statutes. The word "blackmail" in its older sense originated in the sixteenth century from the Scottish border, where it had come to be used for the exaction of payment in return for protection. The *Oxford English Dictionary* cites a deliberately local instance of this original meaning in Scott's *Waverley:* "The boldest of them will never steal a hoof from any one that pays black-mail to Vich Ian Vohr." The word is of course still current for exactions of payment or obedience under threat of injury to life or property, and blackmail in that sense has been a statutory crime since the reign of Elizabeth I. The *O.E.D.* attributes the first modern use to Macaulay in 1840 and defines it as follows: "Any payment extorted by intimidation or pressure, or levied by unprincipled officials, critics, journalists, etc. upon those whom they have it in their power to help or injure." This section of the *O.E.D.* was first published in 1887, yet the dictionary still does not pick up the sense in which the word might be applied to the novels of the eighteen-sixties, until the recent *Supplement,* which adds the definition, "a payment extorted by threats of pressure, esp. by threatening to reveal a discreditable secret."

The late emergence of the word's present-day meaning supports a conclusion that the blackmail plot in the novel actually looks forward in time, and the history of the criminalization of blackmail confirms this. Only gradually, in the course of the nineteenth century, did the trading on reputation that we regard as a crime come to be prohibited as such by the common law. Libel and slander are much older crimes, but they consist in telling untruths. To threaten to tell the truth about someone is much harder to accept as a wrong, and could not readily be prosecuted as a crime until changes in the very nature and tenure of individual reputations had occurred. What happened in the law, roughly, was that threats against reputation for the purpose of exacting payment were construed as a form of robbery. Yet such constructions began only in the late eighteenth century, and then only in a series of cases involving accusations of buggery. In the earliest reported cases, *R v. Jones* (1776) and *R v. Donnally* (1779),

---

heyday of blackmail was in the 1920s and 1930s. Alfred Hitchcock's *Blackmail* and a number of anecdotal studies belong to this period.

sufficient violence had accompanied the threatened accusation for the judges to define the extortion as robbery. In the third, *R v. Hickman* (1784), the defendant who threatened the same accusation was found guilty without any imputation of violence. The principle of regarding such threats as a species of robbery, even when no violence had been offered, was extended in the course of the nineteenth century to include other cases of reputational blackmail. Not until 1895 was it settled in common law that threatening to reveal misconduct short of a crime should itself be regarded as a punishable crime, though a section of the Libel Act of 1843 made it a crime to threaten to publish, or offer to refrain from publishing, any matter "touching any other person," if the intent was to extort money.[4] The men and women of the nineteenth century gradually concluded that some uses of information ought to be prohibited. If a price could be demanded by unscrupulous strangers for silence, then either the older forms of constraint upon such behavior had weakened or the value of information had increased—or both. The reasons for these developments were complex and will be examined in their place. Whether the growing enterprise of blackmailers or the heightened consciousness of their potential victims was the cause, however, the result in law was the modern criminalization of blackmail.

Blackmail has only occasionally and incidentally to do with threatening letters. A confusion arises because of two meanings of "mail" that stem from two different roots altogether. The commoner word of the two refers to the post or to letters and derives from old French *male*, or the bag in which letters were posted. The less common and now obsolete "mail" means payment, rent, or tribute. This word, which is the root of "blackmail," derives from Anglo-Saxon *mäl* and from old Norse *mäl*, a word that meant speech or argument. A reverse etymology, nevertheless, has continued to play about the word "blackmail" and to associate the crime with letters. For one thing, the Waltham Black Act of 1722 made the sending of anonymous threatening letters a capital offense, though that notoriously harsh legisla-

4 The legal history is given by W. H. D. Winder, "The Development of Blackmail," *Modern Law Review*, 5 (1941), 21–50. For an astute analysis of the criminalization of blackmail, see Jeffrie G. Murphy, "Blackmail: A Preliminary Inquiry," *Monist*, 63 (1980), 156–171; and for a rejoinder, Eric Mack, "In Defense of Blackmail," *Philosophical Studies*, 41 (1982), 273–284.

tion had nothing to do with blackmail in the modern sense. The letters Parliament was determined to put a stop to in the early eighteenth century were those threatening to take a nobleman's life or to burn down his barns. They were not threats to his reputation and for the most part had no specific intent of extortion.[5] Still, the severe penalties lingered in the statutes, and the Black Acts may have contributed a direness to the thought of blackmail as late as the end of the nineteenth century. A threatening letter was also evidence of a threat, the only evidence recognized before *R v. Jones*.[6] Letters have another and more important bearing on the rise of blackmail, however. They are among the most obvious of the kinds of evidence the blackmailer can use against his victim, as in Poe's memorable story "The Purloined Letter."[7] In subsequent chapters I shall argue that the theme of blackmail in the later nineteenth century can be tied to developments in communication and in literacy itself.

Because I am persuaded that the art of blackmail responds to sweeping changes in the culture and importantly anticipates conditions of our own day, I intend to begin by examining an instance of that art some fifty years after George Eliot's death, in which both the action and the word for the action are explicit and provide definition such as no dictionary can offer. The work I have in mind is *Blackmail*, Alfred Hitchcock's first talking film and the first such feature-length film produced in England. Released in 1929, *Blackmail* had been planned as a silent film: some scenes were retaken, and sound was added to others. A silent film threatening to talk, threatening to put words to all films from that time, may be thought of as blackmail with a true sense of history. The film accomplishes at least two things that make it an ideal introduction to blackmail as the threatened exposure of a secret and to the literary uses of blackmail: it assumes, by its very title, that its audience understands the word perfectly in its

5 On the Black Act, see Leon Radzinowicz, *A History of English Criminal Law and Its Administration from 1750*, 4 vols. (1948–1968; rpt. London: Stevens, 1974–1975), I, 49–79; and E. P. Thompson, "The Crime of Anonymity," in Douglas Hay et al., *Albion's Fatal Tree: Crime and Society in Eighteenth-Century England* (New York: Pantheon, 1975), pp. 255–308.

6 See James Fitzjames Stephen, *A History of the Criminal Law of England*, 3 vols. (1883; rpt. New York: Franklin [1964]), III, 149–150.

7 "The Purloined Letter" (1844) may be the earliest fiction in which a blackmailer and a detective are opposed. In Dickens's *Martin Chuzzlewit* (1843–1844) the blackmailer employs the detective Nadgett.

modern sense; yet, because the attempted blackmail is so short-lived, the audience is likely to come away wondering why it should be entitled *Blackmail* after all. Hitchcock's film both takes for granted and challenges the definition of the word, and the theme, that most concerns us. Some of the ambiguities of blackmail will be more immediately apparent from the film than from its nineteenth-century forerunners. Moreover, there can be no greater authority on the terror peculiarly instilled by narrative, whether in film or novels, than Hitchcock.

A blackmailer arms himself with neither knife nor poison but with a threatening story—which may or may not be supported by a manuscript, an incriminating letter, or one or more scraps of evidence. In a novel or film, this threatening story is held within the narrative of actual or potential blackmail. Readers or audiences are not threatened by the revelation of the secret, that is, but are treated to a wider view that includes both the secret and its prospective revelation, with a dynamic interplay of motives projected in at least two actors, the blackmailer and his victim, against the background of specific social conditions. Like detective stories, blackmail stories consist of two temporally distinct narratives, that of the incriminating action and that of blackmail or detection. This does not necessarily mean that there must be overlapping lines of suspense, though most detective stories and many blackmail stories conceal full knowledge of the incriminating action until the detection or blackmail is nearly complete. In Hitchcock's *Blackmail* there is little overlapping suspense, for the incriminating action is revealed to the audience before the blackmail action. Other stories, including the popular novel that I shall use to illustrate the art of blackmail among George Eliot's contemporaries, fully exploit a double line of suspense.[8]

It is also important to stress two differences between blackmail and detective stories. The first can be expressed as a difference in motive between the blackmailer and the detective. The latter intends to discover and then to reveal, at the appropriate moment, the concealed

8 Tzvetan Todorov, *The Poetics of Prose*, trans. Richard Howard (Ithaca: Cornell University Press, 1977), pp. 45–46, suggests that the double narrative reproduces, or places "side by side," the two strains that Russian Formalists attributed to every narrative: the story (*fabula*), or what is supposed to have happened, and the plot (*sjužet*), the way it is told. See also Peter Brooks, "Freud's Masterplot," *Yale French Studies*, 55/56 (1977), 280–300. It should be said that I am concerned with a sociology and psychology of these narratives, rather than with a poetics.

crime. The former much more ambiguously needs to discover and threatens to reveal an incriminating fact or action, but shares his victim's interest in concealment, without which he would gain nothing. That some detectives behave like blackmailers, and vice versa, need not obscure this basic distinction, which has important bearings for the social history of blackmail and its psychological interpretation, as well as for narrative. Though a detective is apparently allied with a novelist or storyteller in seeking to make known the original action, the blackmailer is opposed, threatening to reveal but also contriving to conceal secrets. Moreover, if storytelling is a pleasurable, social, and in some sense healthful activity, then blackmail, threatening to tell a story but at the same time not wishing to, is in some sense pathological—more especially as the activity of the blackmailer may be a projection of other persons of the drama. Hitchcock's film is an excellent introduction to the differences between blackmailer and detective, and to the social and psychological implications of this comparison.

The second difference between blackmail and detective stories pertains to the incriminating action, and hence to the scope of the original subject of the story. In the detective story—and again there may be specific or partial exceptions—the subject is an indictable crime. For the blackmail story there may be a much greater range of subjects, since the threatened revelation may be that of a crime, a disreputable act, embarrassing circumstances, or even an innocent mishap. The fear of the criminal, the victim of a detective, can be imagined concretely as the loss of life or liberty at the hands of the state. The fear of the victim of blackmail may include similar conditions or a wide range of less definable but still undesirable states. But whereas the greater range of actions is important to the blackmail story, this difference in the fear of the victim is less so, for in both kinds of stories it is the transition from one state to another, the terror of discovery, that dominates the consciousness of the participant in the incriminating action. In the earliest prosecutions for blackmail, the threatened accusation was that of buggery, which was in fact a crime. But the judges in these early cases apparently reasoned that this accusation was more of a threat to the victim's reputation than a serious attempt to have him prosecuted. Justice Ashhurst, in *R v. Hickman*, argued that "to most men the idea of losing their fame and reputation is equally, if not more terrific than the dread of personal injury";[9] and it was from this perception of the accusation and the terror it induced that the history of regarding reputational blackmail as itself a crime began to take place. In *Middlemarch* Nicholas Bulstrode appreciates that Raffles's story cannot expose him to "the danger of legal punishment or of beggary," yet the revelation of his past seizes him with "the full-grown fang of a discovered lie" and "the agony of terror which fails to kill" (chs. 61, 71). The heroine of *Blackmail* is terrified that she will be arrested for murder, but Hitchcock stresses, in this as in later films, that an "innocent" brush with crime involves terror of revelation as much as of punishment; fear of the abrupt loss of respectability, family, and friends; the violation of intimacy; and a terrible sense of accountability or guilt.

Hitchcock's *Blackmail* begins with the arrest by detectives of a suspect, a police lineup from which the suspect is singled out by a young woman, and the charging and locking up of the suspect (with a little rough handling by the police). All of this is silent, and the dumb show is apparently unrelated to the main action. The latter begins properly in the washroom at Scotland Yard, where the detectives, like the great criminal lawyer Jaggers in *Great Expectations*, are scrubbing their hands at the end of the day's work. Outside a somewhat giddy young woman named Alice White waits in the street for her boyfriend, Frank Webber, one of the detectives making the arrest in the dumb show. They proceed to a tearoom where, as it turns out, Alice is hoping to encounter a certain artist. When this more desirable catch comes along, she succeeds in quarreling with her friend Frank and—shortly afterward—is persuaded to visit the artist's studio. Just as the heroine and her new friend enter at the street door of the studio, they are accosted momentarily by a shabby individual whom the audience recognizes—because of the title of the film, because of his shabby appearance, like Raffles's in *Middlemarch*, and because Alice is compromising herself—as the probable blackmailer.

Alice and the artist climb the stair to the studio and begin a flirtation. For most of this sequence Hitchcock exploits conventions of silent film, as he prepares for several ironic developments. The camera looks aside through the window curtain, glimpsing a policeman on patrol in the dark street below. Within the studio, Alice laughs and points at a fresh painting on the easel of a jester (like the joker in a

9 Quoted by Winder, "The Development of Blackmail," p. 26.

pack of cards), who seems to laugh and point back at her from the canvas. She then tries on the tutu left by the artist's model, and the seduction turns nasty when the gentleman will not give back her own dress. A struggle commences; the camera again glances aside to the police patrol below; the struggle in the studio continues behind the bed curtains. Then a woman's arm emerges from the curtains and gropes successfully for a bread knife on the table next to the bed. The bed curtains sway wildly, a man's arm flops into view, and the curtains fall still. Out into the room comes Alice in a trance, clutching the knife. She swipes at the jester and brings away a hand covered with paint. She is in no condition to conceal any evidence. As she passes out the street door, the shadow of the blackmailer breaks across the lamplight.

Everywhere Alice turns in the London night she confronts images of her guilt, like Pip in the first chapter of *Great Expectations* (though the foremost image, the dead arm of the artist, is something that we, not Alice, have seen through the eye of the camera). At dawn she returns home, nearly around the corner from the scene of the crime, and hides in her bed. At about the same time Frank has been assigned with other detectives to the investigation, for we next see him whistling about the artist's studio, observing the soiled painting of the jester and suddenly, with suppressed alarm, pocketing a lady's glove that he cannot fail to recognize. Alice meanwhile wakes from pretended sleep as her mother brings in her tea and uncovers a caged singing bird. Alice startles at the photograph of Frank, in his police uniform, that hangs on her wall. Her father is a tobacconist, and the family lives behind the shop, which is already alive this morning with news of the murder. She thinks of telephoning Frank from the phone booth in the shop but changes her mind. A neighbor harping on the murder (the sound track sticks deliberately on the word "knife") causes her to drop the family's bread knife on the breakfast table.

At this point Frank enters the shop (visible from the breakfast room). He confronts Alice privately by taking her into the phone booth. No sooner has he pulled the crumpled glove from his pocket than the blackmailer enters. Now Hitchcock leans a little heavier on dialogue instead of pantomime, though the scarcely concealed smirk on the blackmailer's face is something to see. First he remarks that he wants to use the phone to call Scotland Yard; then he changes his

mind and ostentatiously orders a cigar from Alice's father behind the
counter: "I want the best cigar in the house." This is followed by a
friendly: "Any news of the murder?" and by a furtive display of a
glove that matches the one found by Frank. He has his victims where
he wants them, but what exactly does he want them to do? The
shabby blackmailer is enjoying himself so much that he does not have
time to make a significant demand. He makes Frank pay for the cigar
and joins the family for breakfast. Alice's mother does not like this
development at all, but Alice explains hastily that the blackmailer is a
friend. He gives his name as Tracy.

This is the only time we hear the blackmailer's name, but apparently he has an identity, and a record. The camera cuts to the
painted jester (this time signaling an ironic turn in the action) and
then to Scotland Yard, where the artist's landlady is describing the
man who has been hanging about the door lately. "Give me Records,"
the inspector speaks into the phone; the camera flips through a row of
police files; and in no time a call goes out for Tracy's arrest. Back at
the breakfast table in the Whites' home the suspect in question is
whistling the tune of "The Best Things in Life Are Free" while sip-
ping his tea.[10] Frank is summoned to the phone booth, and it is now
his turn to smile to himself, since while listening to the telephone he
is mentally matching the official description sent out by Scotland
Yard with the face of the blackmailer in the back room. This is the
turning point: the blackmailer has become the murder suspect. The
blackmail plot has been so short-lived that we may be inclined to ask,
in retrospect, why the film was so titled in the first place.

Armed with new information in his turn, Frank easily intimidates
the man who has just ordered the best cigar and sat down to breakfast. He orders Alice to lock the door, and the guilt is suddenly all on
Tracy's side. "I wasn't serious," he whines. "I'm not bad really.
Things have been going bad lately." And more defiantly, "It's my
word against hers." When police reinforcements arrive, the blackmailer crashes through the back window and leads a lively chase
across London. A taxi deposits him in Great Russell Street as police

10 I am indebted to Katharine T. Welsh for identifying the tune. The sentiment
may be compared with that of the character Christian in *Felix Holt*, for whom "secrets
were often a source of profit, of that agreeable kind which involved little labour" (ch.
25); or with Raffles in *Middlemarch*, telling Bulstrode "my calling is to enjoy myself
as much as I can. I don't care about working any more" (ch. 53).

vans pull up behind. The blackmailer cowers behind the columns of the British Museum and runs inside past looming objects of ancient art. The chase is punctuated by cuts, with increasing frequency (eight cuts in all), to Alice at home, consulting her conscience. The blackmailer now appears on the Reading Room balcony, then outside on the dome, in the vain attempt to elude policemen and guards. He ascends the dome, turns at the top to point directly at Frank in the forefront of his pursuers. And with the words, "I say, it's not me you want. It's him," he falls backward through the glass to his death in the Reading Room far below.

Alice has by now determined to go to Scotland Yard and confess. As she fills out a form in order to be admitted to Inspector Ward, the friendly uniformed guard asks, "I suppose you're going to tell him who did it?" and she replies, "Yes." There is more irony of this kind, but it is no longer very serious. We are merely being asked to register the heroine's good intentions. A telephone call from some important person intervenes just as Alice is about to speak, and the inspector turns her over to an anxious-looking Frank Webber. To him she confesses that she "did it." "I was defending myself. I didn't know what I was doing." There are more pleasantries exchanged with the guard, as another policeman walks past with the painting of the jester, taken in evidence. The two principals break into hysterical laughter, and the film ends.[11]

The most remarkable turn in *Blackmail* is the ease with which guilt is transferred from the heroine to the blackmailer. Thus the title may refer to the former's state of mind, the impulse that urges her to confess, as much as to the brief and provisional act of extortion. The crime of Alice White is itself ambiguous, an act that the camera has refused to witness directly, as if to permit the audience later to deny that it has occurred. Paradoxically, it is a crime with which the audience can sympathize even as the complicity of the heroine deepens from flirtation to manslaughter. The fluttering curtain and the dead arm of the artist, which the camera persistently recalls as Alice flees

11 *Blackmail* was produced by John Maxwell for British International Pictures. It was written by Alfred Hitchcock, Benn W. Levy, and Charles Bennett, from the play of the same name by Bennett; the director of photography was Jack Cox, the film editor Emile de Ruelle. Anny Ondra played Alice White, John Longden was Frank Webber, Cyril Ritchard the artist, and Donald Calthrop the blackmailer. Joan Barry recorded the dialogue for Ondra. See Donald Spoto, *The Art of Alfred Hitchcock* (New York: Hopkinson and Blake, 1976), pp. 18–24, 503.

from the crime, both signify and conceal what has happened.[12] The crime has become her secret, and when the blackmailer threatens to expose it, in the presence of her parents and of the police, the audience's sympathy goes out to the heroine. In this story the blackmailer actually becomes the murder suspect, displacing Alice's guilt and reversing the paradox of the original action: whereas her partially innocent flirtation had become murder, his malicious intent to profit from her guilt restores her innocence.

Thus Hitchcock treats certain inward relations of blackmail directly in the drama. Where would Alice be now without her blackmailer? The film moves the audience to join in the chase, to hound the blackmailer to his death in the Reading Room of the British Museum, and to forgive and forget Alice's complicity in the process. The eight times that the camera returns to Alice's face during the chase hammer home the equation between his death and her salvation. In the art of blackmail the blackmailer is usually the expendable character,[13] yet he may prove a friend nonetheless. In *Middlemarch* the information that Raffles threatens to reveal—and does reveal in spite of himself—is damaging to Bulstrode but potentially rewarding to Ladislaw and Dorothea. In *Felix Holt* the secrets possessed by the several blackmailers tend more to the benefit than to the injury of Esther Lyon and the man she will marry. As in the Hitchcock film the blackmailers' roles are oddly supportive of the protagonists. The nice feelings of the latter are such that the restitution of their rights is never pursued, yet each novel insists that the full information about the past be brought forward whether or not a hero or heroine is inclined to take advantage of it. The resulting ambiguities—characteristic of blackmail stories—may seem both crude and fragile, but

12 So important is this tactic that the hack who made a novel from the film narrates strictly that which is visible to the camera, refusing to see beyond "the drawn curtains that hid who knew what of horror behind their shimmering folds": see Ruth Alexander (pseud.), *Blackmail: Novelized from Charles Bennett's Play and Talking Film* (London: Rivers, [1929]), ch. 4. Any such curtain or omission or silence, in prose or pictures, conceals a secret from the reader or viewer as well as from other characters. Hitchcock's camera testifies only to an inference, to which the novelist gives a little push, with her "who knew what." But the irony of the film does require that the killing take place. Ruth Alexander has the heroine twice confess the crime prematurely (chs. 8 and 12) and then substitutes a much less interesting irony at the end, by informing the reader that the artist succumbed to a heart attack behind the curtain.

13 In a note to "Raffles and Miss Blandish," George Orwell observed in 1945 that it was "a fairly well-established convention in crime stories that murdering a blackmailer 'doesn't count.'" *A Collection of Essays* (New York: Anchor, 1954), p. 142n.

similar material, I suggest, is the basis of a much more interesting development in *Daniel Deronda*.

Something ought to be said of the typecasting of the blackmailer and his peculiar behavior. Tracy's criminal record (we do not know that he has ever been convicted of a crime) may be less significant than his unemployed status. He has been hanging about the artist's door, either panhandling or possibly blackmailing him in a small way. In the English and Protestant context of the action begging is but a different form of blackmail, which threatens the Christian profession of its victims unless they give something, and part of the blackmailer's scurrility, like that of the beggar, is his classlessness. He exists below the class of his victims but without any definable economic role. He is not working-class; he does not even steal. He is a man without means of making a living who whistles "The Best Things in Life Are Free." He is what you or I might be if we should suddenly lose our clearly defined roles in society. He is without respectability, in short, and this very lack enables him to prey on the respectability of others. For the victim of blackmail may or may not be guilty, but must be subject to shame. The blackmailer is appropriately shameless, and the two have a symbiotic relation. Thus in *Middlemarch* it seems to Will Ladislaw "as if the action begun by that loud bloated stranger [Raffles] were being carried on by that sickly-looking piece of respectability [Bulstrode]" (ch. 61).

The moment arrives, in a blackmail plot, in which respectability confronts its opposite. But worse, the blackmailer seeks intimacy with the blackmailed. He asks for a cigar and sits down to breakfast—of all meals the one for which we are least prepared for company. He threatens even to become a friend.[14] Hitchcock has captured this sensation perfectly in Tracy's behavior. Like Raffles, whose "eagerness to torment was almost as strong in him as any other greed" (*Middlemarch*, ch. 61), Tracy relishes his part so much that he never gets around to making a substantial formal demand. Sharing

14 One of Trollope's blackmailers, Robert Lefroy, in "a coat with frogged buttons that must have been intended to have a military air when it was new, but which was now much the worse for wear," also invites himself to breakfast. The novel subsequently makes much of the disgust of his victim, who has to endure Lefroy's company on a journey as far as San Francisco. See *Dr. Wortle's School* (London: Oxford University Press, 1928), chs. 6 and 7. In the novelization of *Blackmail* (see note 12), Tracy is said to have had "the air of a gentleman run to seed" and to be wearing a "khaki-coloured officer's shirt that might have been clean several weeks ago" (ch. 3).

a secret confers the pleasurable potential of revealing it, but once the secret is revealed, the power and pleasure are gone. The classic treatment of the blackmailer's investment in an intimacy that excludes him is that of Roger Chillingworth in *The Scarlet Letter*, the tormentor who is most distressed by the minister's ultimate confession and who actually tries to prevent it. A blackmailer cannot logically hope for the revelation of that which he threatens to reveal, for then he will enjoy neither payment nor intimacy any longer. He is like a friend who does not want to tell, or a bad conscience that does not want to go away.

Blackmailers differ from detectives, who normally expect to make public the facts as soon as the case is solved. In novels and film, however, and undoubtedly in real life also, some detectives conceal secrets indefinitely. Remember Nadgett, Dickens's first detective, who loves secrets so much that he hates to reveal the results of his private investigations even to his employers. Hitchcock's *Blackmail* is ingeniously plotted so as to elaborate a comparison between detective and blackmailer. Frank Webber has as much reason to conceal the secret as Tracy or Alice. For one thing, the detective is himself a victim of the attempted blackmail, since he is an interested party and also guilty of concealing evidence. But more important, he is the one surviving person besides the heroine who knows that she has killed the artist. Thus if Frank were unscrupulous, it should be easy for him to control the future behavior of his fiancée. The film begins, remember, with Alice's threatened sexual betrayal of Frank. When it ends, they are bound together, whether or not they marry, by the knowledge of her guilt. The audience perceives that Frank is too good a person to take advantage of Alice; he is a scrupulous and sympathetic sharer who has taken the place of the unscrupulous and unsympathetic blackmailer. The intimate who refrains from revelation has also a role to play in the literature of blackmail—such is the role of Daniel Deronda, in fact, from the moment he observes Gwendolen Harleth at the gaming table to the very end of George Eliot's last novel. Hitchcock explicitly compares his detective to the blackmailer by means of the pair of gloves they hold in evidence and by the blackmailer's vain attempt to implicate the detective: "I say, it's not me you want. It's him."

It is even possible, since Tracy's efforts at blackmail are so short-lived, that the title of the film refers equally to Frank's new position of power at the end. But in truth the title embraces not only Frank but all the police, and hence the coercive power of society at large. The heroine is guilty only of flirtation and self-defense, one may say, but she is threatened by a formidable array of legal punishments and with exposure of her noncriminal errors as well. This is the conclusion suggested by the police patrol in the street. Twice we glimpse the blackmailer at the scene of the crime, but twice also the camera glances at the police patrol in the same street, in the light of the same lamp. Alice might call out to that policeman for help, if she knew he was there; he might even prove to be one of Frank's friends. But that is just the point. The policeman is also there to arrest her, and if he were one of Frank's friends, her mere presence in the artist's studio would incriminate her. The purpose of the dumb show with which the film begins is similar: the scenes of arrest and imprisonment express the power of society when wrongdoing is perceived; they hint that individuals are held hostage by this power no matter how they may try to escape. In the scene of the police lineup, a young woman points to the criminal suspect; and in the main action, a young woman is accused by a suspected criminal. In the film, as in the living experience of blackmail, the heroine is caught between a vast disciplinary force of law and respectability and an ambiguous nobody, the blackmailer. Scotland Yard is the representative institution of what might be thought of as official, ubiquitous blackmail; the blackmailer operates on an intimate level and ironically frees the heroine and hero from blame, before being consigned to the Reading Room for good. Suspense in this film does not depend on a question of justice (the death of the artist is unlamented) but on the question of whether Alice White's crime will become known. Blackmail has replaced justice both in the title and in the action of the film. First, will the blackmailer expose the heroine? Second, will the police discover the truth? In the outcome she is spared by a chance and irrelevant telephone call, even though the telephone functions so prominently in the police network of information. Scotland Yard is a repository of information about living individuals, and the British Museum, a repository of information about the dead.

My purpose in explicating this early talking film has been to demonstrate the imaginative reach and possible dimensions of the theme of blackmail. This is a subject that might be pursued in the strictly historical record of modern blackmail, whether successful or failed attempts, but that would be to miss the significance of the idea of blackmail in the modern consciousness. I hope, indeed, to show the ground for such consciousness in nineteenth-century culture, but only fiction is likely to express from an individual point of view the anxiety, the implicit danger and evident risk, inherent in the culture. We have already seen some general similarities in the conception of a theme shared by Hitchcock and George Eliot, despite the unlikelihood of their juxtaposition. George Eliot's fiction can tell us still more of the interplay of guilt and threatened shame that the attempt or the fear of blackmail signalizes. Displacement of guilt from the blackmailed to the blackmailers, if it occurs among fully studied characters, will compel more serious attention than the saving of Alice White. The ambiguities of concealment and revelation will be taken seriously, and the social history of information, dramatized in the blackmail plot, will be seen through the eyes of the most intellectual of nineteenth-century novelists.

2

And a Sensation Novel

In *Blackmail* a fatal and incriminating act occurs in the evening, the attempt at blackmail follows straightway in the morning, and the blackmailer is consigned to the Reading Room floor by the end of the same day. If anything, the life represented in the film is routine: such a startling denouement to an evening of flirtation might occur any day, and the blackmail action meshes easily with a little police work in a plot that swiftly restores everything to normal. Lacking in the film entirely is the common vector of nineteenth-century blackmail, which is the threat of secrets from the past. Most of the secret occurrences that affect characters in nineteenth-century novels have happened elsewhere and earlier in their lives, and not a few streets away on the previous evening.

Why persons inhabiting Victorian fictions should be especially vulnerable to secrets of the past is a profound and puzzling question in itself. Surely our own perception of the sins of the relatively distant past has relaxed somewhat, and it is more possible to live down past sins when they become known. But Victorians on both sides of the Atlantic insist that past actions of a criminal, immoral, or unapproved cast can utterly damn a character in the present. This is primarily an insistence of the fiction, no doubt. People have always gotten away with murder. But the Victorian imagination seems to have dwelt on how awful it was, or would have been, to get away with murder and then to be found out much later.[1] The contempla-

---

1 Still earlier treatments of the theme in fiction include William Godwin's *Caleb Williams* (1794) and Edward Lytton Bulwer's *Eugene Aram* (1832). For the background of these novels, see Maximillian E. Novak, " 'Appearances of Truth': The Lit-

tion of undetected crime seems to have been more challenging than crime itself, whether because the method of discovery had failed, or because the moral agent depended so heavily on discovery as a check to temptation, or because of more subtle conditions that have yet to be studied. Whatever the case, "the full-grown fang of a discovered lie" that grips Bulstrode in *Middlemarch* is the fang of a relatively old story in his life, as are matters of discovery in most such fictions by George Eliot and her contemporaries. The issue of the continuity and discontinuity of personal histories seems to have been paramount, as it was in George Eliot's perception of her own life.

Again it is useful to sample one of the schematic productions of popular art, in which too careful delineation of character or moral principle does not obscure the main outline of the theme. Early in 1862, at about the same time George Eliot was completing her research for *Romola* in the British Museum, Mary Elizabeth Braddon made a decided hit with *Lady Audley's Secret*, a novel typical of the day in its tale of secrets of the past. Lady Audley happens to be a bigamist, but that is only one of her secrets. That she is actually the wife of George Talboys, who has gone to Australia to seek his fortune, is hinted so broadly in the novel that even the dullest reader understands that much. But then there is the question of whether Lady Audley has killed Talboys upon his inopportune return to England. The title of this novel opens up like a series of Chinese boxes: the deep secret is that Lady Audley is mad, and deeper yet is the secret of her mother's madness, which she has inherited.[2]

Like Hitchcock, Braddon combines the actions of blackmail and detection, but in *Lady Audley's Secret* these actions constitute merely the foreground of a double narrative. Unlike the events in *Blackmail*, which are shown in a straightforward sequence, the incriminating actions of the novel have occurred in the past and are unfolded to the reader along with the progress of detection and blackmail. Moreover, the hero of the novel plays both roles, detective and blackmailer. As in Collins's *The Woman in White*, published two years earlier, the main use of blackmail (on the principle that the end justifies the

---

erature of Crime as a Narrative System (1660–1841)," *Yearbook of English Studies*, 11 (1981), 29–48.

2 Elaine Showalter, *A Literature of Their Own: British Women Novelists from Brontë to Lessing* (Princeton: Princeton University Press, 1977), pp. 163–168, wittily argues that the real secret is that Lady Audley is sane.

means) is in the effort of the ostensible protagonist to control his antagonist. As the nephew of Sir Michael Audley, the second husband, Robert Audley uses the information he uncovers about Lady Audley to frighten her: he wants her to go away quietly. Some private detectives undoubtedly employ similar tactics, and Robert Audley has still another motive, since he is commanded by Clara Talboys, whom he loves, to wreak vengeance on the supposed murderess of her brother George. One may easily believe that George Eliot's contemporary outdoes Hitchcock in celebrating the ambiguities of the use of secret information.

Lady Audley's Secret also presents a series of lesser blackmailers, not unlike the series of Jermyn, Christian, and Johnson in *Felix Holt*. The most conventional is Luke Marks, an uncouth fellow who "knew the secret" and "traded on it,"[3] and who prudently marries Phoebe, Lady Audley's maid and the first to guess the secret of the previous marriage. Braddon handles these two rather gently, but not surprisingly so if one keeps in mind the ambivalent role of Tracy and Raffles. Phoebe apparently never makes any explicit demands, though she has deliberately squirreled away the evidence that Lady Audley may have had a child. She also has "a striking likeness" to her victim—"there were certain dim and shadowy lights in which, meeting Phoebe Marks gliding softly through the dark passages of the Court, or under the shrouded avenues in the garden, you might easily have mistaken her for my lady" (ch. 14)—but nothing ever comes of this resemblance in the story. Lady Audley is forced to purchase a rundown inn for the couple to manage, but on the whole the demands of the truculent Luke are modest. Phoebe remains loyal to her mistress even when it is clear that the latter means to burn the inn down in an attempt to rid herself of Robert Audley. A corresponding restraint is apparent on Lady Audley's part, since she never thinks of getting rid of Luke and Phoebe by means of the same arson. The habitually drunken Luke is nevertheless fatally burned in the fire. Only at the end of the novel can we realize that it is not carelessness that leads Braddon into these various improbabilities but an instinctive grasp of the art of blackmail, which portrays a symbiosis of blackmailer and victim. In the next to the last chapter Robert Audley and the reader learn from the dying Luke a secret of which Lady Audley herself is

3 *Lady Audley's Secret* (New York: Dover, 1974), ch. 38.

unaware: namely, that George Talboys crawled out of the deep well into which Lady Audley had pushed him. "I kep' my secret," says Luke, "and let her keep hern" (ch. 38). This exclusively held secret signifies that Lady Audley is guilty of no more than a passionate attempt to kill Talboys: the look-alike maid and her coarse husband have, like the character Tracy in *Blackmail*, relieved the heroine of a degree of guilt. She subsequently dies in a madhouse in Belgium, to which Robert Audley manages to consign her without ever bringing formal charges.

Braddon's novel, then, is a story in which the secrets of the past threaten the tranquillity of the present. It is also a representative Victorian story of blackmail in certain other respects: in the implicit threat to membership in a social class, in the mobility that makes secrets of social origin possible, and in the transformation of justice into a routine of concealment and exposure. Thus Lady Audley's most comprehensive secret is simply her inferior origin, which would undermine her status as Sir Michael's wife even if she were not a bigamist and would-be murderer. The typing of Luke, the blackmailer utterly disrespectful of class, emphasizes this general threat, as does the presence of the maid who instinctively hoards secrets, threatening sham gentility with exposure. Such Victorian anxieties are undoubtedly responsible, in part, for the recognizable literary type of a blackmailer like Raffles and Tracy. We think of Tulkinghorn as the powerful and austere blackmailer in *Bleak House*, whose demise relieves Lady Dedlock's guilt, but should not forget the rabble who, just when Inspector Bucket has taken charge, appear at Sir Leicester's door to sell their secrets: a clamorous consortium of Smallweed, the Chadbands, and Mrs. Snagsby that all but supplants Tulkinghorn as a trader in secrets. In Dickens's novel, as in Braddon's, the distance of Lady Dedlock from her true social origin redoubles the jeopardy of wrongdoing. Exposure of so common a secret as class origin is possible only in a society that provides easy movement from one settlement to another but which still cares deeply about birth and the continuity of individual lives. *Lady Audley's Secret*, with its swift railway journeys between London, Southampton, Liverpool, and the Yorkshire coast, and the obscure bearing of all these places on life at Audley Court, is full of possibilities for blackmail. The investigation by Robert Audley retraces the routes of concealment that crisscross the countryside. *Bleak House* and *The Woman in White* take advantage of the same composite setting, though with greater emphasis on the mixed anonymity and chance connection afforded by the city.

Hitchcock, in the twentieth century, can forego definition of the country by means of the city and vice versa; he takes for granted the mobility of modern populations and concentrates, by means of the camera alone, on the hurrying urban society of strangers under surveillance of the police. The lives represented by Braddon are much more continuously perceived and for that reason more liable to serious interruption. Not that she is a close student of character—her characters, and those of other sensation novelists, are not much more complicated than those of Hitchcock; but the lies of the upstart Lady Audley are more shocking and the honor of Sir Michael more venerable, seen against a background of expected deference and established families in the country. Though we have lately, thanks to the writings of Michel Foucault, been prepared to think of the entire nineteenth century as an age of official surveillance,[4] this emphasis can be misleading if ascribed directly to Victorian fiction. Despite the deep impress of the movement for crime prevention upon society and even upon individual psychology, not all sensation novels employ policemen. No novel of George Eliot importantly involves the police, though a general sense of accountability and the force of public opinion are felt in the later novels especially. For surveillance with something like the connotation of the French verb *surveiller*, one must turn to the urban setting of Dickens's fiction, and even there the representation of official watchfulness is easy to exaggerate.

The process of detection in *Lady Audley's Secret* does seem to be on the way toward substituting for the cause of justice. In part, Braddon obscures the issue of justice by assiduously echoing *Hamlet* whenever she gets a chance.[5] Her hero is sufficiently occupied with questions of what there is to know, whether he wants to know, and whether he should be the one to act, that he begins to doubt whether Lady Audley should be brought to book. A typical meditation on such questions concludes, "Justice to the dead first . . . mercy to the living afterward" (ch. 19), but the main purpose of his investigation

4 Foucault's more influential argument in this regard is *Discipline and Punish: The Birth of the Prison*, trans. Alan Sheridan (1978; rpt. New York: Vintage, 1979), but the idea of a nineteenth-century culture fraught with secrecy receives general support from the epistemologies elaborated in *Les Mots et les choses* (1966).

5 In *Aurora Floyd*, Braddon's next novel of bigamy and blackmail, the heroine is treated more sympathetically and there are echoes of *Othello*: see Robert Lee Wolff, *Sensational Victorian: The Life and Fiction of Mary Elizabeth Braddon* (New York: Garland, 1979), pp. 150–151.

THE ART OF BLACKMAIL

and his threatening of Lady Audley is to make the problem go away.
The hero's task is to discover what has happened and then to cover
things up again. Thus when the woman who has caused all this trouble is tucked away in the *maison de santé* in Belgium, she is deposited
under "a feigned name" (ch. 37). Sir Michael, the aggrieved husband, has "no wish to be told the nature of the arrangements" (ch.
38), just as Harcourt Talboys earlier has refused any communication
with the son who has married beneath the family's expectations.
These characteristic Victorian solutions confirm secrecy as a means
of dealing with untoward or inconvenient acts. When a society strives
to make evil a secret, not surprisingly certain counterefforts of detection and blackmail arise, as well as a literature based on them. The
process of covering and uncovering, uncovering and covering, stands
in the imagination for crime and punishment.

Braddon was neither a very sophisticated psychologist nor especially well informed. But relative lack of sophistication or learning
does not preclude a work of literature from reflecting the responsible
thinking of its time. Arguing from the perspective of Darwinian science, Gillian Beer has suggested that nineteenth-century plots typically represent a widening of knowledge. "Such plot assumes that
what is hidden may be uncovered, and that what lies beyond the
peripheries of present knowledge may be encompassed and brought
within the account by its completion."[6] Sensation novels often seem
to embrace this assumption in the frankest way. They may even seem
to mimic the far-reaching efforts of geology and evolutionary biology
to construct continuous narratives of the past. Such narrative accounts in the sciences often have explanatory power out of proportion
to the sparse and discontinuous evidence on which they are based,
and they can be endlessly enlarged upon when true. Because of the
initial success of Darwinian science, moreover, phylogeny and
ontogeny soon became preeminent in the study of psychology. Freud
was the foremost student of Darwin in this respect, and Freud's
diagnosis and treatment of patients would depend very closely on
narrative. What Beer says of the "completion" of a plot applies more
nearly to legal argument and to psychology, perhaps, than it does to
science per se, and sensation novels often concern themselves with
just these areas of proof.

6 *Darwin's Plots: Evolutionary Narrative in Darwin, George Eliot and Nineteenth-Century Fiction* (London: Routledge, 1983), p. 162.

24

To make a convincing case that nineteenth-century narratives anticipate Freud, it would be better to adduce George Eliot or Dickens
than the general run of sensationalists. Yet any investigation of secrets of the past—often sexual in nature—that bears upon present
chances for happiness and a confrontation of essential innocence with
guilt and unease—sometimes of threatening criminal implications—
may be translated into psychoanalytic terms. Sensation novels offer
passages like the following, from a novel by Collins first published in
Household Words in 1857:

> After passing the door-way, she slowly advanced a few steps,
> and then stopped, waiting with every sense on the watch, with
> every faculty strung up to the highest pitch of expectation—
> waiting in the ominous stillness, in the forlorn solitude, for the
> vague Something which the room might contain, which might
> rise visibly before her, which might sound audibly behind her,
> which might touch her on a sudden from above, from below,
> from either side.[7]

Though every sensation has been tuned to the right pitch, this is not a
ghost story. The young lady voluntarily finds herself in this situation
as the result of a long investigation and many scruples about the pro-
priety of using certain kinds of information, and "the vague Something" that she is about to confront happens to be some words on a
few sheets of paper. The terrible secret of the novel has to do with
one of those quaint deceptions in the past that threaten the social
standing and peace of mind of the Victorian protagonist. At the same
time, the evidence being sought consists of words that supply the key
to a complete narrative, as if in a successful psychoanalytic inquiry.

A more famous novel by Collins appeared in *All the Year Round*
in 1868. Because of its several careful investigations and an apparent
study of inhibited sexuality—and because the innocent Franklin
Blake has been guilty all along—*The Moonstone* has attracted by
now a considerable psychoanalytic literature.[8] Collins also provided a
role in the novel for a medical investigator, Ezra Jennings, that is at

7 *The Dead Secret* (New York: Dover, 1979), bk. V, ch. 5.
8 See especially Charles Rycroft, "A Detective Story: Psychoanalytic Observations," *Psychoanalytic Quarterly*, 26 (1957), 229–245; and Albert D. Hutter,
"Dreams, Transformations, and Literature: The Implications of Detective Fiction,"
Victorian Studies, 19 (1975), 181–209. Hutter's notes provide additional bibliography.

least as important as that of the detective, Sergeant Cuff. The hero
has to be persuaded to reenact the circumstances of the day on which
the diamond disappeared, and in order to lend authority to this undertaking, Jennings gives him passages to read from the writings of
two Victorian doctors, William Carpenter and John Elliotson, whose
researches were partly psychological. Carpenter's brief contribution
to the novel, a passage on the persistence of memory, echoes an important theme of sensation novels themselves. "There seems much
ground for the belief," he writes, "that *every* sensory impression
which has once been recognised by the perceptive consciousness, is
registered (so to speak) in the brain, and may be reproduced at some
subsequent time, although there may be no consciousness of its existence in the mind during the whole intermediate period."[9] The principle that nothing is ever irretrievably lost from the mind, a principle
supported by Elliotson's experiments with mesmerism as well, was
becoming common at this time and would be taken up in due course
by psychoanalysis. It was a principle regularly endorsed by sensation
novels over a much wider field of evidence, outside the mind. Traces
of the past could always be presumed to survive, like a fossil record or
telltale embryo; secrets of social life were never entirely secure, and
therefore might surface at any time. The risk to certain individuals
tended to be moralized in sensation novels, and Sergeant Cuff could
boast—or complain—that "in all my experience along the dirtiest
ways of this dirty little world, I have never met such a thing as a trifle
yet."[10] Yet the traces were scattered, and might therefore never turn
up. As we shall see, there was an appeal to the exceptional or disrup-
tive piece of evidence in this way of thinking that would be exploited
also by Freudian logic. The smallest trace, if it reappeared, loomed
very large. The slightest evidence became the best possible evidence.
Detectives and psychoanalysts can study this paradox to advantage,
and so can blackmailers.

9 *The Moonstone*, ed. J. I. M. Stewart (Harmondsworth: Penguin, 1966), p. 440.
The passage, from *The Principles of Human Physiology*, 4th ed. (1852), p. 781, has
been identified by Ira Bruce Nadel, "Science and *The Moonstone*," *Dickens Studies
Annual*, 11 (1983), 251–252. This portion of Carpenter's book was expanded as
Principles of Mental Physiology in 1874. See also his "On the Unconscious Activity of
the Brain," *Proceedings of the Royal Institution*, 5 (1868), 338–345.

10 *The Moonstone*, p. 136. D. A. Miller, "The Novel and the Police," *Glyph*, 8
(Baltimore: Johns Hopkins University Press, 1981), 144, compares a statement of
Sherlock Holmes: "there is nothing so important as trifles."

The sensation novelists competed for readership just at the time George Eliot began to write fiction. That she should have been significantly influenced by their work seems doubtful and perhaps not very much to the point. Her surviving allusions to Braddon betray only a wry awareness of that novelist's commercial success.[11] She was acquainted with Dickens and Collins, and acquainted with the latter on a fairly informal basis. When George Eliot's identity became publicly known, Dickens promptly asked her to contribute a novel to *All the Year Round*, to follow *A Tale of Two Cities* and Collins's *The Woman in White*.[12] She and George Henry Lewes, needless to say, were also aware of the work of Carpenter and Elliotson, whom Collins's Ezra Jennings invoked as authorities on the unconscious activities of the mind. We know for certain that she read and responded enthusiastically to *The Scarlet Letter* and *The Blithedale Romance* soon after those novels were published in England.[13] But the entire question of literary influence pales before the wider cultural reasons for the obsessions with secrets at this time and the particular circumstances that made George Eliot take an interest in secrets.

George Eliot's early fiction subscribes to the moral doctrine, pronounced in many sensation novels, that secrets must eventually and inevitably be discovered. In an important interpretation of *Adam Bede*, Murray Krieger unerringly picks up this doctrine and relates it to the idea of community in the early fiction. "Clearly secrecy is the enemy of the communal, which requires a continuing shared openness in its human relations," Krieger writes. "What is open is healthily exposed to the air; what is secret can only fester by being closed in upon itself." His argument is focused on the affair of Hetty Sorrel and Arthur Donnithorne, and the symbolic opposite of community is not urban society, as we might expect, but the wood in which the affair is consummated. Partly on the basis of similarity in names— Hetty and Hester, Arthur Donnithorne and Arthur Dimmesdale—he contends that "the fatal function of secrecy and the role of the wood in fostering it" derive from *The Scarlet Letter*.[14] These observations,

11 To John Blackwood, 11 Sept. 1866, *G.E.L.*, IV, 309–310. Cf. G. H. Lewes to Blackwood [27 Feb. 1877], VI, 345.

12 Gordon S. Haight, *George Eliot: A Biography* (Oxford: Clarendon, 1968), pp. 311, 371.

13 To Mrs. Peter Alfred Taylor, 19 Aug. 1852, *G.E.L.*, II, 52. Cf. V, 55n6; 311n5.

14 *The Classic Vision* (Baltimore: Johns Hopkins University Press, 1971), pp. 203–206.

then, add up to a convincing account of at least one theme of *Adam Bede*, and some resemblance of the moral to that of *The Scarlet Letter* seems undeniable. But *Adam Bede* is one of George Eliot's earliest treatments of secrecy, and it may be that a more profound impression of Hawthorne shows itself in her later novels.[15] By the time she was writing *The Mill on the Floss*, for reasons that I shall attempt to describe, the novelist exclaimed in a letter to Charles Bray in Coventry, "I only wish I could write something that would contribute to heighten men's reverence before the secrets of each other's souls, that there might be less assumption of entire knowingness."[16]

While certain attitudes incident to intellectual life colored this reflection, George Eliot's personal experience also informed her understanding of modern society as portrayed in the later novels, each of which has some action resembling blackmail. By the completion of the series, she still valued openness but also openly countenanced some secrets. Except for the extortionate plans of Mirah Lapidoth's shiftless father, *Daniel Deronda* contains no blackmail plot in the criminal sense. In Grandcourt's knowledge of Gwendolen's knowledge of Lydia Glasher, however, the manipulation of secrets as a means to power is strikingly demonstrated. Grandcourt in his way is a devoté of the art of blackmail, and the novel as a whole depicts secrecy as an unavoidable condition of individual and social life. What sensation novels apparently taught George Eliot was the endless potential for blackmail in the modern consciousness of that which is hidden, whether from others or from oneself. In Hitchcock's film a curtain conceals from view a murder, but the film itself is like the opening and then closing of a curtain upon an episode that includes the unseen murder within a story of the management of guilt. *Daniel Deronda* opens and closes to view a similar story.

Before examining George Eliot's career and the specific contribution of the novels after *The Mill on the Floss*, however, I wish to review some of the general conditions for blackmail in the later nineteenth century. Two of the assumptions of this study are that literary fashions are never merely literary and that invented fictions

15 A more important American influence on George Eliot's early fiction is that of Harriet Beecher Stowe. Quite simply, the latter was the best possible example of the moral achievement possible to "writing above the common order." See especially the letters to Stowe in 1869, *G.E.L.*, V, 29–31, 47–49, and Ellen Moers, *Literary Women* (New York: Anchor, 1977), pp. 59, 70–72.

16 To Charles Bray, 26 Sept. 1859, *G.E.L.*, III, 164.

contribute to our understanding of history. If it is the case that black-mail actions in the novel are a marked historical phenomenon, then it ought to be possible to establish a context for them. Such a context will not have fixed limits, but among the most important develop-ments to consider are the growth of knowledge and communication in the nineteenth century, the rise of publicity and division of public and private life, and attitudes toward evidence attendant upon the commitment to crime prevention. Though much is known to histori-ans about these developments, they are so pervasive that they are perhaps more easily understood from their side effects. Reputational blackmail, I suggest, is one unintended result of the information revo-lution, and fictions of blackmail perhaps better represent the anxieties and displacements at work than the real thing. Far more persons have now imagined or read about blackmail than there are persons who have actually been blackmailed. George Eliot was never black-mailed—at least not quite.

I I

The Pathology of Information

The discovery of a law of nature is very like the discovery of a murder. In the one case you arrest a suspected person, and in the other you isolate a suspected cause. . . .

But what has been said of nature is true of commerce. "Nature," says Sir Charles Lyell, "has made it no part of her concern to provide a record of her operations for the use of men"; nor does trade either—only the smallest of fractions of actual transactions is set down, so that investigation can use it. Literature has been called the "fragment of fragments," and in the same way statistics are the "scrap of scraps." In real life scarcely anyone knows more than a small part of what his neighbour is doing, and he scarcely makes public any of that little, or of what he does himself. A complete record of commercial facts, or even of one kind of such facts, is the completest of dreams. You might as well hope for an entire record of human conversation.

—Walter Bagehot, *Fortnightly Review*,
1 February 1876

3

More and More Knowledge

It would be difficult to overestimate the degree to which knowledge in the abstract is a condition of modern life. Knowing, in the sense of awareness or of applied skills, is an inseparable part of being human; but the spread of knowledge with a life of its own is a fact of history, traceable in the institutions of writing and education, science and technology, printing and recording, and what is now manfully called "information science." The institution of knowledge, in the latter sense, is one of relatively slow beginnings and increasingly rapid development, whether it can be said to precede, to parallel, or to follow industrial development. Thus some observers are persuaded that knowledge is displacing industry as the organizing principle of social life.[1] The phenomenon is hard to grasp, because of its ubiquitousness, its size, and its burgeoning growth, outdistancing mere Malthusian bursts of population and the most rapid industrial improvements. Perhaps half the economy of industrial nations today can be characterized, for lack of a better term, as knowledge industry, yet even retrospectively it is hard to estimate the role that knowledge has played in the development of such economies.

There are, I propose, indirect means of understanding such omnipresent conditions. In the first volume of a projected eight-volume work entitled *Knowledge: Its Creation, Distribution, and Economic Significance*, the economist Fritz Machlup speculates at one point

[1] See Peter F. Drucker, *The Age of Discontinuity: Guidelines to Our Changing Society* (London: Heinemann, 1969), and Daniel Bell, *The Coming of Post-Industrial Society: A Venture in Social Forecasting* (1973; rpt. New York: Basic Books, 1976); but the general case is now conventional wisdom.

that he might be willing to pay Tom and Dick for "something they know about Harry." Machlup is illustrating the value of this something in terms of an exchange: "I am curious, but they do not divulge their little secret," he writes, as if parodying Max Beerbohm's parody of Henry James. "I would be willing to pay them for 'letting me in' on their secret. . . . It may be worth a few dollars to me to have my curiosity satisfied—the amount of my payment depending on how much I care about Harry and, of course, on the size of my income."[2] Of such imponderables is the positive science of economics built. But how much more swiftly and dramatically might Tom and Dick arrive at the value of their little secret if Harry would pay for their silence—especially in view of Machlup's interest. In that case, according to our modern understanding of blackmail, Tom and Dick would be involved in a crime, the size of Harry's income would be a factor in the outcome, and he, rather than the investigator, would help determine the value of the information. To turn Machlup's tale of value on its back in this way is, quite simply, to prepare the subject for pathology. Moreover, this narrative, whether in Machlup's version or my own, pretends to be no more than a fiction. The blackmail version is more compelling than the original perhaps and, like most crime stories, is imaginative pathology. Crime stories tell of the system gone wrong, and are easier to construct than stories of the functioning of the system—not merely because the latter are dull, without surprises, but because the system, as we understand the conditions of individual and social life, has virtually no bounds. The project of a crime story, to put it another way, is more manageable than the project of scientific realism, and thus many of the greatest novels that have pretended to realism have crime stories within them. The same can be said for screen plays. Alfred Hitchock's *Blackmail* is an imaginative pathology, one that examines the loss of innocence and the displacement of guilt, the parallels between extortion and the power of the police, the hazards of private blackmail and of the official system of information, and the confusion of information with justice. Hitchcock's juxtaposition of the files of Scotland Yard, a facility for social pathology, and the British Museum, a facility for knowledge generally, is both shrewd and prescient.

2 *Knowledge and Knowledge Production* (Princeton: Princeton University Press, 1980), pp. 208–209. Machlup's earlier book, on which Drucker depends, is *The Production and Distribution of Knowledge in the United States* (Princeton: Princeton University Press, 1962).

The advantages of pathology, practical or imaginative, are well known. Psychoanalysis is sometimes criticized for basing a theory of human psychology on the study of neurosis, but clearly the same criticism might be directed at the science of medicine as a whole. In truth the study of illness not only addresses immediate suffering but affords something easier to understand scientifically than the nature of health. Of the social sciences the most obviously pathological is criminology, but one does not have to seek far for other examples. Thus the study of pressure groups has radically advanced the understanding of democracy; the study of business depressions, economics; or the study of warfare, diplomacy. It can be argued that most inductive sciences advance rapidly through observation of something "wrong" in the field of view. The generalized technique known as systems analysis typically constructs a model of a system and then joggles the model this way and that to find how it works—a process like that of inducing aberrations among a fictitious Tom, Dick, and Harry. Though "pathology" today usually refers narrowly to the medical specialty of that name, in the nineteenth century it could refer to all these kinds of investigation and more. Pathology had an especially prominent role in nineteenth-century positivism. Between 1830 and 1842, Auguste Comte outlined a "positive method" for all sciences that comprised observation, experiment, and comparison. Pathology, in his scheme, was indirect experiment, whether in biology or in social science: that is, pathology studies any disturbances in a normal system as if they were experiments, and some such indirection is of course essential to social science. "This is the nature and character of the indirect experimentation that discloses the real economy of the social body in a more marked manner than simple observation could do. It is applicable to all orders of sociological research . . . and to all degrees of the social evolution, from which, unhappily, disturbances have never been absent."[3] Though the prophetic philosophy of Comte never gained a very significant following, it was common in England to conceive of pathology in similar terms. For example, in 1861 Henry Thomas Buckle could write:

Pathology aims at ascertaining the causes which determine every departure from the natural type, whether of form or of function.

3 *Cours de philosophie positive*, bk. VI, ch. 3, in *Auguste Comte and Positivism: The Essential Writings*, ed. Gertrud Lenzer (New York: Harper, 1975), pp. 243–244. See also the selection from bk. V, ch. 1, pp. 166–170.

> Hence it is, that no one can take a comprehensive view of the actual state of knowledge, without studying the theoretic relations between pathology and other departments of inquiry. To do this, is the business, not of practical men, but of philosophers, properly so-called. The philosophical pathologist is as different from the physician, as a jurist is different from an advocate . . .

Buckle happens to be describing the eighteenth-century medical research of William Cullen, but in his next paragraph he asserts that Cullen's "method in pathology is analogous to that which Adam Smith adopted at the same time, though in a different field."[4]

In the spirit of such definitions of pathology, which George Eliot knew and did in part believe, I propose to comprehend "the actual state of knowledge" in the England of her time. By any direct means, this would be an impossible undertaking; the system of knowledge is not only very large but all-encompassing, in many respects redundant and in others self-interfering—since knowledge of knowledge is still knowledge. Nevertheless, such a system developed historically, and so were its illnesses experienced, or foreseen, in the nineteenth century. All of the imaginative pathology that one could ask for, in fact, has already been prepared by the novelists of the period, some of whom further anticipated a psychopathology of information in the play of consciousness. Reputational blackmail is one of the "disturbances" in the system and frequently an action in the novels of the time, which also range over a much wider set of conditions for possible scandal. I shall be as exact as possible in tracing the indirect experiments with information conducted by George Eliot in her later novels, but I shall also use "blackmail" to refer loosely to the pathological conditions by which the system of knowledge can be understood. Here too, illnesses are of greater immediate concern to us than health, and there may be no better means of coming at that system in any case. Conversely, there may be no better way of explaining the incidence of blackmail plots, or the anxiety represented by blackmail, than systematically.

Because of the computer and microprocessors, we are experiencing an information revolution that makes the industrial revolution slow by comparison. Even the precedence of the two revolutions is in doubt, since printing itself was perhaps the earliest instance of as-

4 *History of Civilization in England*, 3 vols. (London: Richards, 1903–1904), III, 419.

sembly line, mass production, and uniform commodity, and knowledge has been essential to every stage of industrialization.[5] By some information specialists today the industrial revolution is almost scornfully regarded as the deployment of increasing amounts of mechanical energy. It was, of course, and still is, a much more complex development. Though this is not the place to try to describe that development, it might be well to paraphrase Phyllis Deane's summary: (1) widespread and systematic application of knowledge to production; (2) specialization of production for distant markets; (3) urbanization; (4) enlargement and depersonalization of production; (5) shift of emphasis from primary products to manufacturing and services; (6) intensive and extensive use of capital resources; (7) emergence of new classes in relation to the means of production rather than land.[6] Not merely the first but each of these conditions has been brought about in some degree by knowledge in the abstract and has affected conditions of knowledge in turn.

The information revolution is as difficult to characterize as the industrial revolution. Herbert Simon has reasonably suggested that there have been three information revolutions in human history: the developments of writing, of printing, and of the computer.[7] But when did these three developments occur? The truth is that even literacy, the first, did not become widespread until the nineteenth century. Literacy is extremely difficult to measure: neither the number of books nor the number of schools is a sure indication of what fraction of a population is able to read and write (hence the redundancy, "functionally illiterate"). Until literature was mass-produced, there does not seem to have been a reading public, and Richard D. Altick's judgment is that until the last decade of the eighteenth century the literacy rate in England was about what it had been in the reign of Elizabeth I.[8] The political ferment of the seventeen-nineties gave lit-

5 Marshall McLuhan, *The Gutenberg Galaxy* (1962; rpt. Toronto: University of Toronto Press, 1966), p. 124. Cf. Morse Peckham, *Beyond the Tragic Vision* (New York: Braziller, 1962), p. 27, on the "communications revolution" in the nineteenth century, which, "though a part of the industrial revolution, may well have been the most important of its results."

6 *The First Industrial Revolution* (Cambridge, England: Cambridge University Press, 1965), p. 1.

7 "What Computers Mean for Man and Society," in *The Microelectronics Revolution*, ed. Tom Forester (Oxford: Blackwell, 1980), p. 420.

8 *The English Common Reader: A Social History of the Mass Reading Public, 1800–1900* (1957; rpt. Chicago: University of Chicago Press, 1963), p. 30. The history

eracy its first push upward, and the availability of paper and rapid printing assured its climb to near universality in Great Britain over the next hundred years. At the same time, the production of paper and print apparently advanced to meet this demand. Though the printing of books was an invention of the fifteenth century, the true revolution may again be said to have taken place in the nineteenth century, after the Fourdrinier machine and the rotary press came into use. The increase in paper production gives some idea of this advance. From 1800 to 1860, as the population of Great Britain about doubled, paper production increased sevenfold. Production in England rose from twenty-five hundred tons in 1715 to seventy-eight thousand tons in 1855. Some very rough estimates of annual consumption of paper are one-quarter pound per person in 1600, one and one-half pounds in about 1716, two and one-half pounds in 1800, eight pounds in 1860.[9] In general, publishing as an industry was much younger than the invention of printing or the making of paper by hand, and it arose in the face of deliberately constraining taxes on newspapers, on advertising, and on paper that the Victorian reformers called "taxes on knowledge." Reading grew in close conjunction with this industry, as did the lending libraries, mechanics' institutes, and public library movement.

Moreover, the computer, the "third" phase of the information revolution, had its inception in the nineteenth century, as printing had its inception in the fifteenth century and writing before recorded history. Charles Babbage began work on his calculating machines in

---

of literacy is simply not very well known. Quantitative studies such as Lawrence Stone, "Literacy and Education in England, 1640–1900," *Past and Present*, no. 42 (1969), 69–139, and R. S. Schofield, "Dimensions of Illiteracy, 1750–1850," *Explorations in Economic History*, 10 (1973), 437–454, rely almost exclusively on the signatures or lack of the same in marriage registers. The best general essay on the subject is Jack Goody and Ian Watt, "The Consequences of Literacy," in *Literacy in Traditional Societies*, ed. Jack Goody (1969; rpt. Cambridge, England: Cambridge University Press, 1981), pp. 27–68. See also Robert Darnton, "Reading, Writing, and Publishing," *The Literary Underground of the Old Regime* (Cambridge: Harvard University Press, 1982), pp. 167–208.

9 D. C. Coleman, *The British Paper Industry, 1495–1860* (Oxford: Clarendon, 1958), pp. 201, 15, 105, 202. In the second half of the nineteenth century the number of workers in the paper, printing, book, and stationery trades increased at about eight times the rate of the general population: see the figures in B. R. Mitchell, *Abstract of British Historical Statistics* (1962; rpt. Cambridge, England: Cambridge University Press, 1971), p. 60.

1819. If there was an intimate relation between industrialization and reading, so there was between industrialization and computing. Babbage's analytic engine was to be controlled by a Jacquard loom,[10] and his entire effort, as we shall see, was inspired by close observation of industrial processes. A generation later Boolean algebra was born, with the insight that computation could include logical statements as well as magnitudes. According to George Boole, "that which renders Logic possible, is the existence in our minds of general notions,—our ability to conceive of a class, and to designate its individual members by a common name. The theory of Logic is thus intimately connected with that of Language." At the same time he was determined to wrest logic away from metaphysics, as he said, and place it firmly in the hands of mathematics.[11] Farsighted as these Victorians were, they perhaps never dreamed of the quantitative leaps that would accompany the triumphant advance of information in later times. With each advance in the capacity of modern computers, there is inevitably a formidable advance in the sheer amount of information to be handled. In the five-year period from 1978 to 1983 in the United States, the production of office papers increased 21 percent in tonnage. This period is too late to reflect merely the introduction of office copying machines; the increase has to reflect the introduction of office computers as well.[12]

Many early Victorians were highly conscious of their role in the advance of knowledge. With few exceptions they regarded the advantages of literacy as self-evident and were proud of the increase of newspapers and books. The agitators for the repeal of the taxes on knowledge took their victories in stride and modestly inclined to the belief that nothing, in the long run, could stand in the way of knowledge.[13] A kind of furor about knowledge was raised in and about the

10 J. M. Dubbey, *The Mathematical Work of Charles Babbage* (Cambridge, England: Cambridge University Press, 1978), pp. 173, 199. See also *Charles Babbage and His Calculating Machines*, ed. Philip and Emily Morrison (New York: Dover, 1961), and Anthony Hyman, *Charles Babbage: Pioneer of the Computer* (Princeton: Princeton University Press, 1982).

11 George Boole, *The Mathematical Analysis of Logic, being an Essay toward a Calculus of Deductive Reasoning* (1847; rpt. New York: Philosophical Library, 1948), pp. 4–5, 13.

12 Figures from the American Paper Institute, *Los Angeles Times*, 11 Jan. 1984, pp. 1, 14.

13 See Collet Dobson Collet, *History of the Taxes on Knowledge*, 2 vols. (London: Unwin, 1899), for a posthumous account of the reforms.

year 1832. That George Eliot set both *Felix Holt* and *Middlemarch* at the time of the first Reform Bill, in fact, has more to do with the enthusiasm for knowledge in those years than it has to do with politics. In the one novel the political message is that people need education far more than they need the vote; in the second, after a curious relaxation of this stand and with a host of characters pursuing knowledge in one form or another, the satire of Mr. Brooke and his newspaper adventure captures well the spirit of the time. In *England and the English*, published a year after the Reform Bill, Edward Lytton Bulwer addressed a long paean to knowledge. Like other radicals (at the time), Bulwer foresaw in literacy a true emancipation of the people in a "vast commonwealth of knowledge," and he went out of his way to call attention to the latent power of those characteristic productions of the period, the parliamentary reports:

> When all may pour their acquirements into the vast commonwealth of knowledge—it is impossible to calculate the ultimate results to human science, and the advancement of our race. Some faint conjecture may be made from a single glance at the crowded reports of a parliamentary committee; works containing a vast hoard of practical knowledge, of inestimable detail, often collected from witnesses who otherwise would have been dumb for ever; works now unread, scarce known, confined to those who want them least, by them not rendered profitable: when we recollect that in popular and familiar shapes that knowledge and those details will ultimately find a natural vent, we may form some slight groundwork of no irrational guesses towards the future; when the means of knowledge shall be open to all who read, and its expression to all who think.[14]

For all his oratorical style, Bulwer was shrewd enough to realize that the facts and figures already routinely collected in the reports would provide a basis for Victorian reform in areas other than the strictly political; many of the reports, as we know, found their way into the pages of *Das Kapital*.

It would be hard to exaggerate the significance of knowledge in the conscious efforts to bring about social change in England at the time. The expert in a particular field—not necessarily one who performed original research, but one who could assemble all the facts—began to

14 *England and the English*, ed. Standish Meacham (Chicago: University of Chicago Press, 1970), pp. 254–255. Babbage was also caught up in the spirit of reform in these years: see Hyman, *Charles Babbage*, pp. 75–122.

rival the politician whose authority was based in a traditional constituency. In M. Jeanne Peterson's words, "the rise of the expert required social acceptance, not of the *fact* of expertise . . . but of the equation of expertise and authority. . . . The power of the experts was not the power to do, but the power to know, and therefore to judge." In a deep sense, the ascendancy of knowledge over doing and judging made leadership and political choice almost redundant. Secularization further dislocated traditional authority, as "knowledge, expertise, and science all offered an alternative system for understanding and explaining the 'real' world, no longer defined in transcendental terms but in terms of the body and the material universe."[15] By mid-Victorian times it was taken for granted that any position in public affairs ought to be supported by statistics, reports, press coverage, and expert testimony of various kinds. Yet the ground was prepared for these changes, not so much by experts or social reformers, let alone revolutionaries, as by partisans of the Society for the Diffusion of Useful Knowledge, who organized in 1826 for the purpose of promoting literacy and cheap reading matter. The publisher Charles Knight, no expert but one who wrote widely on topics from literacy and printing to labor, emerged as the most active hand. By satirizing the S.D.U.K. in *Crotchet Castle* as the Steam Intellect Society, Thomas Love Peacock suggested the link between its program and the industrial revolution.[16]

In the period before the Reform Bill, knowledge was something of a class issue. It may be hard for us to imagine the case today, but a dying eighteenth-century political establishment anxiously resisted, in one way or another, increased literacy and education. The resistance had the effect of further dividing knowing from doing. Precisely because the early enthusiasts of knowledge were aware of the class issue, they strove to counter it by stressing the neutrality of facts and figures. The statistical movement, especially, benefited from this effort to depoliticize knowledge, since numbers apparently express no opinions whatever. The rise of statistics, and of statistical societies, nevertheless marked a significant break with earlier times. Controversy over the population of Great Britain produced the first

15 *The Medical Profession in Mid-Victorian London* (Berkeley: University of California Press, 1978), p. 286.

16 See Robert K. Webb, *The British Working Class Reader, 1790–1848: Literacy and Social Tension* (London: Unwin, 1955), pp. 66–72.

census in 1801 and hence the first meaningful figures for the change in population in 1811. A Statistical Department was founded at the Board of Trade in 1832, and the Statistical Society of London—later the Royal Statistical Society—in 1834. The Registration Act was passed in 1836. J. R. McCulloch's *Statistical Account of the British Empire* was published by Knight and the S.D.U.K. in 1837. McCulloch and Babbage were both involved, with other persons of distinction, in the founding of the Statistical Society, as was a foreign visitor to Cambridge in 1832, Adolphe Quetelet.[17] This enthusiasm for statistics actually preceded most applications of statistics in natural science.[18]

But notice what becomes of the apparently neutral vision of *l'homme moyen.* The early statistical movement was not so evidently preoccupied with average life as with crime, poverty, and disease. It affords a striking instance of the way in which a sincere effort to gather information of all kinds concentrates in a pathology. The statisticians disclaimed any social program, and above all the program of socialism, but were patently engaged in social pathology. Quetelet himself had an abiding interest in crime, suicide, and disease. The historian of the Royal Statistical Society, looking back over its first fifty years, remarks that "the failures of society, whether from misfortune, misconduct, vice, or the unfavourable conditions somewhat inseparable from life in aggregation . . . have occupied much of the time, and filled many pages of the transactions of the Society."[19] A glance at the early volumes of the *Journal of the Statistical Society*—still a useful collection of facts on many subjects—confirms this. A favorite project was to plot the incidence of crime against some measure of literacy, since literacy, the necessary condition of being well informed, is one thing a statistician must believe in. Many were the

17 Frederic J. Mouat, "History of the Statistical Society," *Jubilee Volume of the Statistical Society* (London: Stanford, 1885), pp. 14–15. For an assessment of Quetelet, the author of *Sur l'homme et le développement de ses facultés, ou essai de physique sociale* (1836), see Paul F. Lazarfield, "Notes on the History of Quantification in Sociology," in *Quantification: A History of the Meaning of Measurement in the Natural and Social Sciences*, ed. Harry Woolf (Indianapolis: Bobbs-Merrill, 1961), pp. 164–181.

18 Some forty years later James Clerk Maxwell could refer in the same sentence to the mathematician Laplace and to Quetelet's disciple Buckle: see John Theodore Merz, *A History of European Thought in the Nineteenth Century*, 4 vols. (1904–1912; rpt. New York: Dover, 1965), II, 598–601. Merz's chapter "On the Statistical View of Nature" describes the mixture of social and natural science on this ground.

19 Mouat, "History of the Statistical Society," p. 24.

efforts to refute A. M. Guerry, the French statistician who found a positive correlation between literacy and crime.[20]

The knowledge that is meant by statisticians—by McCulloch and Babbage, and by economists and computer scientists today—is knowledge that can be stored and subsequently applied to work. It is knowledge that can be expressed in symbols, whether in letters or numbers, and is not limited to one user. It is not to be confused with wisdom, or practiced skills, or what is called common sense. The difference is expressed in Peacock's satire. Dr. Folliott, who speaks common sense in *Crotchet Castle*, consistently opposes Mr. Mac Quedy, who is a caricature of McCulloch. Folliott is against "every thing for every body, science for all, schools for all, rhetoric for all, law for all, physic for all, words for all, and sense for none." Rather, he favors "law for lawyers, and cookery for cooks"—knowledge defined by the specific task it accomplishes, for which apprenticeship would be more appropriate than schooling.[21] Needless to say, "the march of mind," the rapid contemporary advance of another sort of knowledge rather neatly summarized as "words for all," does not receive fair play in *Crotchet Castle*. Knowledge of this kind—which usually is called "information" today[22]—must be capable of storage and retrieval; it cannot remain intrinsic to one mind but must be separable and potentially exchangeable. In the words of one recent writer—words that would further anger Dr. Folliott—"For information to exist, it does not have to be recallable by a specific knower; it does not have to be in the mind of any particular individual. Indeed, information as such may be in no one's mind, and all that may be known to anyone is its location. Information is not the attribute of an individual, it is the attribute of a culture."[23] This does not mean that information "as such" played no role in earlier times—

20 M. J. Cullen, *The Statistical Movement in Early Victorian Britain: The Foundations of Empirical Social Research* (Hassocks, Sussex: Harvester, 1975), pp. 139–144. Guerry's principal work was his *Essai sur la statistique morale de la France* (1833).

21 Thomas Love Peacock, *Crotchet Castle*, ch. 2; published with *Nightmare Abbey*, ed. Raymond Wright (Harmondsworth: Penguin, 1969).

22 I have favored "knowledge" thus far because that is the term most frequently used by the early nineteenth-century writers. In their time the more common meaning of "information" was almost certainly the legal one: a complaint entered in a court of law, analogous to an indictment. An "information" in this sense almost preempts my argument of the general bearing of this state of knowledge on blackmail.

23 Alvin W. Gouldner, *Enter Plato: Classical Greece and the Origins of Social Theory* (New York: Basic Books, 1965), pp. 270–271.

it is as old as civilization. But the growth of information, and the uses of information, began to accelerate rapidly about two hundred years ago.

At any given time most information *is* stored. So if knowledge is understood to include full use and application, then information is latent knowledge. Information is knowledge that is tucked away—hidden, in fact—until it is brought forth. As we shall see again and again, its value hinges upon its release, which may occur through deliberation or by chance. Valuable information is usually valuable as someone either reveals or conceals it, and the information revolution was a condition for secrecy as well as for increased productivity. Value for one person does not always coincide with value for another, and the seeming impartiality of information depends on a utilitarian averaging of human interests. A satirist or philosopher is bound to scorn information: that which is reserved for use can be withheld; that which is hidden may be unseemly; that which is impartial is mean. Yet civilization, especially industrial civilization, banks on more and more information. There may be an underside to this development, which in essence is as old as writing. It may be that the alienation of the self that Plato associated with writing widened in the nineteenth century, as literacy and publication spread rapidly in a culture still deeply committed to individual being. Mere language bestows some limited capacity, in memory and repeated speech, for the storage and exchange of thought; but memory and speech always involve some personal modification or distortion from one repetition to the next. Writing is another matter: Socrates attacks writing, in the *Phaedrus*, precisely because of its virtues as a medium of record and communication. He argues that writing weakens memory—but of course it provides a record independent of individual or collective memory. He argues that written words are divorced from the self—but words must be free of intent, reservation, or inflection if they are to be efficiently exchanged at a distance. Writing, printing, and key-punching are stages in the industrialization of language.

Printing is a multiplication of writing, and to the rotary press and steam power in the early nineteenth century fell the work of multiplying printing. At the brink of the greatest advance of literacy in the ancient world, Plato opposed copying in any form; at the brink of mass literacy in his time, Charles Babbage celebrated copying of all sorts.[24] In the latter's irregular but characteristic work, *On the Economy of Machinery and Manufacturing*, first published in 1832, the longest chapter is quite unabashedly devoted to copying. It is impossible to imagine any less Platonic enthusiasm than Babbage's. "The art of printing, in all its numerous departments, is essentially an art of copying. Under its two great divisions, printing from hollow lines, as in copper-plate, and printing from surfaces, as in block-printing, are comprised numerous arts." Words, in short, are but one of many subjects suitable for copying, and ordinary letterpress is but one of about sixty subcategories of the main operations of printing from cavities, printing from surfaces, casting, molding, stamping, punching, elongation, and copying with altered dimensions. The reason for this elaborate survey is clear: mass production is a fine art of copying. Babbage unhesitatingly includes writing with every other conceivable design. He emphasizes the marvel of repetition, of producing like copies. Of course there is still an original—the engraving, type, or mold—but its value is strictly in producing copies: "Almost unlimited pains are, in some instances, bestowed on the original, from which a series of copies is to be produced; and the larger the number of these copies, the more care and pains can the manufacturer afford to lavish upon the original."[25]

Though Babbage wrote also of the application of power, the division of labor, and other aspects of the industrial revolution, his genius is most evident in the emphasis on copying. The book on manufacturing (he explains also the calculations and processes by which *it* is made) is the key to his vision of the calculating machine. He was a mathematician who happened to be fascinated by industry. He observed the application of machinery, often one step at a time, in factories, and he was aware that in France logarithmic tables had been prepared by teams of clerks possessing little knowledge of mathematics beyond addition and subtraction.

> We have already mentioned what may, perhaps, appear paradoxical to some of our readers,—that the division of labour can be applied with equal success to mental as to mechanical opera-

24 See Alexander Welsh, "Writing and Copying in the Age of Steam," in *Victorian Society and Literature: Essays Presented to Richard D. Altick*, ed. James R. Kincaid and A. J. Kuhn (Columbus: Ohio State University Press, 1984), pp. 30–45.
25 *On the Economy of Machinery and Manufactures*, 4th ed. (1835; rpt. New York: Kelley, 1971), pp. 69–70.

tions, and that it ensures in both the same economy of time. A short account of its practical application, in the most extensive series of calculations ever executed [the logarithmic tables], will offer an interesting illustration of this fact, whilst at the same time it will afford an occasion for shewing that the arrangements which ought to regulate the interior economy of a manufactory, are founded on principles of deeper root than may have been supposed, and are capable of being usefully employed in preparing the road to some of the sublimest investigations of the human mind.[26]

Throughout Babbage's account of manufacturing, both in description and prescription, he assumes the value of a store of knowledge that accumulates well in excess of immediate need. For example, a Report of the Commissioners of Revenue Inquiry could not have been supposed to provide data permitting manufacturers to increase production and cut costs; but Babbage argues that the statistics on personal income in the report should enable manufacturers to calculate an increase in sales from a given reduction in price. He presents a few tables of prices, over a period of years, from firms in Birmingham, and of costs of supplies for Cornish mines. Such actual figures, he argues, ought to be collected with care "in *all* our manufacturing and commercial towns." The point is that one never knows how useful such information may prove. Information can be exchanged, "collected from as many different quarters as possible." If knowledge is power, in other words, information is power to operate at a distance. With typical self-reflection on the task at hand, Babbage also devotes a few pages to "the method of observing manufactories," or the collection of such information as he is setting before us in his book. He recommends using a "skeleton" or questionnaire, and even having one printed up, so as to record data rapidly and efficiently in writing.[27]

"The greatest invention of the nineteenth century," according to Alfred North Whitehead, "was the invention of the method of invention." To see this, "we can neglect all the details of change, such as railways, telegraphs, radios, spinning machines, synthetic dyes" and "concentrate on the method in itself; that is the real novelty, which has broken up the foundations of the old civilisation. . . . The whole change has arisen from the new scientific information."[28] Babbage

26 Ibid., p. 191.
27 Ibid., pp. 119–120, 152–156, 114–118.
28 *Science and the Modern World* (New York: Macmillan, 1925), p. 136.

had not the historical overview of Whitehead, yet he now appears as one of the most shrewdly self-conscious of projectors. He understood the method of invention as one of continuous adjustments in industrial process. By copying such adjustments, from one process to another, he proposed to improve the techniques of copying that constitute mass production. Moreover, he saw production and marketing of goods as continuous, the one depending just as certainly on the collection of accurate information as the other. He was the student not only of invention but of the combined system in which goods, labor, land, and money function as commodities. Even the most naive passages of *On the Economy of Machinery and Manufacturers* convey the vision of cumulative knowledge acting at a distance, the vision of an information network that relates production to consumption and invention to both.

What Babbage could not see, beyond the horizon of the march of mind, was the possible detriment of too much information. In his positive view, there could never be too much information, as there might be overproduction of goods. On the practical side, as an inventor, he laid down the rule that invention must begin with a careful review of the scientific literature. Then too, in the course of any inquiry, such as his own into manufacturing, *"it is important to commit to writing all information as soon as possible after it is received."* Just as his understanding of science and industry is thoroughly practical, his vision of the accumulation of information at large is completely untrammeled. Babbage seems to have felt, like some writers on information today, that knowledge differs essentially from all other resources in that its store steadily increases with use.

> Science and knowledge are subject, in their extension and increase, to laws quite opposite to those which regulate the material world. Unlike the forces of molecular attraction, which cease at sensible distances; or that of gravity, which decreases rapidly with the increasing distance from the point of its origin; the further we advance from the origin of our knowledge, the larger it becomes, and the greater power it bestows upon its cultivators, to add new fields to its dominions.[29]

Yet precisely this increase poses the most obvious problem with information. If knowledge increases to a point where tasks of storage

29 *On the Economy of Machinery and Manufactures*, pp. 114, 386–387.

and retrieval are overwhelming, or the whole obscures the useful parts, a state has been reached that is ideally subject to the prescriptions of "information science" but sometimes grows faster, like a cancer, than the known treatment.

The crisis in the rate of growth in knowledge was first proclaimed by librarians in our time and has been studied most ingeniously by Derek de Solla Price.[30] The sheer quantity of scientific information poses a new problem today because its increase, if continued at the present rate, would not only spill into the streets but preclude all other forms of publication, just as the increase of scientists and engineers, projected into the future, would crowd out all other beings. These distinct impossibilities have prompted a sense of crisis. The logistics of science, and of knowledge generally, will compel the rate of growth to slow, but no one knows how. As Price has shown, the rate of growth in scientific publication has been strikingly uniform as well as high, doubling about every fifteen years since the establishment of the first scientific periodicals in the late seventeenth century.[31] Thus scientists have always had to struggle to keep up with the literature and, partially as a consequence of exponential growth, have worked in narrower and narrower fields of specialization. Though nineteenth-century scientists were not widely concerned with unmanageable growth, the whimsical chapter on "A Law of Acceleration" in *The Education of Henry Adams*, comparing the exploitation of energy with that of knowledge, stands as a convenient counterpoint to Babbage's enthusiasm of the eighteen-thirties. Babbage, we have seen, was persuaded that knowledge was not limited by the laws of growth in the material world. Adams, however, places this comparison in a different light:

> If any analogy whatever existed between the human mind, on one side, and the laws of motion, on the other, the mind had already entered a field of attraction so violent that it must immediately pass beyond, into a new equilibrium, like the Comet of

30 See Freemont Rider, *The Scholar and the Future of the Research Library* (New York: Hadham, 1944), cited by Price, *Science since Babylon*, enlarged ed. (New Haven: Yale University Press, 1975), p. 173n4. Rider's main finding was that, for three centuries, research libraries in the United States have been doubling their collections every sixteen years.

31 Price's chapter on "Diseases of Science," *Science since Babylon*, pp. 161–193, is elaborated in his *Little Science, Big Science* (New York: Columbia University Press, 1963).

Newton, to suffer dissipation altogether, like meteoroids in the earth's atmosphere. If it behaved like an explosive, it must rapidly recover equilibrium; if it behaved like a vegetable, it must reach its limits of growth; and even if it acted like those earlier creations of energy—the saurians and sharks—it must nearly have reached the limit of its expansion. If science were to go on doubling or quadrupling its complexities every ten years, even mathematics would soon succumb. An average mind had succumbed already in 1850; it could no longer understand the problem in 1900.[32]

For the most part Victorians were content to celebrate the rapidly expanding horizons of knowledge, yet, as a practical matter, the establishment of the first scientific abstracts in the eighteen-thirties signaled a new awareness of the task of managing the gains.[33]

Though an inventor himself, Babbage also seems to have taken little account of the checks—to use the Malthusian term—exerted by the property interest in knowledge. It is in truth surprising that the proprietors of factories allowed Babbage to take notes so freely, since the concealment of information from competitors was also a factor in industrial profits. The long-appreciated value of craft secrets was multiplied, in effect, by the form of copying called mass production. The information revolution assured that rapidly conveyable formulae, rather than lifelong apprenticeships, would become the key to production and profits. The point to bear in mind is the latent quality of information, available in symbolic form rather than at the craftsman's finger tips, but still not finally of value except for use. That which has value in revelation almost always has value, for someone, in concealment. Except in certain areas such as banking, credit institutions, and military planning, information scientists, like Babbage, take too little notice of this paradox, though the practice of industrial

32 *The Education of Henry Adams: An Autobiography* (1918; rpt. New York: Book League, 1928), p. 496. "Shadows of the Coming Race," in George Eliot's *Impressions of Theophrastus Such* (1879), makes rather similar points.

33 In *Little Science, Big Science*, pp. 33–39, Price enlists the work of one Victorian, Francis Galton, on the distribution of scientific talent; and in *Science since Babylon*, p. 170n3, he refers to J. C. Houzeau and A. Lancaster, *Bibliographie générale de l'astronomie jusqu'en 1880* (Brussels, 1880–1889; rpt. London: Holland, 1964). The preface to the latter summarized the number of articles published in astronomy year by year and decade by decade from 1600 to 1880. The totals for each century are 396; 3,479; and 18,970 (to the year 1880); for the successive decades of the nineteenth century, 979; 863; 1,188; 1,234; 1,782; 2,712; 3,838; and 6,372. The authors, in short, were well aware in the 1880s of the exponential growth of science.

spying, as old as industry itself, should alert them to it.[34] The black-mailer, in his wicked way, understands the paradox very well. As Dickens's Tigg Montague pronounces to his victim, Jonas Chuzzlewit, "My discoveries, being published, would be like so many other men's discoveries in this world, of no further use to me. You see, Chuzzlewit, how ingenuous and frank I am in showing you the weakness of my own position."[35] The weakness of Tigg's position is the weakness, as he points out, of all traders in information, and it grows proportionately with the growth of information in the modern world. The impression that knowledge, unlike physical energy, is inexhaustible, requires this formidable corrective. While the resources of knowledge may be inexhaustible, its value as far as any one interest is concerned occurs in bursts that are immediately exhausted. The human response to the paradox is very evident, in the grasping for fame or royalties as in the fear of blackmail. The weakness of Tigg's position, in the end, is that he is murdered by his victim.

That the moment of revelation governs the value of information fuels the rapid pace of pure science as well as industrial and marketing research. The loss of value after discovery ceaselessly pushes the scientist to publish. "Around 1850," according to Price, "there appears the familiar pattern of explicit reference to previous work on which rests the distinct, well-knit addition that is the ideal burden of each paper." But the individual aims behind such frequent, orderly, and cumulative publication of papers have to do not with the construction of a body of knowledge but the acquiring of "intellectual property."[36] The wish to preempt discovery contributes to the extremely short half-life of scientific papers and helps explain why—despite Babbage's urging—many papers are never consulted by anyone. Science often moves from a kind of jealous secrecy to formal revelation, with anxiety not unlike that which attends the researches of Edward Casaubon in *Middlemarch*. In a mischievous aside in *Daniel Deronda*, George Eliot hits at the inherent temptation of secrecy within the apparent openness of science, though her immediate reference is merely local gossip. "On no subject," she remarks, "is

34 A fragmentary and poorly organized history is available in Jacques Bergier, *Secret Armies: The Growth of Corporate and Industrial Espionage*, trans. Harold J. Salemson (Indianapolis: Bobbs-Merrill, 1975). Spying has frequently been a cause for concern in the rapidly growing computer industry.

35 *Martin Chuzzlewit* (London: Oxford University Press, 1951), ch. 41.

36 *Little Science, Big Science*, p. 65.

this openness found prudentially practicable,—not even on the generation of acids or the destination of the fixed stars; for either your contemporary with a mind turned towards the same subjects may find your ideas ingenious and forestall you in applying them, or he may have other views on acids and fixed stars, and think ill of you in consequence" (ch. 9).

Patents of invention are the social confession, as it were, that the worth of information inheres in its revelation. Such contracts, arbitrarily created by law, negotiate between secrecy and publicity by enabling the inventor to put a price on revelation. They answer to Tigg Montague's complaint about the publication of discoveries by declaring that, for commercial purposes, the moment of revelation shall be equivalent to fourteen years, during which the inventor can enjoy a monopoly in putting to use what he knows. But he is granted this monopoly only in return for revelation; the monopoly is a bargain struck between society and the person or corporation that finds itself in possession of a secret. Note how arbitrary this bargain is held to be. An important invention is not granted a longer or a lesser time for exploitation than a trivial one. The arbitrary grant of fourteen years expresses uneasily the paradox of information, that its realizable worth dissipates upon publication. Patents and copyrights are usually defended as rights to intellectual property, yet they are severely restricted in time as compared to other property rights. Such rights conflict in spirit with the conviction that gives rise to them, that knowledge should be open to all. Patents of monopoly as such are much older than the information revolution and have their origin in political debts. In England, as elsewhere, patents were granted by the crown for monopolies that had little or nothing to do with innovation. Only with the Statute of Monopolies of 1624 were patents generally restricted to new inventions, and as might be expected, patents of invention were few in any case before the nineteenth century. The obfuscous and expensive procedures that Dickens described in "A Poor Man's Tale of a Patent" (he had no need to exaggerate) yielded in 1852 to the Patent Law Amendment Act, after which the number of patents sealed more than tripled.[37]

37 The numbers of patents sealed each year, for census years from 1801 to 1901, were as follows: 104; 115; 109; 151; 440; 455; 2,047; 2,376; 3,950; 10,643; and 13,062 (Mitchell, *Abstract of British Historical Statistics*, pp. 268–269). Allowance has to be made for the change, also in 1852, from English to United Kingdom patents;

There is nothing personal in letters of patent except the ownership of the same. But a whole series of developments in Victorian society, some similarly enhanced by legislation, came closer to home. The modern developments in communication, in the penny post and electric telegraph, bore directly on personal life as well as on scientific, commercial, and government enterprise. These developments (including a postal service in some ways superior to today's) are an essential part of the information revolution. Faster and surer communications increase the distance in the knowledge at a distance that is information; advances in computer technology now seem certain to dominate communications of the future. The newspaper, composed not only of paper and printing but of communication over long distances, was the most notable Victorian institution to depend on the mails; its ascendancy was assured by the combination of the electric telegraph in gathering news and the mails for its distribution. The newspaper was the institution that above all made the people of the nineteenth century aware of information and communication.[38] But every political and economic institution of the time was touched by the Post Office and the telegraph, and so, for better and worse, was private life.

The history of the improvement in the mails is familiar to social historians, as it was to the Victorians themselves. One does not need a pathology to grasp the significance of the penny post, of railway carriage, and the postage stamp, because the system radically altered the service available before 1840, when all these improvements took place. The concept of swift, dependable mails actually preceded the means. The needs of the commercial community pressed increasingly on the old system, and the mail coaches had their great day just before the introduction of the penny post. But uniformity of service and reduction of price were finally introduced as a deliberate gamble for increased volume and wide public participation. The gamble proved to be perfectly safe, and probably no Victorian reform enjoyed a

---

the second burst of increase reflected in these figures corresponds to the Patents, Designs, and Trade Marks Act of 1883. A comparison of patent statistics with scientific publication and with population was ventured by E. Wyndham Hulme, a former librarian of the Patent Office, in *Statistical Bibliography in Relation to the Growth of Modern Civilization* (London: Grafton, 1923).

38 For a survey of newspaper history see Altick, *The English Common Reader*, pp. 317–364, and for circulation statistics, pp. 391–396.

more palpable success than that of the Post Office.[39] The electric telegraph developed rapidly in the same period. Though the telegraph
was introduced by private hands and spread somewhat sporadically
because of the newness of the technology (the first patent dates from
1837), there was again a deliberate calculation that increased volume
from reduced prices would result in a profitable enterprise.[40] The
first newspaper use of the telegraph occurred in 1845. Continuous
transatlantic service was available from 1866, and by 1872 Great Britain was in touch with Australia by cable. In 1870 the domestic telegraph companies were taken over by the Post Office. The factor to
stress in this history is the rapid rate of increase in both postal and
telegraphic communications, well in advance of the increase in population.[41]

"OUR ENGLISH POST-OFFICE IS A SPLENDID TRIUMPH OF CIVILIZA-
TION" was the epigraph, from Macaulay, in a contemporary history
of the service. The author, William Lewins, saw nothing but
"progress and advancement" ahead, for the Post Office was "capable
of infinite extension and growth."[42] Victorians of the S.D.U.K. per-

39 See Howard Robinson, *The British Post Office: A History* (Princeton: Princeton University Press, 1948), pp. 222–320.

40 See Jeffrey Kieve, *The Electric Telegraph: A Social and Economic History*
(Newton Abbott: David and Charles, 1973), pp. 29–100.

41 The growth in communications can be summarized for the United Kingdom by
the following table:

	Thousands of population	Millions of pieces of mail	Millions of telegrams
1841	26,709	196	—
1851	27,369	361	—
1861	28,927	678	—
1871	31,484	1,069	11.8
1881	34,885	1,776	31.4
1891	37,734	2,667	69.8
1901	41,459	3,833	90.4

At the turn of the century the number of telegrams began to decline in favor of the
telephone. The totals for 1961 (excluding southern Ireland) were 10,500 million
pieces of mail, 34 million telegrams, and 4,977 million telephone calls. By 1970 the
number of telephone calls overtook the number of pieces of mail, which is now actually declining. Figures are from B. R. Mitchell, *European Historical Statistics,
1750–1975*, 2nd rev. ed. (New York: Facts on File, 1981), Tables B1 and G8. Inland
telegrams totaled only 2 million in 1981, and the service came to an end in 1982: see
the *Daily Telegraph*, 30 Sept. 1982, p. 6.

42 *Her Majesty's Mails: An Historical and Descriptive Account of the British Post
Office* (London: Sampson Low, 1864), p. 184.

suasion were as impressed by the rapid increase in quantity of mail as by the added convenience. The penny post was a peculiarly satisfying institution because of its patent success and also because the idea had originated from outside the government, in the pamphlet of a schoolmaster. Rowland Hill subsequently directed the system from the inside, and his memoirs tell of a patient but always optimistic struggle of common sense with inefficiency and entrenched habit.[43] It has to be said, nevertheless, that one of the first consequences of the new vitality of the Post Office was a political scandal in 1844 about the opening of letters, by warrant or otherwise, in a room in London called the Secret or Inner Office. The revelation of some rather discreditable practices of long standing now came as a shock, and the government suffered accordingly in the press and in Parliament.[44] Until the introduction of the penny post, persons using the mails probably understood well enough the risks of submitting their business in writing to hands other than their own, but now suddenly it was very clear what kind of trust this act implied and how invidious its violation must be, since the mails were a service to be used by all, on a uniform basis, everywhere in the country. The prognosis of "infinite extension and growth" was a threat rather than a promise if confidence was not assured. As always, the public extension of a service attenuates personal trust and thus requires still finer bureaucratic tuning to make up for the loss. One of the reforms of 1840, the charging for letters by weight rather than the number of sheets, eliminated counting the sheets as an official excuse to open a letter (previous to this time the use of an envelope had incurred the charge for an extra sheet). Still more subtle pressures were brought to bear on confidentiality by the prepayment for delivery by means of the new adhesive stamps. Prepayment was initiated to save the Post Office money, but it thereby presumed the capacity for consistent delivery. There must also be a heightened expectation of confidentiality that is paid for in advance.

Rowland Hill and his postmen provided an efficient and greatly expanded service. What is impossible to measure is the influence of this service on modern life. The availability of the penny post proba-

43 Rowland Hill and George Birkbeck Hill, *The Life of Sir Rowland Hill and the History of Penny Postage*, 2 vols. (London: De la Rue, 1880).

44 See Robinson, *The British Post Office*, pp. 119-125, 337-352; and Lewins, *Her Majesty's Mails*, pp. 150-164.

bly lent impetus to greater literacy; at the same time the increased use of the mails and of the telegraph placed a subtle strain on the trust between individuals. As in all uses of writing, the messages are loosed from their origin to be interpreted elsewhere. They arrive as interruptions to other routines or excitements. Postal or telegraphic connections affect in various ways assumptions of community and personal identity. Lewins, perhaps not unkindly, relates the mishaps of semiliterate users of the post, and especially of course the Irish. "The addresses of the letters of the poorer Irish are generally so involved—always being sent to the care of one or two individuals—that they usually present the appearance of a little wilderness of words." He offers as a specimen of such an address, "To my sister Bridget, or else to / my brother Tim Burke, in care / of the Praste, who lives in the parish / of Balcumbury in Cork, or if not to / *some dacent neighbour in Ireland.*"[45] But if such were the address—and Lewins's orthography and dialect joke are a little too much to the purpose—it speaks to a human community that modern communications have helped to destroy (or to replace with numerical and alphabetic address codes). The changes induced by the Post Office were not, on balance, destructive, but they resulted in a different sense of personal identity, like that summarized by the child Stephen Dedalus in Joyce's novel, fixing his address in Ireland by careful substations of the Universe. The practice of sending and receiving letters demanded clarity and uniformity in the style of address, and therefore a literate community conscious of geography. As in other aspects of modern life, the price of privacy was a degree of uniformity, since as a last resort the Post Office opened poorly addressed mail in the attempt to deliver or return it.[46]

I have needed to say more about the rise of information than about developments in communication because the latter, the more special case, is much better understood than the former. The experience of communication by letter or telegraph has also more frequently been represented in fiction and history, partly because the text of the communication can so conveniently be reproduced in a narrative. Since the eighteenth century, novels especially have exploited the inherent

45 Lewins, *Her Majesty's Mails*, pp. 224-225.
46 Lewins, *Her Majesty's Mails*, p. 289, tells us that "postmasters and their clerks are forbidden to be parties to the deceptions which used to be practised, and which are now sometimes attempted, as to the place of posting of a letter."

surprise or revelation in the receipt of personal letters, and also the temporal measure of experience in any series of letters. Hardly anything need be said, in consequence, of the chief abuse of such writing, which is the purloining of letters. The nineteenth-century experience, however, differs systemically from all earlier experience of communication, because a successful system of communication begets, without villainous intent—without even thinking, in fact—a form of surveillance. This potential can be documented from the history of the Post Office and an entertaining story by Henry James.

The clerks in the dead-letter office, according to Lewins, were bound to "honourable secrecy," yet he quotes one former postman as stating the following:

> A great deal can be known from the outside of a letter, where there is no disposition to pry into the enclosure. Who would not be almost satisfied with knowing all the correspondence coming to or leaving the hands of the object of his interest? From our long training among the letters of our district, we know the handwriting of most persons so intimately, that no attempt at disguise, however cunningly executed, could succeed with us. We noticed the ominous lawyers' letters addressed to tradesmen whose circumstances were growing embarrassed; and we saw the carefully ill-written direction to the street in Liverpool and London, where some poor fugitive debtor was in hiding. The evangelical curate, who wrote in a disguised hand and under an assumed name to the fascinating public singer, did not deceive us; the young man who posted a circular love-letter to three or four girls the same night, never escaped our notice; the wary maiden, prudently keeping two strings to her bow, unconsciously depended upon our good faith. The public never know how much they owe to official secrecy and official honour, and how rarely this confidence is betrayed. Petty tricks and artifices, small dishonesties, histories of tyranny and suffering, exaggerations and disappointments were thrust upon our notice. As if we were the official confidants of the neighbourhood, we were acquainted with the leading events in the lives of most of the inhabitants.[47]

This postman who sees himself as a confidant, and who is really a kind of satirist, a mocker of secrets, may then aptly be compared with a somewhat better known telegraphist in James's story "In the Cage":

47 Lewins, *Her Majesty's Mails*, p. 243.

During her first weeks she had often gasped at the sums people were willing to pay for the stuff they transmitted—the "much love"s, the "awful" regrets, the compliments and wonderments and vain vague gestures that cost the price of a new pair of boots. She had a way then of glancing at the people's faces, but she had early learnt that if you became a telegraphist you soon ceased to be astonished. Her eye to types amounted nevertheless to genius, and there were those she liked and those she hated, her feeling for the latter of which grew to a positive possession, an instinct of observation and detection. There were the brazen women, as she called them, of the higher and the lower fashion, whose squanderings and graspings, whose struggles and secrets and love-affairs and lies, she tracked and stored up against them till she had at moments, in private, a triumphant vicious feeling of mastery and ease, a sense of carrying their silly guilty secrets in her pocket, her small retentive brain, and thereby knowing so much more about them than they suspected or would care to think.

James's confidante is also a satirist of types, it appears, but one capable of projecting her fantasies upon the private lives of those she has so carefully observed. Undeterred by the "official secresy and official honour" of the postman, the telegraphist's thoughts rise to blackmail:

> She quite thrilled herself with thinking what, with such a lot of material, a bad girl would do. It would be a scene better than many in her ha'penny novels, this going to him in the dusk of evening at Park Chambers and letting him at last have it. "I know too much about a certain person now not to put it to you—excuse my being so lurid—that it's quite worth your while to buy me off. Come therefore: buy me!" There was a point indeed at which such flights had to drop again—the point of unreadiness to name, when it came to that, the purchasing medium. It wouldn't certainly be anything so gross as money, and the matter accordingly remained rather vague, all the more that *she* was not a bad girl.[48]

Lewins's unnamed postman is neither as pathetic nor as inventive as James's unnamed telegraphist, though perhaps he is scarcely less the creature of an author's imagination. The anonymity of the first is undoubtedly to protect his real identity, and the anonymity of the

48 "In the Cage," chs. 5 and 11, in *The Novels and Tales of Henry James*, New York Edition, vol. XI (New York: Scribners, 1908).

second, symbolic. The temptation to blackmail of the fictional employee of the Post Office is not what finally distinguishes them. Blackmail is an opportunity afforded to everyone by communication of knowledge at a distance. The communications are exposed—more so by the electric telegraph than by the post—to agents who have no personal relation to the sender or receiver and hence no personal reason to guard their secrets. Lewins's history and James's story are amused accounts of how personal lives have become public in a way that no one intended.

A modern communications system takes from the one what it gives to the many. When the official many are determined to find and punish an unofficial one, communications undoubtedly help. Hence the post and the telegraph, the telephone and the computer, have played a prominent role in the perfection of police work. We have seen such means ironically identify the wrong man in Hitchcock's *Blackmail*. In this line of work the great advance was made by the instantaneity of electrical communication, the point being for the message to travel faster than is possible for a human culprit to travel by any means whatever. The telegraph was quickly pressed into service to help run the railways in Victorian England, but it also helped the police to keep up with the railways' passengers. Scarcely six years after the first use of the electric telegraph in police pursuit in England in 1845,[49] Hawthorne touchingly defended, through the character Clifford in *The House of the Seven Gables*, those pursued, for the telegraph "puts them too miserably at a disadvantage." In Clifford's view the telegraph ought to be used for daily, or hourly, messages of love, such as " 'I love you forever!'—'My heart runs over with love!'—'I love you more than I can!'—and, again, at the next message—'I have lived an hour longer, and love you twice as much!' "[50] And the telegraph has been used for love, with the speed of light and intensity like that of Clifford's nervousness—but love at a distance, note, detached from the sender or recipient, and subject to the observation of an anonymous postman or telegraphist.

In this summary of the growth of information and communications, I have stressed thus far sources of anxiety in quantifiable aspects of social change. From the individual perspective, quantifica-

49 Kieve, *The Electric Telegraph*, p. 39.
50 *The House of the Seven Gables*, ed. Seymour L. Gross (New York: Norton, 1967), ch. 17.

tion itself is often a threat, and at some point the progress of the one and not the many ought to be defended. In the course of the nineteenth century, not solely under the pressure of numbers, the relation of the one to the many changed in significant ways, as did the imagined relation of one to "circumstances," which were revered as never before.

4

Threatening Publicity

The most blatant and sometimes notorious branch of the knowledge industry in the nineteenth century was the public press, closely dependent upon the post and telegraph—proper names for newspapers to this day. In a chapter on the application of machinery to manufacturing, Charles Babbage could conveniently cite the London *Times*. Relays of shorthand reporters and fifty compositors work rapidly on a parliamentary debate in progress until the speeches "re-appear in regular order" on the rotary press. At this point "the hand of man is now too slow for the demands of his curiosity, but the power of steam comes to his assistance."[1] The age was conscious of its newspapers because they in fact embodied public consciousness. Few historians today would deny the influence of newspapers in the age's reforming spirit, including their influence on the Reform Act of the year in which these words of Babbage were written. The relation of the news to the novel has also long been accepted, and the early career of Charles Dickens as a shorthand reporter seems to have borne this out. When Walter Bagehot remarked that "London is like a newspaper," he was commenting on Dickens's novels and inadvertently on an aspect of urban life that is partly product, partly cause, of "disconnected" information.[2] Newspapers were a symptom, in the last analysis, of the information revolution in both its good and bad aspects.

1 *On the Economy of Machinery and Manufactures*, 4th ed. (1835; rpt. New York: Kelley, 1971), pp. 270–272.
2 "Charles Dickens," in *The Collected Works of Walter Bagehot*, ed. Norman St. John-Stevas (London: The Economist, 1965–), II, 87.

As was the case with the penny post, or with the commitment to knowledge and education generally, progressive Victorians widely celebrated the rise of the periodical press. A history of the fourth estate by F. Knight Hunt included the following prophecy, from Lamartine, as an epigraph:

> Before this century shall have run out, Journalism will be the whole press—the whole human thought. Since that prodigious multiplication art has given to speech—to be multiplied a thousand-fold yet—mankind will write their book day by day, hour by hour, page by page. Thought will spread abroad in the world with the rapidity of light; instantly conceived, instantly written, instantly understood, at the extremities of the earth, it will speed from pole to pole. Sudden, instant, burning with the fervour of soul which made it burst forth, it will be the reign of the human word in its plenitude—it will not have time to ripen, to accumulate into the form of a book—the book will arrive too late. The only book possible to-day is a Newspaper.[3]

Though the prophecy has now been more than fulfilled by television, tape recordings, and computer networks, the celebration of instantaneity, especially with its promise of ever expanding print, "the reign of the human word in all its plenitude," must strike us as less satisfying today. The prospect of unbounded growth and unlimited access to information is fraught with problems, and before the nineteenth century had run out, newspapers so threatened influential persons that the right of privacy had to be invented.

The modern law of privacy is often said to originate not from any legislature or court but from a famous American essay by Samuel D. Warren and Louis D. Brandeis, who were in fact responding to what they regarded as intolerable encroachments on privacy by Boston newspapers in 1890. News had become, in the definition of one editor, "something that will make people talk."[4] Warren and Brandeis argued, in part, as follows:

> Gossip is no longer the resource of the idle and of the vicious, but has become a trade, which is pursued with industry as well

3 Quoted in F. Knight Hunt, *The Fourth Estate: Contributions towards a History of Newspapers, and of the Liberty of the Press*, 2 vols. (London: Bogue, 1850), II, 1.
4 Charles A. Dana, editor and publisher of the New York *Sun* from 1868 to 1897, quoted by Robert Ezra Park, "News as a Form of Knowledge," *Society: Collective Behavior, News and Opinion, Sociology and Modern Society* (Glencoe, Ill.: Free Press, 1955), p. 80.

as effrontery. To satisfy a prurient taste the details of sexual relations are spread broadcast in the columns of the daily papers. To occupy the indolent, column after column is filled with idle gossip, which can only be procured by intrusion upon the domestic circle. The intensity and complexity of life, attendant upon advancing civilization, have rendered necessary some retreat from the world, and man, under the refining influence of culture, has become more sensitive to publicity, so that solitude and privacy have become more essential to the individual; but modern enterprise and invention have, through invasions upon his privacy, subjected him to mental pain and distress, far greater than could be inflicted by mere bodily injury. Nor is the harm wrought by such invasions confined to the suffering of those who may be the subjects of journalistic or other enterprise. In this, as in other branches of commerce, the supply creates the demand. . . .[5]

Such contentions, which were hardly legal arguments, eventually provided a basis for twentieth-century privacy law. The authors' key historical observation is that "the intensity and complexity of life, attendant upon advancing civilization," have actually rendered us "more sensitive to publicity," though they do not stop to explain this causal relation. The appeal to "mental pain and distress" exceeds the torts of slander and libel as understood by Victorian jurists. The comparison of mental suffering with "mere bodily injury," however, might be said to echo the opinion in the earliest convictions for blackmail, that fear of the loss of reputation might be worse than fear of "personal injury." Rather than a deliberate threat to reputation it is now the creation of unwanted publicity that is at issue. The twentieth-century law of privacy, a precarious construction at best, seeks to go beyond slander and libel, beyond falsehood and beyond extortion, to defend against publicity where undisturbed anonymity resided before.[6] The very perception of such a thing as a right to privacy is the result of a modern experience, and the arguments in support of it assume modern sociology. When Warren and Brandeis assert that the supply of printed gossip "creates the demand," they

5 "The Right of Privacy," *Harvard Law Review*, 4 (1890), 196. Warren and Brandeis, p. 205, invoke copyright, which can forestall publication, as evidence of "the more general right of the individual to be let alone."

6 Cf. William L. Prosser, "Privacy," *California Law Review*, 48 (1960), 979. Prosser, p. 984, concurs that the question of privacy first arose because of newspapers.

assume an interrelatedness of society that goes beyond classical economics.

The threat to which these American jurists responded had been treated two years earlier by Henry James, in a fiction about a society newspaper, the *Reverberator*, and its vulgar editor, George P. Flack. A "reverberator" has all sorts of appropriate connotations of noise and machinery and happens also to have been a reflecting lamp— hence the ironic light at the center of the editor's boast:

> You ain't going to be able any longer to monopolise any fact of general interest, and it ain't going to be right you should; it ain't going to continue to be possible to keep out anywhere the light of the Press. Now what I'm going to do is to set up the biggest lamp yet made and make it shine all over the place. We'll see who's private then, and whose hands are off, and who'll frustrate the People—the People *that wants to know.*

Yet for all the row among the Proberts in Paris about the publication of gossip about them, any actual damage to the dignity of the French family is hard to pin down. In James's story Francie Dosson and Gaston Probert marry after all, and George P. Flack continues on his way. Much of the story turns not on the difference of manners in two cultures but on the difference between speaking and printing gossip—a difference still held essential in privacy law. As Flack disarmingly defends himself, "Everything *is* different when it's printed. What else would be the good of the papers?"[7] Before conceiving the *Reverberator* James persuaded himself that "one sketches one's age but imperfectly if one doesn't touch on ... the invasion, the impudence and shamelessness, of the newspaper and the interviewer, the devouring *publicity* of life, the extinction of all sense between public and private"; and the cause of it all that he singled out was "the democratization of the world."[8] Before the nineteenth century public and private were not opposed principles in this degree. Gossip occurs whenever more than two individuals comprise a community, and among literate communities some gossip has usually found its way into print and thus become "different"—but not on the scale of the

7 *The Reverberator*, chs. 4 and 13, in *The Novels and Tales of Henry James*, New York Edition, Vol. XIII (New York: Scribner's, 1908).

8 *The Notebooks of Henry James*, ed. F. O. Matthiessen and Kenneth B. Murdock (1947; rpt. New York: Braziller, 1955), p. 82.

nineteenth century, "to be multiplied," in Lamartine's phrase, "a thousand-fold yet."

Both the invasion of publicity that James attacks and the concern of jurists by the end of the century to extend legal protection to privacy contrast with the general enthusiasm for the press, struggling against deliberately restrictive taxation, at the time of the Reform Act. When Bulwer extolled knowledge in *England and the English*, he had chiefly in mind newspapers and journals, and already the emphasis was on the revelation of facts rather than argument. "The Press, by revealing facts, exerts a far more irresistible, though less noisy sway, than by insisting on theories." Though the facts were said to be quiet, the defense of publication was strident. "This spirit of Revelation," Bulwer continues, "is the greatest of all the blessings which the liberty of the press confers . . . As the nature of evidence is the comparison of facts, so to tell us all things on all sides is the sole process by which we arrive at truth. . . . This publicity is man's nearest approach to the omniscience of his great Creator."[9] To be fair to Bulwer, his notion of publicity includes "all sides" and is consciously utilitarian. But he is as free with capitalization and hyperbole as George P. Flack and sometimes resorts to his own intimidating use of the second person.

Attitudes toward newspapers in the nineteenth century thus pose something of a paradox. What eventually emerged as threatening publicity was conceived, for the most part, as a heartfelt commitment to publicity. In truth, publicity is a faith so widespread that, like the growth of knowledge that Bulwer celebrates in the same work, it tends to escape definition until its adverse implications are felt. As the hyperbole makes clear, "publicity" is not an adjunct, like advertising or public relations, to various enterprises but a condition of improvement, of social progress. Nor is it, strictly speaking, a political principle but a rallying ground for the entire political spectrum, hence also for those who distrust politics. Note the exclusion as well as the sweeping inclusion of "the *sole* process by which we arrive at truth." Behind this evaluation of publicity lies a faith in the power of public opinion that is sometimes thought to elide politics. The very idea of publicity rests on a modern, nontraditional idea of society, yet both "publicity" and "society" can be viewed as dubiously as the newspapers they created. From the perspective of individual experience in

9 *England and the English*, ed. Standish Meacham (Chicago: University of Chicago Press, 1970), p. 254.

the modern world, these concepts and the historial developments they stand for cannot be regarded as unmixed blessings.

Publicity had a double justification for Victorian times: as a test of truth (the classic argument for liberty of the press) and as an alternative to politics (conceived as the province of special interests). In its latter aspect it was construed both as a condition for progress and as a force, called "public opinion." That is, the "spirit of Revelation" and "comparison of facts" induce conclusions and commitment, prompting certain actions and precluding others. The dynamics are vague, but the theory was a favorite among thoughtful Victorians. In George Eliot's one supposedly political novel, *Felix Holt*, politics are wholly subordinate to public opinion, the force of which is compared to steam power. "I'll tell you what's the greatest power under heaven," exclaims the hero, "and that is public opinion,—the ruling belief in society about what is right and what is wrong, what is honourable and what is shameful. That's the steam that is to work the engines" (ch. 30). Felix's entire speech is antipolitical, specifically opposed to the extension of the franchise to working men. Victorians of many persuasions preferred public opinion, in principle, to strict reliance on representative government.[10]

The power of public opinion was first preached by the French, in the writings of Jacques Necker and Jean Joseph Meunier and, somewhat cynically, in the sayings of Talleyrand and Napoleon.[11] But as A. V. Dicey persuasively argued at the end of the era, the power counted for more in England than in any other nation.[12] A knowledgeable public opinion was the desideratum; therefore education was important as well as liberty of the press. Changes come about only when the people as a whole have formed a consensus. The dangers of revolution and of faction are avoided. Public opinion resists the power of any one sector of the population and at the same time makes government less powerful, or less necessary. The doctrine was therefore especially attractive to proponents of "noninterference" like

10 Elsewhere I have shown how frustration with public opinion can lead to a demand for greater police power. See *The City of Dickens* (Oxford: Clarendon, 1971), pp. 32–53.

11 See Ferdinand Toennies, "The Power and Value of Public Opinion," *On Sociology: Pure, Applied, and Empirical*, ed. Werner J. Gahnman and Rudolph Heberle (Chicago: University of Chicago Press, 1971) pp. 251–252; and Hans Speier, "The Historical Development of Public Opinion," *American Journal of Sociology*, 55 (1950), 379–380.

12 *Lectures on the Relation between Law and Public Opinion in England during the Nineteenth Century*, 2nd ed. (1914; rpt. London: Macmillan, 1962).

George Eliot's friend Herbert Spencer.[13] The premise of the doctrine is progress, and its unspoken promise, reform—but cautious reform, from which resistance has melted away in advance. In the novel Felix Holt opposed the franchise in 1832; after the reform of 1867 he made a reappearance in *Blackwood's Magazine* in an "Address to Working Men," scarcely disguising his belief that "any large body of men is likely to have more of stupidity, narrowness, and greed than of far-sightedness and generosity" and confirming that "the great function of knowledge" was "to find right remedies and right methods" to relieve "suffering."[14]

Public opinion may be thought of as the social force that makes knowledge efficacious. Much Victorian legislation, in fact, assumed the same inevitable connection between publicity and reformation. By 1854 as many as sixteen new departments of government were empowered to inspect and report on local government and private institutions. In some areas the only administrative innovation was the right to inspect or the requirement that local authorities submit annual returns. Hence the "dominant theme" of Victorian administration can be expressed as "faith in the powers of inspection, reporting, and the dissemination of knowlege."[15] If the appeal to public opinion was politically vague as to means and ends, it was also humane and respectful of the complexity of social life. Dicey's lectures on *Law and Public Opinion in England* concluded with a quotation from another of George Eliot's acquaintances, Mark Pattison: "Deeper than opinions lies the sentiment which predetermines opinion. What it is important for us to know with respect to our own age or any age is, not its peculiar opinions, but the complex elements of that moral feeling and character in which, as in their congenial soil, opinions grow."[16] These are sentiments worthy of George Eliot herself, who as a journalist and novelist also strove to affect opinion.

As a publicist George Eliot was vulnerable to public opinion as

13 E.g., *Social Statics* (1850; rpt. New York: Schalkenback Foundation, 1954), p. 14: "The triumph of the Anti-Corn Law League is simply the most marked instance yet of the new style of government—that of opinion overcoming the old style—that of force." The priority of public opinion to legislation was also a principal theme of Buckle and of Comte.

14 "Address to Working Men, by Felix Holt"; Pinney, pp. 420, 428.

15 David Roberts, *Victorian Origins of the British Welfare State* (New Haven: Yale University Press, 1960), pp. 106–107.

16 Cf. Mark Pattison, "Learning in the Church of England" (1863), *Essays*, 2 vols. (Oxford: Clarendon, 1889), II, 264.

well as one of its authors—more vulnerable than most, because she was a woman and because of her irregular liaison with George Henry Lewes. Her allusion to public opinion as steam power gives little hint of the danger, yet it is worth noting that twice in this connection she alludes to shame. In the novel Felix Holt has defined public opinion as "the ruling belief in society about what is right and what is wrong, what is honourable and what is shameful." In his later appearance he allows that working men "should have made an audience that would have shamed the other classes out of their share in the national vices," among which he numbers "the commercial lying and swindling, the poisonous adulteration of goods, the retail cheating, and the political bribery."[17] Thus George Eliot indirectly points to an underlying source of the power of public opinion—not the near mystical transformation of knowledge into action, in this case, but the power of shaming someone. Deliberate shaming enlists the power of the many against the few, as Felix implies. The distressing failure in tone of the "Address to Working Men" is partially due to the attempt to shame *the masses* into good behavior, and there is something of this same tone in the novel.

John Stuart Mill began to point out some threatening aspects of public opinion as early as 1836, in an essay based on the observation that in "advancing civilization . . . the importance of the masses becomes constantly greater, that of individuals less." Mill credited newspapers with many achievements, including passage of the Reform Act, but he importantly qualified the celebration of public opinion by calling attention to the problem of numbers. "The individual becomes so lost in the crowd, that though he depends more and more upon opinion, he is apt to depend less and less upon well-grounded opinion; upon the opinion of those who know him. An established character becomes at once more difficult to gain, and more easily to be dispensed with."[18] The effect of aggregate numbers is thus twofold: greater reliance on opinion but less on acquaintance; reputation that is harder to build but easier to lose. Mill was hinting that opinion was a form of knowledge at a distance. Rumor and print have taken the place of personal contact. The difference is in part the same "difference" proclaimed without apology by George P. Flack. It

17 "Address to Working Men, by Felix Holt"; Pinney, p. 416.
18 "Civilization" (1836), *C. W.*, XVIII, 121, 132. In some ways this early essay deserves the title "Civilization and Its Discontents."

is also the difference complained of by George Eliot, throughout her career as a novelist, between published reviews of her work that she could not bear to read and the opinion of her friends.

Mill's reservations about publicity in the widest sense were inspired by the first part of Alexis de Tocqueville's *Democracy in America* and particularly by its assault on the tyranny of the majority.[19] Not until twenty years later, with the help of Harriet Taylor and partly as a result of their long friendship, did he compose the major statement in English on this subject. *On Liberty* is a troublesome as well as eloquent essay. So acceptable to most of us is its defense of liberty of discussion, so steadfast the argument from utility, and so familiar the words of the essay, that the whole seems almost dull in its conception. Actually, it yokes two almost contradictory arguments. On the one hand *On Liberty* insists upon the utility of knowledge and free discussion of all kinds; on the other it combats one of the consequences of discussion, the propensity of the loudest voices to suppress the others. The essay is best known for the argument from utility in the chapter "Of the Liberty of Thought and Discussion"; but it was chiefly motivated, I suggest, by the arguments in the chapter "Of Individuality, as One of the Elements of Well-Being," which follows immediately after. The possible contradiction recalls the brief observation in the essay "Civilization" that men and women depend more and more on opinion, but less on the opinion of persons they can count on. Mill's solution was to segregate conduct that affects others from conduct that affects the individual only. But this distinction raises more logical difficulties than he supposed.[20]

In his introductory chapter Mill began by addressing power and

19 See *Democracy in America*, ed. J. P. Mayer, trans. George Lawrence (1966; rpt. Garden City, N.Y.: Anchor, 1969), pp. 246–261. Mill reviewed the first part in 1835 and both parts in 1840 (*C.W.*, *XVIII*, 47–90, 153–204).

20 Dicey, in the 1914 introduction to *Law and Public Opinion in England*, p. liv, remarks that "since 1859 almost every event which has happened has directed public attention to the extreme difficulty, not to say the impossibility, of drawing a rigid distinction between actions which merely concern a man himself and actions which also concern society." In a footnote, he adds, "Mill qualifies, or rather extends, his simple principle by the remark that, where he talks of conduct which affects only a man himself, he means conduct which affects 'only himself . . . directly, and in the first instance.' Mill thereby all but admits that hardly any conduct of a human being can be named (except conduct which does not go further than the realm of thought) which, strictly speaking, affects 'only himself.'" Cf. C. L. Ten, *Mill on Liberty* (Oxford: Clarendon, 1980), pp. 10–41.

tyranny of a particular kind. His defense of freedom is traditional in part, but the danger of oppressive power has changed from political to social. "Society can and does execute its own mandates: and if it issues wrong mandates instead of right, or any mandates at all in things with which it ought not to meddle, it practises a social tyranny more formidable than many kinds of political oppression, since, though not usually upheld by such extreme penalties, it leaves fewer means of escape, penetrating much more deeply into the details of life, and enslaving the soul itself." As this persistent contrast makes clear, Mill's essay is directed only incidentally against government. When Spencer forbids meddling, he is usually fending against nosy sanitary inspectors or stubborn parliamentary majorities; Mill, however, is worried about oppression much more amorphous and inevitable, oppression in which civilization almost conspires. Anticipating Dicey, whom he also clearly influenced, Mill suggests that "the yoke of opinion is perhaps heavier, that of law is lighter," in England than elsewhere in Europe. His attempt to insulate "self-regarding" from "social" conduct announces his true theme, which is the defense of privacy. "Society has expended fully as much effort in the attempt (according to its lights) to compel people to conform to its notions of personal, as of social excellence," he claims, and the metaphor he uses to express this power is once again that of engines (whether military or manufacturing is not clear): "the engines of moral repression have been wielded more strenuously against divergence from the reigning opinion in self-regarding, than even in social matters." All this the world well knows, Mill implies, yet none knows well how to accommodate publicity to the necessary freedom.[21]

An epic voice in *On Liberty* laments the passing of an heroic age; a sense of loss pervades the broad historical significance that Mill attributes to modern civilization. Like Burke at once lamenting and meaning to restore the age of chivalry, Mill believes that the age of individuality is dead and must not be allowed to die—though his true inspiration here was undoubtedly Carlyle. A terrible sameness has beset humankind, so much so that Mill puts an excess value on nonconformity and even eccentricity.[22] Citing De Tocqueville and Wilhelm von Humboldt, he concludes his chapter on individuality with

21 *On Liberty* (1859), *C.W.*, XVIII, 220, 223, 226.
22 Cf. Leslie Stephen, *The English Utilitarians*, 3 vols. (London: Duckworth, 1900), III, 258, 263–267.

unredeemed distaste (what for another writer would be disgust) for the present:

> Formerly, different ranks, different neighbourhoods, different trades and professions, lived in what might be called different worlds; at present, to a great degree in the same. Comparatively speaking, they now read the same things, listen to the same things, see the same things, go to the same places, have their hopes and fears directed to the same objects, have the same rights and liberties, and the same means of asserting them. Great as are the differences of position which remain, they are nothing to those which have ceased. And the assimilation is still proceeding. All the political changes of the age promote it, since they all tend to raise the low and to lower the high. Every extension of education promotes it, because education brings people under common influences, and gives them access to the general stock of facts and sentiments. Improvements in the means of communication promote it, by bringing the inhabitants of distant places into personal contact, and keeping up a rapid flow of changes of residence between one place and another. The increase of commerce and manufactures promotes it, by diffusing more widely the advantages of easy circumstances, and opening all objects of ambition, even the highest, to general competition, whereby the desire of rising becomes no longer the character of a particular class, but of all classes. A more powerful agency than even all these, in bringing about a general similarity among mankind, is the complete establishment, in this and other free countries, of the ascendancy of public opinion in the State.[23]

The list is a veritable catalogue of changes that Mill and most of his fellow Victorians routinely approve. But everything that is getting better, it seems, is actually getting worse.

The underlying trouble is the rise of "society" in the nineteenth century. Just as there was no press, and no publicity, before the period we are concerned with, there was no such thing as society, at least not in the sense that Mill assumes. His sentences insist that society is a substantive agent, not merely an object of study but a subject in its own right: "Society can and does execute its own mandates," or "Society has expended fully as much effort in the attempt . . . to compel people to conform to its notions of personal, as of social excellence." Before there can be social tyranny, there must be

23 *On Liberty*, *C.W.*, XVIII, 274–275.

such a thing as society. The tyranny of the majority that Mill borrowed from De Tocqueville is but one possible outcome of a whole series of conditions that influence modern experience and cause it to differ from that of earlier times. Some of these conditions are as basic as the increase in knowledge and communication, and it can be seen that "extension of education," and "improvements in the means of communication," and "the increase in commerce and manufactures" are among Mill's disturbingly two-sided changes. In general, the conditions that have produced greater publicity have created the issue of privacy. Society has created the need for privacy.

There were in general two ways of thinking about society in the nineteenth century, depending upon whether one stressed political will or economic relations. Early in the century "civil society" and "civilization" were contrasted with a state of nature; a social contract supported the rule of law; the emphasis was on the suppression of violence and avoidance of revolution. Later, in the Victorian era, "society" could be used without modification, and its thriving existence scorned "interference"; the system of production and consumption was self-regulating. It is not altogether evident that these two perspectives, the political and the economic, were consistent with one another. What the two perspectives have in common, however, is the release of both the state and the individual from traditional roles. The authority of the state is no longer divine nor customary but rests upon a contract; the state is the agent of society and can be judged accordingly. The individual is theoretically free to choose, to pass judgments on society, and to join with others in changing it; but he or she is also constrained by the system to pursue personal advantage. Each person, it may be said, seeks to satisfy his or her wants, but also must do so in order for the system to function. A general liberation has occurred that has left both the individual and the state accountable. Position and authority are not to be taken for granted as in the past but produced and sustained. Institutions are to be reformed— that is, rationalized and adjusted to contemporary reality.[24]

24 Though there is broad agreement today that the conditions of social life changed radically at the commencement of the nineteenth century, it is easier to take note of the conditions than to theorize about the change as a whole. By focusing on the abolishment of poor relief, in which "Townsend, Malthus and Ricardo, Bentham and Burke were at one," Karl Polanyi provides one of the most dramatic explanations of the "discovery of society" in *The Great Transformation* (1944; rpt. Boston: Beacon, 1957), pp. 111–129. The concept of the self-regulating market, which Polanyi regards

At a slightly lower level of abstraction, we can discern three conditions of society that affected individuals directly and indirectly intensified the need for privacy or secrecy, and these conditions are interrelated: a self-regulating economy; social mobility and choice of occupation; and representative government. Each depends on the rise of knowledge and communication and partakes of that liberated condition that in turn enforces a new sense of accountability; each contributed to a weakening of the sense of community.

In the first instance, a self-regulating economy requires not only knowledge operating at a distance but people working at a distance— at a distance from each other and from work itself. Men and women in factories work at fragments, divorced from both product and raw materials and measuring their contribution in days and hours; men and women in the distribution system are in similar positions. Capitalists engage themselves with buyers and borrowers whom they have never met; friends and adversaries are agents for unseen parties; money is the lingua franca of all. So much distance places a special burden on trust, or what the historian W. E. H. Lecky called "industrial veracity."[25] Industrial products had to be reliable, and so did the information necessary to their manufacture and distribution. Credit had to be reliable, as did communications.

But people have not yet been eliminated from the self-regulating economy. Various "positions" may be dictated by the system, but people have to be selected for positions—hired and fired, promoted, transferred, or replaced. The process of selection requires that something be known about people who are not very well known at first hand, whose histories are not known. The retention or exchange of positions requires credentials and dossiers; sales require information about customers, and purchases information about suppliers; credit depends on the reputations of unseen persons. So much exposure of

---

as a fiction, also enforced "the institutional separation of society into an economic and political sphere" (p. 71). Hannah Arendt, in *The Human Condition* (1958; rpt. Garden City, N.Y.: Anchor, 1959), pp. 23–69, brings classical and medieval political theory to bear on the argument that modern society is "neither private nor public." Society embraces the fiction, necessary to the science of economics, of "one enormous family which has only one opinion and one interest" (p. 37)—an argument derived in turn from Gunnar Myrdal, *The Political Element in the Development of Economic Theory* (1929; English trans. 1954). These writers treat economic change as primary, though their subject is the very idea of society.

25 *History of European Morals*, 2 vols. (London: Longmans, 1869), I, 143–145.

personal qualities among agents unacquainted or unaccustomed to one another has in turn enhanced the value of privacy and created a need for intimacy. A very natural resistance to publicity has encouraged the sharing of secrets as a deliberate means to intimacy. Secrecy in turn becomes a temptation to betrayal, or to the threat of betrayal that is blackmail.

The foremost student of these subtle relations was the German sociologist Georg Simmel, who concluded that "what is public becomes ever more public, and what is private becomes ever more private." Simmel grasped the fundamental point that social life dependent upon information was a condition for secrecy, or the concealment of information. Similarly, the representation of all economic values by money produced secrets: the "compressibility" of money, its "abstractness and qualitylessness," and its "effect-at-a-distance" could either advertise or conceal value. Essentially Simmel noted the same heightened importance of truth-telling that Lecky had:

> Our modern life is based to a much larger extent than is usually realized upon the faith in the honesty of the other. Examples are our economy, which becomes more and more a credit economy, or our science, in which most scholars must use innumerable results of other scientists which they cannot examine. We base our gravest decisions on a complex system of conceptions, most of which presuppose the confidence that we will not be betrayed. Under modern conditions, the lie, therefore, becomes something much more devastating than it was earlier, something which questions the very foundations of our life. If among ourselves today, the lie were as negligible a sin as it was among the Greek gods, the Jewish patriarchs, or the South Sea islanders; and if we were not deterred from it by the utmost severity of the moral law; then the organization of modern life would simply be impossible; for, modern life is a "credit economy" in a much broader than a strictly economic sense.

Simmel argued not only that honesty was of relatively greater importance in the nineteenth century than earlier but that discretion, comprised of both awareness and respect for privacy, was a modern virtue.[26]

Greater reliance on veracity and greater possibility of concealment,

26 *The Sociology of Georg Simmel*, ed. and trans. Kurt H. Wolff (1950; rpt. New York: Free Press, 1964), pp. 337, 335, 313, 323.

however, are only two of the depths touched by a self-regulating economy. It has to matter to each person temporarily occupying a position in the system how he behaves, just as it matters to the system. The individual is not (in theory) loyal to a leader or to other individuals but to the system as a whole. He has to qualify for his position and to be receptive to communications. The increasing likelihood that he is literate is a mark of his isolation and dependence both. He cannot, let us say, arbitrarily set the price of anything but must calculate the price and name it. He does not subtract from the stock for his own purposes because he is, above all, accountable for what he does and says—accountable not to God or to any human being but to his position. Thus the "sphere in which one is accountable" can be used to define what is "public" as opposed to private.[27] Little in his public position protects him as an individual. In his public role, if he conceals anything and is found out, he loses his place. But accountability in society reaches well beyond this commercial model, to acts subject to constraints of many kinds and to negligence punishable by law. In a sense, the more one knows, the more one is accountable.[28]

A second condition of society is the relative freedom of mobility and choice of occupation. The principal direction taken by social mobility in the nineteenth century can be summed up as urbanization: the population of Great Britain not only increased but concentrated in cities. In a single decade, from 1821 to 1831, the population of the industrial towns of Manchester, Birmingham, Liverpool, Sheffield, Bradford, and Leeds increased by an average of 48 percent.[29] The numbers and locations pretty well attest to the economic motives of this migration, which continued at less precipitate rates throughout the century (in 1841 over half the population of England and Wales was rural; by 1901 only one-fifth lived outside cities, thirty of which

27 Alvin W. Gouldner, *The Dialectic of Ideology and Technology: The Origins, Grammar, and Future of Ideology* (New York: Seabury, 1976), p. 102. "To be 'accountable' means that one can be *constrained* to reveal *what* one has done and *why* one has done it; thus, the action and the reason for it are open to a critique by strangers." Gouldner, pp. 101–103, explains privacy as an overlapping of the economic system with a traditional patriarchy, so that the father is still immune to questioning from the family, his private realm within the public.

28 Dicey, in the 1914 introduction, *Law and Public Opinion in England*, p. lv, writes that "the advance ... of human knowledge has intensified the general conviction that even the apparently innocent action of an individual may injuriously affect the welfare of a whole community" and instances the man who first imported rabbits to Australia.

29 Cf. Asa Briggs, *Victorian Cities* (New York: Harper, 1965), p. 81.

were as large as or larger than eighteenth-century London). But it is by no means clear that economic necessity alone was the cause. People moving to the city, particularly young people, assumed they were exercising a choice.[30] The urban experience that resulted from this migration and unprecedented growth in population, especially the experience of the commercial, skilled, and professional workers who had reason to feel they were free, combined publicity with increased experience of isolation. In closer proximity with one another individuals knew both more and less about their neighbors. About citizens who were neither neighbors nor fellow workers they knew only the outside; the inside was a matter for conjecture. Thus a common fascination of urban life, frequently remarked by novelists, was the sense of being surrounded by other people's secrets.[31] A corresponding sensation was that of being watched by strange eyes. These feelings were not always imaginary, or if imaginary, were still such as could be acted upon. Those who could afford to sought shelter from publicity, in the layout of their apartments or in colonizing the suburbs. The middle class protected themselves from view as best they could and strove to keep watch on the servants and working class.[32]

Social mobility increases publicity and the need for privacy regardless of whether the movement is toward the city. Industrialization has mostly a centripetal effect on population, but commerce and the mechanization of agriculture have a less certain effect. Workers in shipping, railways, and government service move in all directions. All such movement creates a greater preponderance of strangers. It af-

30 J. A. Banks, "The Contagion of Numbers," in *The Victorian City: Images and Realities*, ed. H. J. Dyos and Michael Wolff, 2 vols. (London: Routledge, 1973), I, 105–122.

31 I have in mind not only sensational fiction based on this principle, such as Eugène Sue's *Mystères de Paris* (1842–1843) and G. W. Reynolds's *Mysteries of London* (1846–1855), but explicit comment such as that by Dickens in *A Tale of Two Cities* (London: Oxford University Press, 1949), bk. I, ch. 3: "A solemn consideration, when I enter a great city by night, that every one of those darkly clustered houses encloses its own secret; that every room in every one of them encloses its own secret; that every beating heart in the hundreds of thousands of breasts there, is, in some of its imaginings, a secret to the heart nearest it!" Similar reflections may be found in Thackeray, *The Newcomes*, ch. 29, and Bulwer, *Eugene Aram*, bk. IV, ch. 5.

32 Donald J. Olsen, "Victorian London: Specialization, Segregation, and Privacy," *Victorian Studies*, 17 (1974), 265–278. Olsen uses the architectural record to demonstrate that "the Victorians desired . . . privacy for the middle classes, publicity for the working classes" (p. 271). "The story of the reconstruction of Victorian London reveals the tension between two coexistent but incompatible Victorian ideals: individual privacy and public accountability" (p. 275).

fords opportunities for individuals or families to move away from an old "situation" as well as toward a new one. Thus there become exurbanites, like Silas Marner and Nicholas Bulstrode both, who are strangers. A high degree of social mobility divides individual lives in time and conceals their past from view. It makes a person, in Mill's words, dependent "more and more upon opinion" but "less and less . . . upon the opinion of those who know him." The discontinuity of place opens a person to real or imagined pursuit—it may be by his own family. The discontinuity opens a person to real or imagined blackmail, if he has erred in the past or if he regards his origins as low. When persons live all their lives in one place, the issue of publicity and privacy is less likely to arise. Wrongdoers among them are known and have already suffered disgrace. According to the Victorian writer Robert Vaughan,

> In a neighbourhood where every man is known . . . where all his movements are liable to observation, and the slightest irregularity becomes a matter of local notoriety, a strong check is constantly laid upon the tendencies of the ill-disposed. In such connexions it is felt that should the law fail to punish, society will not. The crowded capital is to such men as some large and intricate forest, into which they plunge, and find, for a season at least, the places of darkness and concealment convenient for them.[33]

By the same token the ill-disposed are not subject to blackmail if they are known and stay in one place: this is why blackmail is usually associated with migration and with urban life.

Social mobility that is voluntary is likely to be upward mobility, a tendency or desire very evident in the nineteenth century. "The desire of rising," Mill writes, "becomes no longer the character of a particular class but of all classes." Not Caesar only, but all men and women are ambitious: from a certain jaundiced view this undifferentiated ambition is pointless and bound to be resentful. It tends to substitute money-making for other values, and to be emulated by dishonest as well as law-abiding persons.[34] Yet money-making and in-

33 Quoted by Briggs, *Victorian Cities*, p. 61.

34 Cf. Max Scheler, *Ressentiment*, ed. Lewis A. Coser, trans. William W. Holdheim (1961; rpt. New York: Schocken, 1972), pp. 56–58, and Lionel Trilling, *Sincerity and Authenticity* (1971; rpt. Cambridge: Harvard University Press, 1974), pp. 14–16.

creasing consumption are motives essential to society. Because ambition is regarded as general, and because goals of excellence, obedience, or craftsmanship seem diminished, each person's vocation is success. One must have a career—nothing more and nothing less. A nineteenth-century word in this sense, a "career" is essentially a race to the finish. It is competitive and more demanding than a traditional "place." It makes ambition accountable and puts an entire lifetime at risk. Villainy is a career that cuts corners; success is a career that cannot be faulted. Temptation is wanting to cut corners—or telling. Without question the upward cast of social mobility in the nineteenth century made everyone more sensitive to publicity.

A third condition is the acceptance of representative government, a form to which even totalitarian societies pretend. Parliament, the institution of representative government in England, evolved over a long period of time: by the Reform Act of 1832 the principle of representation had been accepted, but the means had still not been fully worked out. Recourse to public opinion seemed a safer bet than spelling out too closely which powers adhered to which constituencies. Merely the notion of *self*-government is fraught with difficulty for a people with ample traditional authorities other than self. The notion of any government at all ran counter in some respects to the growing assumption in favor of personal ambition, and especially of "earnestness."[35] Most Victorians were inclined to the belief that the less government the better. They compensated by preaching a good deal of personal self-control, except in the wide area of making money, where selfishness was necessary to the self-regulating market.

Accountability is both upward and downward in representative government. What stands out is the idea of deserving, in both the constituency and representatives. It is to be decided by a series of reform bills who deserves to vote; and it is to be decided, at each election, who deserves to represent the voters. This is an altogether different conception of government from that in which custom or inheritance decides who shall have these powers. The spotlight is on the past, present, and future behavior of the office-seeker or incumbent. This is why the career of politicians is most sensitive of all to fault or betrayal. It also explains why politicians are usually more anxious to protest they have never changed their minds than they are

35 See Walter E. Houghton, *The Victorian Frame of Mind, 1830–1870* (1957; rpt. New Haven: Yale University Press, 1972), pp. 183–195, 218–262.

to accomplish a particular goal. Since policies are debatable, and effectiveness difficult to prove, consistency is everything. Elected representatives are more often brought down for lying than for wrong policies. Consistency is highly vulnerable, subject to any inconsistency whatever. The theory and practice of representative government have thus contributed to the modern sense of the difference between public and private life. As Max Weber argued, "this conceptual separation of private and public was first conceived and realized in urban communities; for as soon as their officeholders were secured by periodic *elections*, the individual power-holder, even if he was in the highest position, was obviously no longer identical with the man who possessed authority 'in his own right.' "[36] Accountability extends to appointed officials, when they are appointed by a representative or when they are appointed on their own merits, on the basis of their career rather than inherited privilege. To be a "representative" or to serve one is to acknowledge the accountability of one's very existence.

Representative government is the practical means of making state power accountable to society. It is also the incarnation of the principle that society itself is accountable for its welfare.[37] In order for representation to work, the constituency has to be highly responsible. This belief in accountability at both ends of the relation causes well-intentioned Victorians like Mill and George Eliot to insist so firmly on education, and on the extension of literacy prior to the extension of the franchise. Their less moderate friends tirelessly preached the accountability of those who are represented. Carlyle urged, "*Be* thyself a man abler to be governed";[38] and Spencer intoned, "It is thus everywhere and in all degrees—misconduct among those in power is the correlative of misconduct among those over whom they exercise power."[39] Mill himself, at least in his younger days, could point a stern finger in the same direction. In arguing that intelligence rather than property should ideally be the test of the franchise, he supposed

36 *Wirtschaft und Gesellschaft*, pt. III, ch. 6, in *From Max Weber: Essays in Sociology*, ed. and trans. H. H. Gerth and C. Wright Mills (1946; rpt. New York: Oxford University Press, 1967), p. 239.

37 Cf. Trilling, *Sincerity and Authenticity*, p. 26.

38 "Downing Street" (1850), *Latter-Day Pamphlets*, no. 3, *The Works of Thomas Carlyle*, Centenary Edition, 30 vols. (London: Chapman and Hall, n.d.), XX, 105.

39 *The Study of Sociology* (1873), ed. Talcott Parsons (Ann Arbor: University of Michigan Press, 1961), p. 363.

that "it would be easy to exclude all who cannot read, write, and ci-
pher. If a higher test be desirable"—and Mill always privately felt
that it was—"there would be no great difficulty in contriving it." But
Mill, in 1835, did not stop here, since "vice" was also a possible dis-
qualification:

> A test of morality would, in the present state of society, be not so
> easy to devise; something, however, might be done towards it.
> To have been seen drunk, during the year previous, might be a
> disqualification at the annual registry. To have received parish
> relief during the same time, might be equally so. Conviction for
> any criminal offence might disqualify for a longer period, or for
> ever.[40]

The linkage of vice with ignorance, illiteracy with crime, and all four
with parish relief, is typical of attitudes toward knowledge at the
time. I cite these suppositions not to display Mill's political views in
any case, but to show how the theory of representation assumes accountability at its source, and this over a period of time. Certain kinds
of past behavior are to count importantly in the present and future.
Mill's apology for "the present state of society" hints at greater and
greater accountability to come.

Finally, there is a danger that society, with its commitment to a
self-regulating economy energized by the striving of all and organized by representatives rather than traditional rulers, will lose its
sense of community. "What makes mass society so difficult to bear,"
in Hannah Arendt's words, "is not the number of people involved, or
at least not primarily, but the fact that the world between them has
lost its power to gather them together, to relate and to separate
them."[41] The danger of fragmentation is a constant assumption of society. The lasting impression one receives from *On Liberty* is the incalculable difficulty of sustaining society. Tremendous good will and
patience are necessary, tolerance for differentiation and variety of activity, acceptance of the uneasy divergence of public and private life.
Not even immense knowledge will be enough if a sense of cohesion
and direction is wanting. "At present," remarks Dr. Kenn in *The
Mill on the Floss*, "everything seems tending towards the relaxation

---

40 "Rationale of Representation," *C.W.*, XVIII, 31–32. A review of Samuel Bailey,
The Rationale of Political Representation (1835).
41 Arendt, *The Human Condition*, p. 48.

of ties,—towards the substitution of wayward choice for the adherence to obligation, which has its roots in the past" (bk. VII, ch. 2). The whole idea of accountability becomes a subject for the novel because it threatens anew. Maggie Tulliver owes no obligation to God or to Dr. Kenn, only to "the reliance others have in us" (bk. VI, ch. 14). George Eliot became increasingly concerned with this problem, and the last words of the finale to *Middlemarch* still reflect on the "incalculably diffusive" nature of human efforts. As J. Hillis Miller has observed, the novelist herself exemplified "the Victorian transformation from a view of society based on a transcendent ground to a view of it as generating itself."[42]

There are some who feel the need for community but lack patience, and many who are so intolerant of diversity that they distrust privacy altogether. For most people, it may be, the notion that they depend for governance on others little different from themselves is frightening. The burden of so much knowledge, education and reading, legislation and earnestness, is very great. Hence there is a temptation to merge public and private spheres once again in the name of some settled principle of solidarity. Community is everything from this point of view, and privacy becomes secrecy in a bad sense. Or rather, we are the community, and those who differ are a conspiracy. They, in fact, are secretly conspiring to steal our secrets.[43] Thus society can produce a kind of sickness more oppressive than that imagined by Mill, and one in which incoherence turns to fear and fantasy. A frequent expression of such feeling in the nineteenth century was the attribution of power to secret societies. For a certain mentality, the experience of self-government and the belief that events took place of their own accord were delusions: rather, whatever came to pass was due to the intrigue of a few highly placed but disguised persons, bound together by secret oaths and inescapable penalties. It is possible that more people believed in the secret power of a few in the nineteenth century than at any other time in history. The advent of

42 *The Form of Victorian Fiction* (Notre Dame: University of Notre Dame Press, 1968), p. 113.

43 Cf. Edward A. Shils, *The Torment of Secrecy: The Background and Consequences of American Security Policies* (1956; rpt. Carbondale: Southern Illinois University Press, 1974), p. 34. In this book Shils is concerned with the so-called McCarthy era in the United States. See also his "Privacy: Its Constitution and Viscissitudes," *Law and Contemporary Problems*, 31 (Spring 1966), 281–306.

society was oddly accompanied by the fond belief in secret socie-ties.[44]

All such assumptions about society, including the idea of its fail-ure, are amply reflected in English novels. The novel came into its own as a literary kind when society came into being; it is, in Arendt's phrase, "the only entirely social art form."[45] By means of the novel, Harry Levin has suggested, society became its own historian.[46] The nineteenth-century English novel, I am arguing, repeatedly dwells on the hero's fear of publicity. The hero almost never consciously op-poses society; heroes and heroines are *of* society, and novels are com-posed strictly from the same point of view. Yet beginning with the Waverley Novels of Scott, novels make clear what the rest of the his-torical record states only imperfectly: namely, that the anxiety of the law-abiding citizen is lest he or she be thought to break the law, or find himself or herself outside the pale of society. The anxiety is ac-tually more apparent than any evidence of improper thoughts. A classic demonstration of such anxiety is *Rob Roy*, the hero of which is not Rob Roy, an extrasocial being, but the young man named Francis Osbaldistone. Young Frank has many near brushes with violence, and he is certainly brave; yet typically he is anxious about his rela-tions with duly constituted authorities, and whether differences in his appearance will "expose him to observation, if not to censure," from other law-abiding folk. Perhaps this anxiety is prominent in *Rob Roy* because the novel is narrated by the hero of society, but the feelings are characteristic of all such.[47] The posture of the hero in nineteenth-century English novels is generally so tame that it scarcely seems worth remarking except when, as in *Felix Holt, the Radical*, the title

44 See J. M. Roberts, *The Mythology of Secret Societies* (London: Secker and Warburg, 1972), esp. pp. 2, 12, 15–17, 356–357. Among novelistic treatments Roberts, pp. 3–8, cites Disraeli's *Lothair* (1870) and, in passing, Dostoevsky's *The Possessed* (1871), James's *The Princess Casamassima* (1886), and Conrad's *The Secret Agent* (1907). The strength of Roberts's book as history is its stress on the popular myth, which greatly exaggerated the true power of the secret societies. On the other hand, as recently as May 1981 an Italian government fell because of a scandal of memberships in an elite Masonic lodge.

45 Arendt, *The Human Condition*, p. 36.

46 "Society as Its Own Historian," *Contexts of Criticism* (Cambridge: Harvard University Press, 1957), pp. 171–189.

47 Scott, *Rob Roy* (Edinburgh: Black, 1886), ch. 21. I have described the posture of the Scott hero toward law and authority in *The Hero of the Waverley Novels* (1963; rpt. New York: Atheneum, 1968), pp. 149–183.

or other such assertion ironically calls attention to the fact. The posture of the entire fiction is that of membership in society; the tensions are between private and public life.

If we were to ask for a single emblem for the conflict of public and private life, it would be Dickens's brilliant portrayal of the clerk Wemmick in *Great Expectations*. Wemmick, with his post-office mouth, is a caricature of public and private spheres, his life radically split between the criminal law office in Little Britain and the tiny "Castle" in Welworth, with its own livestock and cucumber frame defended by moat and drawbridge and secret communication to the outside. "No; the office is one thing, and private life another. When I go into the office, I leave the Castle behind me, and when I come into the Castle, I leave the office behind me."[48] An instance of the more wonderful fantasy that public life has itself become secret is provided by Disraeli's *Lothair*. In that novel both the Roman Catholic Church and "the oldest, the most powerful, and the most occult of the secret societies of Italy" are conceived on the same subterranean plane. As one of the characters remarks, "After all, it is the Church against the secret societies. They are the only two strong things in Europe, and will survive kings, emperors, or parliaments."[49] The convenience of a secret society for the unwinding of novel plots is not to be scorned. For the conflict of private and public life, it becomes possible to invent not only the individual actors but a social force capable of responding quickly and without too much regard for due process. "You have heard, Walter, of the political Societies that are hidden in every great city on the continent of Europe?" At the end of *The Woman in White*, the hero has only to point out Count Fosco to an Italian he knows in order to exploit "the deadly certainty with which the vengeance of foreign political Societies can hunt down a traitor to the cause, hide himself where he may."[50] The private imagination designs Societies in much the same spirit that the official Wemmick invents his Castle.

Novels with blackmail plots register the translation of reputation into information. If the information, or suppression of the informa-

---

48 *Great Expectations* (London: Oxford University Press, 1963), ch. 25.

49 *Lothair*, ed. Vernon Bogdanor (London: Oxford University Press, 1975), chs. 54 and 50.

50 Wilkie Collins, *The Woman in White*, ed. Harvey Peter Sucksmith (London: Oxford University Press, 1975), pp. 534, 540. On secret societies and the novel, see Manfred Mackenzie, *Communities of Honor and Love in Henry James* (Cambridge: Harvard University Press, 1976), esp. pp. 1–25.

tion, can be put up for sale by third parties, patently reputation has broken loose from personal control. In a trial of 1805, *R v. Souther-ton*, Lord Ellenborough ruled that threats, in order to be subject to prosecution, had to be "such as may overcome the ordinary free will of a firm man, and induce him from fear to part with his money." This early ruling, frequently cited by other judges, placed the first burden of defending against blackmail upon the individual concerned, who ought to be able to stand up against threats to his or her character. The law need not take notice of threats that a little firmness of character could repel. But in the course of the century, as the nature of English society itself changed, this judgment can be seen to erode. In *R v. Thomas Smith* in 1849, the court decided in favor of the recipient of a threatening letter, and Chief Justice Wilde modified slightly the standard of "the ordinary free will of a firm man." The case ought not "to depend on the nerves of the individual threatened, but on the general nature of the evil with which he is threatened." What occurred in the common law, I suggest, was not a pampering of the victims of blackmail, but a gradual shift away from an archaic ideal of self-defense toward a recognition that individuals do not have control over the information that affects their reputations.[51] As early as *Martin Chuzzlewit*, Dickens understood that the rules of behavior were changing with respect to reputation. Here is Tigg Montague, again, blackmailing Jonas Chuzzlewit:

> Reason the matter. If you don't, my secret is worthless to me; and being so, it may as well become the public property as mine: better, for I shall gain some credit, bringing it to light. . . . I am not a moral man, you know. I am not the least in the world affected by anything you may have done; by any little indiscretion you may have committed; but I wish to profit by it if I can; and to a man of your intelligence I make that free confession. I am not at all singular in that infirmity. Everybody profits by the indiscretion of his neighbour; and the people in the best repute, the most.[52]

The sociology is packed into Tigg's last sentence, "Everybody profits by the indiscretion of his neighbour; and the people in the best repute the most." Reputation has been reduced to a certain quantity of in-

51 Cf. W. H. D. Winder, "The Development of Blackmail," *Modern Law Review*, 5 (1941), 21–50. Winder fixes on the Ellenborough ruling and tends to argue that judges might still usefully apply it in cases of reputational blackmail.
52 *Martin Chuzzlewit* (London: Oxford University Press, 1951), ch. 41.

formation; detraction of some persons benefits others, as in a self-regulating market. One does not have to enter the market personally, to become a blackmailer or to pay one, to be a publisher or a postman even, to participate in this exchange.

A blackmailer has this curious role, for a villain, of aligning himself with society and also befriending his victim. One of the shrewdest observations by a sociologist in a recent monograph on blackmail is that the blackmailer seems to be enforcing the kinds of behavior demanded by society (and therefore supported by proper heroes and heroines). Mike Hepworth, the sociologist, is making the same point as Tigg Montague: the public would really like to know what the blackmailer threatens to tell them. "If the blackmailer is to profit he must symbolically mobilise the support of legitimate members of society; his threat must be morally sustained by an invisible accusing army."[53] The stress is on "symbolically," since if the public knew, the knowledge would be worthless; on the other hand, if the public did not care, in some sense, there could be no threat in exposure. The victim, at least, must feel the potential shame. Compare Hepworth's metaphor, "an invisible accusing army," with George Eliot's words in *Daniel Deronda* for Gwendolen's fear of Grandcourt: "Her husband had a ghostly army at his back, that could close round her wherever she might turn" (ch. 36). "Ghostly army" because the public is unseen and partly imagined, and because the force is organized and outnumbers the victim. Grandcourt is a powerful blackmailer who exacts obedience rather than money. His power, nonetheless, is allied in this way with publicity.

53 *Blackmail* (London: Routledge, 1975), pp. 66–67.

5

Circumstantial Evidence

Classical metaphors for the body politic were bound to be somewhat uncongenial to liberal theory. Herbert Spencer tried to conceive of government as the "cerebrum" of society, but as T. H. Huxley pointed out, even this updated metaphor was inconsistent with Spencer's belief that public administration was generally harmful.[1] The great exception to liberal distrust of government was an efficient police force, however, and by the end of the Victorian era this so-called arm of the law had become the most visible symbol of society.

Still, the number of police, and especially a police system, grew slowly. A common argument at the beginning of the century was that an official police force was incompatible with a free people—though a deeper objection was the need for paying for police services in advance, prior to the commission of any crime or to any disruption of the public order. The tact and good sense of Robert Peel achieved the Metropolitan Police Act in 1829 and assured the English police a marked civilian character. The County Police Act of 1839 accepted in principle the need for a broader police network but did little to accomplish this. Successive home secretaries had little persuasive power in the matter until the passage of the County and Borough Police Act in 1856, which compelled establishment of a rural police but also paid part of the cost. This astute compromise between central and local responsibility lasted for the next hundred years and did provide a police system. In Leon Radzinowicz's words, "by 1861 the

---

1 Cf. "Administrative Nihilism" (1871), *Collected Essays*, 9 vols. (New York: Appleton, 1894), I, 269–272.

country was covered by a network of professional police charged with the prevention of crime, the detection of offenders and the maintenance of order. Systematic enforcement of the law had replaced suspended terror as the accepted basis of control."[2]

Coincidentally, in 1861 George Eliot published her first novel containing a blackmail plot. Since Dunstan Cass is blackmailing his brother Godfrey by threatening to reveal the latter's secret marriage to their father, *Silas Marner* does not directly involve the police. Except for the constable accidentally killed by Felix Holt, no police are importantly involved in any of George Eliot's novels. Most blackmail plots in the sensation novels of the eighteen-sixties do not involve the police directly. Yet it is striking that just when "systematic enforcement of the law had replaced suspended terror" in social life, suspended terror should become so popular in the fiction of the same decade. One possible explanation of the coincidence is that assured prevention or detection of crime raises a very dull prospect, which may then be compensated for by imaginary crimes. A successful police force is a challenge to a make-believe Count Fosco, who boasts in *The Woman in White* that "the machinery [Society] has set up for the detection of crime is miserably ineffective ... The hiding of a crime, or the detection of a crime, what is it? A trial of skill between the police on one side, and the individual on the other."[3] Should the police suppress crime altogether, moreover, blackmailers must prey on reputations something short of criminal. Blackmailers will have to persecute those who merely imagine their guilt, or who have not always toed the line and are embarrassed by their pasts. It may be that the "suspended terror" by which Radzinowicz characterizes the restraint on criminals heretofore has been replaced by the "terror" of disgrace that Bulstrode is said to experience in *Middlemarch*. These conjectures are a bit strained, but an extraordinary coincidence is not to be overlooked in history any more than in a detective story.

George Eliot's lifetime witnessed a vast change in the attitude toward crime and the institutional means to contain it. Not only were the police established in this period, but the entire criminal law and its administration were treated with new respect as a system of re-

2 *A History of English Criminal Law and Its Administration from 1750*, 4 vols. (1948–1968; rpt. London: Stevens, 1974–1976), IV, p. v. See also T. A. Critchley, *A History of Police in England and Wales, 900–1966* (London: Constable, 1967), pp. 101–139.

3 Wilkie Collins, *The Woman in White*, ed. Harvey Peter Sucksmith (London: Oxford University Press, 1975), pp. 210–211.

straint. In some ways the criminal law, tidied up by legislation and administrative reform, was expected to take the place of religious or traditional prohibitions of unsocial behavior. After George Eliot's death, F. W. H. Myers wrote of a memorable occasion at Trinity College when, "taking as her text . . . the words, *God, Immortality, Duty,*" she had "pronounced, with terrible earnestness, how inconceivable was the *first*, how unbelievable the *second*, and yet how peremptory and absolute the *third.*" In Myers's account, "Never, perhaps, have sterner accents affirmed the sovereignty of impersonal and unrecompensing Law."[4] But duty might also be enforced by law in the narrower sense, with similar conviction that something must take the place of traditional sanctions of behavior. The criminal law and its efficient administration comprised a sanction of publicity, to which everyone must submit. Thus, two years later, James Fitzjames Stephen wrote in *A History of the Criminal Law in England*—the first substantial work on the subject—that a criminal code for England would provide a "sermon" on the violation of duty. The year is 1883, and here are the final words of Stephen's history:

> At many times and in many places crime has been far more active and mischievous than it is at present, but there has never been an age of the world in which so much and such genuine doubt was felt as to the other sanctions on which morality rests. The religious sanction in particular has been immensely weakened, and unlimited license to every one to think as he pleases on all subjects, and especially on moral and religious subjects, is leading, and will continue to lead, many people to the conclusion that if they do not happen to like morality there is no reason why they should be moral. In such circumstances it seems to be specially necessary for those who do care for morality to make its one unquestionable, indisputable sanction as clear, and strong, and emphatic, as words and acts can make it. A man may disbelieve in God, heaven, and hell, he may care little for mankind, or society, or for the nation to which he belongs,—let him at least be plainly told what are the acts which will stamp him with infamy, hold him up to public execration, and bring him to the gallows, the gaol, or the lash.[5]

4 *Century Magazine*, 23 (Nov. 1881), quoted by Gordon S. Haight, *George Eliot: A Biography* (Oxford: Clarendon, 1968), p. 464. Cf. Basil Willey, *Nineteenth-Century Studies: Coleridge to Matthew Arnold* (1941; rpt. London: Chatto and Windus, 1964), p. 204.

5 *A History of the Criminal Law of England*, 3 vols. (1883; rpt. New York: Franklin [1964]), III, 366–367.

The purpose of the police and the nature of the reforms in the criminal law have to be recalled. The nineteenth century inherited an extraordinary array of criminal statutes, too chaotic even to be thought of as a rational code and characterized, if anything, by the severity of punishments. There were far more capital offenses than there had been in the sixteenth and seventeenth centuries. It was as if, in the formative years of "society," the consciousness of civilization had turned hysterically against crime, with a deep sense that law-breaking of any degree was intolerable.[6] On this subject, by the end of the eighteenth century, all shades of opinion were enlightened: the purpose of laws and their administration was not vengeance against the criminal but the prevention of crime. Authorities differed as to how crime was to be repressed, and solutions to the problem were repressive in different modes. Thus extreme punishments were defended and attacked on the same ground. William Paley, one of the great rationalizing minds of all time, favored capital punishments for wildly various offenses, contending that laws which successfully terrified criminals need not be strictly enforced. If executions were indeed more frequent in England than in other countries, that was partly because a free people prefer extreme penalties to such deterrents as a police force, which would restrict their freedom. As for the final and irrevocable nature of death, one ought "to reflect, that he who falls by a mistaken sentence may be considered as falling for his country," since the intent of capital punishment is the general welfare.[7] On the other side, reformers like Samuel Romilly, who argued against extreme punishments, were also determined to suppress crime. They agreed with the observation that extreme punishments were often not exacted, but contended that laws that were not consis-

6 Michel Foucault, *Discipline and Punish*, trans. Alan Sheridan (1977; rpt. New York: Random House, 1979), p. 90, quotes Rousseau, *Le Contrat social:* "Every malefactor, by attacking the social rights, becomes, by his crimes, a rebel and a traitor to his country; by violating its laws he ceases to be a member of it; he even makes war upon it. In such a case the preservation of the state is inconsistent with his own, and one or the other must perish; in putting the guilty to death we slay not so much the citizen as the enemy." Foucault, pp. 73–131, is excellent on the spirit of the new penology taking over from public torture of the body. The movement he calls punishment, however, with the focus on imprisonment, I am calling broadly crime prevention, from its principal motive.

7 *Principles of Moral and Political Philosophy*, new ed. (London: Baldwyn, 1821), pp. 410–412, 418–419, 428. First published in 1785, this work continued to be read and cited widely after Paley's death in 1805. Cf. Radzinowicz, *English Criminal Law and Its Administration*, I, 248–249.

tently enforced failed as a deterrent. The reformers were compassionate, as compared with Paley, and believed that sureness of punishment, rather than terror, ought to check criminal behavior. Experience appeared to be on their side. After Romilly's death in 1818 capital punishments were gradually repealed for many crimes, largely because those who were out of pocket from persistent theft protested that criminals were not being deterred.

The direction of reform in the early nineteenth century is significant. Making the punishment fit the crime was to make punishment more certain, so that no reasonable person could hope to get away with a crime if caught. In this way crime, with its measured consequences, was conceived of as a form of behavior, or misbehavior, to be accounted for in society. The emphasis was on the prevention of crime, for which everyone must care deeply. In a sense, of course, the vast number of noncriminals care more than the criminals: this is why Foucault can say that the punishment, to this way of thinking, is directed "at all the potentially guilty" as well as the guilty.[8] But Foucault has also emphasized that formal punishment becomes hidden in the nineteenth century. This trend is most obvious in England in the long struggle against public executions, which had become offensive to private sensibilities. Much fuss was made that executions hidden from view would not prove sufficiently terrifying, or even would not be believed. Some objected to the "mystery" of executions behind prison walls.[9] There can be little question that Foucault is right about the general trend, however one may differ about the sinister cast he gives it. The most general effect is that punishment "leaves the domain of more or less everyday perception and enters that of abstract consciousness; its effectiveness is seen as resulting from its inevitability, not from its visible intensity; it is the certainty of being punished and not the horrifying spectacle of public punishment that must discourage crime."[10] It is obviously not the case that whatever is hidden

8 Foucault, *Discipline and Punish*, p. 108.

9 In a letter to the *Times*, 17 Nov. 1849, opposing public executions, Dickens waved aside this objection: "The 'mystery' of private executions is objected to; but has not mystery been the character of every improvement in convict treatment and prison discipline effected within the last 20 years?" See *The Letters of Charles Dickens*, ed. Graham Storey et al. (Oxford: Clarendon, 1965–), V, 654; also to Douglas Jerrold, same day, p. 650.

10 Foucault, *Discipline and Punish*, p. 9. Paley, *Principles of Moral and Political Philosophy*, p. 424, takes up a suggestion "of casting murderers into a den of wild beasts, where they would perish in a manner dreadful to the imagination, yet concealed from the view."

is ubiquitous and powerful; yet Foucault expresses feelings of risk and punishment common in England by the later nineteenth century and especially to be exploited in sensation novels. It also appears to be true that guilt may have a history, and that the intensification of feelings of guilt has to do with the effort of society, a self-governing social order, to prevent crime.

Parallel reasoning lay behind the idea of a police force. Reformation and regularization of the criminal statutes were to assure that offenders would be prosecuted, convicted, and sentenced; a police force would assure that they were caught. Again the principle is to enhance the certainty of the process, and the purpose of certainty is deterrence. A system of constant observation, consistent prosecution, and sure conviction will be appreciated by potential criminals, who will adjust their behavior accordingly. That the aim of the police was the prevention of crime, rather than its punishment, is evident from the stated purposes of the reformers, going back to Patrick Colquhoun and to the maxims of Cesare Beccaria.[11] This aim was restated in the first instructions to the Metropolitan Police in 1829: "It should be understood at the outset, that the object to be attained is the prevention of crime."[12] The method of prevention essentially amounted to observation by the police and the collection of information. The choice of the title "Inspector" for police officers reflects this. The title apparently originated in a suggestion of Bentham, but it also anticipates the broad program of Victorian reform. For if "Inspector" achieved a certain dignity for the police, it was to become a title of much greater power and prestige in such fields as health and education.[13] The police were an instrument of knowledge and communication; the social transformation they were expected to achieve would take place primarily from the information they would gather and the awareness throughout society that they were watching, putting two and two together. Criminals or potential criminals cannot opt out of society; it is hoped, rather, that they will be constrained by their knowledge of the information against them.

11 See Radzinowicz, *English Criminal Law and Its Administration*, III, 246–249, 426–428. Colquhoun's *A Treatise on the Police of the Metropolis* was published in 1795; Beccaria's *Dei Delitti e delle Pene*, 1764, had been translated into English in 1769.

12 Quoted by Critchley, *A History of Police in England and Wales*, p. 52.

13 See David Roberts, *Victorian Origins of the British Welfare State* (New Haven: Yale University Press, 1960), pp. 152–206.

Thus it would be hard to exaggerate the difference that the existence of an effective police force makes in the consciousness of society. On the one hand, just as a reformed criminal law can instill "potential guilt" in everyone, the presence of police can generate secrets. It behooves a criminal, enmeshed by an efficient network of information, to cover his tracks. It behooves even the innocent person to avoid questioning by keeping his or her affairs as private as possible. As publicity in general enhances the value of privacy, a police force enhances secrecy, or the deliberate enactment of privacy. The changed consciousness that undoubtedly results, in the legally innocent as well as the guilty, is readily evident in imagination or fiction. The same novels by Wilkie Collins that celebrate detection are likely to capitalize Secrets.

The assertion that something must be done about crime became insistent in the early eighteenth century, and again toward the end of the century—in the program, for example, of the Society for the Suppression of Vice and the Encouragement of Religion.[14] But the means proposed were then typically private and unsystematic. Informers were employed, impunity was offered to accomplices, and rewards were advertised; for the most part criminals were pursued by those who were wealthy enough to make their resentment felt. The general method was to make it worthwhile for someone to discover and prosecute the guilty, and this was the method proposed by the state in most legislation. "Well into the middle of the nineteenth century," according to Radzinowicz, "the State relied largely on the various benefits which accrued to private individuals from the discovery and conviction of offenders, as its main weapon against public disorder and crime." Above all, the state, the voluntary societies, and the victims of crime depended on the institution of the common informer, a person who legally shared in the penalties assessed against the guilty. "Throughout the eighteenth century, and in the early years of the nineteenth, a number of statutes were passed, which so widened the activity of common informers that an important section of the criminal law came to depend upon them for its enforcement. It was hoped to extend their usefulness and vigilance to all the lesser infringements of the law."[15] Here was a thriving market

14 Radzinowicz, *English Criminal Law and Its Administration*, II, 1–29; III, 147–207.

15 Ibid., II, 33, 142. On informers see also J. L. and Barbara Hammond, *The Skilled Labourer, 1760–1832*, 2nd ed. (London: Longmans, 1920), pp. 341–376.

for petty information, if you will, older than the information revolution.

The history of the police can therefore also be seen as the gradual replacement of the common informer by the salaried policemen. Though legislation in the nineteenth century continued to assign informers an official role, the trend was to reduce their influence by reducing their share in penalties. As early as 1834 Richard Mayne, one of the first commissioners of the Metropolitan Police, began to argue that "the power of laying an information should be confined to constables," since common informers had no stake in preventing crime: on the contrary, the informer's business clearly profited as crime was not prevented. Even the institution of police was a little ambiguous in this respect, especially since police in the early nineteenth century also shared in fines and rewards from the conviction of criminals. Ideally, the more successful police are in the prevention of crime, the less they are needed. They are a model of self-denying citizenry. Mayne stressed that "perhaps the most important effect" of doing away with common informers would be to deprive them "of the power of levying money upon persons who have an advantage in breaking the law, and who are allowed to break it with impunity, by buying off the information."[16] In other words, the informers were frequently blackmailers. So are official police in a highly advantageous position for levying blackmail, it must be said, but they are far more constrained by their organization, salaries, and discipline.

Possibly, not only the new police but blackmailers inherited the role of common informers. The socially useful role of the informer is assumed by the police, say, and the lower motives by the blackmailer. In *Middlemarch* Raffles seems to have some notion of this parallel, for when Bulstrode declares that he will "decline to know" him, Raffles shoots back, "Ha, ha! . . . that reminds me of a droll dog of a thief who declined to know the constable" (ch. 53). Actually, like blackmailers, common informers were often low types. As they were permitted fewer lawful opportunities to earn a modest fee, some may have turned directly to guilty parties to demand the equivalent; and if lawbreakers were increasingly siphoned off by the police, the fine degrees of repute among law-abiding victims may have become that much more sensitive to attack. These are possible effects of a suc-

16 Quoted by Radzinowicz, *English Criminal Law and Its Administration*, II, 153.

cessful police, and if one adds the imaginative and fictional possibilities of blackmail, other dimensions of threatening publicity appear. Just as the common informer could be scorned, so in his place could the blackmailer. In fiction the blackmailer can be scorned as a private informer against the self, who therein deflects guilt and despite from the hero or heroine.

There is a sense in which an efficient police, like the higher inspectors of Victorian reform, have nothing to do but accumulate information. Should the police be entirely successful in their object, the prevention of crime, they would have nothing to do but maintain the supply of information and let it be understood that the information was available as necessary. But note that this is information of a special kind. All of it is potentially evidence; and proof of a crime in a strict sense, as the nineteenth-century jurists understood the matter, required circumstantial evidence. "A case regarded as criminal," Bentham wrote, "cannot but include a mixture of circumstantial evidence. For, to constitute a criminal act, one or more facts of the psychological kind are indispensably requisite: in most instances, the sentiment of *consciousness* . . . in all cases, *intentionality.*"[17] Unless by confession, intention can be proved *only* by circumstantial evidence, since no witness can testify directly as to the thoughts of the accused. Opinions differed as to the use and abuse of circumstantial evidence, as they do to this day, but by the end of the century it had become a popular and well-known subject. I shall argue, indeed, that behind the system of police and detection, and the literature based on it, is the notion of circumstantial evidence. In the sense that the police have nothing to do but watch and wait, accumulating information, the information can do their job for them. The information is always there, waiting to be gathered up, and it is relevant information, incriminating information—that is, evidence. The commitment to the prevention of crime—not to strike blows at criminals but to watch them so closely that they dare not move, and to detect them if they do—can be related to the strong fascination of the time with circumstantial evidence. Without reference to this concept, and its popular usage, it is difficult to compre-

17 *Rationale of Judicial Evidence*, ed. John Stuart Mill, 5 vols. (London: Hunt and Clarke, 1827), III, 5. These papers were written, according to Mill's preface, from 1802 to 1812. Bentham's *Traité des preuves judiciaires*, ed. Pierre Dumont (1823), is a shorter compilation.

hend detective or blackmail fictions and the idea of society that lies behind them.[18]

A detective, to be sure, is an expert in sifting the evidence: "The great Cuff opened the washing-book, understood it perfectly in half a minute, and shut it up again."[19] Strictly speaking, however, the evidence is always first at the scene of the crime. A detective is a skilled and often intimidating agent, but the washing-book, the smear of paint, and the like are everywhere. There is always evidence, which keeps its own watch and impress of every event, and which in the popular imagination is both ubiquitous and relevant. The amateur detective and principal blackmailer of *Lady Audley's Secret* badgers the guilty Lady Audley with what he calls "the theory of circumstantial evidence":

> Circumstantial evidence . . . that wonderful fabric which is built out of straws collected at every point of the compass, and which is yet strong enough to hang a man. Upon what infinitesimal trifles may sometimes hang the whole secret of some wicked mystery, inexplicable heretofore to the wisest upon the earth! A scrap of paper, a shred of some torn garment, the button off a coat, a word dropped incautiously from the overcautious lips of guilt, the fragment of a letter, the shutting or opening of a door, a shadow on a window-blind, the accuracy of a moment tested by one of Benson's watches—a thousand circumstances so slight as to be forgotten by the criminal, but links of iron in the wonderful chain forged by the science of the detective officer; and lo! the gallows is built up; the solemn bell tolls through the dismal gray of the early morning, the drop creaks under the guilty feet, and the penalty of crime is paid.[20]

The implied melodrama, mild righteousness, and subtle but favorable comparison of the detective to "the wisest upon the earth," connect this warning unmistakably with the manner of Collins and Dickens.

18 For example, when Robert Nozick, *Anarchy, State, and Utopia* (New York: Basic Books, 1974), pp. 84–87, introduces blackmail to illustrate a nonproductive exchange, he writes in a footnote of "the unique piece of information" that someone might "have stumbled on." This association of blackmail with the fortuitous recovery of circumstantial evidence is extremely common. It is the way we have been taught to think of the subject by detective novels.

19 Wilkie Collins, *The Moonstone*, ed. J. I. M. Stewart (Harmondsworth: Penguin, 1966), p. 147.

20 Mary Elizabeth Braddon, *Lady Audley's Secret* (New York: Dover, 1974), ch. 15.

A reasonably experienced reader of novels would have no difficulty in placing it about the year 1862. But the basic assumption that circumstances slight as straws can hang a man, the elision of due process so evident in the speech of Braddon's hero, is actually prior to sensation novels, deeply wound up with conceptions of science and the law, and roughly coterminus with the idea of society.

Robert Audley, at least, has the dramatic excuse of trying to frighten Lady Audley; but notice the use of similar rhetoric and even some of the same words in an anonymous essay on circumstantial evidence in the *Law Journal* for 1879. The vestiges of a crime may be traced, according to this writer,

> step by step, till the whole secret stands revealed, and that which was before hidden in the deepest and darkest recess of the criminal's memory and conscience, is brought forth to public view. A piece of broken blade, a single hair, a fragment of newspaper, the print of a hand or a foot, a casual glance, the slightest mark on the person or dress, a half-obliterated label, a word dropped from the lips of guilt, a conscious look or terrified start at a random expression, have each opened up or led on the trail by which the criminal is hunted down.

This same enthusiast is eager to explain the "dangers" to the innocent from evidence, and nothing is a surer index of the terrific aspect of the whole conception than this exaggerated caution. It is "more than possible," the writer remarks, "that the most innocent person may, by the ever-varying and singular accidents of human life, become involved in circumstances of so suspicious a character that they may leave him the occupant of the condemned cell, or at least with a dark suspicion so surrounding and haunting him as effectually to blast his life and prospects."[21]

Formal treatises on evidence, written typically by barristers, convey quite clearly the rationale for this popular view. The very existence of such treatises is historically significant, for the law of evidence arises in the eighteenth century and flourishes in the nineteenth: the law was never codified for England, but much writing was devoted to the subject.[22] Most treatises, following Bentham, de-

---

21 "The Value and Dangers of Circumstantial Evidence," *Law Journal*, 6 Sept. 1879, pp. 545, 544. The writer also borrows freely from Thomas Starkie (see note 23).
22 James Fitzjames Stephen, *A Digest of the Law of Evidence*, 3rd ed. (London: Macmillan, 1877), p. vi, comments on the sheer size of the current treatises, which

fine circumstantial evidence as any evidence other than direct testimony. They also employ the term "indirect evidence" and note that before the end of the eighteenth century such evidence was treated as "presumption." They supply standard cautions about the use of circumstantial evidence and discuss its advantages and disadvantages, as against direct testimony, for establishing the truth. One standard work, by Thomas Starkie, expresses very well both the caution and the enthusiasm inherent in the early Victorian approach:

> The consideration of the nature of circumstantial evidence, and of the principles on which it is founded, merits the most profound attention. It is essential to the well-being, at least, if not to the very existence of civil society, that it should be understood, that the secrecy with which crimes are committed will not ensure impunity to the offender. At the same time it is to be emphatically remarked, that in no case, and upon no principle, can the policy of preventing crimes, and protecting society, warrant any inference which is not founded on the most full and certain conviction of the truth of the fact, independently of the nature of the offence, and of all extrinsic considerations whatsoever.[23]

The statement registers the general purpose of crime prevention and the consciousness of secrecy that this purpose has helped to engender. The more crime is suppressed, the more secret it ought to become in pure self-interest; and the determination to suppress it recognizes this much. Circumstantial evidence is a deterrent to crime and can also betray the intent, which is secret unless confessed, as Bentham pointed out. All evidence bears prosecutorial temptations but must never be pressed beyond "the truth of the fact."

At stake are "the well-being" and possibly "the very existence of civil society." Starkie proceeds to a general assumption about the nature of the world and human society that lies behind the sensation novels of the eighteen-sixties and also such major imaginative reconstructions as *Bleak House* and *Middlemarch*—to say nothing of the scientific views of Spencer or Darwin:

were destined to grow still larger. The *Digest* originated from an abortive plan to prepare a code for England similar to the India Evidence Act of 1872, which Stephen had authored.

23 *A Practical Treatise of the Law of Evidence*, 3rd ed., 3 vols. (London: Stevens and Norton, 1842), I, 558–559. The first and second editions were published in 1824 and 1833; a fourth appeared in 1853 after the author's death in 1849.

All human dealings and transactions are a vast context of circumstances, interwoven and connected with each other, and also with the natural world, by innumerable mutual links and ties. No one fact or circumstance ever happens which does not owe its birth to a multitude of others, which is not connected on every side by kindred facts, and which does not tend to the generation of a host of dependent ones, which necessarily coincide and agree in their minutest bearings and relations, in perfect harmony and concord, without the slightest discrepancy or disorder.

This vision of evidence is all the more harmonious because it is retrospective. The "vast context of circumstances" enjoys the incontravertibility of that which has already happened: "it is obvious that all facts and circumstances which have really happened were perfectly consistent with each other, for they did actually so consist."[24]

Starkie divides circumstances and hypotheses based on them into "natural or mechanical" on the one hand and "moral" on the other. In treating the first he becomes somewhat carried away by examples involving broken penknives, pistol waddings, knee patches, and the impression of a key upon flesh, until he sheepishly checks himself with the observation that "there are, in fact, no existing relations, natural or artificial, no occurrences or incidents in the course of nature, or dealings of society, which may not constitute the materials of proof, and become important links in the chain of evidence." His moral proofs are moral in the sense of "moral statistics," or general laws of human behavior. "That a man will consult his own preservation, and serve his own interests; that he will prefer pleasure to pain, and gain to loss; that he will not commit a crime, or any other act manifestly tending to endanger his person or property, without a motive . . . are principles of action and of conduct so clear that they may properly be regarded as axioms in the theory of evidence." No doubt people have always consulted such axioms in reasoning about human behavior. Nevertheless, as with the heightened awareness of the interconnection of all physical events, the notion that man is a maximizing animal is supported by nineteenth-century convictions about society. "The

24 Ibid., I, 560. Cf. Mill, *A System of Logic Ratiocinative and Inductive* (1843), *C. W.*, VII, 379–387: "The whole of the present facts are the infallible result of all past facts and more immediately of all the facts which existed at the moment previous." Mill is careful to insist, however, that observation without experiment "cannot prove causation."

presumption that a man will do that which tends to his obvious advantage, if he possess the means, supplies a most important test for judging of the comparative weight of evidence."[25]

Starkie's enthusiasm stems from the commitment to crime prevention, which has been elevated to a faith that circumstances themselves record wrongdoing, as if the detection and prosecution of crime were independent of human legislation and enforcement. Policemen and smart detectives, common informers or blackmailers, need hardly be brought into play. "Fortunately for the interests of society, crimes, especially those of great enormity and violence, can rarely be committed without affording vestiges by which the offender may be traced and ascertained." Note the peaceful coexistence of circumstantial evidence with the interests of society. The offender has also his part to play, as Starkie's next sentence makes clear, for "the very measures which he adopts for his security not infrequently turn out to be the most cogent arguments of guilt." The same point is made by Robert Audley to Lady Audley in his reference to "the overcautious lips of guilt." Of course this convenient state of affairs does not result from mere luck, but from more general convictions of the time about knowledge and society. To the writer of a law treatise it may seem like luck, however. "Happy it is for the interests of society that forcible injuries can seldom be perpetrated without leaving many and plain vestiges by which the guilty agent may be traced and detected."[26]

Until the mid-eighteenth century "evidence" in a court of law had the primary meaning of testimony. Indirect evidence was known as "presumption" or inference; the introduction of the term "circumstantial evidence" shifted the emphasis from the reasoning process to the array of facts, particularly as they might be temporally reconstructed. Edmund Burke inadvertently publicized the concept during the impeachment of Warren Hastings by leaning on the opinion in *R v. Donellan*, a murder trial of 1781 in which the defendant was convicted entirely on the basis of circumstantial evidence. The judge in the case had observed that "a train of circumstances" affords strong indirect proof because it cannot be readily invented. Burke sought the same means of constructing a case against Hastings, and averred that

25 Starkie, *A Practical Treatise of the Law of Evidence*, I, 562–563.
26 Ibid., I, 559, 562.

all the acts of the party; all things that explain or throw light on these acts; all the acts of others relative to the affair, that come to his knowledge, and may influence him; his friendships and enmities, his promises, his threats, the truth of his discourses, the falsehood of his apologies, pretences, and explanations; his looks, his speech; his silence where he was called to speak; every thing which tends to establish the connexion between all these particulars;—every circumstance, precedent, concomitant and subsequent, become parts of circumstantial evidence.[27]

In early nineteenth-century discussions of evidence Burke's words, especially the last clause, were frequently quoted in conjunction with Paley's aphorism, "Circumstances cannot lie."[28]

A distinct notion of circumstantial evidence arose for reasons both intrinsic and extrinsic to the law. The intrinsic reasons had to do with the new consciousness of the rules of evidence, which in turn depended on the evolution of the jury. In earlier times juries consisted of witnesses; by the seventeenth century they were expected to render judgment as to the facts testified to before them.[29] Jurors became exemplary persons whose duty it was to judge on the basis of knowledge at a distance. But the modern notion of evidence also derives from natural science and the rise of historicism. Since the inference of evidence is from effects to causes, the influence of science is essentially confined to induction based on observation rather than experiment: the applicable "natural or mechanical" and "moral" laws, to use Starkie's terms, are assumed as given, and the relevant facts worked into a hypothesis as to what has happened and why. Thus natural history and, in particular, paleontology provided models for circumstantial evidence, but not physics or chemistry. Natural history, it might be said, was the most influential science of the time, even though it does not strictly include experimentation. Paleontology appealed to the imagination because of the boldness of its con-

---

27 Report to the House of Commons, 30 Apr. 1794, *The Works and Correspondence of the Right Honourable Edmund Burke*, 8 vols. (London: Rivington, 1852), VIII, 95–96.

28 See Paley, *Principles of Moral and Political Philosophy*, pp. 426–428.

29 William Holdsworth, *A History of English Law*, 16 vols. (1903–1966; rpt. London: Methuen, 1966), IX, 127–133, 177–181. See also James B. Thayer, *A Preliminary Treatise on Evidence at the Common Law Court* (1898; rpt. New York: Kelley, 1969), pp. 7–182.

structions from sparse evidence. Hence we find a tribute to Cuvier in a book on circumstantial evidence:

> A profound knowledge of comparative anatomy enabled the immortal Cuvier, from a single fossil bone, to describe the structure and habits of many of the animals of the antediluvian world. In like manner, an enlightened knowledge of human nature often enables us, on the foundation of apparently slight circumstances, to follow the tortuous windings of crime, and ultimately to discover its guilty author, as infallibly as the hunter is conducted by the track to his game.[30]

The simile of the hunter supplies the lawyer with conventional passion, but that of the scientist supplies authority. The beauty of the word "circumstances" is that it implies connections without naming them, summarizes all effects and their causes, and refers to everything not glimpsed at first sight.

Sensation novelists treated circumstantial evidence in its terrific aspect. It is a trap, or innumerable traps, awaiting the unwary, and the threat it represents is almost worse in that it is intangible, consisting of information rather than steel jaws. But novelists were not alone in this regard. They expressed a popular view of the subject, which in turn was based on such sober accounts as we have seen. The very cautions of lawyers for the defense against exclusive reliance on circumstantial evidence sharpened awareness of its dangers. Evidence always poses trouble for someone. The prestige of induction in the modern world surely contributed to the weight of evidence in the popular imagination, especially to the weight of impersonal inference from "the facts." Yet evidence presented in a court of law is more pointed, more narrowly directed at what has occurred, more humanly troubling than evidence confronted by science. The former takes on almost subjective being while the latter appears objective.

Some of the differences between reasoning from evidence in law and in science were enumerated by James Fitzjames Stephen in drafting the India Evidence Act. First, the facts in physical inquiries

30 William Wills, *An Essay on the Principles of Circumstantial Evidence*, 3rd ed. (1850; rpt. Philadelphia: Johnson, 1857), p. 27. Starkie, *A Practical Treatise of the Law of Evidence*, I, 567n, pays a similar compliment to Cuvier on the same grounds. The single fossil bone was a popular symbol of induction. Thackeray, with a compliment to Richard Owen and Louis Agassiz, employs it in *The Newcomes*, ch. 47, to describe the craft of the novelist.

of science are "generally unlimited" and repeatable by experiment, whereas "in judicial investigations the number of relevant facts is limited by circumstances." Stephen compares the law with experimental science rather than with natural history, but notice in any case the double significance of the phrase "limited by circumstances." Circumstances, which everyone since Bentham agrees are unlimited, may still determine what is relevant. *The* circumstances are those that are touched by an event in time and become the evidence for this event, yet the extent of such circumstances is unknown except as presented. Their extent remains unknown after trial, since, as Stephen's second difference from natural science indicates, judicial decisions are limited by time. "In judicial investigations it is necessary to arrive at a definite result in a limited time; and when that result is arrived at, it is final and irreversible with exceptions too rare to require notice." Thus the "result" of induction differs from science: evidence is pointed toward a decision, one way or the other, that will be translated into somebody's cost. Stephen does not help much by stating, thirdly, that judicial cases are "generally complex" and open to doubt. "They affect the passions in the highest degree. They are testified to by untrained observers who are generally not open to contradiction, and are aware of the bearing of the facts they allege upon the conclusions to be established." On the other hand—the fourth point—the necessary generalizations are within the grasp of ordinary experience. And fifthly, "the process of reaching as good a conclusion as is to be got out of the materials is far easier than the process of establishing a scientific conclusion with complete certainty, though the conclusion arrived at is less satisfactory."[31] Such considerations are not at all reassuring, and they show that induction in law is humanly and dramatically much more affecting than in science. Evidence is introduced in court with a disposition or charge as to what is to be proved; in the treatises evidence is classified according to the *probandum*. To the lay imagination all this leads to a foregone conclusion, and "evidence" bears an unmistakable connotation of guilt. Lydgate acknowledges the superior power of circumstantial evidence at the end of *Middlemarch*, when he dwells on the certainty that he will be thought to have been bribed by Bulstrode: "the circumstances would always be stronger than his assertion" (ch. 73).

31 Excerpted in John Henry Wigmore, *Principles of Judicial Proof* (Boston: Little, Brown, 1913), p. 9.

If Starkie is right that "all human dealings and transactions are a vast context of circumstances," it is far from clear why circumstances should bring to the bar only persons who are guilty. A large element of chance is apparent in a theory that sweeps over an unlimited field of evidentiary facts, and it is this element that is ominously elicited by sensation novels and detective fiction.[32] Such works stir anxiety about circumstantial evidence and imply that a good many persons are guilty of one thing or another. Then they proceed to show that the evidence points to only one secret, or that crimes have been committed by criminals after all. To put it another way, they find psychological guilt quite general in the population and then make criminal guilt satisfyingly specific—a narrative procedure that has much in common with psychoanalysis. Yet the same narrative almost always includes a proviso that incriminating information is likely to turn up on its own. Sometimes the impetus is said to be old-fashioned Providence, as when Robert Audley opines that Lady Audley is "a foolish woman, who looked at life as a game of chance, in which the best player was likely to hold the winning cards, forgetting that there is a Providence above the pitiful speculators, and that wicked secrets are never permitted to remain long hidden."[33] More often it is simply chance, the same force in which foolish Lady Audley is said to place her trust, that brings the relevant circumstances to light. Most novelists seem to relish the idea of chance discovery, which closes the gap in their reasoning between all circumstances and the relevant circumstances. In *The Woman in White* we read, "Through all the ways of our unintelligible world, the trivial and the terrible walk hand in hand together. The irony of circumstances holds no mortal catastrophe in respect."[34] It is hard to tell exactly what this means, except that Collins takes pleasure in "the irony." If it is true that the trivial can be terrible—and Collins can hardly intend the opposite or an equivalence of the two—then it is finally true, in his novels, only for the truly guilty.

The Oxford metaphysician Henry Mansel reviewed anonymously twenty-four sensation novels, including Braddon's *Lady Audley's Se-*

32 Cf. D. A. Miller, "From *roman policier* to *roman-police*: Wilkie Collins's *The Moonstone*," *Novel*, 13 (1980), 153–170, and Patrick Brantlinger, "What Is 'Sensational' about the 'Sensation Novel'?" *Nineteenth-Century Fiction*, 37 (1982), 20–28.
33 Braddon, *Lady Audley's Secret*, ch. 29.
34 Collins, *The Woman in White*, pp. 486–487.

cret and Collins's *No Name*, for the *Quarterly Review* in 1863. Mansel astutely recognized that this kind of fiction differed from the gothic novel in that, no matter how improbable, the actions were typically set in "our own days . . . among the people we are in the habit of meeting." The secrets hinted at, though they originate in the past, are hidden at this very moment. "The man who shook our hand with a hearty English grasp half an hour ago—the woman whose beauty and grace were the charm of last night, and whose gentle words sent us home better pleased with the world and with ourselves—how exciting to think that under these pleasing outsides may be concealed some demon in human shape, a Count Fosco or a Lady Audley!" Thus Mansel pointed to the sensation novel's exaggeration of the modern state of privacy as cherished secrecy—indeed a desperately guarded secrecy that cannot, however, be guarded closely enough. He rather mischievously quotes from *No Name* a passage in which Collins, like Braddon, assures us that secrets cannot remain hidden:

> Nothing in the world is hidden forever. The gold which has lain for centuries unsuspecting in the ground, reveals itself one day on the surface. Sand turns traitor, and betrays the footstep that has passed over it; water gives back to the tell-tale surface the body that has been drowned. Fire itself leaves the confession, in ashes, of the substance consumed in it. Hate breaks its prison-secrecy in the thoughts, through the doorway of the eyes; and Love finds the Judas who betrays it by a kiss. Look where we will, the inevitable law of revelation is one of the laws of nature: the lasting preservation of a secret is a miracle which the world has never yet seen.

Mansel forgives Collins's vague secularization of the idea of Providence and comments instead on his logic: "It would be strange, indeed, if the world had seen it, since, in order to see it, the secret must no longer be preserved. The most completely preserved secret is, of course, that whose existence is least suspected; and if ten thousand such secrets existed, the world, simply because they are preserved, could not possibly know them to exist." For Collins the power of circumstantial evidence is caught up in "the inevitable law of revelation." As a proposition about the capacity of the human or natural world for concealment, the statement is a piece of nonsense or tautology. "The marrow of all this wordly wisdom," Mansel concludes, "is contained in the self-evident proposition, that a secret, so long as it is a secret, is a secret."[35]

The aim of preventing crime, through reform of the criminal law and establishment of a police network, contributed broadly to the very idea of society. More obviously than any other institution, criminal law administration holds individuals accountable, and as Foucault has so suggestively argued, the techniques for holding one accountable changed around the beginning of the nineteenth century. Imprisonment and restraint took the place of public torture; surveillance continued before and after imprisonment, with Bentham's wonderful and ominous Panopticon as a model. As recent critics have suggested, in the vein of Foucault, the spirit of surveillance and reporting inhabited the project of the nineteenth-century novel.[36] The agency of surveillance, in such characterizations of the period, is a bit vague, like the popular imagination of the latent threat from circumstantial evidence. Surveillance, of course, has political overtones even without explicit politics, whereas circumstantial evidence apparently depends on laws of natural history. Both ideas—or perhaps, sensations—are closely related to the rise of publicity, and the language of Collins and Braddon, at least, seems to me more often jubilant than sinister. (I would venture the same opinion of the films of Alfred Hitchcock.) Collins's "inevitable law of revelation" is the "spirit of Revelation" of Edward Lytton Bulwer, and his implicit secularization of Providence equivalent to Bulwer's pronouncement that "publicity is man's nearest approach to the omniscience of his great Creator."[37]

The history of the nineteenth century adumbrated in Foucault's *Surveiller et punir* sometimes resembles a sensation novel. While demonstrating that the historical phenomena he describes are widespread and independent of social control, Foucault manages to sug-

35 *Quarterly Review*, 113 (1863), 488–489, 496–497. H. L. Mansel is identified as the reviewer in *The Wellesley Index to Victorian Periodicals;* the paragraph by Collins is from ch. 4 of *No Name* (1862).

36 See Leo Bersani, "The Subject of Power," *Diacritics*, 7 (Fall 1977), 2–21; D. A. Miller, "The Novel and the Police," *Glyph*, 8 (Baltimore: Johns Hopkins University Press, 1981), 127–147; Mark Seltzer, *"The Princess Casamassima:* Realism and the Fantasy of Surveillance," *Nineteenth-Century Fiction*, 35 (1981), 506–534, which touches on journalism as well as fiction; and two essays by Richard Maxwell, "G. M. Reynolds, Dickens, and the Mysteries of London," *Nineteenth-Century Fiction*, 32 (1977), 188–213, and "Dickens's Omniscience," *ELH*, 46 (1979), 290–313.

37 See chapter 4, note 9.

gest that history may be morally implicated in its own unconscious designs. This impression partly results from the readiness to equate social history with the mental operations, conscious or unconscious, of the inhabitants of a particular time and place. But he may also give too sinister a cast to such exuberant celebrations of knowledge and publicity as Bulwer's, whether in England or in France. So were plans for the suppression of crime enthusiastic and unthinking, just as they are today, with reservations expressed chiefly about the costs. The Panopticon, a splendid symbol for the attitudes Foucault wishes to establish, was never built. As the contractor, Bentham hoped to profit from convict labor; but it is hard to say who was more foolish, the philosopher for putting money into the scheme or Parliament for bailing him out. Bentham was far more astute as a philosopher of language than as a businessman. "Publicity and privacy are opposite and antagonizing, but mutually connected, qualities, differing from one another only in degree," he wrote. "Secrecy might be considered as exactly synonymous to privacy, were it not that upon the face of it it seems to exclude gradation, and to be synonymous with no other than the greatest possible degree of privacy."[38] Such a method as this allows for none of the frisson of Foucault's history or of sensation novels. On the other hand, both the history and the fiction register a tendency for secrecy to be generated from the opposition of publicity and privacy.

Granted that not everyone has a secret, circumstances and publicity may chance to create one. For the innocent, especially, the possibility is dramatic. In some words about publicity in the newspaper sense, Henry James wrote of such unpleasant surprises as follows:

> Living as we do under permanent visitation of the deadly epidemic of publicity, any rash word, any light thought that chances to escape us, may instantly, by that accident, find itself propagated and perverted, multiplied and diffused, after a fashion poisonous, practically, and speedily fatal, to its subject—that is to our idea, our sentiment, our figured interest, our too foolishly blabbed secret.

To be caught this way "is to learn to dread reverberation, mere mechanical ventilation, more than the Black Death." James is thinking of

38 Bentham, *Rationale of Judicial Evidence*, I, 511.

the subject of *The Reverberator* again, focusing here on the sensation of publicity within the private self and the creation of a secret. As in Freudian constructions of the same decade, the dread that James complains of is independent of guilt or innocence in the criminal sense. It is more nearly a condition of modern consciousness. Thus he laments, in the same passage, "fine old leisure," which, "in George Eliot's phrase, was long ago extinct."[39] His allusion is to *Adam Bede*, in which the life of former days is briefly personified and contrasted with the present. Old Leisure, George Eliot wrote, knew nothing of "excursion-trains, art-museums, periodical literature, and exciting novels," nor "scientific theorizing, and cursory peeps through microscopes." Old Leisure "only read one newspaper, innocent of leaders, and was free from that periodicity of sensations which we call posttime" (ch. 52). Old Leisure, in short, was not plagued by so much information and communication. Wide changes in publicity, corresponding changes in private life, and chance discovery have contributed more to modern sensations of being watched than has deliberate social policy.

The young James had written perceptively of sensation novels at the time of their vogue, in a review of Braddon's *Aurora Floyd* in 1865 that also treated briefly of Collins. His first observation was similar to that of Henry Mansel and may have been triggered by the review in the *Quarterly*:

> To Mr. Collins belongs the credit of having introduced into fiction those most mysterious of mysteries, the mysteries which are at our own doors. This innovation gave a new impetus to the literature of horrors. It was fatal to the authority of Mrs. Radcliffe and her everlasting castle in the Apennines. What are the Apennines to us, or we to the Apennines? Instead of the terrors of "Udolpho," we were treated to the terrors of the cheerful country-house and the busy London lodgings. And there is no doubt that these were infinitely the more terrible. Mrs. Radcliffe's mysteries were romances pure and simple; while those of Mr. Wilkie Collins were stern reality.

A little irony plays about these last words. Collins's sternness is no doubt a Victorian sternness regarding the law of nature, but one

---

39 Preface to vol. XVIII, *Novels and Tales of Henry James*, New York Edition (New York: Scribner's, 1909), p. xxi. The remarks are prefatory to the story "Flickerbridge."

never knows how seriously to take his sermonizing. James goes on to make a more important point about the modern literature of crime:

> Crime, indeed, has always been a theme for dramatic poets; but with the old poets its dramatic interest lay in the fact that it compromised the criminal's moral repose. Whence else is the interest of *Orestes* and *Macbeth?* With Mr. Collins and Miss Braddon (our modern Euripides and Shakespeare) the interest of crime is in the fact that it compromises the criminal's personal safety. The play is a tragedy, not in virtue of an avenging deity, but in virtue of a preventive system of law; not through the presence of a company of fairies, but through that of an admirable organization of police detectives.

This contrast, of which the irony is unmistakable, goes to the secret of secrets, the way in which the spirit of revelation has supplanted the spirit of justice. Of course we are not as concerned as James pretends with "the criminal's personal safety," but the "interest" of the novels in question turns on discovery or information rather than justice. The "preventive system of law" and "admirable organization of police" are very much part of the society that brings this interest or emphasis into being. Nor does James stop here. He links the theme of information and its inverse motive "safety" to the method of the novels, and their descriptive modality to literary realism and its extension in modern dramatic performances:

> Of course, the nearer the criminal and the detective are brought home to the reader, the more lively his "sensation." They are brought home to the reader by a happy choice of probable circumstances; and it is through their skill in the choice of these circumstances—their thorough-going realism—that Mr. Collins and Miss Braddon have become famous. In like manner, it is by the thorough-going realism of modern actors that the works of the most poetic of poets have been made to furnish precedent for sensational writers. There are no *circumstances* in "Macbeth," as you read it; but as you see it played by Mr. Charles Kean or Mr. Booth it is nothing but circumstances.[40]

In the days of old Leisure there were no penny post and telegraph, no preventive system of law, and fewer reasons to keep records about

40 *Notes and Reviews* (1921; rpt. Freeport: Books for Libraries, 1968), pp. 110–112.

anyone. A different consciousness of social life prevailed; more depended on firsthand acquaintance and less on information. Reputations were supported, in Lord Ellenborough's phrase, by "the ordinary free will of a firm man," and occasionally were repaired by the use of a sword or pistol. In the days of no leisure, the use of information, publicity, and police promised refinements of justice. More elaborate bookkeeping and swifter communication, liberty of the press and public accountability, policemen to keep watch and evidence "tested by one of Benson's watches"—to borrow from Braddon one more time—all could be said to be motivated by the desire to refine justice. The more one knows, the greater impartiality one can muster; the greater the number of people who know, the less possibility of mistake; the more circumstances taken into account, the sounder the judgment. Today we accept more or less routinely, and in the name of justice, not only police records of past and possible future offenders but so-called security clearances and credit references on those who are not expected to offend.[41]

My intention in recalling the information revolution of nineteenth-century England, the rise of publicity, and the concept of circumstantial evidence has been to show the historical and cultural ground of reputational blackmail. No doubt instances of blackmail are as old as humanity, but it is the prevalence of blackmail and above all the consciousness of blackmail that are worth investigating as preconditions of our own social lives. When the Englishman Fielding in *A Passage to India* gazes at the Marabar Hills, their distant beauty is strangely at odds with English preoccupations:

> At this distance and hour they leapt into beauty; they were Monsalvat, Walhalla, the towers of a cathedral, peopled with saints and heroes, and covered with flowers. What miscreant lurked in them, presently to be detected by the activities of the law? Who was the guide, and had he been found yet? What was the "echo" of which the girl complained? He did not know, but

41 According to James B. Rule, *Private Lives and Public Surveillance: Social Control in the Computer Age* (New York: Schocken, 1974), p. 357, the aim of a good credit bureau is to keep records that discriminate finely: "The most unpopular result of abandoning discrimination . . . would be the inevitable inability of corporate agencies to render 'justice' to their clienteles. . . . To deal 'justly' with individual cases means to take account of fine details of clients' lives. And this in turn requires the collection of authoritative personal information and its application in forceful decision-making—in short, the maintenance of mass surveillance and control."

presently he would know. Great is information, and she shall prevail.[42]

This irony is finally of culture and of history. Information does not prevail in Forster's India—there is a trial, but the miscreant escapes detection, and it is never clear what, if anything, happened in the Marabar cave. Information has prevailed in Fielding's own country, as the narrator indirectly states. Great information achieved many things in Victorian England, but there she created secrets after her own kind.

42 E. M. Forster, *A Passage to India* (New York: Harcourt, 1952), ch. 20.

III

The Secret of George Eliot

Here an Archdeacon of the Church of England, one of our friends, is eloquent in praise of the Scenes of Clerical Life and sent me all the "Times" notice of "A. B." I can't tell you, my dear George Eliot how enchanted I am. Very few things could have given me so much pleasure.

1st. That a woman should write a wise and *humorous* book which should take a place by Thackeray.

2nd. That YOU *that you* whom they spit at should do it!

I am so enchanted so glad with the good and bad of me! both glad—angel and devil both triumph!

—Barbara Bodichon to George Eliot,
26 April 1859

In real life she had sought her fortunes elsewhere; and though to look back into the past was calming and consoling, there are, even in the early works, traces of that troubled spirit, that exacting and questioning and baffled presence who was George Eliot herself.

—[Virginia Woolf,] *Times Literary Supplement*, 20 November 1919

6

Writing and Identity

Marian Evans became the pseudonymous George Eliot as well as, or instead of, the improper Marian Lewes for reasons that were special and in part fortuitous, but many of the conditions of this transformation have to do with her time and place in history. Her secret authorship partook of the general division of private and public life in the age of information and the peculiar experience of the writer within that culture. All persons whose primary relations with their fellow beings depend on the written word multiplied in print, and whose material and emotional well-being comes to depend on this relation, are already pseudonymous individuals in that their names appear in print rather than on the lips of persons meeting face to face. The terms of private and public acquaintance, and representation, so differ that names may as well differ also. At the same time, the customary rewards and anxieties of personal relations become subject to accidental and remote interpretation.

The letters of George Eliot and George Henry Lewes amply illustrate this common alienation of the writer, exacerbated in her case by social ostracism because of their irregular union. Their letters, as presented and annotated by Gordon S. Haight, sometimes refer directly to the problem. The anonymous and experimental nature of the venture into fiction in 1856 threw the initial burden of correspondence with the publisher John Blackwood upon Lewes. Thus the first criticism of the first story, "The Sad Fortunes of the Reverend Amos Barton," was received by Lewes, and he immediately counseled Blackwood that his friend was "unusually sensitive" and "consequently afraid of failure though not afraid of obscurity." This anxiety he qualified by adding that Marian, whom he masked in masculine pronouns, would view as failure "that which I suspect most writers would be apt to consider success," and he indicated "the sort of shy, shrinking, ambitious nature" of his friend.[1] From this point on Lewes cautioned other correspondents about the novelist's sensitivity and diffidence. Meanwhile he encouraged her with positive criticism and began the practice of carefully vetting the published reviews of her work. George Eliot would later confide this view of her "nature" even to relative strangers—"for I am subject to depression about authorship."[2] How serious were her depressions we do not know, but we receive from such correspondence a very good idea of how she managed them, in part by confessing her weakness, publicizing it, in effect, to that sector of the alien world that was likely to be sympathetic. To Harriet Beecher Stowe, for example, George Eliot offered a particularly frank disparagement of her condition as a sickness: "[your letter] made me almost wish that you could have a momentary vision of the discouragement, nay, paralyzing despondency in which many days of my writing life have been past, in order that you might fully understand the good I find in such sympathy as yours—in such an assurance as you give me that my work has been worth doing. But I will not dwell on any mental sickness of mine."[3]

Such protestations by both Lewes and George Eliot seem almost disingenuous. Though she flinched from criticism, it may be that she was eager for praise to a degree that she herself disapproved.[4] The Leweses did in fact discuss responses to her writing at length, as most couples would, "for it is in vain that she abstains from reading what is written about her; there is always enough reaching her by indirect routes to tell her how her purpose has been misunderstood or has meet with indifference."[5] Repeatedly, however, they explain to correspondents the rules they have adopted for the practical management of such information: Lewes reads to her only the extremes of criticism, the welcome praise or entertaining foolishness.

1 Lewes to John Blackwood, 22 Nov. 1856, *G.E.L.*, II, 276–277. The following argument and some other points in this chapter I first outlined in a review of vols. VIII and IX of the *Letters* in the *Yale Review*, 68 (1979), 589–597.

2 To Charles Ritter, 3 July 1872, *G.E.L.*, V, 287.

3 To Harriet Beecher Stowe, 8 May 1869, *G.E.L.*, V, 29.

4 Cf. her observation in a letter to Sara Sophia Hennell, 5 June 1857, that she has "learned to see how much of the pain I have felt concerning my own family is really love of approbation in disguise" (*G.E.L.*, II, 342).

5 Lewes to Edward Dowden [Feb. 1877], *G.E.L.*, VI, 336.

I hardly ever read anything that is written about myself—indeed, never unless my husband expressly wishes me to do so by way of exception. I adopted this rule many years ago as a necessary preservative against influences that would have ended by nullifying my power of writing. Mr. Lewes reads anything written about me that comes his way and occasionally gives me reports of what he reads if it happens to show an unusual insight or an unusual ineptitude. In this way I get confirmed in my impression that the criticism of any new writing is shifting and untrustworthy. I hardly think that any critic can have so keen a sense of the short-comings in my works as that I groan under in the course of writing them . . .[6]

It seems as if the farther away the correspondent, the easier it is for George Eliot to explain this. She uses her far-reaching public connection to alleviate the groaning that it has helped produce. To a woman in Australia whom she had met once—awkwardly—ten years before, George Eliot writes at about this same time that, because her correspondent has engaged in studies "of a serious kind," she "will all the better understand that I have made it a rule not to read writing about myself." To this is added the frankly personal explanation, "I am exceptionally sensitive, and liable to discouragement, and to read much remark about my doings would have as depressing an effect on me as staring in a mirror—perhaps I may say—even of defective glass." Her husband, however, has read the correspondent's welcome article in the *Melbourne Review* and has told her of some gratifying passages in it before laying it away "in the drawer he assigns to any writing about me that gives him satisfaction. For he feels on my behalf more than I feel on my own—at least, in matters of this kind."[7] The striking thing about such letters is not so much the tortured modesty, but the overt statements about sensitivity. The repeated formula is itself a publicizing act, a way of coping with the intrusion of publicity by reversing its direction, almost by celebrating it. In the last instance, with appropriate and instructive irony, George Eliot's personal reply was itself published in the *Melbourne Review* shortly after her death.

The personality of George Eliot, as inferred from her own and Lewes's statements or as traced by a recent biographer to her rejec-

6 To Elizabeth Stuart Phelps, 16 Dec. 1876, *G.E.L.*, VI, 318.
7 To Catherine H. Spence, 4 Sept. 1876, *G.E.L.*, IX, 182–183.

tion by her family,[8] has to be seen in the light of her special circumstances and of the general conditions of literacy. In his edition of the letters Haight cautions us that "George Eliot bore an unusual number of names: Mary Anne, Mary Ann, Marian, Polly, and Pollian Evans, Marian Evans Lewes, and finally Mary Ann Cross."[9] Not only was the masculine pseudonym a conventional tactic for a female novelist, but it served to negotiate for the Leweses, or helped them to get around, the change of name and identity that women—and women only—conventionally accept when they marry. "George Eliot" itself does not seem strictly original as a name, and many have speculated whether the "George" honored her husband or George Sand. The strangeness of communicating in print, the rewards and anxieties of this relation, were shared by all writers who succeeded in reaching very many readers. Even those of us who are not remembered by a famous pseudonym are addressed variously by different persons, in print or in person, in legal or intimate standing, in directories or letters, at different times of life. The inevitable distancing of a writer's relation to readers diminishes control, and the interval between production and response continually catches by surprise the writer's normal readiness for approval or disapproval. The true secret of George Eliot is the ordinary concealment of writer from reader, and it would be an unusual person whose feelings were not affected by this relation.

Before turning to fiction George Eliot had ample experience of writing as a construction of public from private selves, including the experience of concealing and then revealing her identity—since her translation of Strauss's *Life of Jesus* in 1846 was anonymous, whereas that of Feuerbach's *Essence of Christianity* in 1854 was inscribed, just as she and Lewes were eloping to Germany, "by Marian Evans, Translator of 'Strauss's Life of Jesus.' "[10] Her work with John Chap-

8 Ruby V. Redinger, *George Eliot: The Emergent Self* (New York: Knopf, 1975). Redinger's explanations of George Eliot's behavior are often stimulating; her triangulation with J. W. Cross, *George Eliot's Life as Related in her Letters and Journals* (1885), and other early accounts is valuable. But her account of the life ought to be used in conjunction with Gordon S. Haight's *George Eliot: A Biography* (Oxford: Clarendon, 1968), which is the best guide to the rich materials of *The George Eliot Letters.*

9 List of abbreviations, *G.E.L.*, I, xxxvii.

10 This identification of the translator is especially momentous because of Feuerbach's insistence on sexuality as essential to humanity: see *The Essence of Christian-*

man for the *Westminster Review* made her familiar with the pleasures and frustrations of privately conducting a periodical committed to anonymous writing and reviewing. She was a reviewer herself before becoming the sensitive recipient of the criticism of others. In her most sweeping and forceful review article, she was careful to state, adopting a plural pronoun, "Of Dr. Cumming personally we know absolutely nothing: our acquaintance with him is confined to a perusal of his works, our judgment of him is founded solely on the manner in which he has written himself down on his pages." George Eliot tended to forget this distinction, perhaps, as it might be applied to reviews of her own work, but her disclaimer demonstrates her objective awareness, at least, of the divided being of a writer for publication. Dr. Cumming had, in her opinion, "written himself down" in more than one sense, but at the end of her article she reverted to the distinction, in a not altogether happy apology for him "as a man."[11]

The migration to the city, sensitivity to publicity, and apparently shifting identity experienced by George Eliot epitomize the life of her times and profession. Women do not always explain themselves to their brothers, two years after the fact, with the words "I have changed my name,"[12] because it is possible to refer to legal marriage somewhat less tangentially—but alienation from a family is not uncommon when courtship has been privately carried on at some distance. Family solicitors do not always write "to ask when and where you were married and what is the occupation of Mr. Lewes"[13]—unless of course the bride has run off and offended the family. The call for the credentials of Lewes and proof of marriage, in that strained reply to George Eliot's overtures, assumes a social mobility within which persons *could* marry without their families' knowledge. The anxiety and scarcely veiled threat of the solicitor's letter reflect a public component of feeling that gives blackmail its force—the

---

ity, trans. George Eliot (New York: Harper, 1957), pp. 91–93, 156, 170, 310–315. Harriet Martineau picked up very quickly that Marian Evans had put her name to the translation: see *G.E.L.*, II, 187n8, and U. C. Knoepflmacher, *Religious Humanism and the Victorian Novel: George Eliot, Walter Pater, and Samuel Butler* (Princeton: Princeton University Press, 1965), pp. 44–59.

11 "Evangelical Teaching: Dr. Cumming," *Westminster Review*, 64 (Oct. 1855); Pinney, pp. 162, 189.

12 To Isaac Pearson Evans, 26 May 1857, *G.E.L.*, II, 331.

13 Vincent Holbeche to George Eliot, 9 June 1857, *G.E.L.*, II, 346.

"ghostly army" that imperils Gwendolen in *Daniel Deronda* (ch. 36)—except that the Leweses have precluded blackmail by scorning concealment. When social freedom progresses still further, as it has in twentieth-century England, blackmail may fail for the opposite reason: not for lack of concealment but for lack of public indignation. The family may still care, but will not be likely to express itself through a solicitor and hold itself aloof in quite these terms.

George Eliot was conscious of her position and of her literacy in ways that might not occur to those who have not made such a determined move to transpose their lives from one condition to another. She wrote very amusingly of the difference that literacy makes in *The Mill on the Floss*, where the head miller, Luke, represents almost a different culture from the heroine's. Maggie Tulliver tries to interest Luke in some of her books, illustrated ones "that would be easy" for a confessed nonreader. Perhaps *Pug's Tour of Europe*, with pictures of Dutchmen?

> "Nay, Miss, I'n no opinion o' Dutchmen. There be n't much good i' knowin' about *them*."
> "But they're our fellow-creatures, Luke,—we ought to know about our fellow-creatures."
> "Not much o' fellow creaturs, I think, Miss; all I know—my old master, as war a knowin' man, used to say, says he, 'If e'er I sow my wheat wi'out brinin', I'm a Dutchman,' says he; an' that war as much as to say as a Dutchman war a fool, or next door. Nay, nay, I are n't goin' to bother mysen about Dutchmen. There's fools enoo—an' rogues enoo—wi'out lookin' i' books for 'em."

Maggie is like a little member of the Society for the Diffusion of Useful Knowledge. This conversation continues in what are, after all, quite sophisticated terms, as she proposes a book called *Animated Nature* instead. She seems intuitively aware of the importance of biology for her time, when she names some exotic species and comments, "There are countries full of these creatures, instead of horses and cows, you know." But Luke does not believe in knowledge in the form of information, only in the form of skills necessary to his work:

> "Nay, Miss, I'n got to keep count o' the flour an' corn,—I can't do wi' knowin' so many things besides my work. That's what brings folks to the gallows,—knowin' everything but what

they'n got to get their bread by. An' they're mostly lies, I think, what's printed i' the books: them printed sheets are, anyhow, as the men cry i' the streets." (bk. I, ch. 4)

The contrast of dialect and standard English in such an exchange reflects partly literary convention and partly social class; but in the nineteenth century this contrast also suggests the difference in literacy. As George Orwell pointed out with respect to certain characters in Dickens, [14] though the local character speaks in dialect, the heroine from the same locality pronounces words as she would write them.

The difference in exposure to book-learning involves Maggie and her brother Tom, also. Maggie right away observes that Tom is like Luke—"not fond of reading." She boasts that she "can tell him everything he does n't know," but she has forgotten to feed his rabbits for all that (bk. I, ch. 4). Later at school, Tom ought to have the edge over his sister because he is supposed to be learning Latin with Mr. Stelling. When Maggie covets Stelling's many books, Tom has his chance:

> "Why, you could n't read one of 'em," said Tom, triumphantly. "They're all Latin."
> "No, they are n't," said Maggie. "I can read the back of this ... 'History of the Decline and Fall of the Roman Empire.'"
> "Well, what does that mean? *You* don't know," said Tom, wagging his head.
> "But I could soon find out," said Maggie, scornfully.
> "Why, how?"
> "I should look inside, and see what it was about." (bk. II, ch. 1)

The contention between Maggie and Tom anticipates by a few years certain reiterative scenes in *Our Mutual Friend*. In Dickens's novel, Gibbon's *History* is the book that Silas Wegg, who has the ability to sight-read English ("show me the piece of English print, that I wouldn't be equal to collaring and throwing"), notoriously interprets for Nicodemus Boffin, who has purchased it at a sale despite his inability to read ("print is now opening before me").[15] Literacy was rapidly coming to be taken for granted in the Victorian era but was

14 "Charles Dickens," *A Collection of Essays* (New York: Anchor, 1954), pp. 82–83.
15 *Our Mutual Friend* (London: Oxford University Press, 1952), bk. I, ch. 5.

far from universal. Dickens's imagination was alert to the mystery that print must present to the illiterate, but as with George Eliot, the mystery is also something of a joke. Furthermore, Gibbon's great work is something of joke to these Victorians: a symbol of the Enlightenment that must be acknowledged but need not necessarily be read.

The action of *The Mill on the Floss* takes place early in the century, so there is space for reflection on the difference of knowledge then and now. The musings about old Leisure in *Adam Bede* are repeated here in scarcely different images:

> It was a time when ignorance was much more comfortable than at present, and was received with all the honours in very good society, without being obliged to dress itself in an elaborate costume of knowledge; a time when cheap periodicals were not, and when country surgeons never thought of asking their female patients if they were fond of reading, but simply took it for granted that they preferred gossip . . . (bk. I, ch. 12)

Though the narrator's irony faces both ways, and neither the past nor the present is praised for intellectual power or sincerity, the historical difference is clear, and that difference is marked by the rise of information. Moreover gossip, as we shall see, is not compatible with reputational blackmail, though cheap periodicals are. George Eliot this time is not commenting on the difference of town and country, but on the gradual historical change of the culture as a whole, which she exaggerates nostalgically in her early fiction. She is aware of the changes taking place in her lifetime and not at all convinced that the proliferation of literature is all to the good. Her essay "Silly Novels by Lady Novelists"[16] satirizes the "elaborate costume of knowledge," and no one is more aware of the sheer volume of print that is accumulating than this exceptionally learned essayist and novelist. At a visit to Cambridge in 1877 George Eliot was shown an American typewriter and expressed "the fear lest the type-writer should not only reveal its utterances in print, but should multiply them after the manner of the printing-press, thus adding to the number of worthless books."[17]

Maggie Tulliver differs from the people she lives among in that she

16 *Westminster Review*, 66 (Oct. 1856); Pinney, pp. 300–324.
17 Oscar Browning, quoted by Redinger, *George Eliot*, pp. 363–364.

is smart and literate. She grows into a passionate young woman, to be sure, and gains several sorts of moral superiority by the end of *The Mill on the Floss*, but her basic difference from the people she knows, with the exception of Philip Wakem, is her intelligence and habit of reading, however much her naiveté is also stressed. This basic difference from others, rather than her passionate nature or moral defenses, may be thought of as the essential projection of the novelist herself. Instead of drowning with her arms around her brother, Marian Evans became an intellectual. In moving to London at the age of thirty-one, she deliberately chose this role, which others besides herself were discovering in the nineteenth century. In Warwickshire she had already met persons like Charles Bray and Charles Hennell, and Hennell's two sisters, one of whom married Bray. Such persons deserved the reputation of thinkers and writers, but they had independent means and their immediate intellectual concerns derived from their position in the dissenting religious community of the time. Marian Evans's first intellectual concerns were religious; she first translated a work of German higher criticism of the Bible and later translated Feuerbach, who equated theology with anthropology. Even her movement between these two German writers shows a progress roughly the same as her progress to London and friendship with intellectuals like Lewes and Spencer, who were emancipated from religion and committed to supporting themselves by thinking and writing. Her first essay for the *Westminster Review* was fittingly a review of Robert William Mackay's *Progress of the Intellect*, which she accepted as an opportunity to defend knowledge both "actual" and "retrospective." "Now and then ... we meet with a nature which combines the faculty for amassing minute erudition with the largeness of view necessary to give it a practical bearing."[18] Whatever our conclusions as to George Eliot's emotional and moral life, it would be hard to overestimate the significance of her life in the company of books and other intellectuals, and the detachment it necessarily entailed.

Intellectuals comprise a diverse class, attached to various economic classes and performing various functions, for better or worse. Their two leading characteristics—perhaps their only defining characteristics as a class—are their emancipation from religion and freedom from patronage. Clearly secularization is important, because the in-

18 *Westminster Review*, 54 (Jan. 1851); Pinney, pp. 28–29.

tellectual does not (in theory) adhere to any received body of thought. "So long as a belief in propositions is regarded as indispensable to salvation," Marian Lewes wrote in her article on Cumming, "the pursuit of truth *as such* is not possible, any more than it is possible for a man who is swimming for his life to make meteorological observations on the storm which threatens to overwhelm him."[19] Freedom from patronage is important for nearly the same reasons of objectivity, and Marian Lewes devoted the first half of her second polemic, against the poet Edward Young, to an almost angry study of forms of patronage common in the eighteenth century.[20] The title of that article, "Worldliness and Other-Worldliness," mocks precisely the two characteristics of mental life that intellectuals oppose. Not surprisingly, they are to some extent emancipated from their national culture: witness the international bearing of George Eliot's translations and some of her other work, or Lewes's study of Goethe and wide acquaintance with continental thinkers. Intellectuals are too diverse and disorganized to establish a priesthood, but they are similarly a class apart from the rest of the population, with a "secret" devotion to secular knowledge. In a sense they bear a greater burden than a priesthood, because they conceive of their knowledge as self-grounding, independent of revelation or authority, and to defend such knowledge puts them out on a limb. The notion of accountability in modern society weighs heavily upon them because of their felt independence from tradition. This burden, more persistent than her guilt toward her family, explains George Eliot's earnest insistence that her life and writing have moral worth. It directly influences Marian Lewes's attitude toward the evangelical preacher Cumming. She objects to the "impunity" of such men, the way in which a church pulpit resists the accountability of thought in modern society. "For the Press has no band of critics who go the round of the churches and chapels, and are on the watch for a slip or defect in the preacher, to make a 'feature' in their article: the clergy are, practically, the most irresponsible of all talkers."[21] Notice the extraordinary idea of subjecting the pulpit to the press, of having the clergy undergo the same kind of review as other traders in the marketplace of ideas. Marian Lewes will accordingly address one irresponsible

19 "Evangelical Teaching: Dr. Cumming"; Pinney, p. 167.
20 "Worldliness and Other-Worldliness: The Poet Young," *Westminster Review*, 67 (Jan. 1857); Pinney, pp. 336–349.
21 "Evangelical Teaching: Dr. Cumming"; Pinney, p. 161.

talker in print on grounds where he can be held responsible—his own published writings.

For George Eliot and her contemporaries the end of patronage meant the beginning of dependence on the market, and for intellectuals who were not employed in any other sector of the economy, a dependence on publishing. A mixture of articles, reviews, and books, along with editing, became the practice of many persons successful at making a living by writing; but unquestionably the most profitable course was the writing of popular fiction. George Eliot came to believe that the vocation of "authorship" was possibly in need of "some regulating principle ... which would override the rule of the market";[22] but she believed that authors should be paid and was well aware of her own financial link with her public through her publisher. The apartness of authorship had its perils, but also its compensations—most notably the chance to establish a reputation without personal acquaintance with the public. Pseudonymity was a means of exploiting this opportunity and cannot be regarded as solely a defensive maneuver. In the nineteenth century the practice was especially favored by women, but even its initial use by a writer is only partially defensive, since it immediately fuels speculation and publicity for a successful book. Once adopted, pseudonymity has to be seen as the deliberate management of a secret, in the context of a market for writing and subject to the dictates of public opinion. And here Marian Lewes's special circumstances have to be taken into account. Besides the general conditions of being a writer and an intellectual, she had to cope swiftly with the secrets invented by her and George Henry Lewes: their irregular liaison and the identity of George Eliot. These two secrets, the first of which may be called an "open secret," they managed very differently. They told, even ordered, their friends to address Marian as "Mrs. Lewes"; they concealed, and ordered their friends to conceal, the identity of "George Eliot." In the management of the pseudomarriage, they preempted any possibility of blackmail; in the management of the pseudonym, they inadvertently—but in the end quite usefully—opened themselves to a strange form of blackmail. The two affairs were inextricably related, and both were successfully managed. The aggressive public-relations secret was made to support and finally to subsume the quietly determined private relation that was its principal source.

22 "Leaves from a Note-Book," ed. Charles Lee Lewes (1884); Pinney, pp. 437–442.

The circumstances of the person who became George Eliot, and the skill with which they were accommodated, are a kind of object lesson, despite their unusual nature, in the relation of private and public life in the nineteenth century.

Marian Evans chose, in effect, to live with Lewes in a manner not open to blackmail. The concealments they permitted themselves were only petty ones, the kinds necessary to prevent the eruption of land-ladies. With persons whose opinion mattered to them, they were frank and assertive. In September 1855, six months after returning from Germany with Lewes and before settling in Richmond, Marian Lewes—as she now determined to call herself—wrote these well-known words to Caroline Bray:

> If we differ on the subject of the marriage laws, I at least can be-
> lieve of you that you cleave to what you believe to be good, and I
> don't know of anything in the nature of your views that should
> prevent you from believing the same of me. . . . We cannot set
> each other quite right on this matter in letters, but one thing I
> can tell you in a few words. Light and easily broken ties are what
> I neither desire theoretically nor could live for practically.
> Women who are satisfied with such ties do *not* act as I have
> done—they obtain what they desire and are still invited to din-
> ner.

Women who care to be invited to dinner and conceal their affairs would be subject to blackmail; but Marian Lewes has braced herself for a scandal and actually prefers it to concealment. To her mind the private morality of the step she has taken shall weigh against public infamy, as her ensuing paragraph makes clear:

> That any unworldly, unsuperstitious person [cf. "Worldliness
> and Other-Worldliness"] who is sufficiently acquainted with the
> realities of life can pronounce my relation to Mr. Lewes immoral
> I can only understand by remembering how subtle and complex
> are the influences that mould opinion. . . . From the majority of
> persons, of course, we never looked for anything but condemna-
> tion. We are leading no life of self-indulgence, except indeed,
> that being happy in each other, we find everything easy. We are
> working hard to provide for others better than we provide for
> ourselves, and to fulfil every responsibility that lies upon us.
> Levity and pride would not be a sufficient basis for that.[23]

23 To Mrs. Charles Bray, 4 Sept. [1855], *G.E.L.*, II, 214.

As she frequently does later as George Eliot, Marian remarks the limited capacity of letters to convey feelings safely, but she also takes advantage of writing, even to her friend. Her feelings have been armored in the kind of argument one can only construct in writing, and the defense of her actions is predicated on distance and the withholding of personal confrontation. Her irregular marriage is predicated on these conditions, as is her profession, and these are very literate cross-purposes, which we are privileged to examine years later, in an equally literate way, because of their preservation in writing and print.

The secret of the authorship of *Scenes of Clerical Life* and *Adam Bede* was another matter. The novelist guarded very jealously the identity of Marian Lewes with George Eliot. Again she distinguished between personal friends and the public, but the number of friends who knew of the authorship was kept small and the danger of disclosure was thought to be great, as the following letter to John Chapman, in November 1858, attests:

> I have just heard that you have allowed yourself to speak carelessly of rumours concerning a supposed authorship of mine. A little reflection in my behalf would have suggested to you that were any such rumours true, my own abstinence from any communication concerning my own writing, except to my most intimate friends, was evidence that I regarded secrecy on such subjects as a matter of importance. Instead of exercising this friendly consideration, you carelessly, certainly, for no one's pleasure or interest, and to my serious injury, contribute to the circulation of idle rumours and gossip, entirely unwarranted by any evidence. . . . Should you like to have unfounded reports of that kind circulated concerning yourself, still more should you like an old friend to speak idly of the merest hearsay on matters which you yourself had exhibited extreme aversion to disclosure?[24]

In this case George Eliot's reproof of Chapman and her repeated use of "evidence" betray her vulnerability. Her sternness is justified because no firm line can be drawn, for this secret, between her private and public interest. The motives that caused her to adopt anonymity and then pseudonymity will be questioned; her private life may be

24 To John Chapman, 5 Nov. 1858, *G.E.L.*, II, 494. The incomplete text of this letter, as given here, survives in a sales catalogue.

used to discredit her public role (though she will not admit this). Both Leweses were committed to the anonymous-writing trade, and for secret novel-writing they could invoke the authority of Sir Walter Scott.[25] But now Marian's success changed the aspect of their other secret, which they had refused to treat as such. A scandal that could be withstood in strictly private life was directly injurious to the publicity which George Eliot's success required. That the affairs of unorthodox marriage and pseudonymous writing had become permanently linked is evident from the novelist's joking, in a letter to her new sisters-in-law more than twenty years later, "that I am the criminal usually known under the name of George Eliot."[26] In no sense was the secret of George Eliot criminal unless by association with her illegal marriage to Lewes. She could joke thus freely about it after Lewes's death and her legal marriage to John W. Cross.

Soon after Marian Lewes began to publish stories, she began to assure her friends in veiled words that not merely her selflessness, as she had hinted in her letter to Caroline Bray in 1855, but her future writings would make up for her sexual transgression. The first part of "Amos Barton" was published in *Blackwood's Magazine* in January 1857 and was followed swiftly by "Mr. Gilfil's Love-Story" and the adoption of her pseudonym. In June "Pollian" wrote to Sara Hennell, "If I live five years longer, the positive result of my existence on the side of truth and goodness will outweigh the small negative good that would have consisted in my not doing anything to shock others, and I can conceive no consequences that will make me repent the past." There was to be a deliberate trade-off, then, between the "small negative good" that she had failed in and the "positive result" of the next five years. She quickly corrects an adverse implication of seeming to trade conduct for reputation by adding, "Do not misunderstand me and suppose that I think myself heroic or great in any way. Far enough from that! Faulty, miserably faulty I am—" But then she reverses herself once more and concludes her letter with a bold pentameter refrain, "but least of all faulty when others most blame."[27] On the following day she begins a letter to Mary Cash, nee Sibree, with an admission that "the sense of my deficiencies in the past often presses on me with a discouraging weight." After some paragraphs

25 To John Blackwood, 1 Dec. 1858, *G.E.L.*, II, 505 and Haight's note 4.
26 To Mary, Eleanor, and Florence Cross, 13 June 1880, *G.E.L.*, VII, 298.
27 To Sara Sophia Hennell, 5 June 1857, *G.E.L.*, II, 342.

addressed to her correspondent's activities, she volunteers news about herself, in which her relation to Lewes is again coupled with a veiled promise to make up for it by her writing:

> I am very happy—happy in the highest blessing life can give us, the perfect love and sympathy of a nature that stimulates my own to healthful activity. I feel, too, that all the terrible pain I have gone through in past years partly from the defects of my own nature, partly from outward things, has probably been a preparation for some special work that I may do before I die. That is a blessed hope—to be rejoiced in with trembling.[28]

The immediate reference to "the past" in these two letters is to the past two years with Lewes, though it has the inclusive moral sweep familiar to the making of new resolutions. The balancing out of authorship and sexual behavior suggests that George Eliot's future protestations of sensitivity—"I am subject to depression about authorship"—may derive in part from "the terrible pain" of her affair with Lewes.[29]

The supposed marriage, however, had been kept from Marian's brother and two sisters, who were not told of it directly until this time. The optimism of these letters to old friends, in fact, is partially buoyed by George Eliot's writing the week before to her family about her marriage for the first time—and not having yet received a reply except from her sister Fanny. It is in this family connection that the exchange between irregular marriage and secret authorship comes most to the fore. Though the Leweses did not hide their relation, they resorted to polite silence as far as Marian's family was concerned. Marian Evans, no matter how they might insist, could not legally be-

28 To Mrs. John Cash, 6 June 1857, *G.E.L.*, II, 343.

29 In replying to Barbara Bodichon's delighted congratulations on her authorship, George Eliot wrote on 5 May 1859, "I am a very blessed woman, am I not? to have all this reason for being glad that I have lived, in spite of my sins and sorrows—or rather, by reason of my sins and sorrows" (*G. E. L.*, III, 64). To this friend, in other words, she begins to express the same sort of trade-off ("in spite of") that she had hinted at in her letters two years before, but then switches to a paradox ("by reason of my sins and sorrows") more in keeping with the bold spirit of her correspondent. R. H. Hutton, in an astute analysis of the letters available from Cross's *Life*, argued that George Eliot "intended her work as an authoress to be expiatory of, or at least to do all that was possible to counterbalance, the effect of her own example." See *Essays on Some of the Modern Guides to English Thought in Matters of Faith* (1888; rpt. London: Macmillan, 1900), pp. 289–292.

come Marian Lewes. But by February 1857 she had a new secret identity as George Eliot, and as with all secrets, the power of this one rested with its potential revelation. The Leweses did not have any plan to reveal the identity of George Eliot, as far as we know, but by establishing it the novelist gained confidence to press for recognition from her family: at least we can be sure that *until* she was George Eliot, she did not tackle her brother Isaac Evans. Successful author-ship was probably the only way she could achieve social acceptance; the conventional use of a pseudonym gave her access to a publisher who otherwise would not have dealt with her. By complicating their liaison with secret authorship, the Leweses contrived a formidable identity for Marian, which must eventually be known to the world whether they willed it or not. They could even modestly struggle against the revelation that would bring a form of respectability. Most gratifyingly, because of the deserved fame of George Eliot, the scan-dal of whether she was Marian Lewes or Marian Evans was pretty much overcome within the five years prophesied to Sara Hennell.

The embarrassing but triumphant revelation of the identity of George Eliot took place in an appropriately unintended way. The Leweses were in effect blackmailed, without so much as a threatening letter, by the complacency of a nearly total stranger named Joseph Liggins, who permitted people to believe that *he* was George Eliot. Blackmailers, after all, do not wish to reveal the secret they can profit by—they do their best one way or another to exploit someone else's need to keep a secret hidden. The payoff for Liggins was enjoyment of the glory of authorship. The Leweses had not dreamed, nor Black-wood either, of the secret being manipulated by a third party.[30] At first all three were amused that someone named Liggins professed to have written *Scenes of Clerical Life* and *Adam Bede*, but they be-came upset and unnerved when other outsiders conceived the idea of raising charity for Liggins, who was said to have received no pay for these books from the publisher—as indeed he had not.[31] The Liggins rumor arose as early as June 1857 and was eventually given space in the *Times* in April 1859: two months later George Eliot, who was

---

30 Redinger, *George Eliot*, p. 393, does not fully believe the daring of Liggins either and suggests that enemies of Lewes may have put him up to it. For a sample of contemporary confusion about the man, see a letter of Elizabeth Gaskell to Harriet Martineau, Oct. 1859, in *The Letters of Mrs. Gaskell*, ed. J. A. V. Chapple and Arthur Pollard (Cambridge: Harvard University Press, 1967), pp. 583–586.

31 The irony is Haight's, *George Eliot*, p. 283.

writing *The Mill on the Floss*, determined to keep her secret no longer. It was an altogether amusing, exasperating, and instructive episode. Even Lewes, who knew his way in the writing and publishing business very well, found himself much more deeply involved than he could have expected. Following Scott's precedent he had advocated lying, when necessary, to defend Marian's pseudonym; but the Liggins affair drew him in deeper. Over the signature of "George Eliot" he wrote to the *Times*, "Allow me to ask whether the act of publishing a book deprives a man of all claim to the courtesies usual among gentlemen?"[32] Lewes of course knew that he was not George Eliot, knew also that George Eliot was not a gentleman, and that the courtesies usual among gentlemen did not apply in the realm of print and publicity. Blackwood took the matter more calmly, since his personal pride was not threatened if the motive of concealment should be said to be the illicit marriage; but he was deeply worried about the reputation of his magazine and about future sales of books by George Eliot. He and the author were in negotiations over *The Mill on the Floss*, and she did not mistake, or take very kindly to, his nervousness about the revelation of her identity. Their differences were resolved to Blackwood's satisfaction mainly by his promising himself that he could continue to admit the name "George Eliot" in books but not in *Blackwood's Magazine*.[33] As to Liggins—who was unemployed and wonderfully true to type, like Raffles in *Middlemarch* or Tracy in *Blackmail*—he became a force in literary history. The existence of Liggins exemplifies the strange possibilities of the divorce between public and private life. By doing very little other than refusing to deny that he was George Eliot, he shamelessly exploited the secret of

32 Lewes to the editor of the *Times* [15 Apr. 1859], *G.E.L.*, III, 50.
33 Blackwood also persuaded himself that the moral contribution of the fiction could compensate for the irregularity of the author's private life. He wrote to George Eliot on 28 Nov. 1859, "As to the withdrawal of the incognito, you know how much I have been opposed to it all along. It may prove a disadvantage and in the eyes of many it will, but my opinion of your genius and confidence in the truly good, honest, religious, and moral tone of all you have written or will write [an implied contract, perhaps, as to the tone of her future writing] is such that I think you will overcome any possible detriment from the withdrawal of the mystery which has so far taken place" (*G.E.L.*, III, 217). Nevertheless, the falsehood of Liggins's supposed authorship would be publicly linked to the falsehood of George Eliot's supposed marriage. As a reviewer of Cross's *Life* complained, "It is no more true that the author of *Adam Bede* was Mrs. Lewes than it is true that the author of *Adam Bede* was Mr. Liggins." See the *Saturday Review*, 59 (1885); Carroll, p. 486.

her authorship to his own satisfaction. He demanded nothing, merely shared in the fame of novel-writing.

Marian Evans, alias Lewes, alias George Eliot, was the person most concerned in the unraveling of the secret, and she was moved by the experience. In April 1859 she completed the highly uncharacteristic story "The Lifted Veil," which was published in *Blackwood's* that summer. This rather ghoulish tale of clairvoyance and resuscitation troubled the publisher, who seems to have wondered if the author was upset by her concealed relation to himself, since the tale was about "untrustworthy keepers of secrets." Haight has suggested that the title refers obliquely to the lifting of the incognito,[34] and the story is undoubtedly autobiographical in some sort. The hero Latimer, who narrates the painful experience of being able to penetrate the consciousness of other people, resembles the novelist in his travels around Europe, and Gillian Beer has shown some important parallels between his language and that of *Middlemarch*.[35] The story is puzzling because the lifting of the veil apparently refers to the episode of reviving the dead woman at the end, as well as the penetration of other consciousnesses and possibly the incognito. As in many stories of the supernatural, the author's intentions seem very deliberate even if the reader is not privy to them, yet it may be doubted whether "The Lifted Veil" is finally consistent. Sandra M. Gilbert and Susan Gubar accept the equation of Latimer with George Eliot but then "wrench [them]selves free" to take up his antagonist, Bertha, as another projection of the author: the result is a rather strained interpretation, but one that is in keeping with their wider thesis of unconscious aggression in women writers.[36] Whether its inspiration was aggressive or, as Blackwood thought, unhappy, the story is obviously about secrets and unpleasant discoveries.

The Liggins episode was apparently only one of the discomforts that George Eliot experienced with her incognito, which by May 1859 she hoped to preserve only "a few months longer."[37] The "lie"

34 Haight, *George Eliot*, pp. 295–297.

35 "Myth and the Single Consciousness: *Middlemarch* and 'The Lifted Veil,' " in *This Particular Web: Essays on "Middlemarch,"* ed. Ian Adam (Toronto: University of Toronto Press, 1975), pp. 95–115.

36 *The Madwoman in the Attic: The Woman Writer and the Nineteenth-Century Literary Imagination* (New Haven: Yale University Press, 1979), pp. 443–477. U. C. Knoepflmacher's explication, in *George Eliot's Early Novels: The Limits of Realism* (Berkeley: University of California Press, 1968), pp. 128–161, first gave the story prominence.

37 To Mme Eugene Bodichon, 5 May 1859, *G.E.L.*, III, 63.

of the pseudonym and her awareness that her identity would soon be publicly known prompted her to take an open course with this secret as she had with her marriage. The important consequence of Liggins, and of the whole business of concealment, was that it alerted George Eliot to the respect due to some secrets. When rumors of Liggins's role persisted even after she and Lewes no longer concealed her authorship, and had requested their friends not to do so, she concluded one letter to Charles Bray as follows:

> I am not the first author who has suffered from such annoyances, though they become more intolerable as the years bring with them that increased facility of communication which makes the conjectures and inferences of local ignorance matter for current circulation throughout the Kingdom. I only wish I could do something to save any other author anything like the keen suffering of various kinds that I have endured since the publication of "Adam Bede"—I only wish I could write something that would contribute to heighten men's reverence before the secrets of each other's souls, that there might be less assumption of entire knowingness, as a datum from which inferences are to be drawn.[38]

Each novel written after this time treats secrets curiously if not sympathetically, and each novel proves less content with entire knowingness. The novelist, whose historical sense was acute in any case, had now personal experience of "the increased facility of communication" in her time. The laughter, annoyance, and anger she felt in hearing of the mysterious Liggins during her first two years as a writer of fiction alleviated some of the guilt inhabiting her affair with Lewes. By exploiting the distance between an author and her readers and the improved communications of the time, Liggins drew attention to himself that properly belonged to George Eliot, but such displacement has a potentially good side—as when a blackmailer distracts attention from a guilty party in a novel.

---

38 To Charles Bray, 26 Sept. 1859, *G.E.L.*, III, 164. "Entire knowingness" has specific reference to Charles Holte Bracebridge, perhaps the most officious actor in the Liggins charade; but as with such generalizations in George Eliot's novels, the application is much wider.

7

Pastoral Fictions

At first, George Eliot took advantage of her incognito by drawing more closely on her memory of actual persons and places than prudence afterward allowed.[1] Some of the agitation caused by the Liggins affair was due to his connection with Nuneaton, his acquaintance with persons actually known to George Eliot, and his indirect connection therefore with the materials of her early fiction. Just at the time when the whole game was almost up, in June 1859, a Reverend John Gwyther wrote to Blackwood concerning the authorship and stated flatly that he and his daughter had immediately recognized Amos Barton as a portrait of himself when the first story appeared. His letter was extremely courteous, under the circumstances, and George Eliot could only apologize and admit, through Blackwood, that she had been "under the impression that the clergyman whose long past trial suggested the groundwork of the story was no longer living."[2] In truth, the first of the *Scenes of Clerical Life*, "The Sad Fortunes of the Reverend Amos Barton," was the story of a clown, as the "Sad Fortunes" of the title suggests. The hero, or antihero, is inept in every way, and his pathos is set off by two beautiful women—his wife Milly, whom he keeps getting pregnant, and the Countess, who is falsely rumored to be his mistress. Of this hero, the narrator asks us "to see some of the poetry and the pathos, the trag-

---

1 For a summary, see Gordon S. Haight, "George Eliot's Originals," in *From Jane Austen to Joseph Conrad: Essays Collected in Memory of James T. Hillhouse*, ed. Robert C. Rathburn and Martin Steinmann, Jr. (Minneapolis: University of Minnesota Press, 1958), pp. 177–193.
2 To John Gwyther [15 June 1859], *G.E.L.*, III, 85–86.

edy and the comedy, lying in the experience of a human soul that looks out through dull gray eyes, and that speaks in a voice of quite ordinary tones" (ch. 5). The only thing that might be said for the comfort of John Gwyther is that the action of the story is entirely circumstantial. Amos Barton is no accomplice of his misfortunes, merely a victim.

The fiction composed while George Eliot's identity was still a secret is radically different in atmosphere and setting from her own recent life. The pace of the stories also contrasts with that of her own life, especially if the London years from 1850 to 1854, before she eloped with Lewes, are recalled. Those years were extraordinarily active, with wide acquaintance and new possibilities for Marian Evans, who worked, moved about on her own, and visited with others more than she could or would in the early years with Lewes. *Scenes of Clerical Life, Adam Bede*, and *The Mill on the Floss* all draw on the memory of much younger days and can usefully be thought of as "pastoral" fictions—not because of the setting in itself, but because of the contrast between sophisticated and simple points of view that is built into the narrative. Only *Adam Bede*, in fact, has a strictly bucolic setting, but each of the early fictions employs a device of pastoral distancing, whether this was enhanced by the author's incognito or not. The materials are from George Eliot's past, but the narrative is in a different key from that which is represented. Thus the opening chapter of "Amos Barton," with its celebration of "real farmhouse cream" and chiding of the "miserable town-bred reader," still alludes ironically to "the bucolic mind" or "the rustic mind." The antitheses are not primarily introduced to suggest historical differences between then and now, but to maintain an ironic perspective. There is a good deal of clowning for the reader's enjoyment, and the Shepperton choir is something of a circus, "with a bassoon, two key-bugles, a carpenter understood to have an amazing power of singing 'counter' and two lesser musical stars." The mocking assurances of the opening of the story include the first reference to the hero in a simile, when the walls of Shepperton Church are said to be "smooth and innutrient as the summit of the Rev. Amos Barton's head, after ten years of baldness and supererogatory soap" (ch. 1).

The diction of this first chapter, as throughout George Eliot's fiction, relies on a minute study of natural history. The rather startling reference to Barton's bald head, when we have had no introduction to the character other than the title, follows from a statement that "no lichen will ever again effect a settlement" on the walls of the church—hence the "innutrient" head. A few months before Marian wrote "Amos Barton," the Leweses visited Ilfracombe on the Devonshire coast, where they identified species and observed ecological relations of life at first hand. It was here that Marian also read W. H. Riehl and wrote the essay "The Natural History of German Life" that extended the same scientific spirit to sociology.[3] Both she and Lewes sensed the importance of biology for their time, and the importance of natural history in biology. No less concerned with causality than is physical science, natural science possesses a vision "to which every single object suggests a vast sum of conditions," and "it is surely the same with the observation of human life."[4] With her husband's example and encouragement, Marian Lewes grasped the relation of taxonomy to her own calling as a writer. At Ilfracombe she learned "to know the names of things" and "the distinctive qualities which mark out for us [a] particular object from all others."[5] At first it might seem that such a lively interest in science, or the serious social analysis of the essay on Riehl, is at odds with the pastoralism of George Eliot's early fiction; but it has to be remembered that the pastoralism in question is not an ideal but a perspective, a literary convention of distancing. From the very beginning George Eliot was able to combine the formal perspective of knowledge, typified by natural science, with traditional perspectives of pastoral and satire. The pastoralism tends to drop away in the course of writing *The Mill on the Floss*, and the satire is usually checked by moral design, but the grand

3 "The Natural History of German Life," *Westminster Review*, 66 (July 1856); Pinney, pp. 266–299. In her ranking of the sciences Marian Lewes follows Comte, but her emphasis is on fields of natural and social science where generalizations least apply: "To the laws of quantity comprised in Mathematics and Physics are superadded, in Chemistry, laws of quality; to these again are added, in Biology, laws of life; and lastly, the conditions of life in general, branch out into its special conditions, or Natural History, on the one hand, and into its abnormal conditions, or Pathology, on the other. . . . and no biological generalization will enable us to predict the infinite specialties produced by the complexity of vital conditions" (p. 290). Note how the physical scientist's "laws" give way to the naturalist's "conditions" in this account, and the inclusion of pathology.

4 *The Mill on the Floss*, bk. IV, ch. 1. For a view of biology with similar emphasis on diversity and differences in generalization from the physical sciences, see Ernst Mayr, *The Growth of Biological Thought: Diversity, Evolution, and Inheritance* (Cambridge: Harvard University Press, 1982), esp. pp. 21–82.

5 Journal, 8 May to 26 June 1856, *G.E.L.*, II, 251.

perspective of knowledge, the distance between concrete instance and generalization, and the numerous analogies drawn from science persist through *Daniel Deronda*.

Because George Eliot is such a formidable moralist, it is possible sometimes to forget the degree to which her writings describe individual and social behavior in a scientific spirit, as if she were an anthropologist describing her "people." Most of her nicely observed situations have little to do with morality, and often she refers the feelings that her characters experience as morality to habit or prejudice. Her first hero she treats as a being too limited to be responsible for his sad fortunes. The main action of "Amos Barton" is that of gossip and scandal, before which the curate is passive, and the story affords George Eliot an opportunity to treat almost scientifically her own recent experience with social relations. The second excursus in "Amos Barton," after that on fresh cream, concerns the necessary insulation of individuals from gossip about them. Notice the close cooperation of irony and observation, and the reminiscence of Ilfracombe tide pools:

> It was happy for the Rev. Amos Barton that he did not, like us, overhear the conversation recorded in the last chapter. Indeed, what mortal is there of us, who would find his satisfaction enhanced by an opportunity of comparing the picture he presents to himself of his own doings with the picture they make on the mental retina of his neighbours? We are poor plants buoyed up by the air-vessels of our own conceit: alas for us, if we get a few pinches that empty us of that windy self-subsistence! The very capacity for good would go out of us. For, tell the most impassioned orator, suddenly, that his wig is awry, or his shirt-lap hanging out, and that he is tickling people by the very oddity of his person, instead of thrilling them by the energy of his periods, and you would infallibly dry up the spring of his eloquence. That is a deep and wise saying, that no miracle can be wrought without faith,—without the worker's faith in himself, as well as the recipient's faith in him. And the greater part of the worker's faith in himself is made up of the faith that others believe in him. . . .
>
> Thank heaven, then, that a little illusion is left to us, to enable us to be useful and agreeable,—that we don't know exactly what our friends think of us,—that the world is not made of looking-glass, to show us just the figure we are making, and just what is going on behind our backs! By the help of dear friendly illusion, we are able to dream that we are charming,—and our faces wear

a becoming air of self-possession; we are able to dream that other men admire our talents,—and our benignity is undisturbed; we are able to dream that we are doing much good,—and we do a little. (ch. 2)

The thought that attaches illusion to the day-to-day maintenance of self-confidence and opposes it to mirrors (which would show what is going on behind our backs) anticipates George Eliot's almost casual admission, twenty years later, that "to read much remark about my doings would have as depressing an effect on me as staring in a mirror."[6] The capacity of human beings to live side by side with partial knowledge of each other she likens in the story to a miracle of faith—but primarily faith in oneself. The Pauline authority for the comparison seems to undergo a Feuerbachian translation, before being reduced to a play on faith and good works that is far from objective. The miracle is finally said to be, not of surviving shame, but of doing good; and despite—or because of—the distance Marian Lewes has placed between herself and this first story, I suspect that "the very capacity of good" includes the good of writing stories. Amos Barton is like a clown, the figure of fun most unlike ourselves, suggested here by the orator with wig awry and shirt-lap out, "tickling people by the very oddity of his person"; but clowning traditionally plays on inward sensitivity behind outward appearance. The choice of Barton as a hero and the purely circumstantial cast of his story enabled the author to treat everything from the outside, both what she had observed of gossip and what she knew of herself. Steven Marcus has remarked that "what holds true here [in "Amos Barton"], holds true throughout George Eliot's fiction; we see a great deal of her characters not only in themselves, and occasionally not even primarily or fundamentally in themselves, but in the talk about them that circulates through the society they inhabit."[7]

Though usually regarded as wicked, gossip is actually a cohesive activity of small communities in which everyone is acquainted with everyone else. In treating of the subject so pointedly George Eliot is making another pastoral contrast with her own and her readers' society. Her recent experience no doubt led her to reflect that, fortu-

6 See chapter 6, note 7.
7 "Literature and Social Theory: Starting in with George Eliot," *Representations: Essays on Literature and Society* (New York: Random House, 1975), p. 195.

nately, an individual seldom hears what is said about herself; but in moving to London six years earlier she had left the cosier world of gossip behind her. There ought to be more useful and substantial studies of gossip, but anthropologists seem to concur that it is a function of the closeness of a community rather than the opposite—and this is the suggestion of "Amos Barton" and to some extent "Janet's Repentance." A person or persons who are the object of gossip are usually not within hearing, but the right to gossip defines the group to which they belong. According to Max Gluckman, gossip is a sign of "belonging to the one set which has the duty to be interested in one another's vices as well as virtues . . . for scandal is only virtuous if its aim be to demonstrate some kind of social unity." "The more exclusive a social group is," he contends, "the more will its members indulge in gossip and scandal about one another." Readers of "Amos Barton" might even be said to become honorary parishioners of Shepperton, since "a most important part of gaining membership of any group is to learn its scandals."[8] Such gossip, note, effectively precludes blackmail, since everyone quickly learns the damaging truths or falsehoods about everyone else. In representing gossip George Eliot was turning back from her own experience of urban and sometimes exclusively literary life, though with sharpened awareness of the apartness of all individuals.

In George Eliot's first novel and most pastoral fiction of all, there is again a remarkable attention to these external relations of social life and the management of shame rather than guilt. In *Adam Bede* Hetty Sorrel is treated somewhat like Amos Barton, as too limited to be morally responsible. "The Hidden Dread," which serves as the title for the chapter that first hints of Hetty's pregnancy, is dread of discovery only, and the action that ensues makes sense only as a flight from shame. Her panic and isolation bring her to destroy her child, and of that act she is no doubt guilty—but she has to be forced to confess, to realize her guilt through a conversion administered by Dinah Morris. Because Hetty is conceived to be so simple, so irresponsible as to be nearly unresponsible, the relief from shame—under the threat of death—is diagrammatic and almost comic:

> "You won't leave me, Dinah? You'll keep close to me?"
> "No, Hetty, I won't leave you. I'll stay with you to the last.

8 "Gossip and Scandal," *Current Anthropology*, 4 (1963), 313–315.

... But, Hetty, there is some one else in this cell besides me, some one close to you."

Hetty said, in a frightened whisper, "Who?"

"Some one who has been with you through all your hours of sin and trouble,—who has known every thought you have had,—has seen where you went, where you lay down and rose up again, and all the deeds you have tried to hide in darkness. ... It makes no difference,—whether we live or die, we are in the presence of God." (ch. 45)

From the perspective of the writer's own religion, this is pastoralism with no holds barred. George Eliot apparently does not realize the enormous condescension implicit in this famous scene,[9] and so successful is the pastoral convention of *Adam Bede*, the conviction that this is another world, that most readers do not register disbelief either, despite Hetty's frightened "Who?"

In no other novel does George Eliot portray sympathetically such unqualified theism. The necessary conditions for it in *Adam Bede* are the purity of Dinah's faith, the simplicity of Hetty, and the ancient confusion of pastoral themes with Christian belief. The premise of Dinah's discourse is the omniscience of God, which she states boldly in its most intimate realization. God oversees everything—"every thought" and "all the deeds"—and God is always present—all day long, when one hides, and when one dies. The fear of shame prompts concealment, but there is no concealment from God.[10] Therefore confession is of a secret already known; the terror of shame is less, and what might be called the responsibility of guilt takes its place. Who would worry about discovery if she were totally convinced, like Dinah Morris, of the intimate presence and knowledge of God? Such pure Christian belief takes blame and shame out of the social world altogether, except as the institution of confession was social. George Eliot thought a great deal about confession, and had already written perceptively in "Janet's Repentance" of the choice of confessors:

9 The scene was the "germ" of *Adam Bede:* see Journal, 30 Nov. 1858, *G.E.L.,* II, 502. Donald Stone, *The Romantic Impulse in Victorian Fiction* (Cambridge: Harvard University Press, 1980), p. 208, suggests that "Hetty's most unforgivable offense is her refusal to submit to the idyllic way of life Eliot celebrates in the novel."

10 Compare Maggie Tulliver's temporary adherence to St. Thomas à Kempis in *The Mill on the Floss:* "Here, then, was a secret of life that would enable her to renounce all other secrets" (bk. IV, ch. 3).

The impulse to confession almost always requires the presence of a fresh ear and a fresh heart; and in our moments of spiritual need, the man to whom we have no tie but our common nature seems nearer to us than mother, brother, or friend. Our daily familiar life is but a hiding of ourselves from each other behind a screen of trivial words and deeds; and those who sit with us at the same hearth are often the farthest off from the deep human soul within us, full of unspoken evil and unacted good. (ch. 16)

This secularized and generalized account of confession, as contrasted with Dinah's theism, has wide application in George Eliot's novels and is noticeably modern—almost a commonplace of psychotherapy today. Protestant neglect of the institution of confession may have prompted Hawthorne, George Eliot, and others to take up the subject in novels; it may also have given some impetus to the literary theme of blackmail.

Adam Bede is probably the most popular of George Eliot's novels to this day, and it is certainly the most conventional. Its pastoralism is one of its most pleasing conventions, and if life were simpler, as that convention pretends, then suffering and the relief from suffering would be easier all round.[11] The convention operates even when the message is most anthropological, or Feuerbachian:

surely, if there came a traveller to this world who knew nothing of the story of man's life upon it, this image of agony [the way-side crosses in foreign countries] would seem to him strangely out of place in the midst of this joyous nature. He would not know that hidden behind the apple-blossoms, or among the golden corn, or under the shrouding boughs of the wood there might be a human heart beating heavily with anguish; perhaps a young blooming girl, not knowing where to turn for refuge from swift-advancing shame; understanding no more of this life of ours than a foolish lost lamb wandering farther and farther in the nightfall on the lonely heath, yet tasting the bitterest of life's bitterness.

Such things are sometimes hidden among the sunny fields and behind the blossoming orchards; and the sound of the gurgling brook, if you came close to one spot behind a small bush, would be mingled for your ear with a despairing human sob. No won-

11 For a summary of earlier criticism of the novel as pastoral, see Kenny Marotta, "*Adam Bede* as a Pastoral," *Genre*, 9 (1976), 59–72. The best overview of Christian pastoral themes is Renato Poggioli, *The Oaten Flute: Essays in Pastoral Poetry and the Pastoral Ideal* (Cambridge: Harvard University Press, 1975), pp. 16–20, 105–134.

der man's religion has so much sorrow in it; no wonder he needs a suffering God. (ch. 35)

Et in Arcadia Hetty—and Christ—"*if* you came close." But we are close only by pastoral convention. Since the blossoms, and corn, and sound of the brook are by the same convention a long way off, so is the lost lamb.

Displacements among the principal characters also govern the action of the novel in pleasing ways. Hetty the prize, "the pretty thing that might have been a lasting joy" (ch. 31), is sought and seduced by Arthur Donnithorne, though she becomes engaged to Adam Bede; she and Adam were to be married on the very day she is sentenced to die for child-murder, so it is rather lucky that Arthur did intervene. The novelist makes eminently clear that the juicy but passionless Hetty would never be a lasting joy to anyone. Adam's friend Arthur enjoys her, however, and is apparently beforehand with Dinah also—at least he thinks of giving her his watch and chain to remember him by (ch. 48), which she accepts long before Adam thinks of proposing to her and which she is wearing in 1807 at the close of the novel.[12] The sexuality as well as conscience that Hetty lacks turns up in Dinah, as proved by her inability to return the unaggressive but constant love of Seth Bede. Adam brings himself to displace Seth, but never quite Arthur, who enjoys literary and extraliterary privileges as an English gentleman, notwithstanding some lectures on the morality of consequences from Adam and Mr. Irwine both (ch. 16). *Adam Bede* is a fine novel, with a moving episode in Hetty's journey, a noble hero and heroine, and brilliant characterizations of Mrs. Poyser, Mr. Irwine, Lisbeth Bede, and several lesser figures; but one reason it is popular is that everything works out so tidily. "Adam's initial vision of a paradisiac existence with Hetty is . . . rudely jolted," U. C. Knoepflmacher has written, evoking the grandest of pastoral myths; "but Adam's life with a second Eve allows him to become a Loamshire patriarch whose children will be fruitful and multiply."[13]

12 Bringing Arthur "into a strong moral relation with Dinah," Barbara Hardy remarks, is "one of George Eliot's least convincing attempts to end *Adam Bede* on a note of moral affirmation." See *The Novels of George Eliot: A Study in Form* (1959; rpt. London: Athlone, 1963), p. 73. Hardy, pp. 81–83, also writes of the "conspicuous pairing" of Dinah and Hetty. Most readers, I suspect, are influenced by such displacements without being aware of them.

13 *George Eliot's Early Novels* (Berkeley: University of California Press, 1968), p. 91.

The Mill on the Floss, while also good humored and often witty, is a far more problematic work. The early chapters may be thought of as pastoral, but the initial distancing is that of Wordsworthian recollection, and this introduces a narrative of personal development. Though *The Mill on the Floss* may have been planned as another strictly pseudonymous novel, soon after beginning it George Eliot was resolved not to conceal her identity any longer; and unlike *Adam Bede*, the story centers on a heroine who was at least in part an imaginative projection of the author. A skillful play on the fate of "the dark women" of romance (bk. V, chs. 1 and 2) gives Maggie Tulliver, as a passionate woman without a niche in society, an appeal similar to that of Scott's Rebecca; at the same time, close attention to growth and variety, in both individual and social life, seems to honor the publication of Darwin's *Origin of Species* in 1859. *The Mill on the Floss* is in many ways a major Victorian achievement, which would be even more celebrated if it were not for puzzlement about the ending. The narrative distance supported by humor, the attention to development and to social history, and the use of literary and scientific analogy seem to diminish before the moral debate and apocalyptic conclusion of the novel.[14] The reunion of Maggie and Tom in death may have had satisfaction for George Eliot (serving her and her brother Isaac right) that her readers cannot share; the flood has the arbitrariness of any apocalyptic event and contravenes the careful historicism of the novel. It is the intense and not wholly satisfactory moral debate at the end, however, that most concerns me here, because it presents another exchange of reputation and conscience and therein recapitulates the secret of George Eliot.

Threats of punishment or the loss of love in *The Mill on the Floss*, and the moral debate itself, tend to obscure the degree to which this novel also dwells on shame rather than guilt. The brilliant satire of the Dodson sisters, to begin with, is a study of behavior governed overwhelmingly by notions of good or ill repute. The point of entitling one chapter "A Variation of Protestantism Unknown to Bos-

---

14 F. R. Leavis, *The Great Tradition* (1948; rpt. New York: Anchor, 1954), pp. 55–62, attributed the failure of distance and other difficulties of the last two books of the novel to George Eliot's uncritical identification with the heroine, but this is an oversimplification. For a full summary of the "difficult truths and consoling lies" of *The Mill on the Floss*, see Barbara Hardy's essay in *Critical Essays on George Eliot*, ed. Barbara Hardy (London: Routledge, 1970), pp. 42–58. Defenses of the ending of the novel are now legion.

suet" is to underline how strangely incongruous is their behavior with Christian belief properly understood. "The religion of the Dodsons consisted in revering whatever was customary and respectable ..." (bk. IV, ch. 1). Their storerooms of carefully preserved treasures that are not for use are more reminiscent of the households visited by Telemachus in the *Odyssey* than of any gospel truth, and the famous visit to Aunt Pullet's bonnet (bk. I, ch. 9) is like a breathtaking glimpse into some undisturbed tomb. The mournful Aunt Pullet is merely the lachrymose version of all the Dodsons, whose logic of keeping up appearances finally equates existence with death. "To live respected, and have the proper bearers at your funeral, was an achievement of the ends of existence that would be entirely nullified if, on the reading of your will, you sank in the opinion of your fellow-men, either by turning out to be poorer than they expected, or by leaving your money in a capricious manner, without strict regard to degrees of kin" (bk. IV, ch. 1). George Eliot's description of the Dodsons is both moving and satiric. The "variation" she describes is persuasive,[15] and at the same time demonstrates the limitations of the avoidance of shame as a motive for life. Marian Lewes may be thought to be exorcising the motive altogether.

The narrator explicitly states that "the same sort of traditional belief ran in the Tulliver veins, but it was carried in richer blood, having elements of generous imprudence, warm affection, and hot-tempered rashness" (bk. IV, ch. 1). Though Tom Tulliver's eagerness to punish seems to be prompted by temper and though his inner sense of justice sustains him against opinion, he is chiefly concerned for the honor of his family, and he is capable on more than one occasion of driving his sister accordingly. "If your conduct, and Philip Wakem's conduct, has been right, why are you ashamed of its being known? Answer me that" (bk. V, ch. 5). Though Maggie Tulliver's sense of guilt seems to have been stamped by the reproof she experiences as a child from brother, mother, and aunts, she is also aware of her supposedly awkward manners and appearance. When she cuts off her hair to get even with her tormentors (bk. I, ch. 7), she possibly intends unconsciously to ease her guilt by increasing and fo-

---

15 Again George Eliot is intensely conscious of the difficulties of classification in biology. "Certainly the religious and moral ideas of the Dodsons and Tullivers were of too specific a kind to be arrived at deductively, from the statement that they were a part of the Protestant population of Great Britain" (bk. IV, ch. 1).

cusing her shame. When she runs away to the gypsies, it is to escape "from all the blighting obloquy that had pursued her in civilized life" (bk. I, ch. 11). The shame-culture epitomized by the Dodsons extends further than we might expect at Dorlcote Mill and in the town of St. Ogg's, though in the end Maggie is to triumph over it.[16]

The Mill on the Floss constructs a thoroughly diversified environment for shame. By the end, after Maggie's first boating adventure and before her last, nearly everyone is to judge behavior from the outside. Tom, needless to say, expects "the worst that could happen,—not death, but disgrace," and Bob Jakin, a loyal friend, can only think, "where was Mr. Stephen Guest?" (bk. VII, ch. 1). Stephen himself, unknown to Bob, has argued that Maggie ought to marry him now, despite his quasi-engagement to Lucy Deane, because of appearances: "Dearest . . . you *are* mine now,—the world believes it,—duty must spring out of that now" (bk. VI, ch. 14). Dr. Kenn, "a man who had known spiritual conflict, and lived through years of devoted service to his fellow-men," is inwardly persuaded of the desirability of the marriage also (bk. VII, ch. 2). Subsequently Kenn is "aghast at the obstinate continuance of imputations against her in the face of evidence" and tries to employ Maggie as a governess for his own children, but he is forced to back down (bk. VII, ch. 4). Rather unexpectedly, two of the Dodson sisters remain loyal. Maggie's mother and aunt Glegg decide to outface appearances and befriend her even in disgrace—Mrs. Tulliver from loneliness and maternal instinct and Mrs. Glegg by elevating one Dodson principle, close kinship, above the rest: "Lightly to admit conduct in one of your own family that would force you to alter your will," she recalls, "had never been the way of the Dodsons" (bk. VII, ch. 3). In the midst of her shame Maggie, meanwhile, has constructed a moral argument to cover her case.

Unlike Dinah Morris tutoring Hetty in such matters, Maggie employs no argument that is not consistent with George Eliot's own be-

16 See George Levine, "Intelligence as Deception: *The Mill on the Floss,*" *PMLA*, 80 (1965), reprinted in *George Eliot: A Collection of Critical Essays*, ed. George R. Creeger (Englewood Cliffs, N.J.: Prentice-Hall, 1970), pp. 107–123. "George Eliot is certainly suggesting in the final chapters both the power of public opinion and the need to develop it more consistently to a higher level of social sympathy" (p. 114). This interpretation tends to overlook some ironies that persist even to the end of the novel. "The world's wife," remember, is ready to condemn but also to forgive Maggie—if she would marry too (bk. VII, ch. 2).

liefs. Once or twice she may use an expression for conscience like "the divine voice within us," but she appeals to no revealed truths or moral authorities. Instead, she bases her moral judgment on the facts and derives her idea of what ought to be the case from what is the case—a procedure sometimes known as naturalistic ethics. I do not believe she quite succeeds—to have done so would be to succeed where many philosophers have failed—but it is a worthy argument all the same. Roughly, Maggie contends that for Stephen and her to marry would violate the long-term expectations of those they live among and who have trusted them—would violate their own former expectations, for that matter. The very absence of divine or other sanctions for behavior makes the need to consult their own experience more urgent. The principle is summarized in her question and answer, "If the past is not to bind us, where can duty lie? We should have no law but the inclination of the moment" (bk. VI, ch. 14). Such a "law" or rule of behavior is specific to the case in question, but deducible from its wider context, from relations of more than a moment's duration. Earlier Maggie argued, also with Stephen, "that the real tie lies in the feelings and expectations we have raised in other minds. Else all pledges might be broken, when there was no outward penalty. There would be no such thing as faithfulness." When he protested the insincerity of pledges that persons long to break, she exclaimed:

> Oh, it is difficult,—life is very difficult! It seems right to me sometimes that we should follow our strongest feeling; but then, such feelings continually come across the ties that all our former life has made for us,—the ties that have made others dependent on us,—and would cut them in two. ... I mean, if life did not make duties for us before love comes, love would be a sign that two people ought to belong to each other. But I see—I feel it is not so now: there are things we must renounce in life; some of us must resign love. ... Love is natural; but surely pity and faithfulness and memory are natural too. And they would live in me still, and punish me if I did not obey them. I would be haunted by the suffering I had caused. Our love would be poisoned. Don't urge me; help me,—help me, *because* I love you. (bk. VI, ch. 11)

Stephen responded to that appeal because of his "nobleness," we are told, but of course Maggie's confession of love has not helped

matters. Their seeming elopement has in effect handed him an argument on her own ground. They have now, only half intentionally,
given rise to different expectations from those of the recent past.
They have created the public impression that they have already made
love together, and in any case they have irremediably hurt Lucy
Deane and Philip Wakem. "If the past is not to bind us, where can
duty lie?" But the past now includes some rather telling new events,
for which they are partly to blame, but which are events nonetheless.
It should be said in defense of Stephen's second round of argument
that his notion of the past as a continuous unfolding of events is more
in keeping with the processes of development and of history featured
earlier in the novel than is Maggie's attempt to turn back. It is deci-
dedly more in keeping with the novel as a whole than the stoppage of
time that George Eliot creates by means of the flood, however well
she prepares the reader for that event. Stephen also perceives that
faithfulness (he calls it "outward faithfulness") is not natural in the
same degree that love is natural (bk. VI, ch. 14). Maggie has one un-
answerable argument as far as she is concerned, and that is that she
cannot be comfortable with the thought of enjoying love at others'
expense. But Stephen of course hopes to change that feeling, and
Lucy and Philip are undoubtedly the two most understanding friends
they have. All in all, the remaining ground for Maggie's advocacy of
the recent past as opposed to Stephen's advocacy of the immediate
past is the cultural and Christian preference for selfless as opposed to
selfish actions—but neither Maggie, nor Stephen, nor the narrator
voices a religious appeal. Though not all readers of George Eliot care
deeply for this debate, many have tacitly ceded a moral standoff by
disputing the attractiveness of Stephen, imputing incestuous wishes
to the heroine, or discovering some other reason for her stance.

It is important to see that the debate takes place in two stages, before and after the drifting of the couple out to sea. The intervening
circumstances give weight to Stephen's argument; they complete
Maggie's temptation. But there is something rather contrived about
this continuation of the argument that makes most readers uncomfortable without quite knowing why. It is because the new circumstances of the second stage are not necessary to the moral significance
of Maggie's argument. What has changed? Quite simply, she has lost
her reputation without losing her virtue. The narrator puts the case
succinctly, but just barely, in telling Maggie's thoughts before sun-

rise: "She felt it now [her outlawry?],—now that the consequences of such a fall had come before the outward act was completed" (bk. VI, ch. 14). This hurried thought is to be translated, she will suffer the public reputation of eloping with Stephen without having yet eloped. It is curious how rapidly George Eliot narrates this thought, and how unclear from the context is the "it" that Maggie feels. Yet the design of the denouement hinges on just this point. The contrivance of the plot is to ensure (a) that Maggie is assumed to be a fallen woman and (b) that her virtue is still intact. This seems like a formula for a good-bad woman who is technically pure, but it is more than that. Maggie's virtue is not merely technical—it is downright impressive, as her part in the moral debate demonstrates above all. Moreover, George Eliot is now set to prove that virtue over every other contender in the novel. Maggie's virtue (b) is to be a moral triumph on every side. She is better than Stephen, because she is selfless rather than selfish, believes in choice rather than luck, and knows furthermore that he will go back to Lucy. "Forgive me, Stephen!" she can apostrophize, after his last appeal: "It will pass away. You will come back to her" (bk. VII, ch. 5). She is better than Lucy, by the latter's own admission. Lucy could not give Stephen up: "Maggie . . . you are better than I am. I can't—" (bk. VII, ch. 4). She is better, or perhaps higher, than Philip, who writes of "the new life into which I have entered in loving you" (bk. VII, ch. 3). And she is better than Tom, who realizes in her presence, before their deaths, "a new revelation to his spirit, of the depths of life that had lain beyond his vision, which he had fancied so keen and clear" (bk. VII, ch. 5). Each of these quiet triumphs is enhanced, I suggest, by (a) her disgrace. Once again we have to ask, did George Eliot really need both (a) and (b)? The answer is no; the latter would suffice. The moral argument is strong, its celebration complete. But George Eliot was determined to create, I assume, the same balance of undeserved shame and moral achievement that she hinted to her friends when she secretly designed to become a novelist.[17]

17. *The Mill on the Floss* is the first of George Eliot's strong attempts to portray the struggle of "the outward and the inward" in personality, between constraining circumstances and "unconscious yearning" (bk. III, ch. 5). In the manuscript, where she wrote these words she also wrote, "A girl of no startling appearance, and who will never be a Sappho or a Madame Roland or anything else that the world takes wide note of, may still hold forces within her as the living plant-seed does, which will make way for themselves, often in a shattering, violent manner"—but this sentence was de-

In a famous passage, after Maggie has consulted Dr. Kenn, George Eliot writes of "repugnance to the men of maxims" and calls for "wide fellow-feeling with all that is human":

> The great problem of the shifting relation between passion and duty is clear to no man who is capable of apprehending it: the question whether the moment has come in which a man has fallen below the possibility of renunciation that will carry any efficacy, and must accept the sway of a passion against which he had struggled as a trespass, is one for which we have no master-key that will fit all cases. The casuists have become a by-word of reproach; but their perverted spirit of minute discrimination was the shadow of a truth to which eyes and hearts are too often fatally sealed,—the truth that moral judgments must remain false and hollow, unless they are checked and enlightened by a perpetual reference to the special circumstances that mark the individual lot. (bk. VII, ch. 2)

The passage is justly celebrated and typical of its author, who by the bye rescues one more class of persons, the casuists, from our over-hasty reproach. The odd thing about it is that it seems to be defending against the choice that Maggie did not make.[18] The question at this point would seem to be moot as far as Maggie is concerned, unless the narrator, after all that has gone before, is speculating with the experienced Dr. Kenn that at some point she may still "accept the sway of a passion against which [she] had struggled as a trespass."

---

leted in proof (see *The Mill on the Floss*, ed. Gordon S. Haight, Clarendon Edition of the Novels of George Eliot [Oxford: Clarendon, 1980], p. 206n7). The antiheroic theme seems in no way objectionable; it would be sounded again in connection with yearning in *Middlemarch* and elsewhere. Perhaps the sentence was excised because of the image of parturition; or perhaps because strictly speaking it was inconsistent with the denouement of *The Mill on the Floss*, in which the world takes note of Maggie Tulliver in a bad sense. That clause doubly fails to apply to George Eliot, whom the world took note of in both good and bad senses; therefore it is remotely possible that the sentence was deleted from self-consciousness, by one who was making a way for herself "often in a shattering, violent manner." The final image is botanic, after all, not nearly as aggressive as the comparisons to Sappho or Madame Roland. All one can really insist upon, for purposes of interpreting the novel, is that the constraints on Maggie Tulliver in the end are both moral and social, and that the outward are a glory to the inward.

18 The manuscript of the novel contains wording still less appropriate to Maggie's case, for instead of posing the question "whether the moment has come," it reads, "when the moment comes that a man must resign himself to that lower moral stage where his failures have robbed renunciation of its efficacy, is one," etc.—as if this moment were inevitable. See the Clarendon Edition, p. 437n3.

The conclusion of *The Mill on the Floss* still contains ambiguities. Not even the import of the titles of the last two books in the novel, "The Great Temptation" and "The Final Rescue," is precisely clear.

The chapter of *The Mill on the Floss* that concludes book II and Tom's school days is entitled "The Golden Gates Are Passed." Maggie journeys to King's Lorton to tell Tom that their father has lost the lawsuit and suffered a stroke, and they return home together "into their new life of sorrow." Chapter and book end, "They had entered the thorny wilderness, and the golden gates of their childhood had forever closed behind them." At the beginning of the chapter, however, the same image is used for Maggie's growing up, with particular reference to her relation to Philip Wakem, whom she has seldom seen after her visit as a child when both boys were at King's Lorton.

> When [she and Philip] did meet, she remembered her promise to kiss him; but, as a young lady who had been at a boarding-school, she knew now that such a greeting was out of the question, and Philip would not expect it. The promise was void, like so many other sweet, illusory promises of our childhood; void as promises made in Eden before the seasons were divided, and when the starry blossoms grew side by side with the ripening peach,—impossible to be fulfilled when the golden gates had been passed. (bk. II, ch. 7).

The allusion connects, through the chapter title and the principal event narrated, to the further estrangement of the Tullivers from the Wakems. But in another respect the fall into adulthood is a curious one. Neither knowledge nor sexuality is implied in this fall except by the utmost indirection. Adulthood, rather, signifies the unmaking of a promise and the cessation of friendship. In Eden "the starry blossoms grew side by side with the ripening peach," but now a regular temporal order will descend over the process of generation, and this order is oddly prohibitive of sexual experience. Maggie, we have seen, endures a second curious fall before the end of *The Mill on the Floss*, the fall that comes "before the outward act was completed" (bk. VI, ch. 14); and the novel concludes, extraordinarily but as hinted all along, with a return to the beginning, to family, to childhood, and "the days when [Maggie and Tom] had clasped their little hands in love and roamed the daisied fields together" (bk. VII, ch. 5). The action as a whole can therefore be seen as a fall that does not take place, a gate that is not passed, a turning back from adulthood, or simply the ending of life before a real fall can occur.[19]

To say that a fall does not take place is another way of saying that George Eliot does not admit any discontinuity in the life of her main character. The ingenious arrangements at the end of *The Mill on the Floss* show how a fall might occur, but the author has set out to write a continuous narrative; and by terminating in this planned but arbitrary manner, she succeeds. At the beginning of her career as a novelist George Eliot very naturally used materials from her early life, at first objectively and then more subjectively. She had no need to justify a life in which the past was severed from the present, because her identity was still unknown to the public. Once her identity had been revealed, her separation from her own past was obvious to anyone who cared to think about it, and George Eliot began to write of the discontinuities between past and present lives. Whereas at first pastoralism had sufficed to express the narrator's distance from the scene, she now treated warily and curiously her characters' secrets. She would never need to manage, in her subsequent novels, such a stopping, miraculous ending as that of *The Mill on the Floss*. The fictions of one principal locality give way to what Henry Auster has called "the literature of displacement"[20]—and to quite a few stories of secrets and of blackmail. Beginning with *Silas Marner* displacements occur literally from place to place, as Auster points out, and metaphorically over time. Some of the displacements are also psychological, from one character to another, as in a dream.

Because of actions that are discontinuous and knowledge that is partial, the later novels contain situations in which the management of some revelation of the past is paramount. Thus toward the end of *Silas Marner* the role of Dunstan Cass is discovered, and in the same chapter Godfrey Cass confesses to his wife that he is Eppie's father (ch. 18). The sharp readjustment demanded by such revelations had already been noted in *Adam Bede* and twice compared to a "terrible" light. When Adam sees Arthur and Hetty in the wood and recalls the locket she had dropped at the dance—a bit of circumstantial evidence

19 This interpretation need not preclude the "cosmic irony" that the novel's ending shares with other Victorian works: see Knoepflmacher, *George Eliot's Early Novels*, p. 182.

20 *Local Habitations: Regionalism in the Early Novels of George Eliot* (Cambridge: Harvard University Press, 1970), pp. 177–206.

that he has hitherto been unable to account for—he suddenly understands "everything else that had been doubtful to him"; and to characterize his new knowledge the narrator compares it to prophetic writing—or the reverse of prophetic writing: "a terrible scorching light showed him the hidden letters that changed the meaning of the past" (ch. 27). It is a powerful figure, which George Eliot repeats in more general terms in describing Mr. Irwine's understanding of the same history (ch. 39). In *The Mill on the Floss* there is a quieter, externalized use of the same perception, when Maggie understands that Philip Wakem is making love to her and "a great change came over her face,—a flush and slight spasm of the features such as we see in people who hear some news that will require them to readjust their conceptions of the past" (bk. V, ch. 4). But in these earlier novels of continuous actions the shock is absorbed somehow, partly because the persons making the readjustments are innocent. *Silas Marner* and the later novels dramatize such revelations by the construction of the narrative and challenge the identity of certain characters over time. Godfrey and Nancy Cass have to readjust to a past for which he is directly responsible and she indirectly. Silas Marner's readjustments are at the center of the novel. Though innocent, he too has concealed his past—even from himself—and can remember it only after the gift of Eppie has restored purpose in his life and he has broken silence to Dolly Winthrop.

The importance of the past to a person's identity is firmly asserted in the first two novels but not finally tested. In *Adam Bede* the past is said to inhere in all our feelings and also to be secret, something that divides us from each other: "The secret of our emotions never lies in the bare object, but in its subtle relations to our own past: no wonder the secret escapes the unsympathizing observer, who might as well put on spectacles to discern odours." The reference, oddly, is to Adam's churchgoing, which has been continuous and, as part of the community life, not particularly secret. George Eliot is thinking of her own situation and counting on the pastoral narrative, including an allusion to "early Christians who had worshipped from their childhood upward in catacombs," to reflect the difference (ch. 18). As for putting on spectacles to discern odors (a dismissal of the subject worthy of Mrs. Poyser), this is a far cry from the patient examination of apartness in *Silas Marner*. The very moral of *The Mill on the Floss*—"If the past is not to bind us, where can duty lie?"—insists on the continuity of personal identity over time, and there are several passages discoursing on the subject:

> There is no sense of ease like the ease we felt in those scenes where we were born, where objects became dear to us before we had known the labour of choice, and where the outer world seemed only an extension of our own personality; we accepted and loved it as we accepted our own sense of existence and our own limbs. Very commonplace, even ugly, that furniture of our early home might look if it were put up to auction; an improved taste in upholstery scorns it; and is not the striving after something better and better in our surroundings, the grand characteristic that distinguishes man from the brute,—or, to satisfy a scrupulous accuracy of definition, that distinguishes a British man from a foreign brute? But heaven knows where that striving might lead us, if our affections had not the trick of twining round those old inferior things,—if the loves and sanctities of our life had no deep immovable roots in memory. (bk. II, ch. 1)

Again pastoralism, already projected into a satire of "British man" and enhanced in a sentence to follow by a contrast between "the finest cistus or fuschia" and a humble "elderberry," pulls away from the represented object. It is wonderful writing, with the undercutting of upholstery and all the rest; but the immediate reference is to Tom Tulliver's homecoming from school, and Tom's later material striving is tightly rooted in his upbringing. Usually, of course, it is Maggie's past that matters—but actually, throughout the novel, the heroine seldom recalls her childhood. The narrator recalls it for her.

Modern consciousness, I suggest, assumes a fairly constant reference to a present and past identity, a kind of duplicity even, that George Eliot only gradually begins to explore. In *Adam Bede* most of the characters are sincere, and Dinah Morris is notable for "the total absence of self-consciousness in her demeanour." Even though this beautiful woman preacher's appearance is very striking, she "walked as simply as if she were going to market, and seemed as unconscious of her outward appearance as a little boy. There was no blush, no tremulousness" that could suggest insincerity (ch. 2). And indeed Dinah never blushes until Adam Bede comes upon her unexpectedly one day—when, "for the first time in her life, [she] felt a painful self-consciousness" (ch. 11). She will blush some more at the end of the novel, before Adam quite realizes that he is in love with her, but such is the most conventional behavior of heroines in love.[21] Dinah's lack of self-consciousness, in fact, is meant to contrast with Hetty's constant awareness of her appearance. In *The Mill on the Floss* George Eliot introduced a very different heroine, one with a highly developed moral consciousness, yet no angel like Dinah at all—if anything, more like a witch.[22] Nevertheless, Maggie's sincerity is never supposed to be in doubt, and her concealments are unintended. She meets Philip in the Red Deeps, but not without a "severe monotonous warning [that] came again and again,—that she was losing the simplicity and clearness of her life by admitting a ground of concealment" (bk. V, ch. 3). When she later ventures into society at her cousin Lucy's house, she is somewhat at a loss because she "had never in her life spoken from the lips merely," as others plainly do (bk. VI, ch. 2). The conclusion of *The Mill on the Floss* can be regarded as a conspiracy on the part of George Eliot and Maggie to protect the latter from duplicity however innocent, even the kind experienced over time by Silas Marner.

It has often been contended by critics that Adam Bede's moral consciousness changes. He becomes more cautious in judgment—and changes his love right about from Hetty to Dinah. His progress, I would argue, is so conventional in Victorian novels that it poses no problem whatever of personal identity over time. Heroes are almost always permitted to love more than once as long as the last love is the best, a process of selection not granted to heroines. Rather, it is a person like Arthur Donnithorne, not a hero but a sort of alter ego for Adam, who may step out of bounds and thereby threaten his own existence. Arthur has harbored a secret, and the narrator of *Adam Bede* comes right out and involves the reader in the question of his identity:

> Are you inclined to ask whether this can be the same Arthur who, two months ago, had that freshness of feeling, that delicate honour which shrinks from wounding even a sentiment, and does not contemplate any more positive offence as possible for it?—who thought that his own self-respect was a higher tribunal than any external opinion? The same I assure you, only under different conditions. (ch. 29)

21 The convention has its own precariousness: see Ruth Bernard Yeazell, "Podsnappery, Sexuality, and the English Novel," *Critical Inquiry*, 9 (1982), 339–357.

22 See Nina Auerbach, "The Power of Hunger: Demonism and Maggie Tulliver," *Nineteenth-Century Fiction*, 30 (1975), 150–171.

The well-known discussion that follows, on the moral determination of character by deeds and vice versa, obscures the question of personal identity with which the essay begins.

George Eliot can pose the question of identity because Arthur is not her hero. She is quite aware from her own experience that self-respect may sometimes serve as "a higher tribunal than any external opinion," and after her own identity was known to the public she began to treat the question of whether people might be "the same . . . only under different conditions" with a different emphasis. Instead of immediate translation into a moral lesson about the consequences of one's deeds, she dramatized the problem by narrating lives that were discontinuous as well as secret. This move, more in tune with the melodrama of sensation novels in the eighteen-sixties than with pastoral distancing, enabled her to dwell on the suspenseful management of secrets. But she portrayed such divided experience at first—with the exception of Silas Marner—only in wicked or hateful characters. Romola, the first full-fledged heroine of the later novels, she would strive to make as unself-conscious as Dinah Morris; Tito Melema, in the same novel, she would make far more despicable than Arthur Donnithorne and burden him with all the secrets.

Each of George Eliot's novels after *The Mill on the Floss* explores some life history that is discontinuous yet surreptitiously connected with a past. The discontinuity is social, and nothing strange to the history of the author's own times; but its replication in narrative begins to resemble, through the importance bestowed on the past, the tracing of distortions and finally a transference, the conditions that have come to be known as "the analytic situation." As Paul Ricoeur has written of psychoanalysis and its pursuit of continuous narratives, "the patient is both the actor and the critic of a history which he is at first unable to recount. The problem of recognizing oneself is the problem of recovering the ability to recount one's own history, to endlessly continue to give the form of a story to reflections on oneself."[23] These words will serve to characterize George Eliot's personal commitment to the art of the novel, a commitment that evinces many of the historical conditions for psychoanalysis. She was not prepared to cede the priority of moral demands, but she gradually enlarged her study of consciousness, told of unconscious thoughts and mental suffering inflicted upon the self as well as upon others,

23 "The Question of Proof in Freud's Psychoanalytic Writings," *Journal of the American Psychoanalytical Association*, 25 (1977), 862.

and experimented with narrative reconstructions of both shame and guilt.

A comparison of the project of George Eliot with the project of Freud may need to be qualified in one respect, since the latter almost never treats shame directly as an object of his inquiries. George Eliot and other nineteenth-century novelists, in their creative work, were seldom unconcerned with shame in one way or another. The culture of information and publicity disarmed honor, so to speak, and diffused the possibility of shame in all directions. Avoidance of shame becomes the passive strategem of private life, while threatening shame is the implicit means of control in the rise of public opinion. The novelists of the century repeatedly explore situations conducive to shame, the defenses against it available to protagonists, and the salutary effects on the community when wrongdoing coincides with shame. Guilt and shame are often hard to distinguish, whether as community judgments or as internalized feelings. As the latter, they appeal to the great novelists of character, but because both feelings originate in social life (including the family), it is not difficult for a lesser novelist to imply their existence. The internalizations of guilt and shame are important, and not merely to the psychologist, since these feelings help to enforce peaceful social existence. But whereas guilt can be characterized as internalized punishment, shame is an internalized sense of the self's appearance to others; the one sensation reflects the subordination of the self to more powerful figures, as of the child to a parent, and the other, coordination of the self with fellow beings in the formation of personal identity. Even this definition has to struggle against a Judeo-Christian tradition that conceives of morality and guilt as essentially inward, pride and shame as outward considerations. For this tradition, any regard for shame is less worthy than obedience to conscience.

Freud focused his attention on the internalization of guilt and treated shame rather casually, as one of the elements of repression. He began his researches as a doctor and scientist, with a special interest in the sexual instinct, and not as a student of social relations. Though Darwin, in speculating about the evolution of morality, had emphasized the social habits of animals and early humans, he too tended to override the distinction between shame and guilt. "The nature and strength of the feelings which we call regret, shame, repentance or remorse, depend apparently not only on the strength of the violated instinct, but partly on the strength of the temptation, and still more on the judgment of our fellows."[24] Freud gives less emphasis to the judgment of our fellows and much more to that of fathers, but he similarly conjoins the various "social virtues" in his definition of repression. In his *Three Essays on the Theory of Sexuality*, he regularly groups together "disgust, shame, and morality" as the "moral dams" that impede the sexual instinct. In no other work does he mention shame so frequently, and here, always in this conjunction. He seems to believe with Darwin, though not quite consistently, that these feelings too are instinctive and may be inherited.[25] He never confuses disgust, shame, and morality, but he does take these feelings for granted. Collectively, these are the forces against which human sexuality attempts to reassert itself.

One peculiarity of Freud's belief about shame did not seem peculiar to him, because it had long been a contention of male-dominated psychology: women, as the inferior sex, were supposed to be especially susceptible to shame. This old idea, based on men's greater size and the custom of female modesty, is obviously a projection of male concerns: specifically, projections of the fear of losing in a fight and of the fear of sexual inadequacy. But the idea is very much at home in the culture, and it suited perfectly Freud's intuition that women must be deeply anxious about the lack of a penis. Late in his life, Freud could acknowledge the conventionality of the idea and still hold to his intuition. Thus "shame, which is considered to be a feminine characteristic *par excellence* but is far more a matter of convention than might be supposed, has as its purpose, we believe, concealment of genital deficiency."[26] Freud failed to devote his customary powers to the study of shame, probably because he located the feeling too far away, in the general forces of repression or in the constitution of women. As a man, and a man of his time, he was ashamed of

24 *The Descent of Man, and Selection in Relation to Sex,* 2nd ed. (London: Murray, 1875), p. 114. The entire paragraph was added in the second edition; in the first (1871), Darwin emphasized regret and remorse, two feelings distinguished merely by degree.

25 *Three Essays on the Theory of Sexuality* (1905), S.E., VII, 177–178. But cf. Draft K in the Fliess papers: "Where there is no shame (as in a male person), or where no morality comes about (as in the lower classes of society), or where disgust is blunted by the conditions of life (as in the country), there too no repression and therefore no neurosis will result from the sexual stimulation in infancy" (S.E., I, 222).

26 *New Introductory Lectures on Psycho-Analysis* (1933), S.E., XXII, 132.

shame. This tendency to project the feeling upon the opposite sex might be reversed in the case of a woman. George Eliot may have pressed her diagnosis of shame so forcibly upon Tito Melema, in *Romola*, because she was ashamed of shame.

Shame and guilt may finally be impossible to distinguish clearly, since shaming is often threatened as a punishment and guilt may be a cause of shame. What seems to happen, in the course of psychotherapy as well as in novels, is that certain negotiations take place between shame and guilt.[27] There may be a trade-off, say, in which shame becomes less excruciating because of a strengthened sense of responsibility, or guilt becomes less oppressive through private or public confession. The shifting of a burden from one side to the other is not the same as laying it down altogether, but it brings substantial relief. Psychoanalysis seems to take for granted that shame is constitutive in repression and then quite commonly assists the patient in arriving at an understanding of his or her feelings of guilt—as if one always started with shame, apparent in the resistance to psychoanalysis itself, and converted it to guilt, which is assuaged by speaking of it with the analyst. This pattern is something like the progress of George Eliot's motives as a writer of fiction and even more like the progress depicted in "the analytic situation" of *Daniel Deronda*.

Negotiations with a blackmailer tend to take an opposite tack. Yet by threatening guilt with shame, the blackmailer may do his clients and the public some good. The novels of George Eliot and her contemporaries were first of all great social novels. By beginning with social relations, these novels may end by demonstrating that shame is as basic to Freud's project as it is to their own.

27 Helen B. Lewis pursues this possibility in *Shame and Guilt in Neurosis* (New York: International Universities, 1971). She agrees with Freud that women are more subject to shame than men are (pp. 144–164).

I V

Her Fictions of Discontinuity

A striking figure in these opening chapters is that of Herr Klesmer, a German music-master, who has occasion to denounce an aria of Bellini as expressing "a puerile state of culture—no sense of the universal." There could not be a better phrase than this latter one to express the secret of that deep interest with which the reader settles down to George Eliot's widening narrative. The "sense of the universal" is constant, omnipresent. It strikes us sometimes perhaps as rather conscious and over-cultivated; but it gives us the feeling that the threads of the narrative, as we gather them into our hands, are not of the usual commercial measurement, but long electric wires capable of transmitting messages from mysterious regions.

—[Henry James,] *Nation,* 24 February 1876

8

Turning to Blackmail

The early fiction of George Eliot is traditionally and usefully regarded as pastoral. The settings are rural for the most part, but what really matters is the implied distance between the actions represented and the greater sophistication of the narrator and readers. I have suggested that even the scientific reflections of the author contribute to this perspective rather than work against it; and the early chapters of *The Mill on the Floss* reinforce the pastoral perspective by sharing with the reader an adult view of childhood experience. The later novels exploit some of the same general perspective: unless one counts the Florence of *Romola*, described in the proem as "hardly changed [in] its outline since the days of Columbus," or the nearly contemporary London of *Daniel Deronda*, George Eliot wrote no essentially urban fiction. But after *The Mill on the Floss* and the revelation of her identity as the novelist, she surrendered the comfort of pastoral fiction—always a little flattering to the reader, even when charged with irony—for something quite different. All her later novels contain within the action a marked discontinuity between the present and some experience of the past that has been deliberately or otherwise forgotten. In some—*Felix Holt*, the Bulstrode part of *Middlemarch*, the secret of Gwendolen in *Daniel Deronda*—there is a double line of suspense, as in a detective story, because the reader knows neither what has happened nor how it will be discovered. But all have double narratives, at least in part, and all are concerned with establishing a continuity that has been broken.[1]

1 The best single introduction to the subject is Thomas Pinney, "The Authority of the Past in George Eliot's Novels," *Nineteenth-Century Fiction*, 21 (1966), reprinted

Silas Marner is sometimes grouped with the earlier novels and sometimes with the later. It evidently relies heavily on a pastoral convention: the setting is rural, and the hero and other characters are apparently simpler than the narrator and readers of the story. Raveloe is said to be "never reached by the vibrations of the coach-horn or of public opinion" (ch. 1), and even a pastoral ideal can be glimpsed here, since it is in the countryside that Marner's recuperation can take place. But *Silas Marner* is just as importantly a fiction of discontinuity, the story of a person cut off from his past. Apart from the fairy-tale contrivance of the plot, the main facts about the hero are that his career has been struck asunder by injustice and infamy in Lantern Yard and that he has become a displaced person in Raveloe:

> Even people whose lives have been made various by learning, sometimes find it hard to keep hold on their habitual views of life, on their faith in the Invisible, nay, on the sense that their past joys and sorrows are a real experience, when they are suddenly transported to a new land, where the beings around them know nothing of their history, and share none of their ideas ... Minds that have been unhinged from their old faith and love have perhaps sought this Lethean influence of exile, in which the past becomes dreamy because its symbols have all vanished, and the present too is dreamy because it is linked with no memories. But even *their* experience may hardly enable them thoroughly to imagine what was the effect on a simple weaver like Silas Marner, when he left his own country and people and came to settle in Raveloe. (ch. 2)

The bridge between "even people ... [of] learning" and "a simple weaver" expresses, precisely, the pastoral perspective, but the theme is transportation, or the discontinuity of any life. The deliberate introduction of perspective, whether of pastoral or some other comparison, is a constant with George Eliot, but the action supporting this theme is new. That is why actions of continuity or discontinuity provide a better means of dividing early from late novels in the canon. Potential discontinuity is a theme nearly from the beginning, and a

in *George Eliot: A Collection of Critical Essays*, ed. George R. Creeger (Englewood Cliffs, N.J.: Prentice-Hall, 1970), pp. 37–54. Bernard J. Paris, "George Eliot and the Higher Criticism," *Anglia*, 84 (1966), 59–73, associates the novelist's need "to discover a continuity between past and present" with the Victorians' general reinterpretation of culture and religion.

breaking point is approached in *The Mill on the Floss*. Now the theme will be presented from the point of view of the life that is discontinuous.

When *Silas Marner* was first published, R. H. Hutton noted "the strong intellectual impress which the author contrives to give to a story of which the main elements are altogether unintellectual."[2] Marner, in fact, is like an intellectual without book-learning, since he has some "reputation for knowledge" and "cleverness" among people "mostly not over wise or clever" (ch. 1). No earlier character of George Eliot, unless it is Maggie Tulliver, so differs from the people around him, and Maggie is not alien or utterly alone or deliberately forgetful of her past. Moreover, Maggie stays put, and perishes, where she was born. Now the novelist is dramatizing the plight of a person who has left the past behind as she herself has in becoming George Eliot; and when Marner, having found a new life with Eppie, feels it safe to visit his old home—hard by Prison Street and the jail which assure him "that he was in his native place"—he finds that Lantern Yard has been demolished to make room for a large factory (ch. 20). Such is the sequence of history rather than the flight of pastoral, and there is no going back—though Marner, in talking with Dolly Winthrop, has by now "recovered a consciousness of unity between his past and present" (ch. 16). For every experienced discontinuity George Eliot posits a necessary continuity, even when continuity itself may seem threatening.

The first fiction written wholly after the disclosure of George Eliot's identity was actually "Brother Jacob." Though the story was not published until July 1864, it was written in August 1860, after the publication of *The Mill on the Floss* and the visit by the Leweses to Florence that spring. Eventually it was given to the publisher George Smith for use in *Cornhill,* as a gesture to make up for the loss he suffered in publishing *Romola* in the magazine. "Brother Jacob" is hardly an achievement to place beside *Silas Marner*—Gordon Haight distinguishes it as "unique among George Eliot's works in its complete lack of sympathy for any of the characters, even the idiot."[3] The story certainly has a despicable hero in the confectioner David

2 Review in the *Economist,* 27 Apr. 1861; Carroll, p. 176.
3 *George Eliot: A Biography* (Oxford: Clarendon, 1968), p. 340. U. C. Knoepflmacher, *George Eliot's Early Novels* (Berkeley: University of California Press, 1968) p. 224, calls Faux "perhaps the most unpleasant character in George Eliot's fiction."

Faux, alias Edward Freely, who "dared rob nobody but his mother" (ch. 3). His general posture is a travesty of the morality of consequences:

> David was by no means impetuous; he was a young man greatly given to calculate consequences, a habit which has been held to be the foundation of virtue. But somehow it had not precisely that effect in David: he calculated whether an action would harm himself, or whether it would only harm other people. In the former case he was very timid about satisfying his immediate desires, but in the latter he would risk the result with much courage. (ch. 1)

The irony expended on this character, in truth, points to an arguable refutation of the morality of consequences preached by Adam Bede and Mr. Irwine, among others: it all depends on who is performing the calculations. Almost slapdash in manner, "Brother Jacob" is George Eliot's first story of a discontinuous career, and she treats the subject gingerly and with despite that helps her to maintain her balance.[4] David Faux runs off with his mother's guineas to the West Indies and returns as Edward Freely to a town called Grimworth, where he succeeds for a time somewhat the way Nicholas Bulstrode succeeds in Middlemarch, though with a different demeanor. The mobility of the man is associated with "the inevitable course of civilization" that introduces commercial products instead of homemade cakes and pastry in Grimworth (ch. 2).

The narration of "Brother Jacob" is sportive. The choice of confectioner as vocation for the hero sets the tone and hints at self-indulgence from beginning to end. Faux is not deeply bent on his vocation and will try his hand at anything: "If you question me closely as to whether all the money with which he set up at Grimworth consisted of pure and simple earnings, I am obliged to confess that he got a sum or two for charitably abstaining from mentioning some other people's misdemeanours" (ch. 3). That is, Faux is also a blackmailer on the side. Recall that Bulstrode, no confectioner but a banker, is both subject to blackmail himself and prone to use his intimate knowledge of Middlemarch affairs to force people to give him his way. Both of

---

4 Lawrence Jay Dessner, "The Autobiographical Matrix of *Silas Marner*," *Studies in the Novel*, 11 (1979), 265–271, details some of the venomous humor of "Brother Jacob."

these outsiders and fated victims of public exposure are also intrusive insiders. Both at first endure a good deal of suspicion from the community.

> But when the confectioner ceased to be a novelty, the suspicions also ceased to be novel, and people got tired of hinting at them, especially as they seemed to be refuted by his advancing prosperity and importance. Mr. Freely was becoming a person of influence in the parish; he was found useful as an overseer of the poor, having great firmness in enduring other people's pain, which firmness, he said, was due to his great benevolence; he always did what was good for people in the end. (ch. 2)

In Faux are anticipated Bulstrode's hypocrisy, his righteousness, and his whole career; but Bulstrode never changes his name, and he takes himself much more seriously. Moreover, the reader of *Middlemarch* is forced to take him seriously.

One should not find it surprising that so perturbed a theme should first be sounded by the novelist in so light a manner. "Brother Jacob" is to the later novels as "Amos Barton" is to the earlier. Both stories treat from a great distance themes of particular interest to the author. Amos Barton, with his sad fortunes, she created as something of a clown in order to study the variance between even minimal inward being and outward reputation. Brother Jacob she created an idiot, in order to blackmail, in effect, his calculating and morally even more simple-minded brother. The first story has been deemed important for the development of George Eliot as a novelist in part because of its serious commitment to realism; the second has been neglected, in part, because of its lack of seriousness. But the action of the second is not purely circumstantial. It is set into motion by dull greed and elaborated rather slyly in the double life of Mr. David Faux as Mr. Edward Freely. The title "Brother Jacob" does not refer to the main actor in this story but to the tenacious idiot who is Faux's "Nemesis" (ch. 3). The theme of personal identity over time is ironically and boldly inscribed in the action, but the secret sharer in the knowledge of the past is also featured large. The people of Grimworth, and especially Miss Penny Palfrey, have reason to be thankful to brother Jacob.

Though *Silas Marner* is a much more serious work than "Brother Jacob," the story of Godfrey Cass and his brother Dunstan is less serious at first than that of Marner. The narrator scorns the divided life of Godfrey, with his secret marriage that has taken place before the present action of the novel, as "an ugly story of low passion, delusion, and waking from delusion" and characterizes it as "vicious folly." She also refers to "a movement of compunction" that brought about the marriage and to delusion "partly due to a trap laid for him by Dunstan, who saw in his brother's degrading marriage the means of gratifying at once his jealous hate and his cupidity" (ch. 3). Godfrey has been set up for blackmail, and the blackmailer is more hateful than his victim. Though George Eliot is severe with both—in marked contrast with her sympathy for Marner—Dunstan's sneering and general nastiness at least make Godfrey's weakness tolerable. But then she carefully brings the two story-lines together, and this relatively shallow blackmail plot makes its contribution to the first of the multiplot novels. Though *Silas Marner* is a short work and is sometimes called a "fable," it has this important position in George Eliot's canon. As Fred C. Thomson has argued, the double plot and theme of discontinuity henceforth become her principal means of testing the relation of individuals to society.[5]

There are two differences between Godfrey Cass's situation and that of Arthur Donnithorne: Godfrey has actually married the girl, and he has in his brother a blackmailer of "diabolical cunning" (ch. 3). Notice that marriage has given weight to the pastness of the secret life simply by making it weigh for the future from which it is disconnected: this is one reason that sensation novels of the period prefer bigamy to adultery as a secret. It is doubtful that Arthur Donnithorne could have been blackmailed for getting Hetty with child, and George Eliot just noticeably refrains from explaining Godfrey Cass's "delusion." I take it that "low passion" by itself would not have got Godfrey in such trouble, and if not for "waking from delusion" he might have remained married. George Eliot is writing of a completed action and from a different angle than that of *Adam Bede*. Arthur's fall was not complete, any more than Maggie Tulliver's fall was complete—though it goes without saying that hers would have been if she had gone as far sexually as he. His reputation suffers, and he has to leave Loamshire for a while to ease a greater threat to the reputation

5 "The Theme of Alienation in *Silas Marner*," *Nineteenth-Century Fiction*, 20 (1965), 82–84. Cf. Jerome Thale, *The Novels of George Eliot* (New York: Columbia University Press, 1959), p. 75.

of the Poysers. On the other hand, he does not enjoy the advantages of being blackmailed that Godfrey Cass enjoys, which are the advantages of becoming a victim in turn. Godfrey can take out his feelings on his brother Dunstan, and so can the reader. By this means the character, the novelist, and the reader are able to "get over" a past life and repair a personal identity.

This process would be more apposite if Godfrey had a career, which he has not—all he really needs to save him is the death of his first wife, so that he can marry again. It is noteworthy that subsequent victims of blackmail in the works of George Eliot do have careers, and not in confectionery either, but in such fields as politics, banking, and mercenary marriage. In the other plot of *Silas Marner*, the hero can be said to have a career, though a humble one. Indeed, the point is that Marner has two careers, the first having been destroyed, along with his religious faith, promised marriage, and social life, by the treachery of one William Dane. The latter is not a blackmailer like Dunstan Cass—blackmailers do not destroy their prey—but he is parallel to Dunstan to the degree that the other has set a "trap" for his brother, and the early victimization links Godfrey and Silas Marner together before they are linked as the two fathers of Eppie.[6] It is also true that if Marner had set up shop in Raveloe in some more ambitious style, instead of becoming a recluse, he might have been subject to blackmail because of the circumstances under which he left Lantern Yard. But Marner has taken even his false conviction upon himself, and it has made a deeper alteration in his character than a blackmailer might effect. He has, in fact, a good deal in common with his author: a reputation for cleverness, a kind of knowledge, a loss of faith, removal to another place, a measure of infamy, semiseclusion, increasing capital, and an adopted child. He has not really fallen, has not stolen a penny, and has not opened himself to blackmail as Godfrey Cass has.

Of the characters with discontinuous careers in *Silas Marner*, the author apparently sympathizes with Marner and judges Godfrey. Readers are likely to respond similarly, scarcely realizing how divided this response is. For those tempted to scorn someone who has been unable to make the two halves of his life meet, Godfrey Cass

6 Cf. David R. Carroll, "*Silas Marner:* Revising the Oracles of Religion," in *Literary Mongraphs*, ed. Eric Rothstein and Thomas K. Dunseath, vol. I (Madison: University of Wisconsin Press, 1967), pp. 175–181.

suffices as a target. To yield to this response, however, is curiously to side with the much more despicable Dunstan Cass. One of the uses of a blackmailer in fiction entails this contradiction: the figure is antithetical to the protagonist (both protagonists in this case) and yet functions in some helpful way. Dunstan, perversely enough, is the one who threatens to make Godfrey accountable for his actions; he threatens to tell what ought to be confessed. He is at once more careless of responsibility than his brother and a bad conscience. Dunstan, like David Faux, is a thief as well as a blackmailer; and by stealing Marner's gold, just before Godfrey's child wanders in the door, he assists in the second and healthier change in Marner's life. Still more obligingly, he steps into the stone pit with the gold and drowns. Dunstan has his uses, and when both actions of *Silas Marner* meet, his is the pivotal role.

While reproving Godfrey Cass's behavior as a young man, the narrator launches into a sermon against trusting in chance. "Favourable Chance is the god of all men who follow their own devices instead of obeying a law they believe in." Five examples of "the worship of blessed Chance" are set forth, with elaborate parallel irony, rounded out by a reductio ad absurdum: "The evil principle deprecated in that religion is the orderly sequence by which the seed brings forth a crop after its kind" (ch. 9). What is Dunstan's role in this thicket of irony? Like many blackmailers, including our friends Tracy and Raffles, he personifies the risk inherent in the religion of chance and in all concealment. He is the narrator's cat's-paw, more on the side of the sermon than its object. Yet what is his further role in the action of *Silas Marner?* It is he who gives the lie to the sermon, by creating the principal interruption or violation of "the orderly sequence by which the seed brings forth a crop after its kind" in the novel, the improbable chance that makes possible the fairy-tale transformation of gold coin into a golden child. The chapter that brings Dunstan to the edge of the stone pit (ch. 4) is a model of George Eliot's ability to narrate circumstances, character, and the character's rationalizations in brief compass, but this effective realism scarcely conceals the commitment of the double plot to chance. Dunstan's presence also helps obscure the fact that Godfrey's salvation—Godfrey, the original hapless idolator of Chance—comes about at this time through the pure chance of the death of his first wife. Dunstan Cass performs so well for George

Eliot because he is so eminently expendable, and he is apparently so wicked that he makes good the operation of chance.[7]

When Silas Marner comes to himself after experiencing the epileptic fit that is still another coincidence at the conjunction of the two actions, he first imagines that the child on his hearth is his gold and then that it might be "his little sister come back to him in a dream." Such images of dead children are common in Victorian novels: infant mortality was common, and the dead children are sharp reminders of the continuing life of the siblings, through childhood and mature age. Here Eppie seems to Marner "somehow a message . . . from that far-off life" in Lantern Yard that he has not been able to bring himself to think about in Raveloe. The dreamlike reminder even awakens in him "old impressions of awe at the presentiment of some Power presiding over his life" (ch. 12). So the child from its earliest appearance recalls continuity and design, and chance happenings may be providential. As soon as Marner resolves to keep Eppie near him and care for her, he conceives "that the child was come instead of the gold,—that the gold had turned into the child" (ch. 14). This is the chief miracle of *Silas Marner*, purely anagogic and resting on triple coincidence. Its significance is that Marner has already begun to recover "a consciousness of unity between his past and present" (ch. 16). The play on the meaning of "gold" is the stuff of fairy tales, skillfully handled and condoned by the pastoralism of the novel, which still views Marner as more simple than the novelist and reader.

Gold literally makes an appearance in George Eliot's fiction only at this time, in "Brother Jacob" and *Silas Marner*. Greed for gold is repudiated in both stories—laughed at in the first and frowned upon in the second as the sterile obsession of misers. It has been suggested that this interest reflects George Eliot's own embarrassment of riches after her first success as a novelist, and there is surely some truth in this argument.[8] One of the minor embarrassments of having old

---

7 Something similar might be said of the expendability of Molly Cass. Novelists can be almost routinely cruel, and the coincidence of Molly's death is presumably acceptable because she is a drug addict and meditating "vengeance" (ch. 12). *Silas Marner* is still a fairly early experiment for George Eliot, however: one cannot imagine Mrs. Glasher in *Daniel Deronda* sinking down on the snow, though Mrs. Glasher is both an inconvenience and a blackmailer.

8 See Ruby V. Redinger, *George Eliot: The Emergent Self* (New York: Knopf, 1975), pp. 338–340, and Peter Simpson, "Crisis and Recovery: Wordsworth, George

friends and former acquaintances know that she was a successful novelist was their possible speculation as to her income. The whole experience of negotiating for considerable sums, and having publishers compete for her work, was new to her. Money seemed a little wicked, but also a good, just as in fairy tales. It was a difficult time for George Eliot. As a writer with a new public and private identity, she was determined to work on something different and ambitious, but she found it impossible to begin. Hence "Brother Jacob" and *Silas Marner* were written after *Romola* was first conceived, and it seems likely that some of her difficulty resided in the tensions of the market for writing that now surrounded her. Negotiations with Blackwood over *The Mill on the Floss* had not been easy, and she now permitted herself to break with Blackwood on mercenary grounds—though in order to protect her own idea of her work she settled for less for *Romola* in 1862 than Smith originally offered her. The break with Blackwood proved not to be permanent, but until it was over, George Eliot was not altogether comfortable about her financial connection to her world. All that is gold does not glitter.

Eliot, and *Silas Marner*," *University of Toronto Quarterly*, 48 (1979), 108–109. Dessner (see note 4) makes a similar point but wildly exaggerates George Eliot's "unhealthy appetite for money."

9

Romola and the Past

In June 1860 George Eliot had written to Blackwood from the continent that she had a new project. Being "anxious to keep it a secret," she would not tell him about it by letter, but wrote that it would "require a great deal of study and labour" and that she was "athirst to begin."[1] In August she broke to him "the secret," describing only a historical romance set in Florence at "the close of the fifteenth century, which was marked by Savonarola's career and martyrdom," and already confessing misgivings about completing it.[2] After writing "Brother Jacob" and *Silas Marner*, and after a second journey to Italy in the spring of 1861, she still experienced difficulty—probably more so than in beginning any other novel. The writing was finally under way, and given a name, in January 1862. It may be less important to fathom George Eliot's immediate difficulty—*Romola* was, after all, very different in setting and period from her other novels—than to ask why, according to her own perception, the experience of writing it marked such an epoch in her life. There really does appear to be an early and a late George Eliot, marked by *Romola* and the two stories that preceded it. Cross interrupts the sequence of letters and journal entries that comprises his record of her life to remark, "The writing of 'Romola' ploughed into her more than any of her other books. She told me she could put her finger on it as marking a well-defined transition in her life. In her own words, 'I began it a young woman,—I finished it an old woman.' "[3]

If George Eliot told Cross why the writing of *Romola* was pivotal,

1 To John Blackwood, 23 June 1860, *G.E.L.*, III, 306.
2 To John Blackwood, 28 Aug. 1860, *G.E.L.*, III, 339.
3 J. W. Cross, *George Eliot's Life as Related in Her Letters and Journals*, Illustrated Cabinet Edition, 3 vols. (New York: Merrill and Baker, n.d.), II, 277.

he does not say. The answer lies within the novel and in the two lesser fictions that the writing of *Romola* subtended, each of which had to do with the need for reconciling past and present experience in some continuous narrative of identity. New beginnings, or epochs of personal experience, tend to be prominent in the large-scale narrative of any life, and Romola's life is no exception. We read of Romola's response to her brother Dino's death, "It seemed to her as if this first vision of death must alter the daylight for her forevermore" (ch. 15); or of Romola's first venture beyond Florence, "For the first time in her life she felt alone in the presence of the earth and sky, with no human presence interposing and making a law for her" (ch. 40); or of her time in the green valley, "The experience was like a new baptism to Romola" (ch. 69). Yet the most common new beginning of all, marriage, is almost elided in the text. Romola's marriage takes place only after Tito Melema's character is thoroughly made known to the reader, and hence only after a curtain of dramatic irony has descended over the action. The epochal style of narrative is finally more insistent than it is persuasive. In the venture beyond Florence a new beginning is arrested after a single paragraph by the appearance of Girolamo Savonarola and what seems to be, in retrospect, Romola's most important epoch of all. No sooner do we breathe freely with her alone "for the first time" than we read, "It was the first time she had encountered a gaze in which simple human fellowship expressed itself as a strongly felt bond" (ch. 40). Such a false start, or superimposition of beginnings, results from the strained flirtation with discontinuity in the life of Romola. It is a flirtation only: George Eliot finally conceives of Romola's life as continuous, or nearly so. Discontinuity is pronounced nefarious and displaced onto Tito Melema, as it had been onto David Faux and the brothers Cass. Yet the novelist herself later accepted that a life could fall into two parts, because she began *Romola* as a young woman and finished it as an old woman.

Romola's experiences, like Maggie Tulliver's, have a tendency to stop short. The successive changes in Maggie's life, however—both true epochs like the fall of Mr. Tulliver and childish moments that are narrated because of their traumatic import—seem to occur more simply than changes in the life of the more deeply rebellious Romola. Maggie rebels as a child but not as an adult; she wishes to choose, as she tells Stephen Guest, but she chooses to conform. Romola chooses freedom and has her choice thrown back in her teeth by Fra Girolamo: "You wish your true name and your true place in life to be hidden, that you may choose for yourself a new name and a new place, and have no rule but your own will." Words like these arouse Romola's "anger" and "stronger rebellion," and the dramatic encounter argues that she is more in need of external control than Maggie was. But she is nevertheless "shaken," moved by the "bond" she feels and by the "authority" of the monk. "And you are flying from your debts,—the debt of a Florentine woman, the debt of a wife. You are turning your back on the lot that has been appointed for you; you are going to choose another. But can man or woman choose duties? No more than they can choose their birthplace or their father and mother." Fra Girolamo argues, in short, very much along the lines Maggie Tulliver argued with herself and Stephen. For Romola, significantly, this argument is articulated most forcefuly from without, and it is hard to say what would have followed if God had not sent his "messenger" at this moment (ch. 40).

Romola's experience ought to be more extensive than Maggie's. She has had a more imposing intellectual role in relation to her father; she is herself more imposing in every way, if we can trust her initial description (ch. 5). She is also married, though she does not have children. Yet the narrative glosses over both her true relation to her father and her marriage, most especially by withholding nearly all her thoughts and feelings for twenty-six chapters. When the narrative subsequently "goes behind" Romola, the reader begins to be better informed about both relations. Then it appears that "Romola had had contact with no mind that could stir the larger possibilities of her nature; they lay folded and crushed like embryonic wings, making no element in her consciousness beyond an occasional vague uneasiness" (ch. 27). Therefore "the larger possibilities" of Romola have no more been fulfilled by study with her father or eighteen-months' marriage to a young man of great ability than Maggie's possibilities were fulfilled by much lesser fare. Her relation to Savonarola comes closest to satisfying her, but that too concludes in a standoff, for reasons that I shall try to describe. The very backing and filling of the argument, I suggest, shows that George Eliot was bent on narrating a disruption of life such as she and her heroine had not countenanced in *The Mill on the Floss*, and hence on portraying a "consciousness" beyond mere uneasiness.

On the eve of Romola's second and final return to Florence and before she is aware of the arrest of Savonarola or of Tito's death, we read:

The memory of her life with Tito, of the conditions which made their real union impossible, while their external union imposed a set of false duties on her which were essentially the concealment and sanctioning of what her mind revolted from, told her that flight had been her only resource. All minds, except such as are delivered from doubt by dulness of sensibility, must be subject to this recurring conflict where the many-twisted conditions of life have forbidden the fulfilment of a bond. For in strictness there is no replacing of relations: the presence of the new does not nullify the failure and breach of the old. Life has lost its perfection: it has been maimed; and until the wounds are quite scarred, conscience continually casts backward, doubting glances. (ch. 69)

Notice how carefully Romola's position is circumscribed—by the indirect style, by the generalization over "all minds" except the insensible, and above all by the contrived situation of the plot. Romola's first "flight" was aborted and atoned for; the second can hardly be regarded as unjustified. It is not she who has run away from "what her mind revolted from," but Tito who has repeatedly run out on her. The moral weight of their respective characters differs as earth from air. Nevertheless these "conditions of life have forbidden the fulfilment of a bond." That concession, from the perspective of *The Mill on the Floss*, is a grave complication of the represented life. While still laboring to justify and to elevate the heroine, *Romola* does concede that a bond has been broken.

The true discontinuity represented in the novel cannot be read without mapping upon the story of Romola's life the story of Tito's. Many readers, from the time of the novel's first publication, have found Tito more interesting than Romola. Henry James, by asserting that Tito was "the leading figure in *Romola*," no doubt intended to be critical as well as provocative.[4] But in another sense of "leading" James was precisely correct, for the narrative begins with Tito and

4 "Tito is the leading figure in *Romola*. The story deals predominantly, not with Romola as affected by Tito's faults, but with Tito's faults as affecting first himself, and incidentally his wife. Godfrey Cass, with his life-long secret, is by right the hero of *Silas Marner*." James goes on to say that *Felix Holt* has a heroine but no hero, and that Hetty Sorrel or Arthur Donnithorne should be thought of as the hero of *Adam Bede*. In this formulation the character with a secret, or about whom there is a secret, is the hero. See "The Novels of George Eliot," *Atlantic Monthly*, 18 (1866), reprinted in *A Century of George Eliot Criticism*, ed. Gordon S. Haight (Boston: Houghton Mifflin, 1965), pp. 47–48.

stays with him, except for a few chapters, through the death of Bardo; and consequently for a long while the reader knows more about Tito than about Romola, and far more about Tito than Romola knows. The arrangement is a somewhat awkward one for George Eliot. Tito partially exists, like David Faux, for the novelist and reader to strike at; therefore to give this "Shipwrecked Stranger" (ch. 1) such a prominent role in the first third of the novel, berating his weakness and secretiveness, strains our expectations of the author's fairness and compassion. William Butler Yeats perceived the harshness of accusation here and remarked that George Eliot "plucks her Tito in pieces with as much assurance as if he had been clock-work."[5]

The prominence of Tito and the antipathy toward him can be explained by studying the grouping of the characters in the novel, or what Barbara Hardy has called George Eliot's "habit of antithesis." The contrast and opposition of Tito and Romola are firmly based in resemblance and parallelism. "Tito's growth in treachery is strong and rapid: he betrays Baldassare, then Bardo, then Romola, then Florence. It is paralleled by Romola's sacrifice: for Bardo, for Savonarola, for Tito, for Florence, and, in the end, for Tessa and Tito's children."[6] The antithesis, which Hardy spells out further, has also been traced among the symbolic details of the novel by George Levine.[7] It remained for Dianne F. Sadoff to marshal similar evidence for a psychoanalytic reading of the author's unconscious wishes at work in the novel.[8] Tito is everything that Romola is not. In his re-

5 Quoted by Joan Bennett, *George Eliot: Her Mind and Her Art* (1948; rpt. Cambridge, England: Cambridge University Press, 1962), p. 148.

6 *The Novels of George Eliot: A Study in Form* (1959; rpt. London: Athlone, 1963), pp. 85–88. Hardy's chapter "Character and Form" provides a lesson on how to read the plots of the novels through contrasts and resemblances.

7 "*Romola* as Fable," in *Critical Essays on George Eliot*, ed. Barbara Hardy (London: Routledge, 1970), pp. 84–88. Laura Comer Emery, *George Eliot's Creative Conflict: The Other Side of Silence* (Berkeley: University of California Press, 1976), pp. 84–85, notes that Romola and Tito "begin to look like opposing aspects of one psyche."

8 *Monsters of Affection: Dickens, Eliot, and Brontë on Fatherhood* (Baltimore: Johns Hopkins University Press, 1982), pp. 88–94. Sadoff believes that the writing of *Romola* was traumatic in a psychoanalytic sense. She boldly interprets Tito as a "figure" for Romola's desires, including the desire to abandon fathers. "Every major male character in the novel represents a father or brother; Romola herself is a figure for the young Mary Ann Evans" (p. 92). Such multiple projections are, at least, psychoanalytically consistent, and Sadoff's pages on *Romola* are the most persuasive part of her book.

pudiation of his stepfather, Baldassare, and in his craven fear of discovery, he represents the personality who has broken entirely with his past. Thus he is given one opportunity after another "of retrieving that moment on the steps of Duomo, when the Past had grasped him with living quivering hands, and he had disowned it" (ch. 34), but he cannot bring himself to do so. Whereas Romola's conflicts are subtle and hedged from the reader's view, Tito's are visceral and fully displayed—concealed only from the other characters.

Romola stands for remembrance and the continuity of the present with the past, but the tension of her stance becomes apparent by cross-reference to Tito. In one of several passages toward the end of the novel that hover between indirect style and frank description of the heroine's state of mind, George Eliot crosses over to Tito's role in the plot and illuminates Romola's thought by a single question:

> She was thrown back again on the conflict between the demands of an outward law, which she recognized as a widely ramifying obligation, and the demands of inner moral facts which were becoming more and more peremptory [note the carefully hedged source of her conflict]. She had drunk in deeply the spirit of that teaching by which Savonarola had urged her to return to her place. She felt that the sanctity attached to all close relations, and, therefore, pre-eminently to the closest, was but the expression in outward law of that result towards which all human goodness and nobleness must spontaneously tend; that the light abandonment of ties, whether inherited or voluntary [filial or conjugal], because they had ceased to be pleasant, was the uprooting of social and personal virtue. *What else had Tito's crime toward Baldassare been but that abandonment working itself out to the most hideous extreme of falsity and ingratitude?* (ch. 56, my italics)

One does not like to break into George Eliot's prose in order to focus the reader's attention in this manner, but *Romola* is the most dreamlike of her novels, both in its details and in its overall construction.[9] Even without this allusion to abandonment "working itself

---

9 Dreamlike construction is roughly what Levine means, I believe, when he urges us to regard the novel as a "fable." Felicia Bonaparte, in *The Triptych and the Cross: The Central Myths of George Eliot's Poetic Imagination* (New York: New York University Press, 1979), prefers to call *Romola* a "poem" (p. 5) or a "symbolic narrative" (p. 10). By tracing countless allusions in *Romola* Bonaparte creates a wonderful compendium of sources, but by reading the allusions *as* the text, she turns the whole into an allegory of the history of civilization.

out," a reader coming to the novel a second or third time realizes that Tito is fractional as well as "extreme." He is not so much an entire person as a representation of extreme freedom from guilt and terror of shame. George Eliot makes a point of stating that Tito's "mind was destitute of that dread" of divine retribution, or of any "vague fear at . . . wrong-doing," or "terror of the unseen," that is "the initial recognition of a moral law." His "mere sensual cowardice" does not rise to anything like guilt (ch. 11). But he is instinctively fearful of "scorching looks and biting words" (ch. 16).[10] In general, Romola feels guilty for what she has not done and scarcely thought of doing, whereas Tito is stirred by "inward shame" (ch. 9) at what he has done and will continue to do. It is the latter who is obviously set up for some kind of blackmail, since he is both completely incautious of wrongdoing and terrified of discovery; and what is finally most dreamlike about Tito is his situation with respect to Baldassare. For Baldassare both is and is not Tito's "father," both is and is not alive to him. "It will lighten your wonder," Tito says to the barber Nello, who has admired his Italian, "to know that I come of a Greek stock planted in Italian soil much longer than the mulberry-trees which have taken so kindly to it. I was born at Bari, and my—I mean, I was brought up by an Italian—and, in fact, I am a Greek, very much as your peaches are Persian" (ch. 3). From this initial merry obfuscation to the last fatal encounter—"Tito knew him; but he did not know whether it was life or death that had brought him into the presence of his injured father" (ch. 67)—there is hardly a scene between Tito and Baldassare that is not anomalous, or that would be plausible in waking life. Whereas Romola is like a creature in a deep study—not unlike the guilty woman whom R. H. Hutton perceived in George Eliot after reading Cross's *Life*[11]—Tito is like a creature in a bad dream.

In the first place, the reader of *Romola* is asked to believe that Tito ought to be combing the Aegean to discover whether his stepfather is alive and enslaved by pirates. The facts are not stated; we are ap-

10 Bonaparte, *The Triptych and the Cross*, pp. 154–160, contrasts Tito's "fear" with "moral dread." By observing a difference of shame and guilt, one can analyze the opposition and displacement between Tito and Romola without this recourse to a "mystery" as the sanction of morality.

11 "George Eliot's Life and Letters," *Essays on Some of the Modern Guides to English Thought in Matters of Faith* (1888; rpt. London: Macmillan, 1900), pp. 271–310.

prised of this conclusion after the "importunate thought" strikes Tito and he reaches a negative conclusion. *"If it were certain"* that Baldassare were alive, then perhaps Tito should attempt to find and ransom him; since it is not certain, he won't. "He had always equivocally spoken of [Baldassare] as 'lost'; he did not say to himself,—what he was not ignorant of,—that Greeks of distinction had made sacrifices, taken voyages again and again, and sought help from crowned and mitred heads for the sake of freeing relatives from slavery to the Turks." Here then is a typical source of shame, a failure to rise to the expectations of others. Lest the reader cannot enter wholeheartedly into the idea, George Eliot adds in somewhat incongruous nineteenth-century vocabulary, "Public opinion did not regard this as exceptional virtue." She also generalizes about the misfortunes of the aged, "dimmed and faded human beings"—"if there is any love of which they are not widowed, it must be the love that is rooted in memories and distils perpetually the sweet balms of fidelity and forbearing tenderness." And she tells for the first time, or rather intimates, how Baldassare rescued Tito "from blows" when he was only seven and "a very bright lovely boy."[12] But Tito does not set out in search of his stepfather, to renew a relation that has become "irksome" with a man whose thoughts "have long taken the character of monotony and repetition." Was his stepfather dead or alive in any case? "It was a great relief to be quit of Baldassare, and he would have liked to know *who* it was that had fallen overboard" (ch. 9). Fourteen years later in *Daniel Deronda* George Eliot was to face directly a question of who had fallen overboard in the Mediterranean and who had wished him dead, but for *Romola* she dipped her pen in the ink of Greek romance and determined that only the despicable Tito entertained such thoughts.

The reader is further asked to accept that, once Tito has equivocated about Baldassare's existence and the latter actually shows up,

---

12 "A youth of even splendid grace," the description continues, "who seemed quite without vices, as if that beautiful form represented a vitality so exquisitely poised and balanced that it could know no uneasy desires, no unrest,—a radiant presence for a lonely man to have won for himself" (ch. 9). It is just possible that George Eliot intended a homoerotic relation, with a murderous Baldassare later dreaming of "plunging that dagger into a base heart, which he was unable to pierce in any other way" (ch. 34). In such case the reticence surrounding the narrative of the early relation would be deliberate—but I cannot believe she would develop such a relation as melodramatically as she does later in *Romola* or write of "justice" at its conclusion (ch. 67).

the young man dare not recognize the older or be recognized by him, lest he be shamed by his own previous inaction and silence. The plausible explanation for Tito's subsequent behavior in the novel is thus the inevitable snowball effect of lying. But note how the imagined inferences threaten to unroll as in a dream, to expose a now portentous secret—namely, that Tito has "secretly" thought about his stepfather:

> Tito's talent for concealment was being fast developed into something less neutral. It was still possible,—perhaps it might be inevitable,—for him to accept frankly the altered conditions, and avow Baldassare's existence; but hardly without casting an unpleasant light backward on his original reticence as studied equivocation in order to avoid the fulfilment of a secretly recognized claim . . .

This analysis begins with a moral observation such as the novelist might have applied to Arthur Donnithorne, switches to indirect narrative of Tito Melema's thoughts, and penetrates to the fear that even secret thoughts may be inferred from outside. At the bottom of the rational moralizing lies a nightmare of circumstantial evidence—"to say nothing," the sentence continues, "of his quiet settlement of himself and investment of his florins, when, it would be clear, his benefactor's fate had not been certified" (ch. 11). In narrating Tito's subsequent career George Eliot invents ample rational scheming and evasions for the character to pursue, but at the core of his relation to Baldassare she posits blind terror. The proof of the dreamlike quality is that Tito never decisively acts against Baldassare. Is it possible that a young man with no scruples and no love, wonderfully ambitious and successful in the labyrinthine politics of Florence, could not find a means to eliminate the doddering, vengeful Baldassare? But instead of arranging the murder of which he is so obviously capable, Tito is himself pursued—with about equal effectiveness and still as in a dream—by his stepfather. The action with Baldassare has to be seen as a return of the repressed.

George Eliot accounts for Tito's inaction against Baldassare by labeling it "characteristic." She wishes all her characters to behave consistently. But the result in this case is to diminish Tito still further, to reduce him to a mere figment. For one thing, he is a physical coward: "Tito shrank with shuddering dread from disgrace; but he had also that physical dread which is inseparable from a soft plea-sure-loving nature, and which prevents a man from meeting wounds and death as a welcome relief from disgrace." But the argument that Tito does not prefer death to disgrace for himself hardly precludes his secretly killing another. On the other hand, unlike Arthur Don-nithorne or Godfrey Cass, Tito never thinks of confessing his trou-bles to anyone. As a creature of pure shame, "he never thought of that." And in sum, "he never thought of any scheme for removing his enemy. His dread generated no active malignity, and he would still have been glad not to give pain to any mortal. He had simply chosen to make life easy to himself . . ." (ch. 19). Such softness and the ab-sence of much human nature in Tito prompted Leslie Stephen, in a strenuous libel of the second sex, to put him down as a woman:

> [Romola's] husband, Tito, is frequently mentioned as one of George Eliot's greatest triumphs. The cause of her success is, as I take it, that Tito is thoroughly and to his fingers' ends a woman. I do not intend to condemn the conception, for undoubtedly there are men whose characters are essentially feminine. Tito is of the material of which the Delilahs are made, the treacherous, caressing, sensuous creatures who involve strong men in their meshes as Tito fascinates the rather masculine Romola.[13]

In this haphazard criticism Stephen apparently assumes that women are some nastier kind of men. Possibly, however, the dreamlike plot of *Romola* drew from him this response, since the strangely incom-plete Tito embodies the temptations, the unconscious "abandon-ment" of ties, of the heroine.

Romola the heroine is conceived as altogether sincere, like Dinah or Maggie, and possesses both "girlish simplicity" (ch. 5) and "boy-like frankness" (ch. 9); and while the first third of the novel affords the reader ample opportunity to observe Tito's insincerity and "tal-ent for concealment" (ch. 11), Romola "was as simple and unre-served as a child in her love for Tito" (ch. 17). Very much like Dinah, she walks "without the slightest conscious adjustment of her-self" (ch. 5), and her first "self-consciousness" only arises in love (ch. 20). Her sincerity is effectively enhanced by the reluctance of

---

13 *George Eliot*, English Men of Letters (London: Macmillan, 1902), p. 139. Ste-phen may have recalled a line about Tito in the *Westminster Review*, Oct. 1863; "He is Hetty, but a man, and not a fool." See Carroll, p. 217.

the narrative, or at least its neglect, to explore her thoughts at the outset of the action. Reluctance is a fair enough term, in fact, because the narrative plays down two important events: her marriage to Tito and her father's death. The careful avoidance of involving the heroine too deeply in her marriage protects her from blame when it turns out badly, but the equally determined avoidance of Bardo's death is more startling. Though the death occurs before the opening of book II, which advances the action eighteen months after the marriage (ch. 21), it is not mentioned for several more chapters, when the reader is casually informed, "[Romola] had been present at no festivities since her father had died,—died quite suddenly in his chair, three months before" (ch. 27). This is the chapter, and the casual announcement, which begins the serious narrative of Romola's life, including her thoughts.

Before this hiatus we have had Tito, and more especially the shameful repudiation of Tito's mysterious stepfather and tutor. While Tito has been doing his best to forget Baldassare, the narrative has succeeded in forgetting Bardo. But now Tito is off somewhere, Bardo is remembered, and Romola's simplicity is compromised: "it belongs to every large nature, when it is not under the immediate power of some strong unquestioning emotion, to suspect itself, and doubt the truth of its own impressions, conscious of possibilities beyond its own horizon." Her marriage, we learn, has been disappointing; she hopes that a "true marriage" can begin. "But the sense of something like guilt towards her father in a hope that grew out of his death, gave all the more force to the anxiety with which she dwelt on the means of fulfilling his supreme wish [to save his library for posterity]. That piety towards his memory was all the atonement she could make now for a thought that seemed akin to joy at his loss." There might indeed be grounds for a better marriage now, since "joy at his loss"—that is, her father's death—parallels the "great relief" Tito hoped for if only his father had died. Romola's "father's place was empty—there was no longer any importunate claim to divide her from Tito . . . and their true marriage could begin" (ch. 27). Compare with this "importunate claim" the "importunate thought" that is Tito's first consciousness of Baldassare.

When the construction of the narrative is thus taken into account, it seems that Romola and Tito lead parallel lives. Husband and wife might have got along famously if they had been able to meet on purely selfish grounds for the resistance to tiresome fathers. An extremely careful reader may have suspected trouble as early as the first description of Romola with her father, when "a fine ear would have detected in her clear voice and distinct utterance a faint suggestion of weariness struggling with habitual patience" (ch. 5). But Tito is constrained only by shame, Romola by "something like guilt"; the first seeks escape from past ties, the second "atonement." The novel brings the two quests into daring proximity. Remember that when Romola loses her father, she knows not even of the existence of Baldassare—as Tito has known and not known all along by willful forgetting. The concealed parallel in their situations is also to be the prime cause of their estrangement, even before Tito sells the precious library. For "the terrible resurrection of secret fears, which if Romola had known them would have alienated her from him forever, caused him to feel an alienation already begun between them,—caused him to feel a certain repulsion towards a woman from whose mind he was in danger" (ch. 27). The relation thus dramatizes his terror and her conscience.

"If Romola had known"—the double plot hinges precariously on the narrative status of such conditions as this. If the condition is to be accepted as authoritative rather than dramatic, then the reader is being prepared for another triumph of conscience such as concluded *The Mill on the Floss*: Romola's knowledge, her discovery of Tito's secret fears and their object, will override every other consideration in their relation; he will stand condemned and she will triumph. But as soon as one presses such an interpretation, it begins to tangle with the principle of economy in narrative. Why need *Romola* have a double plot if the net outcome is to be the same as in the earlier novel? To read the condition dramatically, on the other hand, as indirect narrative of Tito's anxieties only, is scarcely adequate to Romola's subsequent discovery of the secret and her reactions. Instead of seeking a single interpretation the reader has to understand, at least intuitively, that a double plot has been set up to accommodate inconsistency on one side or the other, and further, that the inconsistency is on the side least exposed to view, the Romola side. The secrets of Tito we know almost as well as he can, thanks to a merciless narrative that conceals them—for purposes of dramatic irony and moral hygienics—from the heroine.

The inconsistencies can only be revealed over time, and without the heroine's cooperation. Romola wants to preserve *all* connections, and hardly needs coaching from Savonarola on this score. Thus her loyalties have already been strained by the behavior of her brother Dino, who has forsaken their father for the Church. Even in such a small problem as this, Tito's unknown duplicity is a useful distraction. Unaware of the secret known to the reader, Romola addresses him: "Even you, Tito, would find it hard to forgive" a son who has forsaken his father (ch. 13). The reader almost winces for poor Tito. Would not Romola in the long run make an exception for him, too, as she is tempted to do for Dino? Such a small irony illustrates the various binds of the double plot. In its broadest sense the plot is easier to understand allegorically then psychologically, in terms of the passage from chapter 56 quoted earlier: Romola exemplifies "the sanctity attached to all close relations"; Tito, "the light abandonment of ties . . . working itself out to the most hideous extreme." These two not only have something in common—tiresome fathers—but are briefly married to each other. The ties and close relations represented in the novel come to include the marriage, which—still diagrammatically— Tito abuses and Romola tries to preserve. Loyalty and disloyalty are thereby crossed, guaranteeing inconsistency even on the consistent side: Romola adheres to and receives credit for adhering to the very person who exemplifies the abandonment of ties, including the abandonment of herself. The double plot forces the heroine into inconsistency despite herself, in a sort of whipsaw of martyrdom. Only a heroine can believe it possible to keep up all the relations in life.

Girolamo Savonarola first enters Romola's life uninvited, with warnings and commands that are little more than outward expressions of her own conscience—warnings about willfulness and inconsistency, commands to stay and to serve. Savonarola does not always practice what he preaches, however, and his role in the novel emerges almost at the opposite side, as a figure of contradiction. He attracts and repels Romola, who finally is able both to empathize with him and to judge him wanting. The obvious resemblance is to Tito, but Tito's doubleness is shallow, self-indulgent, fearful, and finally unnecessary, whereas Savonarola's doubleness is profound, the almost inevitable contradiction of the leader caught up in history—"the doubleness which is the pressing temptation in every public career, whether of priest, orator, or statesman" (ch. 65). Romola moves closer and closer to Savonarola, but never all the way. In this relation

George Eliot is able to exploit the example of Scott in historical romance: the historical leader can be sympathetically observed, and even followed for a while, without following him over the brink.[14] So the doubleness of Savonarola is almost to be expected, even as that of Tito is to be exorcised:

> Under this particular white tunic there was a heart beating with a consciousness inconceivable to the average monk, and perhaps hard to be conceived by any man who has not arrived at self-knowledge through a tumultuous inner life: a consciousness in which irrevocable errors and lapses from veracity were as entwined with noble purposes and sincere beliefs, in which self-justifying expediency was so inwoven with the tissue of a great work . . . that it was perhaps impossible, whatever course might be adopted, for the conscience to find perfect repose. (ch. 64)

Quite evidently George Eliot treats this "consciousness" seriously, entertaining compromises in the historical person that she will not countenance in her heroine. "Whatever falsehood there had been in him, had been a fall and not a purpose; a gradual entanglement in which he struggled, not a contrivance encouraged by success." The confession of Savonarola she treats almost as if it were her own recent experience: "perhaps this confession, even when it described a doubleness that was conscious and deliberate, really implied no more than that wavering of belief concerning his own impressions and motives which most human beings who have not a stupid inflexibility of self-confidence must be liable to under a marked change of external conditions" (ch. 71). Notice how the exception that certifies Savonarola's merit—"human beings who have not a stupid inflexibility of self-confidence"—echoes the exception that favors Romola two chapters earlier—"all minds, except such as are delivered from doubt by dulness of sensibility" (ch. 69). At the end, when Savonarola has to endure "the hooting and the spitting and the curses of the crowd," and then "the hard faces of enemies made judges," and finally "the horrible torture," Romola is made to feel very close to him and to side with him against the crowd. "As Romola thought of the anguish that must have followed the confession . . . that anguish seemed to be

14 Judith Wilt, *Ghosts of the Gothic: Austen, Eliot, and Lawrence* (Princeton: Princeton University Press, 1980), pp. 198–203, treats Savonarola as a "Gothic antihero." But this is a type who sometimes overlaps with the historical or semihistorical characters in Scott.

pressing on her own heart and urging the slow bitter tears." It is Savonarola, finally, who is ceded the title "martyr" and linked with early images of Romola in the novel through his "greatness" (ch. 71).

Tito is a creature of shame and lies, Romola of guilt and loyalty, and Savonarola of history. The division of labor in the novel assures that Romola can keep her head up. "Her life could never be happy any more, but it must not, could not, be ignoble" (ch. 36). The same displacements that protect Romola's simplicity and nobility, however, are the measure of her complexity. It is as if the title of the novel named not only the character but a wider organization. Though Tito is capable of having children by Tessa, and Savonarola of surrendering himself to a great cause, neither is capable of "love" like that of Romola for her father:

> Romola was nervously anxious to have in her possession a copy of the only portrait existing of her father in the days of his blindness, lest his image grow dim in her mind. The sense of defect in her devotedness to him made her cling with all the force of compunction as well as affection to the duties of memory. Love does not aim simply at the conscious good of the beloved object: it is not satisfied without perfect loyalty of heart; it aims at its own completeness. (ch. 28)

George Eliot's astuteness is all the more evident for its indirection. "Sense of defect," "force of compunction," and "duties of memory" are not love. Nearly every phrase employed for Romola's state of mind changes the definition of love to guilt. Why "nervously"? Why "in the days of his blindness," instead of simply when Bardo was alive? Only taken-for-granted affection ("as well as affection") remains to the idea of love. Such a preamble throws the sincerity and meaning of the last sentence in doubt. The sentence begins by saying that love is not entirely unselfish—a confession that itself seems noble—but stops short of saying that love is selfish. And what can the "conscious good" of Bardo consist in now that he is dead? Since he is dead, it would be fairer to say that love in the present circumstances aims *only* at its own completeness. "Completeness" does not mean selflessness plus desire, as it appears on first reading, but the capacity for guilt; and "perfect loyalty of heart" is enforced by guilt.

And what of the object of this love or guilt? The double plot of *Romola* enforces a comparison of Bardo with Baldassare, the late father with the half-alive stepfather.[15] When the former was alive he was blind and a bit of a bore, demanded too much of his children, and held a low opinion of the mental powers of women. But such faults are more bearable than those of Baldassare, who "belonged to a race to whom the thrust of the dagger seems almost as natural an impulse as the outleap of the tiger's talons" (ch. 23), and who is at this moment lurking about the streets of Florence. Baldassare survives and haunts, on quite a different level of representation than that which Bardo inhabited. The memory of Bardo may make Romola anxious, but the gradual reappearance of Baldassare for Tito is almost supernatural. He appears first in the evidence of a ring upon Tito's finger (ch. 1), then in the reticences of Tito's speech (ch. 6), as the importunate thought that Tito keeps to himself (ch. 9), in the searching glance of Fra Luca and the delivery of a letter (ch. 10), and shortly after the death of Bardo—as we learn later—as a clutch on the arm: "'Some madman, surely,' said Tito" (ch. 22). Baldassare is not mad, the narrator assures us, "for he carried within him that piteous stamp of sanity, the clear consciousness of shattered faculties." Yet for purposes of effective action it would have been just as well if he had remained a ghost, since his gothic presence is far from scary. His soliloquy to the effect that nobody loves him fails as pathos and as a plausible account of his motive (ch. 30). It all seems very clumsy for George Eliot. The impotence of Baldassare, however, like the ineffectiveness of Tito's defense, is due to the dreamlike action of *Romola*. Daggers break and encounters fail to materialize. Despite Baldassare's supposed killer's instinct, his real weapon is that of the blackmailer: "He could search into every secret of Tito's life now: he knew some of the secrets already, and the failure of the broken dagger, which seemed like frustration, had been the beginning of achievement." Baldassare is exactly what Tito deserves and what chain mail is helpless against. He is the object and walking proof of Tito's oldest secret betrayal. Now his purpose will be "to find the sharpest edge of disgrace and shame by which a selfish smiler could be pierced . . . to send through his marrow the most sudden shock of dread" (ch. 38). Bardo was even less like this blackmailer than he was like a tigerish killer; but Bardo's ghost undoubtedly had very similar feelings about Tito.

15 Hardy, *The Novels of George Eliot*, p. 120, compares the two fathers; and Emery, *George Eliot's Creative Conflict*, p. 87, remarks that "Baldassare is an exaggerated version of Romola's father."

Savonarola happens to be preaching "The day of vengeance is at hand!" and Romola happens to be in the Duomo on the day Baldassare first appears in Florence and clutches, also by accident, Tito's arm. The heroine has a good look at her stepfather-in-law, "for gray hairs made a peculiar appeal to her, and the stamp of some unwonted suffering in the face . . . stirred in her those sensibilities towards the sorrows of age, which her whole life had tended to develop" (ch. 24). Such is the beginning of a beautiful, if somewhat grotesque, relationship. Henceforth whenever their paths cross, a potential revelation is near. He is the one who knows much, and learns more, of what she should know about Tito. Two years later Romola comes upon Baldassare near death, amid the famine and pestilence that has descended on Florence. "Now at last, perhaps, she was going to know some secret which might be more bitter than all that had gone before" (ch. 42). Baldassare discovers first who she is, however, and has the pleasure of accepting enough *grossi* from her hand to buy a new hunting-knife (ch. 44). Before long he conceives that he has a hold over Romola as well as Tito, since he can inform her about Tessa (ch. 50). Twice she catches sight of him in the Duomo again, where both have gone to hear Savonarola (ch. 52). At last, twenty-four chapters after the narrative has disclosed the death of her father, Baldassare reveals himself to Romola with the words, "Ah! you would have been my daughter!" He then tries to assert the identity of their interest against Tito. "He made you love him . . . [and] he made *me* love him." He casts in her face the news about Tessa and her children. "You hate him . . . There is no love between you; I know that. I know women can hate; and you have proud blood. You hate falseness, and you can love revenge." And he proposes that she persuade Tito to leave his armor off so that he, Baldassare, can have another go at him (ch. 53). With some justification Sandra Gilbert and Susan Gubar conclude that Baldassare is a double for the heroine who offers "a Satanic response to Romola's situation."[16]

The functions of Baldassare as a ghostly father and secret sharer are reasonably clear. If his character and behavior are not what one should expect from the general practice of George Eliot, the excep-

16 *The Madwoman in the Attic* (New Haven: Yale University Press, 1979), p. 495. With odd understatement, George Eliot at this point writes, "It seemed to Romola as if every fresh hour of her life were to become more difficult than the last" (ch. 53). One thinks of Maggie in *The Mill on the Floss:* "Was her life always to be like this,—always bringing some new source of inward strife?" (bk. VI, ch. 9).

tion may prove the degree of projection, displacement, and cross-plotting in *Romola*. There is in truth one highly imaginative side to the conception of Baldassare, which has to do with his learning and his lack of it, his previous scholarship and "consciousness of shattered faculties." Both "fathers" in *Romola*, remember, are formidable exponents of classical learning.[17] It is almost as if George Eliot were rehearsing, in this new experiment, the subject of her first serious periodical contribution, R. W. Mackay's *The Progress of the Intellect*, which had as its subtitle *The Religious Development of the Greeks and Hebrews*. Now her heroine is brought into close proximity to two scholars of antiquity, one of whom is blind and the other missing certain other faculties. Baldassare's knowledge has come and gone: he is the one who is trying to enforce memory in his thankless protégé, but his own memory has failed him in the very enterprise of scholarship in which he has made his mark. By the time he has reached Florence he can no longer read Greek. "Could he by long gazing at one of those books lay hold of the slippery threads of memory?"

> He was tempted, and bought the cheapest Greek book he could see. He carried it home and sat on his heap of straw, looking at the characters by the light of the small window; but no inward light arose on them. Soon the evening darkness came; but it made little difference to Baldassare. His strained eyes seemed still to see the white pages with the unintelligible black marks upon them. (ch. 30)

Surely the pathos of this is successful. It is, more than that, a deeply disquieting occurrence, since there is no indication that black marks constituting Italian or any other language would have any more inward meaning for Baldassare than Greek. That so much of human memory can be entrusted to writing, and then writing become indecipherable, is a terrifying thought to any literate person and to any writer or reader by definition.

Baldassare is he who is preparing—on behalf of the narrator, Romola, and the reader, as it were—to expose Tito, who has deserted

---

17 R. H. Hutton, again, in the *Spectator*, 18 July 1863, addressed the theme of scholarship and passion for learning in *Romola*. "The powers of language" seemed to him to be pitted against "religious, or even . . . animal raptures." See Carroll, pp. 200–201.

both Baldassare and scholarship and has been eager to dispose of Bardo's library. Yet, as in a nightmare of his own, when he tries to explain who he is and to accuse Tito of what he is, Baldassare is asked to locate in the text of Homer the scene depicted on the ring, which once belonged to him and has now been purchased from Tito by Bernardo Rucellai. The situation of this trial, which has suddenly become Baldassare's trial rather than Tito's,[18] already tells against him because he has broken in upon the supper in the Rucellai gardens. "He was aware that something was being demanded from him to prove his identity, but he formed no distinct idea of the details. The sight of the book recalled the habitual longing and faint hope that he could read and understand." But he fails so piteously to make any sense of the pages of Homer in this public scene that even Tito is moved (ch. 39). Baldassare's failure of learning and Bardo's blindness—ultimately linked with Casaubon's failure and even Lydgate's in *Middlemarch*—are conditions of the double plot that cry out for interpretation. What does this wider failure—for it is not only Baldassare's Greek but his knowledge, his "faculties" and "threads of memory," that have failed him—what does this failure of knowledge signify about his principal intention and role in the novel, which are to shame Tito into acknowledging the past? Is the retardation of the exposure of Tito in the novel motivated by reservations about "entire knowingness"—to use the phrase from George Eliot's letter to her friend Charles Bray? The strangeness of Baldassare suggests that there is some ambivalence in the drive to expose Tito's forgetfulness, just as the higher "doubleness" of Savonarola tends to mitigate against utter contempt for Tito's duplicity. If Baldassare were a fully realized character, one might be able to argue that his love for Tito explained his ambivalence or loss of memory. But Baldassare is more like an agent of the narrator or even of the heroine than a character in his own right. The most blatant coincidences in *Romola*—and there are a good many—almost all involve Baldassare. If anyone is likely to encounter the other principal characters purely by accident, that person is Baldassare. In other words, he may have lost his knowledge of Greek and his wits besides, but he has an uncanny knowledge of the plot.

The supper in the Rucellai gardens is not the first time in *Romola*

18 The reversal parallels that of Tracy in Hitchcock's *Blackmail*, though here the action is much more dreamlike.

that an incident has confounded the memory of a personal past with the memory that constitutes more general knowledge. When Romola and her father first meet Tito, Bardo is eager to hear if there is any record of Baldassare's researches. "There *was* such a record," Tito replies, but "the only record left is such as remains in our—in my memory." Bardo comforts himself with the reflection, "Doubtless you remember much, if you aided in transcription"; and he adds, by way of comparing boys with girls, "I constantly marvel at the capriciousness of my daughter's memory." It is this somewhat gratuitous remark that brings about the first communication between Tito and Romola, of the kind that is possible between boys and girls before a blind parent:

> When Bardo made this reference to his daughter, Tito ventured to turn his eyes toward her, and at the accusation against her memory his face broke into its brightest smile, which was reflected as inevitably as sudden sunbeams in Romola's. Conceive of the soothing delight of that smile to her! Romola had never dreamed that there was a scholar in the world who would smile at a deficiency for which she was constantly made to feel herself a culprit. (ch. 6)

Quite possibly George Eliot developed Tito's capriciousness of memory—notably with Tessa, falling asleep or otherwise forgetting himself in her lap—in order to make his character consistent. The soft side of his nature is necessary to explain why so crafty and ambitious a schemer could fail to dispose of such weak opposition as Baldassare affords. But there is also in Tito almost a principle of forgetfulness, which at first attracts Romola.[19] The principle becomes explicit, again in proximity to books and knowledge generally, when the two differ over the disposal of Bardo's library, and Tito is urging Romola to leave Florence with him. "I like people who take life less eagerly," he tells her; "and it would be good for my Romola, too, to see a new life. I should like to dip her a little in the soft waters of forgetfulness" (ch. 32). He has, in fact, already sold the library—the chapter is entitled "A Revelation"—while she is entrenched in memory, insisting on continuity with the past and also the business of preserving li-

---

19 Bonaparte, *The Triptych and the Cross*, pp. 104, 111, remarks the "Bacchian" tendency to forgetfulness; and Levine, *"Romola* as Fable," p. 92, registers "how Tito operates to intensify [Romola's] freedom."

braries. The neat opposition between memory and forgetfulness is soon thrown into doubt again, however, by the strange behavior of Baldassare, a father who has forgotten what he knows and almost who he is, though his mission is to destroy or to expose Tito.

There is a question of how seriously to take Romola's "deficiency." If her father is correct about her memory—and she herself feels she is a "culprit"—then her effort to preserve all connections in life and one library may be uphill work for her. George Eliot's determination to endow her with heroic stature may be understandable. In the same early chapter in which Tito first calls in the Via de' Bardi—that chapter is entitled "Dawning Hopes"—his bright face

> seemed like a wreath of spring, dropped suddenly in Romola's young but wintry life, which had inherited nothing but memories,—memories of a dead mother, of a lost brother, of a blind father's happier time,—memories of far-off light, love, and beauty, that lay embedded in dark mines of books, and could hardly give out their brightness again until they were kindled for her by the torch of some known joy. (ch. 6)

These memories are none too happy, least of all the ones in dark mines of books. The memories that Romola later struggles to maintain are not pleasant either—the love of her father that is more like guilt, the stepfather whom "she dreaded to know more about" (ch. 43). Tito first enters her life as an alternative to a life of "nothing but memories," only to be rejected as a falsehood and a false hope. In the epilogue Romola will again have nothing but memories and Tito's children by Tessa, and those memories must be the least cheerful of all. As she explains her idea of heroism to one of the children, "this sort of happiness often brings so much pain with it that we can only tell it from pain by its being what we would choose before everything else."

The continuous narrative of *The Mill on the Floss* includes one major episode of forgetfulness, when Maggie and Stephen drift down the river with the tide. "Memory was excluded," and with it prudence and consideration. "Thought did not belong to that enchanted haze in which they were enveloped,—it belonged to the past and the future that lay outside the haze" (bk. VI, ch. 13). Maggie later does her best, with George Eliot's help, to place this episode back into perspective. There is a corresponding, less immoral episode in *Ro-*

mola, when the heroine awakens on the shore of the green valley to a moment of "oblivion," characterized by "a bliss which is without memory and without desire" possible only to youth (ch. 68). But far more important, *Romola* invents more than one life story, the first of which, Tito's, is discontinuous in time. There can be little doubt that George Eliot is still on the side of memory and truth—we have met the enemy, and he is Tito. But the very hitting at Tito, the heroism of Romola, and the combined actions also produce a work of great subversive power. It is not surprising that George Eliot suffered much difficulty in writing *Romola*, for taken as a whole it is probably the most charged with contradiction of all her works.

> To close the doors and windows of consciousness for a time; to remain undisturbed by the noise and struggle of our underworld of utility organs working with and against one another; a little quietness, a little *tabula rasa* of the consciousness, to make room for new things ... that is the purpose of active forgetfulness, which is like a doorkeeper, a preserver of psychic order, repose, and etiquette: so that it will be immediately obvious how there could be no happiness, no cheerfulness, no hope, no pride, no *present*, without forgetfulness.

These words are not George Eliot's but Nietzsche's, in his essay on guilt that begins by questioning whether the making of promises is natural. *Romola* too speaks to the human costs of memory and says in more than one way that forgetfulness is natural. Though she writes from an opposing camp, George Eliot might agree with Nietzsche that memory "involves no mere passivity to rid oneself of an impression ... but an active *desire* not to rid oneself, a desire for the continuance of something desired once, a real *memory of the will.*"[20] And George Eliot had the wit and experience to grasp that human commitments make sense only in the wider culture of knowledge. In some such Nietzschean terms the "straining gaze" of Baldassare upon the page of Homer (ch. 39) can be understood as linked to the heroism of Romola, and the futility of the one to the pain of the other.

"The happiest of women," the narrator quips in *The Mill on the Floss*, "like the happiest of nations, have no history" (bk. VI, ch. 3). In *Romola* George Eliot ponders the ironies of that sentence as a series of problems. It would be a great mistake, furthermore, to un-

20 *On the Genealogy of Morals*, trans. Walter Kaufmann and R. J. Hollingdale (New York: Vintage, 1969), pp. 56–57.

derestimate her awareness of what she was doing, or to read the yearnings of her heroine and lapses in the narrative as unconscious products of the author's personal needs. No doubt she is unaware of some of the ways in which Tito, Savonarola, and Baldassare substitute for Romola herself, but all the essential parallels and contrasts are of her own deliberate construction. Similarly, though the author drew on her own experience to write the novel, and especially her sense of discontinuity from her own past life, she did not write *Romola* for herself but for her readers—and she never wrote merely for her readers' entertainment. This novel was a major enterprise, with a new publisher and higher expectations, with the act of writing for the public very much in mind. As readers of *Romola* have sensed from the beginning, it was consciousness of what she was doing, rather than the opposite, that made the writing ponderous and finally less readable than her other novels. Quite obviously George Eliot took up the theme of personal identity over time, of memory and of consciousness itself, because she believed it important for her particular moment in history. For the story of Bulstrode in *Middlemarch* she would take up the subject of memory in still more strenuous terms:

> Even without memory, the life is bound into one by a zone of dependence in growth and decay; but intense memory forces a man to own his blameworthy past. With memory set smarting like a reopened wound, a man's past is not simply a dead history, an outworn preparation for the present: it is not a repented error shaken loose from the life: it is a still quivering part of himself, bringing shudders and bitter flavours and the tinglings of a merited shame. (ch. 61)

If Romola's memories are unhappy and the cause of unhappiness, Bulstrode's are certainly no better. It is worth noting that Dickens also at this time took up, again and again, the theme of memory and insisted especially that unpleasant recollections of the past had important moral bearing in the present. His reasons were undoubtedly personal also, and of a different bent from George Eliot's, but though the moral of his stories of memory is sometimes contorted, the need to fix identity over time is paramount. Forgetfulness would leave no self.[21]

21 See Alexander Welsh, *The City of Dickens* (Oxford: Clarendon, 1971), pp. 101-117, 196-203, and Ruth F. Glancy, "Dickens and Christmas: His Framed-Tale Themes," *Nineteenth-Century Fiction*, 35 (1980), 53-72. The five separately pub-

Romola is eventually able to break away from Savonarola because of their sharp difference over the execution of still another paternal figure in the novel, her godfather, Bernardo del Nero. It is then that she declares to Savonarola, in ringing words, "God's kingdom is something wider,—else, let me stand outside it with the beings that I love" (ch. 59). There is nothing like a clash between two authorities a person has accepted for herself to prove the impossibility of maintaining all the connections in life. As a result "all clinging was at an end for her" (ch. 60) and she is able to leave Florence for the second time. All the same, much of George Eliot's deliberate study in the novel is to interpret Savonarola as an actor in history and as a "public" man with whom the heroine can associate, with whom Romola can sympathize in his defeat and whose portrait adorns her wall in the epilogue. The doubleness of Savonarola is the consequential and fateful counterpart of the divided consciousness that the heroine conceals even from herself.[22] Thus, "in the career of a great public orator who yields himself to the inspiration of the moment, that conflict of selfish and unselfish emotion which in most men is hidden in the chamber of the soul, is brought into terrible evidence: the language of the inner voices is written out in letters of fire" (ch. 52).

Savonarola's career, in which conflict normally "hidden in the chamber of the soul" is writ large, reflects George Eliot's own unaccustomed role as a publicist after her identity was known, just as Romola's singleness reflects her uncompromising ideal and clinging to the past. But again it would be a mistake to reduce *Romola* to an indulgence of the author's personal experience. In this part of her novel in particular she had the most ample of literary precedents in the historical romance of Scott. This precedent governs the relation of her heroine to the main historical figure and permits the former to wait out, to observe and benefit from, the more consequential actions of the latter. Thus Romola, differing from Savonarola over the case of Bernardo, "was enduring one of those sickening moments, when the

lished Christmas books gave way to the major autobiographical project of *David Copperfield*, but as Glancy shows, the importance of memory continued to be stressed in the Christmas numbers of *Household Words* and *All the Year Round*.

22 This is apparently George Eliot's meaning when she writes to R. H. Hutton on 8 Aug. 1863, "the great problem of [Romola's] life, which essentially coincides with a chief problem in Savonarola's, is one that readers need helping to understand" (*G.E.L.*, IV, 97).

enthusiasm which had come to her as the only energy strong enough
to make life worthy, seemed inevitably bound up with vain dreams
and wilful eye-shutting." Her dissociation from the fanaticism that
moves events in history is like that of Henry Morton in *Old Mortality*. "If Romola's intellect had been less capable of discerning the
complexities in human things, all the early loving associations of her
life would have forbidden her to accept implicitly the denunciatory
exclusiveness of Savonarola." The visions of Camilla, like the effect of
the wilder Covenanters upon Morton, stir Romola's indignation
against Savonarola, and she experiences "a sudden insurrection of
feeling" that calls into question all of his teaching and leadership (ch.
52).

The importance of the Waverley Novels as a model for subsequent
English fiction should not be forgotten, and George Eliot read this
precedent expertly. The objectivity of Scott's hero that is associated
with a political establishment, she treats as the objectivity of a responsible intellectual position. As in Scott, an "insurrection of feeling" in heroine or hero can substitute for actual participation in the
movement of history.[23] But the public conclusion of the action in
Romola is less satisfying than in a typical novel of Scott, and the heroine's sense of identity is finally uncertain. For the author of *Waverley*, who died in 1832, national ascendancy confirmed the settlement
of 1688 as ample ground for political faith, even if his secularism was
to affect "the first unsettlement" of Mary Ann Evans's religion.[24] The
author of *Romola* was a conservative in the age of information, and
her one attempt at historical romance differs accordingly.

> Where were the beings to whom she could cling, with whom she
> could work and endure, with the belief that she was working for
> the right? On the side from which moral energy came, lay a fa-
> naticism from which she was shrinking with newly startled re-
> pulsion; on the side to which she was drawn by affection and
> memory, there was the presentiment of some secret plotting,
> which her judgment told her would not be unfairly called crime.
> And still surmounting every other thought was the dread in-
> spired by Tito's hints, lest that presentiment should be con-

23 Avrom Fleishman, *The English Historical Novel: Walter Scott to Virginia
Woolf* (Baltimore: Johns Hopkins University Press, 1971), pp. 161–163, comments
on Romola's "rejection of history."
24 Cross, *George Eliot's Life*, I, 369.

verted into knowledge, in such a way that she would be torn by irreconcilable claims.

This formulation of the conflict in fiction follows Scott's example quite closely, but it has been reduced to the difference between a "presentiment" and "knowledge." Accordingly, the resolution of George Eliot's novel has less to do with any concrete historical event. This particular chapter ends with Romola groping for "some immediate beneficent action" that may substitute for "wider faith"—"but when she turned around, she found herself face to face with a man who was standing only two yards off her. The man was Baldassare" (ch. 52).

The private conclusion of the novel resides in the carefully arranged death of Tito at the hands of Baldassare. The latter cannot quite be said to kill Tito for Romola: in a last great coincidence the nearly dead Tito washes up at his feet, and the old man gathers enough strength to seize Tito's throat and hang on until both are dead.[25] Then comes the narrator's comment: "Who shall put his finger on the work of justice and say, 'It is there'? Justice is like the Kingdom of God,—it is not without us as a fact, it is within us as a great yearning" (ch. 67). The comment on justice is more acute than many people realize, as the word "yearning," closely associated with George Eliot's heroines, ought to alert us. It is quite possible that the yearning in this case embraces all three characters—Baldassare, Tito, and the absent heroine. Moreover, there is an echo of the narrator's question, "Who shall put his finger on the work of justice and say, 'It is there'?" in what Cross tells us his wife told him about *Romola*: "She told me she could put her finger on it as marking a well-defined transition in her life." The verbal echo, which may be purely accidental, should not lead us to conclude that *Romola* is about George Eliot herself. But in writing the novel, and specifically in canceling out Tito by means of Baldassare, and Baldassare by means of Tito, she made a difference in her life and in the canon of her novels. At least in retrospect, she thought, "I began it a young woman,—I finished it an old woman."

25 Cf. Sadoff, *Monsters of Affection*, p. 98: "When Baldassare kills Tito, and with his [adopted] son himself, he acts out Romola's revenge as well as his own."

10

Blackmail and Opinion

Because *Romola* differs from the other novels in kind, narrative, and setting, it is sometimes regarded as a diversion rather than an important turning in the George Eliot canon. In point of fact these differences were productive and, by establishing perspective and dispelling emotion, contributed to the novels that followed. *Romola* is not merely an interruption in the series of novels about English life, and the author's own estimate of it ought to be respected.

Romola is George Eliot's only historical novel. It is possible to feel that she was mistaken to write about the distant past and history gleaned from books, and to welcome her return to near contemporary England as a silent confession of failure. But *Romola*'s dislocation and deliberate historicism almost certainly contributed to the objectivity of the later novels. History in George Eliot's time provided a more assured perspective than pastoralism or even then the avowed antiromantic realism of *Adam Bede* and *The Mill on the Floss*. As Georg Lukács construes the course of the novel since the eighteenth century, "the historical novel transforms the social novel into a genuine history of the present";[1] and if Lukács is right with respect to the novel generally, the same may be true of *Romola* in the development of George Eliot's realism. Of course, "a genuine history of the present" will still be conventional in some sort; and if Baldassare, for example, corresponds to a type of mad avenger popular in Renaissance literature, the crass Christian of *Felix Holt* or Raffles in *Middlemarch*

---

1 *The Historical Novel*, trans. Hannah and Stanley Mitchell (London: Merlin, 1962), p. 169.

corresponds to a nineteenth-century type of blackmailer who is equally literary: the real in narrative, whether of fact or fiction, is always conventional. But by consciously imagining bygone times and foreign types she freed herself to write a history of her own times.

Romola is George Eliot's highly personal novel centering on a single character. It is nearer to *The Mill on the Floss* in this respect than to any subsequent novel, and after *Romola* too close identification of the novelist with her heroines is not a problem. The idealization of Dorothea Brooke that F. R. Leavis carefully delineated[2] results from a willingness to accommodate readers' expectations rather than from a glorified projection of the author. The second marriage of Dorothea might even be seen as a descent from the austere life of Romola. Indeed the first marriage of Dorothea is probably not as disturbing to most readers as Romola's marriage, because a chorus of characters place it in comic perspective and promise that it shall be mended somehow. Dorothea's and Casaubon's awakening to their marriage is much more finely described than anything in *Romola*, but the imperatives of memory and promising are rehearsed with greater precision in the realist narrative of *Middlemarch* only to be aborted by Casaubon's death, which opens the author to the charge that she has manipulated an action otherwise carefully developed.[3] The realism of *Felix Holt* and *Middlemarch* is achieved more by recourse to convention than to personal history. Dorothea Ladislaw, Mary Vincy, and Esther Holt conventionally give birth to a postnarrative brood of children, whereas Maggie and Romola—and Gwendolen Grandcourt—are childless, as George Eliot herself was childless. In so far as families extend forward as well as back in time, the convention of the marriage ending may be thought of as realistic, whereas heroines or novelists who are without children may be especially wedded to the past.[4]

2 *The Great Tradition* (1948; rpt. New York: Anchor, 1954), pp. 93-101. Virginia Woolf, *The Common Reader* (1925; rpt. New York: Harcourt, 1953), pp. 172-176, anticipated Leavis in complaining of the heroines.

3 Cf. Carol Christ, "Aggression and Providential Death in George Eliot's Fiction," *Novel*, 9 (1976), 130-140. The mathematician Sofia Kavalevskaya made a similar observation to the novelist herself, who replied that death intervenes in just this way in life: see Raymond Chapman and Eleanora Gottlieb, "A Russian View of George Eliot," *Nineteenth-Century Fiction*, 33 (1978), 363-365.

4 For some differences between *Romola* and *Middlemarch* that reflect George Eliot's career, see Susan M. Greenstein, "The Question of Vocation: From *Romola* to *Middlemarch*," *Nineteenth-Century Fiction*, 35 (1981), 487-505.

The later novels are decentralized, while *Romola* is both centrifugal and centripetal. No other novel of George Eliot relates characters so closely to a central ego by displacement, since Tito, Baldassare, and even Savonarola partially enact motives that may finally have to be understood as belonging to Romola herself. The psychological plot is the most intricate that George Eliot devised: Romola remains nearly uncompromised as the heroine—a martyr to consistency, in fact—but is also, through the agency of these other characters, the most compromised of women. The actions involving the next heroines are scarcely at all generated by this kind of displacement, and their degree of emancipation makes its own contribution to realism. Whereas in *Romola* the person hiding from the past has married the heroine, and her loyalty is inevitably shadowed by his opposite disloyalties, the problem of a discontinuous life in *Middlemarch* is effectively concentrated in the character of Bulstrode. Raffles, in fact, threatens to reveal a story pertaining to Ladislaw's origins, but the person he threatens to reveal is Bulstrode, not the second husband of Dorothea. The story of Bulstrode is still more tangential to the story of Mary Garth, the one story a model of discontinuity and the other of continuity. As Peter K. Garrett observes, "The presence of the past, the landscape of memory which expresses security in the context of Fred and Mary's story expresses guilty terror in Bulstrode's."[5]

The relative disengagement of the heroine is evident in *Felix Holt*, the novel that immediately followed *Romola*, even though Esther Lyon is drawn directly into the affairs of the Transome family by a marriage choice and the property question. To explain Esther's rejection of Harold Transome and property, the novelist stresses the singleness of her devotion to Holt: "she never speculated on possible relations yet to come. It seemed to her that she stood at the first and last parting of the ways." But at this point the narrator both implies and denies that such a youthful vision of marriage as one continuous life is an illusion. "And, in one sense, she was under no illusion. It is only in that freshness of our time that the choice is possible which gives unity to life, and makes the memory a temple where all relics

5 *The Victorian Multiplot Novel: Studies in Dialogical Form* (New Haven: Yale University Press, 1980), p. 165. Garrett's description of the plot of *Middlemarch*, which he purposefully contrasts with the "tightly linked" plots of Dickens and "sharply stylized" plots of Thackeray (p. 135), can also be used to point up the contrast with *Romola*.

and all votive offerings, all worship and all grateful joy, are an unbroken history sanctified by one religion" (ch. 44). The danger that Esther may suffer a Romola-like problem of memory is thus handled at arm's length. It is a problem that does not even occur to Esther, we are assured, only to the narrator, who passes along the thought for what it is worth. At the same time the novel affords an obvious comparison with the heroine in the person of Mrs. Transome, an older woman with secret memories.[6] Whereas Esther is not conscious of her past—the birthright that, through a series of chances, makes her heir to the Transome estate—Mrs. Transome is all too conscious of the adulterous affair that gave birth to Harold Transome. Both pasts are concealed at first from the reader, but it is the second that supplies a depth of "consciousness"—a word that becomes more and more insistent in *Middlemarch* and *Daniel Deronda*—and makes Mrs. Transome by far the more interesting of the two characters. For all her superior interest, nevertheless, she is finally held up as a bad example. The narrator never deviates from a standard social judgment upon her; there is simple contrast between Esther and Mrs. Transome, no buried connection. This arrangement contributes to the realism of *Felix Holt*: Mrs. Transome lives out her unhappy life with her senile husband; nothing can be achieved for romance or allegory by killing her off, say, as Tito is killed in the previous novel.[7]

One result of the diminished use of displacement in the novels after *Romola* is a less marked division between shame and guilt. George Eliot will not again separate these two responses as sharply as she had in the characterization of Tito and Romola: instead she will examine their conjunction. When Christian offers to sell Harold Transome information about the inheritance, for example, the latter reflects, "More people besides Jermyn know about his evidence, it seems. The whole thing may look black for me if it comes out. I shall be believed to have bribed him to run away, whether or not." On these thoughts the narrator comments, "Thus the outside conscience came in aid of the inner," and further states, "We are very much indebted to such a

6 The parallel is traced by Barbara Hardy, *The Novels of George Eliot* (1959; rpt. London: Athlone, 1963), pp. 137–139. Miriam Allott, "George Eliot in the 1860's," *Victorian Studies*, 5 (1962), 96–98, argues that Mrs. Transome is the novelist's "only imaginative success" of this time.

7 "Killed Tito in great excitement," reads George Eliot's journal entry for 16 May 1863. See *George Eliot's Life as Related in Her Letters and Journals*, ed. J. W. Cross, 3 vols., Illustrated Cabinet Edition (New York: Merrill and Baker, n.d.), II, 278.

linking of events as makes a doubtful action look wrong" (ch. 36). Transome's misgivings about the appearance of bribery and the narrator's comments clearly anticipate the more careful exploration of "inside" and "outside" constraints on behavior in *Middlemarch*, in which Bulstrode's terror of shame and temptation to murder become a mental process of gradation, and the components of Lydgate's complicity in the same action—his relation to Bulstrode, his probity and professional knowledge, his pride and financial embarrassment—are still more finely mixed:

> There was a benumbing cruelty in [Lydgate's] position. Even if he renounced every other consideration than that of justifying himself,—if he met shrugs, cold glances, and avoidance as an accusation, and made a public statement of all the facts as he knew them, who would be convinced? It would be playing the part of a fool to offer his own testimony on behalf of himself, and say, "I did not take the money as a bribe." The circumstances would always be stronger than his assertion.

Lydgate is not Bulstrode, and Lydgate is not in a court of law when the accumulation of circumstantial evidence tells against him more powerfully than his own testimony can speak for him. "But then came the question"—prompted by such outside considerations— "whether he should have acted in precisely the same way if he had not taken the money?" (ch. 73).

In general, with respect to genre and narrative, the differences between *Romola* and the later novels may be summed up by saying that George Eliot's efforts in *Felix Holt*, *Middlemarch*, and *Daniel Deronda* are much more efforts of representation than of projection. That a novelist will project her own conscious and unconscious states of mind in her characters to some degree can be taken for granted, but after the invention of Romola George Eliot's personal investment in her heroines becomes less apparent. In fact it has been common in recent years to claim that among the triumphs of characterization in the later novels it is Edward Casaubon who emerges most brilliantly from the novelist's inmost perception of herself.[8] It is as if "the work

8 See especially Richard Ellmann, *Golden Codgers: Biographical Speculations* (New York: Oxford University Press, 1973), pp. 19–30; also Neil Hertz, "Recognizing Casaubon," *Glyph*, 6 (Baltimore: Johns Hopkins University Press, 1979), 24–41.

of justice" in the simultaneous deaths of Tito and Baldassare and the completion of *Romola*, that historical romance, had sufficed to restore "a consciousness of the unity" of past and present in the novelist's being—as the series of coincidences had in Silas Marner's life—and thus freed her to conduct her researches into human behavior in general. The themes of a career and of knowledge she did not give up. The emphasis on inviolate memory and classical learning in *Romola* tends to give way to blackmail and opinion in *Felix Holt*, to reputation and knowledge in *Middlemarch*, and finally to ideology in *Daniel Deronda*, but the contentions and mixed feelings about Bardo's library run deep—and surface again in the library at Lowick.

If the return from *Romola* is to be seen as a return to representation and to the present, then something ought to be said of the precise setting of the next two novels. In both the historical moment is the same, the time of the Reform Bill of 1832, and this choice is not accidental. George Eliot began writing *Felix Holt* in March 1865 and completed it in May 1866. The coincidence of this, her most nearly political novel, with the debate preceding the Reform Bill of 1867 is evident, though the novel's topicality defers to 1832. The purpose of this mapping of the present upon the past is to make the political message—very sharp for George Eliot—less insistent, no doubt, but also to make the novel more representative, as *Middlemarch* would be representative. The Reform Bill of 1832 is a great turning point of nineteenth-century England, and was immediately recognized as such. For conservatives and liberals alike its passage was prophetic, and historians still single out the spirit of reform as perhaps the most pervasive of all Victorian concerns. The Reform Bill stood to the Victorian present as the Revolution of 1688 stood to the time of Scott and Austen, but with more troubling connotations of changes still in process. It could not be regarded as a triumphant compromise so readily as a beginning; its very premises were such as could be applied over and over to every social condition. Implicit in reform was a consciousness of responsibility, of diffused power and restraint. Reform assumed that public and private interests must somehow cohere, but also tended to subordinate the latter to the former. In the eighteen-thirties John Stuart Mill began to formulate his thoughts on the divergence of the two.[9]

9 See chapter 4. Larry M. Robbins, "Mill and Middlemarch: The Progress of Public Opinion," *Victorian Newsletter*, 31 (1967), 37–39, connects the treatment of public opinion in *Middlemarch* with *On Liberty*.

The era of the Reform Bill inaugurates a public theme, since an assumption of reform is that institutions can be made to conform to human will. But the will ought to be free and in the last analysis private, and therefore a strong understatement of individual responsibility is soon apparent.[10] Perhaps the most frequently quoted line from *Felix Holt* is the narrator's assertion that "there is no private life which has not been determined by a wider public life." The context is as follows:

> These social changes in Treby parish are comparatively public matters, and this history is chiefly concerned with the private lot of a few men and women; but there is no private life which has not been determined by a wider public life, from the time when the primeval milkmaid had to wander with the wanderings of her clan, because the cow she milked was one of a herd which had made the pastures bare. . . .

Thus the well-known observation is playfully couched in terms of social migration and economic supply. The reference to "social changes" in this updating of a pastoral experience assumes awareness and objective study of something called society and a division of public and private interests. In a semifacetious, almost Thackerayan manner, George Eliot elaborates the point and prophesies the "mutual influence of dissimilar destinies" in her own story:

> For if the mixed political conditions of Treby Magna had not been acted on by the passing of the Reform Bill, Mr. Harold Transome would not have presented himself as a candidate for North Loamshire, Treby would not have been a polling-place, Mr. Matthew Jermyn would not have been on affable terms with a Dissenting preacher and his flock, and the venerable town would not have been placarded with handbills, more or less complimentary and retrospective,—conditions in this case essential to the "where" and the "what," without which, as the learned know, there can be no event whatever. (ch. 3)

Just as the passing of the Reform Bill results from the confluence of earlier events, so does each private happening. With the typical strat-

---

10 For George Eliot's position on free will, see George Levine, "Determinism and Responsibility in the Works of George Eliot," *PMLA*, 77 (1962), 268–279; and Elizabeth Ermath, "Incarnations: George Eliot's Conception of 'Undeviating Law,'" *Nineteenth-Century Fiction*, 29 (1974), 273–286.

egy of Victorian realism—from one point of view a modified historical romance—the novelist will exploit the pastness of these events as a sign of their inevitability, though the irony and reflexiveness of the passage betray the author's uneasiness. That she should gibe at "the learned" and question the possibility of narrating any event "whatever" are points to keep in mind in reading each of her subsequent novels.

Above all, the Reform Bill sounds the themes of knowledge and opinion. The wider spirit of reform assumes a role for knowledge that can be applied, in this or that institution or enterprise, as a need arises: in short, the preparation and potential use of information, such as the demography that was the most compelling argument for the bill itself, or the reports that preceded the New Poor Law of 1834, or the countless assemblages of evidence that justify the habit of legislation from this time forth. A history of the Reform Bill contemporary with the writing of *Felix Holt* characterized it as "an exemplification of the power of public opinion at a time when there were fewer means of giving expression to it than we possess at present."[11] In the novel George Eliot stressed the role of opinion, first, because public opinion *was* the evident means by which the English constitution was changed in 1832 and, second, because in the months prior to 1867 she believed that public opinion was still a safer means of reform than extension of the franchise. In *Middlemarch* she would create what Quentin Anderson has called, in contrast to the visible landscape of *Adam Bede*, "the landscape of opinion."[12]

Through Felix Holt and to a lesser extent through Rufus Lyon, the novelist pretty clearly states her views. In his speech against the franchise Holt avers that he wants "the working-men to have power," but not the wrong kind. The readily perceived difference between the two sorts of power is moral—"power to do mischief,—to undo what has been done with great expense and labour, to waste and destroy, to be cruel to the weak, to lie and quarrel, and to talk poisonous nonsense," as opposed to power to do good, which is not as explicitly defined but associated with skills of carpentry and agriculture, and with

11 W. N. Molesworth, *The History of the Reform Bill of 1832*, 2nd ed. (London: Chapman and Hall, 1866), p. v.

12 "George Eliot in *Middlemarch*," in *From Dickens to Hardy*, ed. Boris Ford (1958); reprinted in *George Eliot: A Collection of Critical Essays*, ed. George R. Creeger (Englewood Cliffs, N.J.: Prentice-Hall, 1970), p. 148.

wisdom. Behind the moral difference is the difference of ignorance from knowledge:

> Ignorant power comes in the end to the same thing as wicked power; it makes misery. It's another sort of power that I want us working-men to have, and I can see plainly enough that our all having votes will do little towards it at present. I hope we, or the children that come after us, will get plenty of political power some time. I tell everybody plainly, I hope there will be great changes, and that some time, whether we live to see it or not, men will have come to be ashamed of things they're proud of now.

To explain the relation of knowledge to political will, Holt adopts an analogy to steam power—specifically the relation of physical force to the machinery it drives. "All the schemes about voting and districts and annual Parliaments and the rest are engines, and the water or steam—the force that is to work them—must come out of human nature, out of men's passions, feelings, desires." This analogy makes "passions, feelings, desires" more fundamental even than knowledge, but the force "must come out of" this source of energy, and it comes in the form of "public opinion." The latter is a kind of energized knowledge, which is constitutive and prior to the design of machinery. Put another way, knowledge and public opinion are *in*forming.

> I'll tell you what's the greatest power under heaven . . . and that is public opinion,—the ruling belief in society about what is right and what is wrong, what is honourable and what is shameful. That's the steam that is to work the engines. . . . And while public opinion is what it is,—while men have no better beliefs about public duty,—while corruption is not felt to be a damning disgrace,—while men are not ashamed in Parliament and out of it to make public questions which concern the welfare of millions a mere screen for their own petty private ends,—I say, no fresh scheme of voting will much mend our condition.

Holt clinches his point by arguing that "thirty sober men" can be outvoted by "seventy drunken and stupid." This difficulty would not obtain if men had "real opinions." The trouble is that "Jack can't read" (ch. 30).

No Victorian faith is more common than that which makes education prior to enfranchisement. Public opinion is thought to mediate between desire and action in a way that is healthfully dependent upon knowledge. What is especially remarkable in George Eliot's formulation of her working-class hero's views is the way in which the power of shame, rather than moral principle alone, enters into this process of mediation. Thus, "what is right and what is wrong" becomes equivalent to "what is honourable and what is shameful"; at present "corruption is not felt to be a damning disgrace," and "men are not ashamed in Parliament and out of it"; but someday "men will have come to be ashamed of things they're proud of now." Such equations reveal a second dimension of the "opinion" in public opinion. On the one hand that concept refers to the specific judgments, the "real opinions" arising from shared knowledge, which can be applied to questions of public policy. On the other hand the concept appeals to the shaming force—*"that's* the steam"—of collective pre-judgments. The power of public opinion depends on the rise of information in the modern world but also on information in the sense of possible indictment. It is in the nature of public opinion to depend more on shame than on morality.[13]

We know relatively little about George Eliot's reasons for writing *Felix Holt:* as Fred C. Thomson has concluded, after examining all the evidence, "the idea seems to have come to her quite suddenly."[14] In retrospect the novel seems mainly an exercise in preparation for *Middlemarch,* and the doubleness of public opinion, as promise and threat, is one indication of this. The two novels are set in the era of the Reform Bill and treat of private life in relation to public life, and each combines themes of knowledge and reputation, the first by fairly crude juxtaposition and the second by justly famous case studies. Knowing and being known (or remaining unknown) are closely associated in both novels, as learning and loyalty were in the dreamlike projections of *Romola.* The lesser novel, in the implicit coercion of "there is no private life which has not been determined by a wider

13 This emphasis on shame can be compared with Darwin's account of the social virtues in *The Descent of Man, and Selection in Relation to Sex,* 2nd ed. (London: Murray, 1875), pp. 97–127. George Eliot defined shame in *Romola* as "the reflex of that outward law which the great heart of mankind makes for every individual man, a reflex which will exist even in the absence of sympathetic impulses that need no law." The individual in question is Tito Melema, who lacks the good impulses of a "brute," but still can be made to blush (ch. 9).

14 Introduction, *Felix Holt, the Radical* (Oxford: Clarendon, 1980), pp. xiii-xvii.

public life" and the appeal to a race who "will have come to be ashamed," seems to bear within it the inspiration of the pathology of information to be studied in *Middlemarch*. At the same time, the hero's determination "to apply force where it would tell, to do small work close at hand," anticipates the meliorism of the finale of *Middlemarch* and underscores its risks. To achieve something painstakingly little by little makes the loss of it a potential disaster—hence Holt's first definition of mischief is "to undo what has been done with great expense and labour" (ch. 30). But thus far George Eliot does not portray the inherent connections or the depressant side effects of her doctrine.

In *Felix Holt* the promise and threat of opinion are linked primarily by juxtaposition.[15] In one place the novel openly advocates the power of public opinion; in another it rehearses a number of actions of blackmail, including one so unfeeling that a former sexual partner, Jermyn, threatens to expose his mistress, Mrs. Transome, and their son, Harold. Indeed, in the grasping for secrets, betrayal of origins, and threats to inheritance, the novel is more "sensational" than in its tale of adultery. On the one hand it proffers serious social history and advocacy and on the other all this blackmail, and readers are left to make the connection, if any, for themselves. Buried among the literary allusions in the novel is the slightest of possible clues: the Debarry sisters have just finished reading Bulwer's *Eugene Aram*, a novel of 1832 in which a former accomplice in crime preys on the hero's present reputation, founded on his vast learning. A year later Bulwer published his principal contribution to the era of Reform, *England and the English*, a veritable compendium of contemporary thinking on the role of science, information, and the press, which also preached that "reformed opinion precedes reformed legislation."[16] Both within Bulwer's novel and by comparison of its blackmail theme with the themes of *England and the English*, one can perceive a juxtaposition of the celebration of opinion and the threat of discovery broadly similar to that in *Felix Holt*.

The blackmailer in the novel written a third of a century earlier, however, is a former criminal accomplice in a capital crime. The

15 Cf. Barbara Hardy, *The Novels of George Eliot*, p. 89, who compares the film technique of "cross-cutting."

16 *England and the English*, ed. Standish Meacham (Chicago: University of Chicago Press, 1970), p. 381.

story of Eugene Aram can be read in the Newgate Calendar; the risk of discovery to him, in the novel as in real life, is nothing less than hanging. The secrets of later Victorian sensation novels are as likely to be disgraceful circumstances or petty contrivances as capital crimes, and the blackmailers more often scurrilous third parties who threaten only the reputation of their victims. Instead of Bulwer's deeply flawed hero of Faustian ambition, Satanic isolation, and fateful love, a host of mildly flawed, unfortunately weak, and conventionally married persons populate sensation novels. Their fictional world is one of general apprehension, since the evidence of anyone's past exists more or less haphazardly, and the trace of some misdemeanor is likely to surface at any time. A set of blackmailers, not criminal in themselves but without anything better to do, prepare to make use of information that comes their way; but fortunately for all, the information that does come to light damns only those who deserve to be damned. Some such anxiety and some such relief typify the sensation novels of George Eliot's time[17] and are apparent in *Felix Holt*. It seems that there is much still to be learned before society, through the operation of public opinion, can be mended; and much that ought to be known, and perhaps will be known, about the individuals who comprise society. The latter are accountable to no faith and to no king, and therefore ought to be accountable to themselves and to their own pasts. Harold Transome is the product of "much knowledge which he had set himself deliberately to gain" (ch. 8) and a would-be radical politician of the type who sought to apply knowledge widely in the early nineteenth century; but he is not yet aware of that which he ought to be aware of—and his constituents ought to be aware of—his tainted birth and threatened inheritance. A number of would-be blackmailers are therefore eager to trade on the potential discovery.

The blackmailers in *Felix Holt* are on the lookout for information, like salesmen seeking a new product, or archivists pursuing genealogies, or even geologists tapping rocks. They are not already in possession of the facts, like Eugene Aram's former accomplice, Houseman, but are purposeful investigators and cultivators of information. They do not desire to publish but to control the timing and direction of their discoveries or to suppress them altogether. Theirs is

17 Cf. Patrick Brantlinger, "What is 'Sensational' about the 'Sensation Novel'?" *Nineteenth-Century Fiction*, 37 (1982), 1–28.

the underside of the power of knowledge, and the word "power" emerges in this context as in the discourse on public opinion in the novel. After Mr. Lyon has consulted the lawyer Jermyn about the evidence of the past that has come into his hands, the latter enjoys "a state of comparative triumph in the belief that he, and he alone, was now in possession of facts that, once grouped together, made a secret that gave him new power over Harold" (ch. 18). And, after he has amassed more information, he says to himself, "I have the matter entirely in my own power. . . . I shall hold all the threads between my thumb and finger. I can use the evidence or I can nullify it" (ch. 21). Since "Mr. Harold," Jermyn's natural son, is the object of most of these maneuverings, the action recalls Baldasarre's vague hope to control his stepson Tito: blackmail is being employed by the older generation to exert some power over the younger. But Jermyn's efforts are also professional, a conscious mastering of circumstantial evidence. He thinks of "facts . . . grouped together" and of "all the threads" of narrative that he can either complete or destroy. In the background is much research, and in the foreground the resultant knowledge, prepared for blackmail: "I am the only person who has the requisite knowledge," he threatens Harold, and "if I engage not to use my knowledge against you, you must engage in writing that . . . you will cancel all hostile proceedings against me" (ch. 35). It is only later that, hurt to the quick, he surrenders his last secret, and consequently the last of his power, by exclaiming in public, "*I am your father*" (ch. 47).

George Eliot insists on the ubiquity of information in *Felix Holt*. If Jermyn were the only person with fateful knowledge of the past, he might figure in a gothic fiction with psychological and tragic overtones. But Jermyn is not alone, he is a lawyer, and he has semiprofessional competitors for secrets. Unlike the secrets in a gothic novel and unlike those in *Romola*, the secrets in *Felix Holt* are paradoxically in the public domain; and George Eliot represents the modern world, as in a sensation novel, as a kind of strip-mine of information, from which anything may turn up. The representative blackmailers are therefore third parties like Christian and Johnson, similarly on the lookout for information. Christian observes Jermyn at work and thinks, "What was the real meaning of the lawyer's interest . . . ? Here was a secret; and secrets were often a source of profit . . ." "The only problem was to find out by what combination of independent knowledge he could outwit Jermyn" (ch. 25). Later Christian decides that "the most profitable investment" he can make of his knowledge is with Harold Transome (ch. 36); and in the following chapter Johnson decides to approach Esther Lyon with what he knows (ch. 37). The world of secrets—the same as the world of information—is so open that a character with ambitions like Jermyn's is bound to be frustrated; one expert in circumstantial evidence cannot master the whole, and lesser blackmailers are able to spoil the master's game by dropping the merest truth. Jermyn is "entirely ignorant of those converging indications and small links of incident which had raised Christian's conjectures" and "did not see the course of things that could have disclosed and combined the various items of knowledge which he had imagined to be his own secret." Therefore when he learns from Mrs. Transome that Esther already knows her birthright, he is "confounded"; and worse, "the more fatal point was clear: he held no [further] secret that could help him" (ch. 42). No action could be more clearly designed to show that information of itself is useless, and that only the ephemeral moment in which it is revealed or put to work is worth monopolizing.

It seems fair to conclude that George Eliot knew what she was doing when she included this frenetic blackmail activity in a novel celebrating public opinion. The power of public opinion counts on literacy, education, and the rise of information but also, as Felix Holt's own eloquence shows, on shame. No wonder Mill was so concerned to separate social from private spheres, if the very same forces counted on for order and progress in society make almost anyone's business of interest to third parties. By the time of *On Liberty* Mill could write scornfully of "the modern *régime* of public opinion" and compare it to "the Chinese ideal of making all people alike." But the rule of public opinion follows from his own arguments about the collective basis of truth. However arrived at, a conclusion is not sound unless it can be challenged by "every variety of opinion" and examined in "all modes in which it can be looked at by every character of mind." Propositions that are true and propositions that are false must be treated in the same way; beliefs cannot be held with conviction unless they are open to dispute, and open indefinitely. Yet it is the same openness that has begun to rub. Turned around, so that a person becomes the object instead of the subject of scrutiny, openness disturbs and pains deeply. Mill's conception of truth and of society treads in a circle of knowing and being known, and the more one thinks about this circle, the more one needs to draw a curtain before strictly private conduct, "the part which merely concerns himself" or "his own body and mind."[18] In the one direction, for this vision, everything ought to be looked into; and in the other, something had better be concealed.

Mill never fully acknowledges that scrutiny, investigation, and debate help to establish control in the liberal society. The work of cognition goes forward incessantly, and nothing is easy to decide. Yet this activity must result in what Mill calls a "consolidation" of opinion that is both necessary and desirable. *On Liberty* is a passionate defense of small craft sailing against the tide of public opinion, but the tide arises, in the first place, from the increase in knowledge. Arguably, the commitment to truth places the severest of all constraints upon freedom:

> As mankind improve, the number of doctrines which are no longer disputed or doubted will be constantly on the increase: and the well-being of mankind may almost be measured by the number and gravity of the truths which have reached the point of being uncontested. The cessation, on one question after another, of serious controversy, is one of the necessary incidents of the consolidation of opinion; a consolidation as salutary in the case of true opinions, as it is dangerous and noxious when the opinions are erroneous. But though this gradual narrowing of the bounds of diversity of opinion is necessary in both senses of the term, being at once inevitable and indispensable, we are not therefore obliged to conclude that all its consequences must be beneficial.[19]

These words make quite clear what Mill has known all along. Learning is a process of surrendering personal opinions, and social behavior

18 *On Liberty, C.W.*, XVIII, 274, 232, 224. The ironic result of this deliberation is the proposed further separation of public and private life. Mill writes, "To individuality should belong the part of life in which it is chiefly the individual that is interested; to society, the part which chiefly interests society" (p. 276), as though urging us to render to Caesar the things that are Caesar's.

19 *On Liberty, C.W.*, XVIII, 250–251. Perhaps the best elucidation of Mill's view is that of his self-appointed adversary, James Fitzjames Stephen. Basically, the latter thought of persuasion and coercion as functions of specific institutions, such as the newspapers or the courts, not as a generalized power of "society." See *Liberty, Equality, Fraternity*, ed. R. J. White (Cambridge, England: Cambridge University Press, 1967). The first edition was published in 1873 after Stephen's return from India; Mill, who died that year, did not have a chance to reply to the book.

is a sacrifice of cherished eccentricity. Knowledge itself constricts freedom of thought, and the progress of civilization based on knowledge affords less and less privacy. Mill is reduced to saying, in effect, that if we cannot help what is happening, we are not bound to like it. The experience he writes of is a global one, not a specific instance of persecution for unpopular belief; and a sense of loss is what he chiefly leaves his reader. He goes on, in this passage, to "confess" that he would like "the teachers of mankind" to provide some substitute for the diversity and eagerness of opinion that was once possible. This rather grim and limited role for teachers—the jogging of minds that no longer have any place to go—may remind us of Felix Holt in the novel. George Eliot has roughly the same faith in knowledge and progress as Mill, and her hero designs to be such a teacher, with very little prospect of influencing history one way or the other.

Felix Holt touches upon another problem, which is the seemingly arbitrary behavior of information itself. Like some other novels in the sensational mode, it implies that information cannot be monopolized by anyone: the story of Matthew Jermyn is not tragic, merely one of frustration. But the strangest thing is the way in which the information about Esther's birthright surfaces in the first place because of a practical joke and series of extraordinary chances, which make the discovery of the past arbitrary in the extreme. In the episode in question, Christian, acting as messenger, places Philip Debarry's pocketbook in his coattail next to a notebook that he had been carrying about for years; Scales, the head butler, snips off the coattail while Christian is asleep in the park and flings it away; Felix Holt, coming through the park in the evening of the same day, stubs his foot on the coattail and, too proud to return the contents to the Debarrys himself, conveys them to Mr. Lyon for the purpose; and Mr. Lyon duly discovers, from the notebook and the locket and chain that had come into Christian's possession long ago, the connection with Esther's real father (chs. 12 and 13). Serious students of George Eliot are likely to be offended by these contrivances, the joke compounded by the outrageous train of circumstances—to say nothing of the coincidence of Esther Lyon's residence in Treby Magna near the Transome estate and the timely death of Tommy Trounsem.[20]

20 For the narration of practical jokes in realistic literature, see Alexander Welsh, *Reflections on the Hero as Quixote* (Princeton: Princeton University Press, 1981), pp. 81–123.

The contrivances are first of all defensive. George Eliot does not believe that there is a special providence in the fall of a sparrow or in the fortunes of any human being. She subscribes only to the modern belief in circumstances, which are interconnected but not necessarily in a personally satisfying way. *Felix Holt* and *Middlemarch* endorse something like the proposition of Thomas Starkie, that "all human dealings and transactions are a vast context of circumstances, interwoven and connected with each other, and also with the natural world, by innumerable links and ties."[21] But like most of us, George Eliot wishes to discern some particular continuity in this universe. In order to establish continuity (a kind of design threading its way through the context) she noisily insists upon it in this episode, exaggerating the chance connections in order to forestall the reader's and her own sense of probabilities, on the principle that the best defense is an attack. Some conscious irony is evident in her choice of a practical joke to begin the business, as if to admit that some human contrivance will be necessary here. But more, unintended, irony reveals itself in the bullying of circumstances to produce a discovery. If the improbable possibilities are as improbable as all that, something in the novelist must be protesting that no continuity can be discerned after all. Even if everything in the universe is connected, it does not follow that all the connections can be known.

If it were not for this joke and train of circumstances, then, the most important—or seemingly most important—information in *Felix Holt* would never be communicated. To the themes of blackmail and of public opinion in the novel must be added this highly unpredictable sequence of events, which poses the question of whether information so hedged and potentially so well concealed (the implication of so many coincidences working to bring it to the surface) is to be interpreted as a risible source of entertainment of the sort confined to fiction or an exaggerated statement of the dependence of information upon chance in the real world. In *Felix Holt* George Eliot addresses this last problem in the mode of sensation novels, and not surprisingly she fudges the issue with a little attempted humor and exaggeration. Such novels inadvertently argue on two sides of the question: on the one hand, information is available just about anywhere, and some of it may be incriminating or potentially rewarding for some-

21 See chapter 5, note 23.

one; on the other, information of dramatic portent may well remain hidden, never affecting anyone personally and thereby having only negative effect. The very novels that proclaim the inevitable revelation of secrets steadily imply that most secrets remain hidden, since those uncovered are uncovered so ingeniously or through such unlikely chances. Strip-mining is not nearly as effective, when it comes to information, as stubbing a toe against the evidence and carrying it unerringly to the one person who is able to interpret it. What are we to make of "the momentous information that Esther was the surviving Bycliffe" (ch. 42)? We have learned from the novelist's elaborate correspondence with Frederick Harrison,[22] as well as from the novel itself, that Esther's inheritance was just barely tenable; it had to be intricately researched by a lawyer and a novelist as well as by the several schemers within the fiction. "Momentous information," then, or mere chance? Esther, we note, has the spirit not to make use of the information, just as Will Ladislaw will refuse to make use of the information supplied by Raffles. Heroic disdain may be the motive in both cases, but if so, it is disdain for these kinds of connections. *Felix Holt* may seem to look askance at its load of information, or with contempt at favorable chance operating at its center. The narrator's tongue begins to resort to the cheek, perhaps, as it does when Raffles first makes his appearance in *Middlemarch*. These are fictional worlds in which assiduous blackmailers and the occasional practical joker are much in demand, and no wonder a smile sometimes plays about the lips of either.

In *Silas Marner*, as we have seen, an action characterized by triple coincidence is accompanied by a sermon directed against belief in "Favourable Chance" (ch. 9). In *Romola*, in which the coincidences are less startling because there are more of them, Tito is implicitly criticized when the narrator remarks how "trivial incidents" interfere with "a clever man's calculations." If one is going to gamble, then he had better be prepared for the risks, but for Tito "life was so complicated a game that the devices of skill were liable to be defeated at every turn by air-blown chances, incalculable as the descent of thistle-down" (ch. 47). The trouble with preaching against reliance on chance, or apparently mocking the operation of chance in the antics of the plot as well as of the blackmailers in *Felix Holt*, is that such

22 See the exchange of letters of early 1866, *G.E.L.*, IV, 215–240; and Martha S. Vogeler, "George Eliot and the Positivists," *Nineteenth-Century Fiction*, 35 (1980), 406–431.

implicit criticism bears rather nervously on the task of evidence in a court of law, say, or the path of induction in certain sciences, which also depend heavily on chance or do their best to account for it. In a criminal case—or a business enterprise, for that matter—information may be systematically gathered and sifted for relevance; but if key facts are not represented, there is often no case—or opportunity for profit. In any science that depends on observation, large differences in conclusions result from very small chances of discovery—such as a single fossil, an anomaly in a set of data, or accident in the laboratory. One of the reasons for the partnership of elaborate proofs with happenstance in the novels of this period is undoubtedly the felt importance, and felt limitations, of induction in the modern world. Though blackmail and the virtues of public opinion are merely juxtaposed in *Felix Holt*, and the bearing of chance upon the use of information is wrapped in a joke, the novel introduces a number of problems associated with knowing and being known that are explored further in *Middlemarch*.

It remains to say something of meliorism, a corollary to the commitment to public opinion, in *Felix Holt*. A faith in the gradual improvement of human life was common in the nineteenth century and closely associated with the advance of knowledge. Though progress is inevitably checked on this side or that, incremental improvement in the world is possible and deserves, according to George Eliot, the name of heroism.[23] The most memorable passage of *Felix Holt* in this regard embraces the "illusions" of Rufus Lyon:

> For what we call illusions are often, in truth, a wider vision of past and present realities,—a willing movement of a man's soul with the larger sweep of the world's forces,—a movement towards a more assured end than the chances [n.b.] of a single life. We see human heroism broken into units, and say this unit did little,—might as well not have been. But in this way we break up a great army into units; in this way we might break the sunlight into fragments, and think that this and the other might be cheaply parted with. Let us rather raise a monument to the soldiers whose brave hearts only kept the ranks unbroken, and met death,—a monument to the faithful who were not famous, and who are precious as the continuity of the sunbeams is precious, though some of them fall unseen and on barrenness. (ch. 16)

23 The word "meliorism" was probably the author's coinage: see her letter to James Sully, 19 Jan. 1877, *G.E.L.*, VI, 333-334.

It is another passage to place beside the finale of *Middlemarch*. The conventional military language for heroism is crossed with the natural image of the sunlight that perhaps more persuasively, for modern times, conveys the ideas of growth and continuity independent of the single life.

The sentiment is then curiously compromised by the paragraph that follows and concludes the chapter: "At present, looking back on that day at Treby, it seems to me that the sadder illusion lay with Harold Transome, who was trusting in his own skill to shape the success of his own morrows, ignorant of what many yesterdays had determined for him beforehand" (ch. 16). George Eliot explicitly contrasts her meliorism, grounded in the evolutionary science of the day and expressing continuity with the danger of a life that is discontinuous, out of touch with its past. One kind of "illusion," or partial knowledge, can be redeemed by the future, but the other is somehow fatal; and this even though Harold Transome's ignorance of his past, unlike his mother's knowledge, is mostly someone else's doing. At stake are really two different ways of regarding actions in a multiform world of chance and information, and the radical who trusts to formal representation in Parliament is going to have to learn that he is a bastard and to suffer from public opinion accordingly.

The strength and hope of the sunbeams have also been oddly undercut in advance, because the same image for continuity simply vanishes when it is employed earlier for Mrs. Transome, the only character with fine consciousness of the past. For "a woman's hopes are woven of sunbeams; a shadow annihilates them"; and the shadow "was the presentiment of her powerlessness" (ch. 1). Moreover, this fragile hope early in the novel apparently reflects what George Eliot herself claimed to feel about sunshine: "I cannot feel hopeful without the sunlight," and "the sunshine [is] to me the greatest visible good of life—what I call the wealth of life, after love and trust."[24] The truth is that Mrs. Transome has something like full knowledge, as opposed to the "illusions" of Harold or Mr. Lyon, either one; she is the only character in the novel with substantial consciousness or true presentiments. Yet even after the writing of *Romola* George Eliot does not know quite what to do with Mrs. Transome and her past, perhaps because, in the process of descending from the dreamlike

24 Letters to John Blackwood, 15 July 1871, and to Harriet Beecher Stowe, 4 Mar. 1872; *G.E.L.*, V, 165, 252.

projection of *Romola* to a represented world, the first need was to do something conventional. Mrs. Transome is constrained by being a fallen woman. *Felix Holt* at once chafes against convention and succumbs to it. The character with the fullest knowledge is simply trapped.

If Mrs. Transome is a fallen woman and her son the wrong sort of radical, the titular hero of the novel is almost a travesty of the hero of society invented for the purpose by Scott. As Arnold Kettle has complained, "that Felix should be imprisoned for his part in a riot he has tried to quell is a fact conveyed by George Eliot without a breath of irony."[25] Felix Holt is so passive a hero that the most he can hope for is "not much." "This world is not a very fine place for a good many of the people in it. But I've made up my mind it sha'n't be the worse for me, if I can help it. They may tell me I can't alter the world,—that there must be a certain number of sneaks and robbers in it, and if I don't lie and filch somebody else will. Well, then, somebody else shall, for I won't." Furthermore, he attributes his resolve to a "conversion" he has experienced. His is a heroism confined to not lying or stealing, and this only after a conversion brought about "by six weeks' debauchery" (ch. 5). Unlike the heroes of Scott, Holt works for a living; and his dedication to knowledge is evident in the repudiation of the false medicine of his father, his celebration of public opinion, and his determination to be a teacher. But it is curious that one so dedicated to knowledge should have such negative and minimal goals.[26] If we believe six weeks' debauchery is the operative cause, then how explain Holt's determination unless as the result of a perpetual blackmail of the self? Holt never says whether the six weeks were enjoyable or otherwise but just recites the fact as information about himself. By threatening to tell about it, he forces himself to behave perhaps. In some ways he is a representative Victorian.

25 *"Felix Holt, the Radical,"* in *Critical Essays on George Eliot*, ed. Barbara Hardy (London: Routledge, 1970), p. 108. Linda Bamber, "Self-Defeating Politics in George Eliot's *Felix Holt*," *Victorian Studies*, 18 (1975), 419–435, and Catherine Gallagher, "The Failure of Realism: *Felix Holt*," *Nineteenth-Century Fiction*, 35 (1980), 372–384, also trace some of the novel's weaknesses to the hero.

26 The goals, of course, are understated, and from another point of view are grandiose. Donald Stone, *The Romantic Impulse in Victorian Fiction* (Cambridge: Harvard University Press, 1980), p. 228, protests that the author's "own role in *Felix Holt* is synonymous with that of her righteous hero, exhorting others to submit but himself wielding the most romantic fantasy of power."

11

Knowledge in *Middlemarch*

Felix Holt and *Middlemarch* both contain actions in which certain characters whom we now recognize as blackmailers—though George Eliot and her contemporaries did not use this term—have in their possession stories that they are willing to tell or to refrain from telling for a price. The stories are essentially the stuff of old-fashioned gossip, except that they are linked to evidence and offered to sale to the parties most likely to be helped or injured. Reputation and accountability have become so impersonal that third parties are able to make a commodity of such stories, which might be given away free as gossip. In the introduction to *Felix Holt*, where the stress is on bygone days, a coachman named Sampson claims to know "fine stories" about the Transomes but never says what they are. The narrator explains that "fine stories" is to be taken "ironically," as "stories not altogether creditable to the parties concerned." At the end of *Middlemarch*, after Raffles has either died or been killed by Bulstrode—and it may not matter which, since Bulstrode has prayed for his death as well as given him the brandy—it seems that the blackmailer, with a certain poetic justice, has already inadvertently given away his story in the form of boastful gossip. A horse dealer named Bambridge has picked up in the neighboring town a "fine story" about Bulstrode that leads to the banker's undoing (ch. 71).

The irony of fine stories, it would seem, is not easily exhausted. By a very characteristic strategy, however, in the same introduction to the novel that is itself the best introduction to *Middlemarch*, George Eliot asks the reader to contemplate another interpretation of "fine stories," one that substitutes for the irony of "fine," in the sense of

216

discreditable to others but enjoyable to us, an imaginative awareness of the suffering of others. She argues that this different interpretation of "fine" is not ironical; but in truth she is substituting one irony for another, her irony being that the "stories" of others are finally unknown to us. She makes this turn as follows:

> And such stories often come to be fine in a sense that is not ironical. For there is seldom any wrong-doing which does not carry along with it some downfall of blindly climbing hopes, some hard entail of suffering, some quickly satiated desire that survives, with the life in death of old paralytic vice, to see itself cursed by its woeful progeny,—some tragic mark of kinship in the one brief life to the far-stretching life that went before, and to the life that is to come after, such as has raised the pity and terror of men ever since they began to discern between will and destiny. But these things are often unknown to the world; for there is much pain that is quite noiseless; and vibrations that make human agonies are often a mere whisper in the roar of hurrying existence. There are glances of hatred that stab and raise no cry of murder; robberies that leave man or woman forever beggared of peace and joy, yet kept secret by the sufferer,—committed to no sound except that of low moans in the night, seen in no writing except that made on the face by the slow months of suppressed anguish and early morning tears. Many an inherited sorrow that has marred a life has been breathed into no human ear.

The paragraph anticipates a well-known passage in *Middlemarch* that similarly invokes "tragedy" and emphasizes what is unknown, contrasting the "roar" of existence once again with a "silence" (ch. 20). The emphasis in the introduction to *Felix Holt* on stories "unknown," "kept secret," and "breathed into no human ear" continues in *Middlemarch* and in *Daniel Deronda*, and may finally be more important than tragedy or moralism. Not even George Eliot's acumen and the omniscience of a fictional narrator can penetrate to all secrets, and these novels stand counter to entire knowingness.

Still another turn occurs in a final short paragraph of the introduction, as the narrator invokes ancient stories of souls imprisoned in trees to express the idea of hidden suffering:

> The poets have told us of a dolorous enchanted forest in the underworld. The thorn-bushes there, and the thick-barked stems

have human histories hidden in them; the power of unuttered cries dwells in the passionless-seeming branches, and the red warm blood is darkly feeding the quivering nerves of a sleepless memory that watches through all dreams. These things are a parable.

The immediate reference is to Canto XIII of the *Inferno,* as we realize from an earlier comparison of the coachman of the introduction to "the shade of Virgil in a more memorable journey." Poets are referred to in the plural because Dante, in inventing the wood of suicides, drew upon classical sources in Virgil, Ovid, and Seneca. It is a powerful allusion, not because it places Mrs. Transome with the suicides or wasters of their substance, but because of the commonplace experience behind the ancient stories—the wonder at how so palpably alive a thing as a plant, with a vascular system and varied growth, could lack consciousness. The noiseless kingdom of plant life appeals strongly to the naturalist in George Eliot.[1] She is also thinking of Dante's conception of souls excluded from the knowledge of events following their deaths, a discontinuity of the self that is the most consistently poignant experience, always in the foreground, in *The Divine Comedy.* The "pity" that the character Dante braces himself to withstand at the commencement of his journey George Eliot adopts as her own stance in her later work, even as she prepares faithfully to imagine the lives of her own characters. Her use of analogy here, both the literary analogy and the experience of confronting the silence of a forest, has also to be seen as a method of *Middlemarch.* Whether the thorn bushes or the veiled stories of the previous paragraph are the "parable" she refers to is unclear, but in order to fulfill her implicit promise to hidden lives, the novelist must resort to analogy.[2]

Except for some glances at Mrs. Transome—*Felix Holt*'s most sensitive study of a life partially discontinuous—that novel is not

1 In the last chapter of *The Physiology of Common Life,* 2 vols. (Edinburgh: Blackwood, 1860), II, 430–436, Lewes cites Bichat's distinction between the "internal" life of plants and the "manifold relations" of animals to their world, but argues that the life of plants is also in some degree intermittent, like the waking and sleeping of animals. The Dantean, and classical, image modulates over distinctions of this kind.

2 The introduction itself sets up analogies, and the same can be said of the chapter epigraphs that first appear in *Felix Holt.* The latter practice is borrowed from Scott but is new in George Eliot's art, playing an important part in *Middlemarch* and *Daniel Deronda.*

very Dantean. Its secrets are for the most part impersonal, of the kind that can be picked up anywhere, it would seem, in advanced society; and one indication of this is that Jermyn, the other partner in the personal secret, is willing to employ his knowledge so unfeelingly. The deepest criticism of society that the novel has to offer is to be found in the juxtaposition of the celebration of public opinion on the one hand and the crass manipulation of evidence on the other. A fact, a datum of information, becomes a dubious thing in *Felix Holt*. The novel represents a field for discovery and then implies, through the practical joke and studied coincidences at the center of the plot, how much there is in the field that might elude discovery if it were not for sheer chance. The antics of the eager blackmailers do not give a fine name to truth, and the part played by chance casts induction itself in a doubtful light. The novel about opinion is also about the hoarding of information and the limitation of what can be known. These matters, however, are much more deeply pondered in *Middlemarch*, with its eschewal of jokes and searching gaze into that which is "not unusual," like the response of Dorothea Casaubon to her marriage:

> Some discouragement, some faintness of heart at the new real future which replaces the imaginary, is not unusual, and we do not expect people to be deeply moved by what is not unusual. That element of tragedy which lies in the very fact of frequency, has not yet wrought itself into the coarse emotion of mankind; and perhaps our frames could hardly bear much of it. If we had a keen vision and feeling of all ordinary human life, it would be like hearing the grass grow and the squirrel's heart beat, and we should die of that roar which lies on the other side of silence. As it is, the quickest of us walk about well wadded with stupidity. (ch. 20)

As in the introduction to *Felix Holt*, the movement of thought is from a consideration of the tragic in human experience to what cannot be known, and toward a comparison between human and other forms of life. Instead of a sensational past, secret adultery, we have the not unusual present, "some discouragement, some faintness of heart," of a girl recently married. The modern cast of thought here immediately expresses itself as the possible multiplication of experience—like the "many Teresas" of the prelude to the novel—conformable to the notion of society, as the novelist speculates that "the very fact of frequency" ought to spawn some revisionist theory of tragedy. For a moment she seems bent on prophesying what has "not yet" but must inevitably come to pass, and the tragedy meant can only be multiplication, the repeatedness of experience that denies identity. Then just as suddenly George Eliot withdraws from the revisionist enterprise she has embarked upon, in the name of the safety of the perceivers of what is not unusual—"our frames could hardly bear much of it." Superficially less Dantean than a story of a bleeding thorn bush, the writing moves from specific sighting and swift interpretation to a response of the narrator as if she were a participant—a double strife of the journey and the pity—that is Dantean in its method and modern in its burden.

The explanation of why the novelist hurries on is the famous condition contrary to fact, expressed in a naturalist analogy: "If we had a keen vision and feeling of all ordinary human life, it would be like hearing the grass grow and the squirrel's heart beat, and we should die of that roar which lies on the other side of silence." The half-ventured theory of tragedy based on frequency of occurrence has to be withdrawn, then, because of still more evident limitations of knowledge.[3] We do not have access to all ordinary human life; there is more life than we could possibly know, let alone respond to; there is more information in general than we can cope with, and if very much of it came at us all at once, we could not physically withstand it. In the introduction to *Felix Holt* the sound was "the roar of hurrying existence" that nearly obliterates the "whisper" of individual suffering. In the echo of the passage in *Middlemarch* the "roar" has become everything living that we cannot hear at all. The contrafactual should not be read hastily to mean that we do not want to hear, or even that we would suffer from hearing. We cannot, in the first place, hear at all. We hear only the light chatter on this side of silence, an occasional hint or understatement, in the specific application of the passage, of some discouragement or faintness of heart in the occasional girl like Dorothea. "As it is, the quickest of us walk about well wadded with stupidity." That "well wadded" is nicely ambivalent as between ef-

3 Ian Adam, "A Huxley Echo in *Middlemarch*," *Notes and Queries*, 209 (1964), 227, compares this sentence to a similar one in T. H. Huxley's "The Physical Basis of Life," published in the *Fortnightly Review* in February 1869. Note, however, that "the roar of hurrying existence" in the introduction to *Felix Holt* predates Huxley's essay.

fectively wadded and fortunately wadded; and "stupidity" is another playful term, because of its common use in discharging the burden of ignorance upon others. But the operative term is "wadded," and there are no exceptions: "the quickest of us" go on the same journey in the same state.

The purpose of the present examination of George Eliot's work is to show how it belongs to the modern culture of which it is a part and how it elucidates a weakness in the strength of that culture. In particular I am concerned here with the rise of information in the culture and all that follows therefrom. But I do not wish to distort or give too narrow a view of George Eliot, especially not of her greatest work, which is *Middlemarch.* As her reflections at the beginning of her most nearly political novel remind us, even at its most topical her work participates in a tradition of Christian representations of reality into which Dante himself was born. Erich Auerbach summarizes this tradition by observing that "human destiny and the history of the world became once more an object of direct and compelling experience, for in the great drama of salvation every man is present, acting and suffering; he is directly involved in everything that has happened and that happens each day."[4] I would hope that anything I say about *Middlemarch* can be received as a narrower historical interpretation of the same tradition as it survived and was transformed in the nineteenth century, by George Eliot and others. Auerbach writes of Dante as a poet of the secular world; George Eliot was preeminently a novelist of the secular world, though the world had changed a great deal since the twelfth century.

With this much preamble and precaution, let me posit that the single most inclusive theme of *Middlemarch* is knowledge, and that the theme keeps resolving, in one way or another, into statements of the limitation of knowledge. This is not a new position to take: readers from the first have noted how much knowledge is contained and expressed in *Middlemarch.* Academic reviewers like Sidney Colvin responded with enthusiasm, found the novel "all saturated with modern ideas, and poured into a language of which every word bites home with peculiar sharpness to the contemporary consciousness."[5] Henry James judged the "philosophic" George Eliot superior to the

4 *Dante: Poet of the Secular World,* trans. Ralph Manheim (Chicago: University of Chicago Press, 1961), p. 20.

5 *Fortnightly Review,* 19 Jan. 1873; Carroll, p. 331.

"didactic" Fielding, but complained that the discursive portions of the novel were "too clever by half." He seemed to find the burden of learning unliterary: "*Silas Marner* has a delightful tinge of Goldsmith . . . *Middlemarch* is too often an echo of Messrs. Darwin and Huxley."[6] Lord Acton, in a perceptive review of Cross, saw the writing of George Eliot's fiction as the means of coping with the discontinuity of her life, and the importation of so much knowledge as a strategy for coping with the age's unbelief:

> After the interrupted development and the breach with the entire past, only her own energy could avail in the pursuit that imparted unity to her remaining life. It was the problem of her age to reconcile the practical ethics of unbelief and of belief, to save virtue and happiness when dogmas and authorities decay. To solve it she swept the realm of knowledge and stored up that large and serious erudition which sustains all her work, and in reality far exceeded what appears on the surface of the novels or in the record of daily reading.[7]

But it was not until the mid-twentieth century, after the publication by Anna T. Kitchell of the notebook called the "Quarry for *Middlemarch*," that students of George Eliot began to have a practical idea of how some of the knowledge found its way into the novel.[8] In the same decade techniques of the New Criticism were brought to bear, and critics were able to demonstrate that the interconnectedness of things, such as the novelist frequently urged, was imaged forth in her text. Reva Stump expounded in detail what she believed to be "the governing image" of *Middlemarch*, the web;[9] Quentin Anderson, selecting the same image, suggested that it might be thought of as "a vast switchboard in which every signal is interpreted differently by each receiver, and each receiver is in its turn capable of propagating in response a signal of its own with equally dissonant consequences."[10] Anderson's slightly anachronistic translation of the

6 *Galaxy*, March 1873; Carroll, p. 359. See also Carroll's introduction, pp. 27–32.

7 *Nineteenth Century*, March 1885; reprinted in *A Century of George Eliot Criticism*, ed. Gordon S. Haight (Boston: Houghton Mifflin, 1965), p. 154.

8 A Supplement to *Nineteenth-Century Fiction*, 4 (1950); reprinted in *Middlemarch*, ed. Bert G. Hornback (New York: Norton, 1977), pp. 607–642.

9 *Movement and Vision in George Eliot's Novels* (Seattle: University of Washington Press, 1959), pp. 138–154.

10 "George Eliot in *Middlemarch*," in *From Dickens to Hardy*, ed. Boris Ford

image is worth pausing over, because it intuits the degree to which the famous "web" of the novel is an information network and at the same time indicates that the network is imperfect. For all the vast knowledge that George Eliot incorporated in her work, by *Middlemarch* she had arrived at a position somewhat critical of her own and her age's faith in knowledge, and her wariness extended both to the grounds for knowing anything and to the social implications of the theme.

Our understanding of sources and our appreciation of the integument of imagery and analogy in *Middlemarch* has tended to supplant the older estimation of George Eliot as the brilliant exponent of character and morality.[11] There have, of course, always been studies of the ideation in the novels, but now a shift has become discernible in the general critical assessment of her achievement. Once the form of her novels was defended against the strictures of Henry James; now, the echoes of Darwin and Huxley are defended and frequently celebrated. Twenty years ago Bernard Paris studied the intellectual development of George Eliot in order to offer a thematic interpretation of the novels,[12] and U. C. Knoepflmacher employed a similar investigation in a comparative study.[13] But even this approach has undergone a subtle shift, from a study of the ideas of George Eliot to her critique of knowledge. Knoepflmacher wrote of *Middlemarch* as essentially an inquiry into truth; later he began to stress that "rationalizations abound" among the characters of the novel, and still more recently he has observed that the novelist "turns her knowledge of science against the presumption of those scientists who fail to admit that they, too, are allegorists, makers of fictive models of reality."[14] Having examined Darwin's language and narratives, including his "inextricable web of affinities," Gillian Beer has drawn careful atten-

---

(1958); reprinted in *George Eliot: A Collection of Critical Essays*, ed. George R. Creeger (Englewood Cliffs, N.J.: Prentice-Hall, 1970), p. 148.

11 A notable exception is Martin Price, *Forms of Life: Character and Moral Imagination in the Novel* (New Haven: Yale University Press, 1983), pp. 147–175.

12 *Experiments in Life: George Eliot's Quest for Values* (Detroit: Wayne State University Press, 1965).

13 *Religious Humanism and the Victorian Novel* (Princeton: Princeton University Press, 1965).

14 *Laughter and Despair: Readings in Ten Novels of the Victorian Era* (Berkeley: University of California Press, 1971), pp. 173–174, and "Fusing Fact and Myth: The New Reality of *Middlemarch*," in *This Particular Web*, ed. Ian Adam (Toronto: University of Toronto Press, 1975), pp. 70–71n14.

tion to the implicit model of evolutionary science in George Eliot's novel.[15] In general, from a better understanding of the knowledge in *Middlemarch* has emerged an appreciation of the problem of knowledge, the epistemology, of *Middlemarch*.

A mainstay of recent studies has been patient examination of the long, and generally forgotten, work by George Henry Lewes called *Problems of Life and Mind*, a compilation of psychology, logic, metaphysics, philosophy of science, and general reflection that Lewes had been working on for years and the last two volumes of which George Eliot prepared for the press after his death.[16] Though parts of the work are somewhat jumbled and the argument is often vague, it contains a flexible view of science and of scientific hypotheses that George Levine, most notably, has used to elucidate attitudes toward knowledge and the limitations of knowledge in *Middlemarch*.[17] At the same time, with a point of view derived from the writings of Jacques Derrida rather than *Problems of Life and Mind*, J. Hillis Miller has seen George Eliot's novel as an even more radical critique of knowledge. For Miller, the novel deconstructs the metaphysical system that it apparently affirms, and indeed its radical stance cannot finally be traced to the author, let alone Lewes, but must be seen as a propensity of any text. Thus the "universal propensity for misinterpretation which infects all the characters in *Middlemarch*" is ambivalently universal, as between the set of all characters in the novel and the set of all sentient beings anywhere. "The concepts of origin, end, and continuity are replaced by the categories of repetition, of difference, of discontinuity, of openness, and of the free and contradictory struggle of individual human energies, each seen as a center of interpretation, which means misinterpretation, of the whole"[18]—both

15 *Darwin's Plots* (London: Routledge, 1983), pp. 149–180.

16 *Problems of Life and Mind*, 5 vols. (London: Trübner, 1874–1879), was published in three series. For George Eliot's role, see especially K. K. Collins, "G. H. Lewes Revised: George Eliot and the Moral Sense," *Victorian Studies*, 21 (1978), 463–492.

17 "George Eliot's Hypothesis of Reality," *Nineteenth-Century Fiction*, 35 (1980), 1–28; and *The Realistic Imagination: English Fiction from Frankenstein to Lady Chatterley* (Chicago: University of Chicago Press, 1981), pp. 260–269. See also Michael York Mason, "*Middlemarch* and Science: Problems of Life and Mind," *Review of English Studies*, 21 (1971), 151–169.

18 "Narrative and History," *ELH*, 61 (1974), 466–467. See also Miller's "Optic and Semiotic in *Middlemarch*," in *The Worlds of Victorian Fiction*, ed. Jerome H. Buckley, Harvard English Studies 6 (Cambridge: Harvard University Press, 1975),

because George Eliot perceived as much in certain figures employed in *Middlemarch* and because such is the case in every text, once the metaphysics inherent in the language has been peeled back.

Miller and others have increasingly relied, for the interpretation of *Middlemarch*, on the brief essay by George Eliot entitled "Notes on Form in Art," which she sketched in a notebook and dated 1868. As Thomas Pinney commented in first publishing it, the essay shows a distinct modification of or turning away from the mimetic theory of her earlier period. The argument begins as a meditation on what is meant by "Form." The interesting kinds of perception, George Eliot suggests, are of "separateness" and lead to "discrimination of wholes & then ... discrimination of parts," as in later theories of Gestalt. The consequent forms of art, as opposed to "mere" or "direct" imitation, are like hypotheses about the relation of parts to whole. "What is structure but a set of relations selected & combined in accordance with the sequence of mental states in the constructor, or with the preconception of a whole which he has inwardly evolved?" George Eliot seems to allow for other kinds of perception ("massive impression") as well, but the kinds that lead to art depend so evidently on separateness and discrimination that the theory seems to have what we would call a structuralist bias: "Fundamentally, form is unlikeness, as is seen in the philosophic use of the word Form in distinction from Matter; & in consistency with this fundamental meaning, every difference is form."[19] This is the sentence from which Miller quotes in support of his conclusion that *Middlemarch* is "an example of form arising from unlikeness and difference" and "an example of form as difference in its effect on its readers."[20]

By linking form to perception and hence to knowledge generally, "Notes on Form in Art" undoubtedly says something authentic about knowledge in such a novel as *Middlemarch*. But the apparent structuralism of the essay is specific to perception and reasoning, not to the sum of knowledge or experience. Rather, the successive perception of unlikenesses is a process that contributes to knowledge as shaped by experience over time, which is then replicated in "the

---

pp. 125–145; and John P. McGowan, "The Turn of George Eliot's Realism," *Nineteenth-Century Fiction*, 35 (1980), 171–192.

19 "Notes on Form in Art"; Pinney, pp. 432–434.

20 Miller, "Narrative and History," pp. 469–470.

highest Form" of art. That form is organic, because an organism is the best available metaphor (or metonomy) for complex experience:

> As knowledge continues to grow by its alternating processes of distinction & combination, seeing smaller & smaller unlikenesses & grouping or associating these under a common likeness, it arrives at the conception of wholes composed of parts more & more multiplied & highly differenced, yet more & more absolutely bound together by various conditions of common likeness or mutual dependence. And the fullest example of such a whole is the highest example of Form: in other words, the relation of multiplex interdependent parts to a whole which is itself in the most varied & therefore the fullest relation to other wholes. Thus, the human organism comprises things as diverse as the finger-nails & tooth-ache, as the nervous stimulus of muscle manifested in a shout, & the discernment of a red spot in a field of snow; but all its different elements or parts of experience are bound together in a more necessary wholeness or more inseparable group of common conditions than can be found in any other existence known to us. The highest Form, then, is the highest organism, that is to say, the most varied group of relations bound together in a wholeness which again has the most varied relations with all other phenomena.[21]

What emerges from this difficult meditation on form is not the principle of unlikeness by itself, but that principle as it is embedded in biological science, which George Eliot and Lewes had studied together for more than a decade. She understood the importance of diversity to that science even as she understood the drive of other sciences to discover sameness. Diversity was the evidence of evolution, and she associated greater specialization with higher organization. Not even biology, if by biology was meant "the laws of life," was adequate to the task of describing and analyzing organic being in its special conditions, which require natural history and pathology.[22]

"The tendency of George Eliot's law," in Elizabeth Ermath's words, "is not toward ever greater uniformity but towards ever greater individuality and multiplicity."[23] The structure of knowledge (and of art) and the laws of science (as it is usually understood) yield

21 "Notes on Form in Art"; Pinney, p. 433.
22 "The Natural History of German Life"; Pinney, p. 290.
23 "Incarnations: George Eliot's Conception of 'Undeviating Law,'" *Nineteenth-Century Fiction*, 29 (1974), 282.

to particular conditions. Both Lewes and George Eliot could be vague about the meeting point of "law" and "conditions," but that is hardly surprising when the difference in the thrust of inquiry between evolutionary and other sciences is scarcely understood today. In an important letter about her belief in 1874, George Eliot wrote:

> the consideration of molecular physics is not the direct ground of human love and moral action, any more than it is the direct means of composing a noble picture or of enjoying great music. One might as well hope to dissect one's own body and be merry doing it, as take molecular physics (in which you must banish from your field of view what is specifically human) to be your dominant guide, your determiner of motives, in what is solely human. That every study has its bearing on every other is true; but pain and relief, love and sorrow, have their peculiar history which make an experience and knowledge over and above the swing of atoms.[24]

The humanism of such a statement may be vague but is not privileged. What is human is never the same. It is always the product of a specific sequence of events, a "peculiar history" not duplicated anywhere. The same is true of all existence, in time, "over and above the swing of atoms." The evolutionary bent of the statement places conditions and perception, "experience and knowledge," higher than the laws governing the swing of atoms, but even this typical rhetoric of higher and lower does not strictly convey any privileged standing to "human love and moral action." Strictly speaking, what is higher is simply later.[25]

It seems hardly surprising, especially when so much recent interpretation has prepared us to see *Middlemarch* in this way, that

24 To the Hon. Mrs. Henry Frederick Ponsonby, 10 Dec. 1874, *G.E.L.*, VI, 99.

25 As the conjunction of experience and knowledge suggests, knowledge accrues over time. Perception of likeness and unlikeness over time and awareness of conditions are functions of intelligence, according to Lewes, in the volumes of *Problems of Life and Mind* edited by George Eliot: "When we call a man intelligent, we mean that he shows a readiness in adapting his actions to circumstances; and he is more intelligent in proportion as he recognizes similarities amid diversities, and diversities amid similarities of circumstance, by these means guiding his conduct. To know an object is to reproduce in memory the various experiences which we or others have had when this object has been presented under different conditions and to different senses. . . . Intelligence is the sum of all our various registered experiences. No amount of knowledge *in general* suffices to replace particular experience" ("The Intelligence," *Problems of Life and Mind*, 3rd series, II, 391–392).

George Eliot's own "highest Form" in art should have so much to do with problems of knowledge. She shared this concern with her major characters, however, and through them studied ways in which a commitment to knowledge comes to include the condition of being known. Most of the principal characters in *Middlemarch* have as their aim, in one form or another, the pursuit of knowledge. Edward Casaubon and Tertius Lydgate are the two most obviously dedicated, and determined to make a name for themselves, in this pursuit. Each envisions his research as systematic, over a unified field: hence Casaubon is preparing his famous Key to all Mythologies, and Lydgate believes that a "fundamental knowledge of structure" (ch. 15) is important to medical practice. Neither finds his task smooth going, and Casaubon finds it particularly rough going against the narrator's very evident skepticism and scathing commentary. "Such capacity of thought and feeling as had ever been stimulated in him by the general life of mankind had long shrunk to a sort of dried preparation, a lifeless embalmment of knowledge" (ch. 20), for example—and even the "such" is sharply qualifying. In the course of the novel George Eliot impugns Casaubon's scholarship (ch. 21) and finally dismisses the Key as something a good deal less than scientific "error," which sometimes leads to truth.[26] "Mr. Casaubon's theory . . . was not likely to bruise itself unawares against discoveries"; it is "not tested," not falsifiable, in fact, and therefore not science (ch. 48). The novelist sympathizes with Casaubon and is close to him in some ways—both she and Lewes associated the character with themselves[27]—but clearly she is much more respectful of Lydgate's pursuit of knowledge. The latter's "clearest eye for probabilities" and "fullest obedience to knowledge" are to his credit, despite his shallow regard for women's knowledge and other blindnesses. He has, at least in science, a "testing vision of details and relations" and a readiness "to invent tests." And Lydgate is very modern in his stated preference for information over something called justice: "People talk about evi-

26 For this point the novelist may be indebted to Huxley: see W. J. Harvey, "The Intellectual Background of the Novel: Casaubon and Lydgate," in *"Middlemarch": Critical Approaches to the Novel*, ed. Barbara Hardy (London: Athlone, 1967), p. 36.
27 George Eliot wrote to Harriet Beecher Stowe in 1872, "I fear that the Casaubon-tints are not quite foreign to my own mental complexion"; and twice in letters of the same year Lewes jokingly referred to himself as Casaubon. See *G.E.L.*, V, 322, 291, 332.

dence," he remarks, "as if it could really be weighed in scales by blind Justice. No man can judge what is good evidence on any particular subject, unless he knows that subject well" (ch. 16). His pride, of course, is exposed in nearly all such accounts of his mind, and he will come to realize that he can be trapped by circumstances notwithstanding his knowledge and essential probity. Though George Eliot is kinder to him than she is to Casaubon, Lydgate's pursuit of knowledge also entails forms of blindness.

But why always Casaubon and Lydgate? Just because knowledge is a deep subject, let us not forget Mr. Brooke. As Beer has observed, "One should always pay attention to Mr. Brooke."[28] With his "documents" (ch. 2) and "love of knowledge, and going into everything" (ch. 5), he is like a caricature of Casaubon and Lydgate. "Those germinal ideas of making his mind tell upon the world at large which had been present in him from his younger years, but had hitherto lain in some obstruction, had been sprouting under cover," with the result that Mr. Brooke has purchased the *Pioneer* and is bent upon influencing public opinion (ch. 37). He is, in truth, the single character in the novel most closely associated with public opinion, which in its positive aspect has become almost a joke, presented in Dickensian high spirits: "and what do we meet for but to speak our minds—freedom of opinion, freedom of the press, liberty—that kind of thing?" (ch. 51). It is astonishing how quickly George Eliot has moved from a celebration of public opinion in the abstract in *Felix Holt* to this lighter treatment; and a corresponding adjustment has occurred in regard to the Reform Bill. It is the same bill and the same period in both novels, but viewed seemingly from greater distance now. Mr. Brooke may be a fool, but there is a greater tolerance for fools and for reform in *Middlemarch*.[29] He is a person with good intentions and

28 "Myth and the Single Consciousness: *Middlemarch* and 'The Lifted Veil,' " in *This Particular Web*, ed. Ian Adam, p. 94.

29 The difference presumably comes about because of the passing of the Reform Bill of 1867, a fait accompli between the writing of the two novels. The finale of *Middlemarch* refers kindly to "those times when reforms were begun with a young hopefulness of immediate good which has become much checked in our days," and the journalist Will Ladislaw is permitted to become what the working-class Felix Holt would scorn to be, a member of Parliament. See Jerome Beaty, "History by Indirection: The Era of Reform in *Middlemarch*," *Victorian Studies*, 1 (1957), reprinted in *A Century of George Eliot Criticism*, ed. Gordon S. Haight, pp. 306–313, and Graham Martin, "*Daniel Deronda*: George Eliot and Political Change," in *Critical Essays on George Eliot*, ed. Barbara Hardy (London: Routledge, 1970), pp. 139–141.

"plenty of ideas and facts," who merely needs Will Ladislaw "to put them into shape" (ch. 34). Knoepflmacher has suggested that Mr. Brooke has a representative nineteenth-century mind,[30] and before he is dismissed as merely silly, or his silliness deemed unworthy, it ought to be remembered that he bears some family resemblance to Dorothea Brooke, who also longs to accomplish some good, and who imagined she would find purpose in "the fellowship in high knowledge" (ch. 48). Similarly, Camden Farebrother, one of the least blameworthy characters in *Middlemarch*, is more interested in natural history and in the scientific literature of the day than he is in his ministry, and is furthermore reported—somewhat scandalously for a man in his position—to favor "Brougham and Useful Knowledge" (ch. 38).

Nicholas Bulstrode also pursues knowledge, though his researches may not be directly apparent because what he deliberately seeks is error. "To point out other people's errors," we are told, "was a duty that Mr. Bulstrode rarely shrank from" (ch. 13), and there can be no doubt that he has acquired valuable information in fulfilling this duty. If the powerlessness of Mr. Brooke's knowledge is self-evident, and his influence upon public opinion something of a joke, the power of Bulstrode is real. Indeed, in Middlemarch only Bulstrode is in a position to realize the adage that knowledge is power, and his power takes a peculiarly unpleasant cast:

> Mr. Bulstrode's power was not due simply to his being a country banker, who knew the financial secrets of most traders in the town and could touch the springs of their credit; it was fortified by a beneficence that was at once ready and severe ... He would take a great deal of pains about apprenticing Tegg the shoemaker's son, and he would watch over Tegg's church-going; he would defend Mrs. Strype the washerwoman against Stubb's unjust exaction on the score of her drying-ground, and he would himself scrutinize a calumny against Mrs. Strype. His private minor loans were numerous, but he would inquire strictly into the circumstances both before and after. In this way a man gathers a domain in his neighbours' hope and fear as well as gratitude; and power, when once it has got into that subtle region, propagates itself spreading out of all proportion to its external means. It was a principle with Mr. Bulstrode to gain as much

30 *"Middlemarch:* An Avuncular View," *Nineteenth-Century Fiction,* 30 (1975), 61–62. See also Robert Kiely, "The Limits of Dialogue in *Middlemarch,"* in *The Worlds of Victorian Fiction,* ed. Jerome H. Buckley, pp. 108–110.

power as possible, that he might use it for the glory of God. (ch. 16)

Thus Bulstrode knows, watches, scrutinizes, and inquires his way to power. The last sentence is the clue to the systematic claim of his project. His belief in Providence is as firm as Casaubon's in the common origin of myths or Lydgate's in the common structure of living tissue, and a lot steadier than Brooke's faith in the march of mind. He believes he has access to that body of knowledge which is divine Providence, as later chapters of the novel make clear. "He was doctrinally convinced that there was a total absence of merit in himself; but that doctrinal conviction may be held . . . with intense satisfaction when the depth of our sinning is but a measure for the depth of forgiveness, and a clenching proof that we are peculiar instruments of the divine intention" (ch. 53). Bulstrode, too, is a man of ratiocination and proofs, and he is a man of truth, a man who "shrank from a direct lie with an intensity disproportionate to the number of his more indirect misdeeds" (ch. 68).

Any such partial catalogue of the characters of *Middlemarch* argues that this study of provincial life, first, invents a good many quests for knowledge and, second, calls every one of the quests in doubt. The epic theme, moreover, is confirmed by the hero and heroine who stand against knowledge in the abstract, who are the conservative and least modern of all the characters, and who enjoy the nearly unqualified admiration of the novelist, a writer of no little erudition herself. I refer, of course, to Caleb Garth and his daughter Mary, whose main action is to keep well clear of the other heroes and heroines and to rescue from the incongruous effects of a classical education one Fred Vincy, in order to perpetuate their conservative race. Caleb Garth is George Eliot's hero of work, of getting things done. He can think and calculate, but his head is never divorced from his hand, and his knowledge is therein equivalent to skill. He is notably not one to keep a close accounting of what others owe him. He works for work's sake and not because he is driven by the market. He loves to contemplate the "myriad-headed, myriad-handed labour by which the social body is fed, clothed, and housed," but this is his practical and organic idea of community, not a systematic idea of society. "His classification of human employments was rather crude, and . . . would not be acceptable in these advanced times." Only "business," defined as practical work, interests him, and "learning" is pointedly one of the activities his classification leaves to one side:

> He divided [employments] into "business, politics, preaching, learning, and amusement." He had nothing to say against the last four; but he regarded them as a reverential pagan regarded other gods than his own. In the same way he thought very well of all ranks, but he would not himself have liked to be of any rank in which he had not such close contact with "business" as to get often honourably decorated with marks of dust and mortar, the damp of the engine, or the sweet soil of the woods and fields. (ch. 24)

The daughter of this man of business is Mary Garth, a young woman of great steadiness and loyalty who considers her father and mother "the best part of myself" (ch. 25) and who would rather be at home than go off to be a teacher (ch. 40). She utterly rejects "preaching" as an employment for Fred Vincy and patiently waits until he can be helped into "business" by her father. When they marry, Fred will have forgotten his Greek and Latin (ch. 86), and in the finale of the novel we read that Mary gives her own children—who are boys, un-like Rosamond Lydgate's girls—"little formal teaching."

Middlemarch is not only concerned with the limitations of knowl-edge but with the close bearing of motives of reputation on knowl-edge. In *Felix Holt* the juxtaposition of a positive public opinion and crude blackmail expresses this relation; in *Middlemarch* the relation of knowing to being known is persistently and finely drawn in each of the stories, so that the extreme case of blackmailing Bulstrode is but one of four relevant actions. Casaubon, Lydgate, Brooke, and Bul-strode are every one susceptible to threatening publicity. It is as if George Eliot were saying that the pursuit of knowledge, in modern society, is not separable from questions of publicity. If knowledge it-self is remote, storable in "documents," exchangeable, publishable, and sometimes concealable, then the same effects of distance that gov-ern its being govern also its practitioners, who are thereby subject to exposure in a way very different from Caleb Garth's experience. Garth is known personally for the work he does and can do; the seek-ers of knowledge have placed themselves at risk in a culture of infor-mation, a culture that can inform against them.

George Eliot makes abundantly clear that virtually the sole motive of Casaubon's scholarship is fame, and that this relation between his knowledge and his being known runs far deeper than mere vanity, his pleasure in sitting for the portrait of St. Thomas Aquinas and the like. Casaubon is both vain and "resolute in being a man of honour," a person "unimpeachable by any recognized opinion"; but he is subject to the deepest terror by authorship. He will be judged in absentia from his writings, and already is so judged, as he fears. Authorship entails risks that are less within his control than his personal conduct.

> In conduct these ends [of honor] had been attained; but the difficulty of making his Key to all Mythologies unimpeachable weighed like lead upon his mind; and the pamphlets—or "Parerga," as he called them—by which he tested his public and deposited small monumental records of his march, were far from having been seen in all their significance. He suspected the Archdeacon of not having read them; he was in painful doubt as to what was really thought of them by the leading minds of Brasenose, and bitterly convinced that his old acquaintance Carp had been the writer of that depreciatory recension which was kept locked in a small drawer of Mr. Casaubon's desk, and also in a dark closet of his verbal memory. These were heavy impressions to struggle against, and brought that melancholy embitterment which is the consequence of all excessive claim: even his religious faith wavered with his wavering trust in his own authorship, and the consolations of the Christian hope in immortality seemed to lean on the immortality of the still unwritten Key to all Mythologies.

The independent life of writing, divorced from its author, becomes a strong reason for not writing at all, lest some terrible failure in the Key—like a previous mistake in a dedication of a Parergon to Carp— open the author "to ridicule in the next age" or to "be chuckled over by Pike and Trench in the present" (ch. 29). George Eliot knew of the terror herself, as the recension put away in the locked drawer may suggest by resemblance to the drawer to which Lewes consigned even those writings about the novelist that he approved. Scholarship has its good days, and Dr. Spanning's praise of "my late tractate on the Egyptian Mysteries" puts Casaubon in a rare good humor (ch. 37), but on the whole the perils outweigh the pleasures. When Will Ladislaw, "not at all deep himself in German writers," criticizes Casaubon's failure to consult the Germans who "have taken the lead in historical inquiries," the narrator comments wryly that "mortals are easily tempted to pinch the life out of their neighbour's buzzing glory, and think that such killing is no murder" (ch. 21). The equation of this diminishment of reputation with murder, however lightheartedly represented as insecticide, connects with the one murder case in *Middlemarch*, which is in response to blackmail, and may recall that at the beginning of this century blackmail was popularly referred to as "moral murder."[31]

The importance of Lydgate's relation to his public is more evident because he is a doctor. In the nature of such a career, he must not only know what he is doing but be perceived as knowing. His success is bound to depend on public relations that ostensibly have little to do with medical science. Lydgate's particular failure, therefore, follows from his neglect and scorn for this aspect of the practitioner's life, just as his ironic success in later years depends more on being fashionable than on scientific achievement. But Lydgate is more than just a doctor, and is far closer than Casaubon to George Eliot's idea of an intellectual. His troubles both personal and professional conflict with an ideal. "Only those who know the supremacy of the intellectual life— the life which has a seed of ennobling thought and purpose within it—can understand the grief of one who falls from that serene activity into the absorbing soul-wasting struggle with worldly annoyances" (ch. 73). Some of Lydgate's troubles result from his finely described "commonness," or unconscious snobbery—a taking for granted of status that fatally ignores opinion. He does begin to understand, what had not occurred to him, that even popularity may interfere with a career, as when his talent attracts Rosamond "because it gives him prestige, and is like an order in his button-hole or an Honourable before his name" (ch. 58). Lydgate's is the most sharply differentiated talent in *Middlemarch*: in his intellectual aim and in his specialization he is the most modern hero of the novel, and the constraint that his marriage places upon him is partly due to what Georg Simmel analyzed as the typically differentiated relations of modern men, which prompt concealment in several directions at once.

> These differentiated friendships which connect us with one individual in terms of affection, with another, in terms of common intellectual aspects, with a third, in terms of religious impulses, and with a fourth, in terms of common experiences—all these

31 Mike Hepworth, *Blackmail* (London: Routledge, 1975), pp. 21–22.

friendships present a very peculiar synthesis in regard to the question of discretion, of reciprocal revelation and concealment. They require that the friends do not look into those mutual spheres of interest and feeling which, after all, are not included in the relation and which, if touched upon, would make them feel painfully the limits of their mutual understanding.[32]

The analysis is extremely suggestive of Lydgate's partial relations with his fellow doctors, with Bulstrode, with Farebrother, with Ladislaw, with his family, and with his own wife, no one of which relations admits of frank intimacy. Without question Rosamond's concealments from her husband are stunning, but as perceptive students of that marriage have begun to comment, he is not open with her.[33] Nor can Lydgate, the most promising and undoubtedly talented seeker of knowledge, be open with any of the Middlemarchers: it is this isolation that makes Dorothea's befriending of him so touching. George Eliot hints at some tragic flaw in the "commonness" of Lydgate (ch. 15), but succeeds brilliantly in portraying the common relations of a modern person with his fellows. This intellectual's embroilment with Bulstrode and his recognition that even "valid evidence" will not clear him (ch. 73) dramatize his position beyond a doubt. It is the nature of his position in society that it will not support him by close friendships, and it is the nature of opinion and circumstances to indict.

George Eliot studies the connection between the pursuit of knowledge and the opinion of others with a reserved pathos in the case of Casaubon and with marvelous subtlety in the case of Lydgate. For Mr. Brooke she deploys some light comic reversals that can be enjoyed by all. It is only right that a fool who longs to exercise his love of knowledge "and that kind of thing" in the public arena should learn at first hand how he is regarded by the public. Hence Brooke as publisher of the *Pioneer* meets with an unflattering description of himself in the *Trumpet* (ch. 38), and is told to his face by his tenant Dagley that his "charrickter" in Middlemarch is nothing to be proud of (ch. 39). For Bulstrode, also, there is a sharp reversal in store, in

32 *The Sociology of Georg Simmel,* trans. and ed. Kurt H. Wolff (New York: Free Press, 1964), p. 326.

33 See Kathleen Blake, "*Middlemarch* and the Woman Question," *Nineteenth-Century Fiction,* 31 (1976), 285–312, and Sandra M. Gilbert and Susan Gubar, *The Madwoman in the Attic* (New Haven: Yale University Press, 1979), pp. 515–516.

which poetic justice takes a somewhat melodramatic turn. Since Bulstrode's power flows from his knowledge of the errors or weaknesses of others, it is only right that he should fall victim to Raffles's blackmail and inadvertent revelation of his secret.[34] The novelist sets up Bulstrode for a fall just as surely as she sets up Brooke, but the fall is to be singular and complete—not the fall of a great criminal, as in an old form of tragedy, but of a man of high pretensions. "For the pain, as well as the public estimate of disgrace, depends on the amount of previous profession. To men who only aim at escaping felony, nothing short of the prisoner's dock is disgrace. But Bulstrode had aimed at being an eminent Christian" (ch. 53). If the demonstration in some respects is rather crude, in other respects, such as the relation of Bulstrode to his wife, it is very fine. Moreover, the applications of this fall are to be taken to heart by all. "Who can know how much of his most inward life is made up of the thoughts he believes other men to have about him, until that fabric of opinion is threatened with ruin?" (ch. 68).

The rare characters in *Middlemarch* who are immune to opinion and uninterested in scandal are the very same—the Garths—who stand against knowledge in the abstract. Caleb Garth is present when Raffles first accosts Bulstrode, but he immediately takes himself off: "if there was anything discreditable to be found out concerning another man, Caleb preferred not to know it" (ch. 53). Nevertheless—and this is one of the final ironies of the novel—Garth is instrumental in bringing about Bulstrode's fall. He cannot abide a life that is double: therefore, as soon as he has heard the story, he ceases to work for one who "can't get his life clear" (ch. 69). Though Garth says nothing to anyone, his ending of his employment is taken in Middlemarch to be a direct criticism of the banker, "so that even a diligent historian might have concluded Caleb to be the chief publisher of Bulstrode's misdemeanours" (ch. 71). George Eliot deliberately calls attention to Garth's role even as she exonerates him: his is the stern judgment against which a divided life finally breaks. Without some such tribunal blackmail itself would be futile, and by making Garth seem to be, though he is not, "the chief publisher" of Bulstrode's faults, the nov-

34 Cf. "Quarry for *Middlemarch*": "The idea which governs the plot about Bulstrode is, that there is nothing which the law can lay hold of to make him responsible for: the Nemesis is wrought out by the public opinion determined against him" (*Middlemarch*, ed. Bert G. Hornback, p. 634; Ms. p. 22).

elist admits that Raffles operates with the best opinion positively behind him.

Garth's daughter Mary is similarly disinclined to interfere in the affairs of others. She guards against even the appearance of wrong when she nurses Featherstone on his deathbed (ch. 33); she "looks about her, but does not suppose that anybody is looking at her" (ch. 40). Dorothea Casaubon, on the other hand, is a curious exception in this regard. Her actions are not dictated by "the world's opinion" either (ch. 48), and she believes "that people are almost always better than their neighbours think they are" (ch. 72), yet unlike Mary or Caleb Garth she is one of the seekers after knowledge in the novel.

A formidable case for Dorothea has been made by the very students of George Eliot who have made of *Middlemarch* a book of knowledge—or a book of wisdom. By carefully tracing the ways in which Lydgate and Dorothea are complementary characters, U. C. Knoepflmacher shows how the Arnoldian balance of virtues tips in her favor: "Lydgate's gradual fall and Dorothea's gradual ascendancy" argue that she gains, in the course of the novel, "the true disinterestedness that was lacking in his . . . idealism."[35] After reviewing the role of hypothesis, of imagination, and of active feeling that Lewes, especially, stressed in scientific work, George Levine has taken the comparison with Lydgate one step further and suggested that Dorothea is ironically "the better scientist."[36] And David Carroll has analyzed the way in which "the ideas of perception, hypothesis, and evidence" enter into the series of actions near the end in which Dorothea weighs the facts and reaches important conclusions with respect to Lydgate and Ladislaw. For in "the climax" of the novel it is up to Dorothea to make a clear judgment of "the circumstantial evidence" seeming to link Lydgate financially with Bulstrode and Ladislaw sexually with Rosamond. Carroll shows how the heroine, in remaining flexible and forcing herself to be disengaged, can arrive at the true facts much as a scientist ought to. "The mind must move flexibly and disinterestedly among the circumstances, untrammelled by deduction. . . . Instead of excluding the circumstances which threaten her beliefs, she must absorb them into a more comprehen-

35 Knoepflmacher, *Religious Humanism in the Victorian Novel*, pp. 78–96.
36 Levine, *The Realistic Imagination*, pp. 265–271.

sive hypothesis."[37] In other words, when Dorothea returns to the foreground of the action in *Middlemarch*, she copes successfully by employing scientific methods that have little resemblance to the "high knowledge" that she dreamed of at the beginning.

If such interpretations are correct in their tendency, then one still has to wonder a little about the apparent exemption of the heroine from the desire of fame, and from the onus of reputation as well. Two explanations of Dorothea's exemption are possible. Recent defenses of her devotion to truth are so congruent with the Leweses' ideas of science, that one has to step back from them a little and recall that she is not, after all, engaged in an activity very much like scientific research. Dorothea is trying to understand what is happening among the people she knows and forcing herself, in the case she cares most about, to extend the benefit of doubt. Neither in her marriage choices nor in other personal relations does she concern herself with public opinion. Carroll makes a special point of her "act of belief" in Lydgate, and so does George Eliot (the expression is Lydgate's own, in direct discourse). In truth, the heroine's direct, personal response to Lydgate ignores both public opinion and the evidence. Carroll's use of the word "nobility"[38] suggests the archaic quality of her response, and in effect the relations of society are abridged by this heroic performance.

The other possibility is that Doreathea is no exception at all to the other characters' interest in fame, once her performance has been publicized by the writing of *Middlemarch*. With corrosive insight Calvin Bedient has written of the "famished need for recognition" in the novel and of fame as its theme. "The effort—and failure—of self-monumentalization embraces almost the entire cast. Nearly every important character tries to carve his name on the world—to become as permanent as history, as significant as all mankind." Bedient's hyperbole has the ring of outrageous truth, and if Dorothea's personality is unlike the rest of the cast's, her presentation in the prelude and finale of the novel tells another story. The argument of the former is that modern girls cannot look forward to the fame of Saint Teresa, and of the latter, that it is a shame they will rest in unvisited tombs. Within the novel proper the superiority of the heroine exerts itself so

37 "*Middlemarch* and the Externality of Fact," in *This Particular Web*, ed. Ian Adam, pp. 86–90.
38 Ibid., p. 87.

as to make her lack of fame all the more regrettable. In this inverted interpretation of *Middlemarch* Dorothea remains central, and Bedient has glimpsed her helplessness before the culture of information.[39]

In the present interpretation of the novel I am conscious of fighting shy of Dorothea, as we know—from the maintenance of a multiple plot, the study of the other side of her marriage, and the expenditure of humor at her expense—that the novelist herself fought shy of the heroine, without entirely succeeding. Dorothea is significantly less modern than any of the other seekers of knowledge—Casaubon, Lydgate, Brooke, Bulstrode, and even Farebrother. Her plight as a woman is hardly specific to the nineteenth century, as the example of Romola partially attests. If George Eliot had wished, she might have given her heroine a career, but convention and inclination were against it.[40] She may project the "common yearning of womanhood" (the language of the prelude is obscure) in Dorothea more than in any other character, but the novels given much to projection—*Romola* and to a lesser extent *The Mill on the Floss*—are now well behind her. In Dorothea's two marriages there is not a marked question of discontinuity, as we might expect, but rather a kind of persistent virginity in the face of both.[41] I am less struck, finally, by the degree to which Dorothea changes in the course of the novel than the degree to which, like many heroines, she remains a given. In almost the first sentence of *Middlemarch* we read that this heroine has "the impressiveness of a fine quotation from the Bible—or from one of our elder poets—in a paragraph of today's newspaper" (ch. 1). That comparison, to say nothing of the one with Italian paintings of the Virgin, immediately registers the archaism of the character and opposes her to the print culture of the nineteenth century.

Two other of the seekers of knowledge are also rather static, and the manner in which they are presented is essentially sportive, comic

39 *Architects of the Self: George Eliot, D. H. Lawrence, and E. M. Forster* (Berkeley: University of California Press, 1972), pp. 87–94. Bedient is not slamming the Victorian novelist: "this feverish yearning for fame," he writes, "makes George Eliot our contemporary" (p. 87).

40 Cf. Lee R. Edwards, "Women, Energy, and *Middlemarch*," *Massachusetts Review*, 12 (1972), 223–238.

41 The imbalance in *Middlemarch*'s treatment of sexuality has been demonstrated by Barbara Hardy, *The Appropriate Form: An Essay on the Novel* (London: Athlone, 1964), pp. 105–131.

as well as partial. Casaubon and Brooke are alike in the futility and
the internal disconnectedness of their enterprises—the clutter of no-
tations awaiting pigeon holes. Brooke is the more nearly static of the
two, but Casaubon is not much better: all he ultimately learns is that
marriage to a young woman is extremely uncomfortable for him.
There is a strong element of the comic in the conception of Brooke
and Casaubon both, less of the comic in Dorothea and Farebrother,
but a sense in which all three male characters, at least, stay pretty
much in place. They belong in the neighborhood, and their lives are
not threatened by discontinuity in the sense that we have been remarking. Lydgate and Bulstrode, on the other hand, do not belong to
Middlemarch, do not live continuous lives, do have careers that matter, and are profoundly changed in the end. The lives of Lydgate and
Bulstrode tend least to comic resolution, and they are, especially as
they appear in combination, the most modern of the characters concerned with knowledge. The two, indeed, are closely tied together in
the narrative, and I hope to move closer to the significance of information, and of blackmail, in *Middlemarch* by thinking about their
relation.

From the meeting of the board of the infirmary early in the novel
to the occasion of Raffles's illness and death, with its "malignant effect on Lydgate's reputation" (ch. 71), the banker and the doctor are
bound together in a special way.[42] Significantly, they are not friends
and have antithetical feelings and personalities; they are brought into
conjunction by their specialized functions within a modern social organization. Lydgate "did not intend to be a vassal of Bulstrode's" (ch.
18), and the choice of word for the excluded relation is significant. It
is part of Lydgate's modern consciousness that he needs only "a medium for his work" or "a vehicle for his ideas," no personal and distinctly archaic relation to another more powerful than himself; and
likewise Bulstrode's power is not based on fealty in the community
but on information and credit. Nonetheless it is Lydgate's connection
with Bulstrode, mirrored by his alienation from his wife, that comes
to symbolize the most arcane power of circumstances in the novel,
and thus George Eliot's most radical representation of society.

42 The board meeting marks the beginning of the combined novel *Middlemarch* as
we know it: see Jerome Beaty, *"Middlemarch" from Notebook to Novel: A Study of
George Eliot's Creative Method*, Illinois Studies in Language and Literature 47 (Ur-
bana: University of Illinois Press, 1960), pp. 3–42, summarized p. 42.

"On this occasion," the narrator informs us, "Bulstrode became identified with Lydgate," and she presents the meeting of the infirmary board as Lydgate's first real brush with circumstances:

> For the first time Lydgate was feeling the hampering threadlike pressure of small social conditions, and their frustrating complexity. At the end of his inward debate, when he set out for the hospital, his hope was really in the chance that discussion might somehow give a new aspect to the question, and make the scale dip so as to exclude the necessity for voting. I think he trusted a little also to the energy which is begotten by circumstances,— some feeling rushing warmly and making resolve easy, while debate in cool blood had only made it more difficult. (ch. 18)

If there is a recollection of Lilliput in the first image, it merely puts a satiric edge to the description of individual and social perplexity. The following image, of the balance scale, brings together Lydgate's science with the operation of opinion, since he hopes that discussion will render voting unnecessary. The dipping of a laboratory scale, on which some scientific truth depends, is already an image that makes knowledge seem fragile; and the same implication extends to opinion at the meeting. That a scientist who has been unable to decide a question calmly by himself trusts to feelings at a meeting to decide it for him is not a slap at Lydgate alone, but a reflection on how collective decisions are arrived at. The thought anticipates, to be sure, the ironic conclusion of the scene in which Lydgate, goaded by one of the other doctors, casts the deciding vote for Bulstrode's candidate for chaplain of the infirmary, but the study of this deservedly famous scene is precisely the interaction of relative strangers at a meeting, so familiar as a modern institution. Such hospital or other committees are replications in small of the wider combinations of society, and questions of discretion and concealment, revelation and power are implicit in the information that is debated there.

A Mrs. Taft in Middlemarch, "who was always counting stitches and gathered her information in misleading fragments caught between the rows of her knitting, had got it into her head that Mr. Lydgate was a natural son of Bulstrode's, a fact which seemed to justify her suspicions of evangelical laymen" (ch. 26). But Lydgate is no more a natural son to Bulstrode than he is his vassal. The doctor and banker are thrown together even though they have no personal liking for one another, and each is aware of the mixed reputation that the other enjoys in the town. They have a good deal in common, besides their association with the infirmary, in their susceptibility to comment and in the concealment of their private selves from the public. No doubt the concealments of Bulstrode are of a guilty kind and those of Lydgate less contorted, but in each the concealment is deepened by the professional role. Both lives are divided between public and private being, and the crossing of that division is experienced like a burn. In danger of exposure Bulstrode thinks of leaving Middlemarch in order to escape the "scorching" contempt of his neighbors (ch. 68), and Lydgate habitually "shrank, as from a burn, from the utterance of any word about his private affairs" (ch. 63). The professional relation of the two begins in the carefully delineated circumstances of the meeting of the board and concludes amid circumstances that make them appear accomplices in murder, "circumstances [that] would always be stronger" than anything Lydgate might say on his own behalf (ch. 73). Both characters occupy a world in which the relation of outward to inward being can only be deduced from circumstances, and in which gossip itself pretends to reason. The seeming collusion of Bulstrode and Lydgate "was soon to be loudly spoken of in Middlemarch as a necessary 'putting of two and two together' " (ch. 71).

When the younger man's medical opinions, too rational to be readily understood perhaps, have come into dispute in the town, "Mr. Toller remarked one day, smilingly, to Mrs. Taft, that 'Bulstrode had found a man to suit him in Lydgate; a charlatan in religion is sure to like other sorts of charlatans' " (ch. 45). Again slander points to the true connection. There are plenty of grounds for arguing, from the superior vantage point of George Eliot and the reader, that Bulstrode's religion is false and Lydgate's science true, but what the two have in common is the career that opens them to attack. Implicit in the career are a progressive investment in knowledge on the part of the individual *and* consistent approval or acquiesence on the part of those who employ the career—the people who purchase medical services or bank loans. At first hearing, Lydgate's career seems very modern and Bulstrode's tinged with outdated and discredited religion, but as Alan Mintz has argued, "Bulstrode the banker embodies an almost classical unity of religious conviction and economic practice." The classical representation he has in mind is the vocation of the capitalist sketched by Max Weber, and as such Bulstrode is nearly as modern as Lydgate. Even if he is "the most thoroughly corrupt character in the novel,"[43] corruption is also endemic to his situation. Bulstrode is notoriously a hypocrite, but in a sense Lydgate would have to learn hypocrisy if he were to be a success in Middlemarch. One thinks of the statement in *Romola* of "the doubleness which is the pressing temptation in every public career."[44]

George Eliot goes rather far in the blasting of Bulstrode, and there is undoubtedly deep antipathy in her portrayal of the pious banker. But we should read carefully the famous passage in which she explains that Bulstrode was not a "coarse hypocrite." Fielding, the "great historian" with whom George Eliot compares herself earlier in the novel (ch. 15), had singled out hypocrisy in his preface to *Joseph Andrews* as one of the sources of "the true Ridiculous" and thus fair game for the satirist. The leading hypocrite in *Middlemarch* is not held up for ridicule but treated as the victim of blackmail, and we are invited to consider the cause of his vulnerability as if it were our own. An untruthful personality that may be laughed to scorn in the eighteenth century has become something of a problem in the nineteenth century, because of the increasing division in all personality between public and private experience. When Raffles appears on the scene with his "By Jove, Nick, it's you!" he performs the needling that the satirist used to perform, but with a difference. That "peculiar mixture of joviality and sneering" (ch. 53) typifies the blackmailer's manner because he finds the idea that anyone has any real privacy so very amusing. Persons are now exposed *by* their careers, which usually evoke a pretense of private virtues from what are in reality impersonal relations. Bulstrode, according to George Eliot, "was simply a man whose desires had been stronger than his theoretic beliefs, and who had gradually explained the gratification of his desires into satis-

43 *George Eliot and the Novel of Vocation* (Cambridge: Harvard University Press, 1978), p. 18, also pp. 146–150. Mintz provides an extensive analysis of Lydgate's career, pp. 73–96.

44 *Romola*, ch. 65: see chapter 9. Judith Wilt, *Ghosts of the Gothic* (Princeton: Princeton University Press, 1980), pp. 203–204, suggests that "in *Middlemarch* those who think they know what they are to be—Bulstrode, Casaubon, Lydgate—are literally unmade. These stride confidently forward in response to a clear 'vocation,' like Romola's brother Dino, thinking, as Lydgate does of Farebrother, that 'a pitiable infirmity of will' ails the Fred Vincys, the Will Ladislaws, the Dorotheas, who drift in this less than epic age. But they are defeated, whereas the drifters survive."

factory agreement with those beliefs. If this be hypocrisy, it is a process which shows itself occasionally in us all, to whatever confession we belong." And "there is no general doctrine which is not capable of eating out our morality if unchecked by the deep-seated habit of direct fellow-feeling with individual fellow-men" (ch. 61). The difficulty is that modern society, as instanced in banking and medical careers, does not permit direct human relations to become habitual.

Lydgate and Bulstrode are strangers to Middlemarch. They have come there to engage in professions, to relate functionally to the Middlemarchers and not because they are indigenous members of a community—so it is hard to see what "deep-seated habit of direct fellow-feeling" can guide them in their social role. They are men with discontinuous lives whom society, for its part, is prepared to assimilate to its purposes, at least until some question is raised. "No one in Middlemarch was likely to have such a notion of Lydgate's past" as the narrator herself supplies. "Not only young virgins of that town, but gray-bearded men also, were often in haste to conjecture how a new acquaintance might be wrought into their purposes, contented with very vague knowledge as to the way in which life had been shaping him for that instrumentality" (ch. 15). There is irony here, since George Eliot implies that Lydgate's past must affect his performance in Middlemarch, but the townspeople, regarding him as an instrumentality, overlook this. Bulstrode, a much less likable man, is "considered to have done well in uniting himself with a real Middlemarch family" (ch. 11), but some "wished to know who his father and grandfather were, observing that five-and-twenty years ago nobody had ever heard of a Bulstrode in Middlemarch" (ch. 13). Instead of the narrator's sharing her irony with the reader in this case, we have hints and premonitions of a missing past that, when revealed, will overturn completely the man's reputation and foreclose his usefulness at one stroke.

In the twentieth century, with social mobility still more common, it is hard to imagine that anyone who dealt with Bulstrode would be gravely upset to discover how he carried on three decades ago in London, or that he himself would be much threatened by the revelation. The shady activity of those days, it turns out, is itself symbolic of unfortunate discontinuities, since "the business was a pawnbroker's" (ch. 61): quite apart from the possible criminal link of trading in stolen goods, a pawnbroker profits from pledges that are never redeemed, offered by persons who are trying to hold their personal estates together and who fail. The feeling for continuity among Victorians had to be very strong for such fine stories, which are not even given in the text, to grip the imagination in this symbolic way. The feeling *was* strong because continuity was threatening to change into the absence of continuity. Whereas Lydgate's failure in Middlemarch only gradually becomes evident, the experience of Bulstrode, verging upon the gothic, is like a nightmare: "it was as if he had had a loathsome dream, and could not shake off its images with their hateful kindred of sensations,—as if on all the pleasant surroundings of his life a dangerous reptile had left his slimy traces" (ch. 68).

The reptile is Raffles, another stranger to Middlemarch, and of course it is Raffles who indirectly drags down Lydgate too, because of the medical consultation at Stone Court, the loan from Bulstrode, and the previous association of the two men. Who or what does Raffles represent? Among the carefully studied characters in the novel, many famous in their own right, or among the lightly sketched local characters, "this loud red figure" is something of an excrescence, a literary type who has seemingly wandered into the wrong company. The narrator names him, among other things, "an incorporate past" that has risen before Bulstrode (ch. 53), but that hardly assures the reader of his real being. At least two recent commentators have associated Raffles with the characteristic devices of Dickens rather than of George Eliot. Peter K. Garrett calls him "the shabby double who parodies [Bulstrode's] rationalizing doctrines and revives his repressed guilt" and underlines the nightmare quality of the relation.[45] In one of the most searching attempts to come to terms with this portion of the novel, David Carroll also invokes Dickens and argues that Raffles and Bulstrode "have each become the other's threatening extension" and "between them . . . make up one person." Moreover, Carroll sees the violent relation of the two as "a clear means of understanding what is happening in several other important relations—

---

45 *The Victorian Multiplot Novel* (New Haven: Yale University Press, 1980), pp. 164-165. In the ascription of guilt to Bulstrode, however, some words of Barbara Hardy, *The Novels of George Eliot* (1959; rpt. London: Athlone, 1963), p. 183, ought to be kept in mind: "It may look like the haunting of guilt, and yet it presents a kind of innocence. What is innocent is Bulstrode's fear—he is afraid of the past only as something which might be discovered. Set in counterpoint against George Eliot's insistence that he is what the past has made him, is his hope that he is free, except from being found out."

those between Casaubon and Dorothea, and Lydgate and Rosamond
... the same pattern of tampering with the evidence of reality, of
bribery, of blackmail, the rapid escalation of demands on each side,
plotting and counter-plotting, and finally open hostility." Carroll
treats the relation as far more gothic than I would—if one is to assign
a generic name to this portion of *Middlemarch*, it should be sensational rather than gothic. The sensational element is apparent in the
stress on evidence and the way in which Raffles serves as a conduit
for information. "Certain facts have been wilfully excluded from the
scheme of things," as Carroll explains. "They come roaring back in
the shape of Raffles. . . . He comes back talking compulsively and
blackmailing his briber. It is almost as if the unpleasant facts have
taken on a life of their own."[46]

The course of action adopted by Bulstrode is murder, but the roles
of the several characters are blurred. The chapter in which the
banker, against the doctor's orders, makes brandy available to Raffles
is headed by an epigraph of George Eliot's own composition: "Our
deeds still travel with us from afar, / And what we have been makes
us what we are." The application is obviously to Bulstrode, but no
doubt also to Lydgate, and most immediately to the sick man. "Bulstrode's first object after Lydgate had left Stone Court," the chapter
begins, "was to examine Raffles's pockets, which he imagined were
sure to carry signs in the shape of hotel-bills of the places he had
stopped in, if he had not told the truth in saying that he had come
straight from Liverpool . . ." Curious transpositions occur here: Bulstrode is the hunted victim, but he goes through the blackmailer's
pockets in search of evidence; Lydgate is the doctor in charge, but his
prescription for the treatment of alcoholism is so advanced, and so
contrary to received opinion, that the banker can easily risk altering
it. Bulstrode's being, his "what we are," is uppermost in the text, but
Lydgate we care more about, and Raffles is the one who has most recently traveled "from afar"—as if to embody the transience of the
other two. Bulstrode prays for his blackmailer's death, and his
prayer—assisted by the brandy—is answered. "As he sat there and
beheld the enemy of his peace going irrevocably into silence, he felt
more at rest than he had done for many months. His conscience was

46 "*Middlemarch* and the Externality of Fact," in *This Particular Web*, ed. Ian
Adams, pp. 79–84.

soothed by the enfolding wing of secrecy, which seemed just then like an angel sent down for his relief" (ch. 70). Of the three strangers to Middlemarch in the chapter, one has been sacrificed, the second experiences some temporary relief from the information that threatens to ruin him, and the third has become still more enmeshed in circumstances that tell against him.

Raffles, the stranger so sacrificed, has scarcely more character than the eminently dispensable Tracy in Alfred Hitchcock's *Blackmail*. Next to Bulstrode or Lydgate he weighs almost nothing at all, and he must clearly count for what rather than who he is in the novel. His role in the fine story of Bulstrode is obviously essential, and he is thus important to the story of Lydgate as well. If it will help to make his presence felt, he ought to be compared with Will Ladislaw—a much more substantial character, but one whom readers have also judged too lightweight for the part.[47] It is astonishing how often Ladislaw, the only other stranger of note, is perceived by other characters as threatening, and precisely because he bears information of some kind. When he appears in Middlemarch as editor of the *Pioneer*, Mr. Hawley claims to recognize the foreign type—"some emissary," as he says (ch. 37). Bulstrode unhappily is forced to associate Ladislaw directly with Raffles's presence in the town and tries to buy him off, as if in danger of blackmail from this quarter also. "It was the first time he had encountered an open expression of scorn from any man higher than Raffles"; but after talking with Ladislaw the banker comforts himself with the reflection that he, at least, is not likely to "publish" their conversation (ch. 61). Later Ladislaw remarks to Lydgate that he is surprised gossip has not accused him of plotting "with Raffles to murder Bulstrode" (ch. 79). There is no getting around the fact that this stranger poses a certain threat from the past to Casaubon, also, and that he is the first to inform Dorothea of her husband's inadequate scholarship (ch. 21). Dorothea Casaubon scorns Mrs. Cadwallader's comparison of Will to an Italian with white mice.[48] For her

47 This judgment is now being seriously contested. Eugene Hollahan, "The Concept of 'Crisis' in *Middlemarch,*" *Nineteenth-Century Fiction*, 28 (1974), 453–457, argues that Ladislaw generates the plot of the novel as a whole; Gordon S. Haight, "George Eliot's 'eminent failure,' Will Ladislaw," in *This Particular Web*, ed. Ian Adam, pp. 22–42, argues that he is "the true hero" and "the only coherent focus" of the plot.

48 Can George Eliot have been thinking of Count Fosco and his white mice in Collins's *The Woman in White* (1860)?

"he was a creature who entered into every one's feelings, and could take the pressure of their thought instead of urging his own with iron resistance" (ch. 50). The contrast is with her husband, and the terms—"entered into every one's feelings"—describe a welcome intrusion: Ladislaw and Raffles are entirely unlike personalities, the one antithetical to the other. Yet both bear information against some of the Middlemarchers.[49]

Raffles figures most importantly in the novel not as a character but as a catalyst in the drama of information and circumstances. It may be better to disregard him as a person altogether and concentrate on the reaction taking place around him. As George Eliot and her commentators have been careful to point out, the threads of connection run this way and that in *Middlemarch;* the very process of the novel's composition from multiple actions signals that connections and parallels, however slight, can usually be found. There are no true limits to the actions of circumstance, which extend indiscernibly backward and forward in time; and a reality so construed invites ironic overstatement of the particular turnings it takes. An event that can be identified as anything approaching a beginning can be expected to be very slight, and in a just narrative of circumstances ought to be the slightest and most inconspicuous circumstance of all. Yet the information that identifies that circumstance and enables blackmail, that threatens to connect various narratives within the narrative as a whole, craves notice as a melodramatic beginning. Some such contradictory desiderata inspire the improbable narrative in chapters 12 and 13 of *Felix Holt*, in which a practical joke, lost pocketbook, stubbed toe, heroic reticence, and matching information deliberately overstate the odds against discovery in order to apologize, as it were, for narrating the beginning of the main action. To introduce Raffles and the blackmail action in *Middlemarch,* George Eliot does something quite similar—in shorter compass, with much greater finesse, and with shrewd reference to her theme of knowledge.

49 Once the novel is interpreted as *about* knowledge, their roles seem to relate to one another. David Carroll, as we have noted, sees Raffles as a personification of "the unpleasant facts," and George Levine, *The Realistic Imagination,* pp. 297–308, sees Ladislaw as the exponent of a kind of learning characterized by freedom and receptivity. It is interesting that Raffles, among other things, pretends to an education (ch. 41).

Chapter 41 of the novel is the deliberate introduction of a line of suspense, in the course of which we see a little more of Joshua Rigg—the least important stranger to Middlemarch—and a representative action of the new character, John Raffles, attempting to extort a little money from Rigg. There is a certain amount of exposition concerning the past relation of the two men and the tobacco shop belonging to Rigg's mother in a seaport town. The epigraph from the clown's song in *Twelfth Night*—"By swaggering could I never thrive, / For the rain it raineth every day"—describes Raffles, who is said to have "the air of a swaggerer" and wishes to pass as "having been educated at an academy." The complete song would seem to reflect on Raffles's aging, his unflattering sexual relation to Rigg's mother, and his propensity to drink. But all of the really useful exposition is compassed by the words at the opening and closing of the chapter that introduce the line of suspense, hint at the main action in which Raffles will be involved, and mysteriously concern writing. The opening paragraph is a single sentence informing us that Bulstrode and Rigg—now bearing the name Featherstone and occupying Stone Court—have in the course of business exchanged "a letter or two." The second paragraph consists of the following digression:

> Who shall tell what may be the effect of writing? If it happens to have been cut in stone, though it lie face downmost for ages on a forsaken beach, or "rest quietly under the drums and tramplings of many conquests," it may end by letting us into the secret of usurpations and other scandals gossiped about long empires ago,—this world being apparently a huge whispering-gallery. Such conditions are often minutely represented in our petty lifetimes. As the stone which has been kicked by generations of clowns may come by curious little links of effect under the eyes of a scholar, through whose labours it may at last fix the date of invasions and unlock religions, so a bit of ink and paper which has long been an innocent wrapping or stop-gap may at last be laid open under the one pair of eyes which have knowledge enough to turn it into the opening of a catastrophe. To Uriel watching the progress of planetary history from the sun, the one result would be just as much of a coincidence as the other. (ch. 41)

The digression is one of mock solemnity and superb irony, and of economy that can fully be appreciated only by reading *Felix Holt* and

Middlemarch entire. The subject, "the effect of writing," is developed by analogy between any scrap of paper and inscriptions in stone that through time may become archaeological discoveries, and by simultaneous comparison between writing and speech—specifically gossip or whispering. A quotation from Sir Thomas Browne's *Urne-Burial* announces the theme of time and accident, suggests the fragility of evidence for entire lifetimes in the past, and promises an exposition both scientific and fantastic.[50] As opposed to gossip then or now, writing may occur at one time and be read at another, and as evidence may therefore both conceal secrets and reveal them. With her fine metaphysical image of the whispering gallery George Eliot elaborates this difference: one can actually construct a reliable means to deliver gossip across a large space, as in a whispering gallery; paradoxically, the more permanent record of writing is subject over time to greater effect of chance. Cause and effect have long been featured in the novelist's moral and historical teaching, but the "curious little links of effect" preserving a decipherable stone or paper are oddly diminished; instead of a formidable operation of cause and effect it is the element of chance that brings access to information. The placing of the writing "under the one pair of eyes which have knowledge enough to turn it into the opening of a catastrophe" recalls precisely what happened in *Felix Holt*, in the elaborate series of chances that placed the appropriate bit of writing under Rufus Lyon's eyes; because the eyes are those of "a scholar" and the ancient writing may "unlock religions," a more immediate reference is to the wrong Key of Edward Casaubon. Reduction of "the secret of usurpations" to "other scandals" and the contrast of "long empires ago" with "our own petty lifetimes" have been implicit in the antiromantic thesis of George Eliot's realism since *Adam Bede*, but here the comparisons have to do with information and with writing in particular. In the full context of *Middlemarch*, moreover, we understand the comparison between evidence of use to archaeologists, who are third parties to usurpations and scandals of the ancient world, and evidence of use to

---

50 *Hydriotaphia: Urne-Burial, or, a Brief Discourse of the Sepulchral Urnes Lately Found in Norfolk* was published in 1658. George Eliot quotes from the first sentence of chapter 5, and her irony picks up from Browne's treatment of "these minor monuments." I wish to thank Gwin Kolb, Jr., for helping to identify the quotation; Robin Grey has pointed out to me that the entire paragraph is in the style of Browne.

blackmailers, who are third parties to stories of the more recent past. Both kinds of agents need only information to become informants.[51]

The comparisons ironically exalt blackmailers at the expense of scholars, in fact, but thus far the novelist is not telling what the low writing consists of. In her opening paragraph she has hinted that it is a letter, and in the closing sentence of the chapter she specifies "a letter signed *Nicholas Bulstrode,*" but this careful withholding of information through the course of the chapter later appears as still greater overstatement, since the paper does not turn out to be an incriminating letter at all, but merely evidence to Raffles's eyes—which "have knowledge enough," like the scholar's—that Bulstrode is in Middlemarch. The signature at the close no doubt suggests the real subject of the chapter, but the reader does not yet know enough of Bulstrode's past to connect it, even by analogy, to the sleazy past of the new character, Raffles. The digression itself contains a hint in the reference to Uriel, from whose perspective on the sun a catastrophe induced by a bit of paper and ink cannot be distinguished from a discovery important to history. The allusion to Uriel adumbrates a fall for someone, while in effect apologizing for the narrative suspense, since even angels lack foreknowledge of the plot. The archangel Uriel, stationed on the sun in *Paradise Lost,* encountered Satan on his way to earth and even pointed the way, because he could not penetrate Satan's intentions. The "false dissembler" goes unperceived:

> For neither Man nor Angel can discern
> Hypocrisy, the only evil that walks
> Invisible, except to God alone,
> By his permissive will, through Heav'n and Earth.[52]

51 Raffles quite professionally records information. He complains to himself, "Sometimes I'm no better than a confounded tax-paper before the names are filled in," and when he succeeds in recalling "Ladislaw," he "immediately took out his pocket-book, and wrote down the name, not because he expected to use it, but merely for the sake of not being at a loss if he ever did happen to want it" (ch. 53). George Eliot's own notebook gives a glimpse of his reasoning as a blackmailer in the early days: "He knew that the marriage was pending between Bulstrode & the widow York, & hence debated with himself to which of the two he should carry his information. He determined for Bulstrode, conjecturing that he should get more money there for silence than in the other direction for speech, & in no case should he lose the claim for speech ultimately." See "Quarry for *Middlemarch,*" in *Middlemarch,* ed. Bert G. Hornback, p. 633; Ms. p. 20.

52 *Paradise Lost,* III, 682–685.

Since Bulstrode is a hypocrite and one who expressly believes that he walks invisible by God's permissive will, the allusion seems pointed.

As we later understand, just because Bulstrode has continued to walk invisible, he has concluded that he is favored with a special Providence. When he first encounters Raffles in person, therefore, the difference between "spiritual relations and conceptions of divine purposes" and the prospect of public exposure of his story is marked:

> Five minutes before, the expanse of his life had been submerged in its evening sunshine which shone backward to its remembered morning: sin seemed to be a question of doctrine and inward penitence, humiliation an exercise of the closet, the bearing of his deeds a matter of private vision adjusted solely by spiritual relations and conceptions of the divine purposes. And now, as if by some hideous magic, this loud red figure had risen before him in unmanageable solidity,—an incorporate past which had not entered into his imagination of chastisements. (ch. 53)

Suddenly it is Raffles who is the devil, and it is clear why George Eliot has chosen Bulstrode as the exemplary victim of modern blackmail. Her purpose is not to whip a form of hypocrisy that is peculiarly distasteful to her, still less to belittle evangelical Christianity or its Puritan forebears. Rather, she writes as the novelist of a secular age, conscious of belief and unbelief. She chooses Bulstrode, in her own providential gesture as novelist, in order to argue that if divine Omniscience is no longer a plausible threat to behavior, then the fortuitous knowledge of blackmailers may take its place. Her choice of Bulstrode, with his outdated religious pretensions, may have been learned from Hawthorne's Puritan subjects; and the "loud red figure" of Raffles, who rationally conceived incorporates merely the "past," serves ambiguously as the Devil had served before him, both to persecute the victim and to share the blame.

Blackmailers, after all, can shore up the inward conscience with the outward demands of society: to be private is no longer, in the nineteenth century, assuredly to be alone with God, and therefore to be private is not wholly in the interest of society. "It was an hour of anguish for [Bulstrode] very different from the hours in which his struggle had been securely private, and which had ended with a sense that his secret misdeeds were pardoned and his services accepted. Those misdeeds even when committed—had they not been half sanctified by the singleness of his desire to devote himself and all he possessed to the furtherance of the divine scheme?" But the test of deeds and of devotion is no longer divine but social. Blackmail poses the threat of shame rather than conscience, and the threat therefore strikes deepest at the career that is a secular legacy of Puritanism: "For who would understand the work within him? Who would not, when there was the pretext of casting disgrace upon him, confound his whole life and the truths he had espoused, in one heap of obloquy?" (ch. 53). Later on, in a franker statement about Bulstrode's "misdeeds," a statement less in the indirect style, George Eliot will imply that a belief in Omniscience has never been a sufficient check to behavior, since many misdeeds are "like the subtle muscular movements which are not taken account of in the consciousness . . . and it is only what we are vividly conscious of that we can vividly imagine to be seen by Omniscience" (ch. 68). A blackmailer, as opposed to a personal conscience, usually hints pretty clearly what he has seen, and he may even exaggerate a little.

Chapter 41 does not yet give us Bulstrode directly, only the scrap of paper that Raffles uses to wedge his flask in its leather cover and on which he eventually discovers the name of the banker. The story we are given instead is that of Raffles, "a man obviously on the way towards sixty, very florid and hairy," who has become the second companion to the frog-featured woman who is Joshua Rigg's mother, a parasite of the tobacco shop and of the mother's income from the frog-faced son. George Eliot's original readers could not foresee the eerie resemblance to the short-lived ambition of Tracy in the tobacco shop of Hitchcock's *Blackmail;* and readers of *Middlemarch* for the first time still cannot foresee the parallel with Bulstrode's earlier life as the second husband to the pawnbroker's wife, whose daughter married the son of Casaubon's aunt; or the way in which Bulstrode has also thrived at the expense of an absent child, who became Will Ladislaw's mother. The air of prostitution, much filtered when Bulstrode's story is later given directly, is heavy in chapter 41. "Having made this rather lofty comparison" between ancient and modern inscriptions and their results, the narrator comes down, "I am less uneasy in calling attention to the existence of low people by whose interference, however little we may like it, the course of the world is very much determined." Something might be done "by not lightly giving occasion to their existence," she says—alluding to the sexual transaction that produced the "superfluity" who is Joshua Rigg. "But those who, like Peter Featherstone, never had a copy of themselves demanded, are the very last to wait for such a request either in prose or verse" (ch. 41). The riposte of George Eliot's own prose is very skillful, the play on "copy" bowing toward the preceding paragraph on "the effect of writing" but also glancing back to the "copy of himself" that Mr. Casaubon has not achieved, having "not yet succeeded in issuing copies of his mythological key" (ch. 29). But just as there is indignation about Casaubon's impotence beneath the surface of *Middlemarch*, there is scarcely concealed contempt for unattractive sexuality associated with the woman who is Rigg's mother and Raffles's paramour. The failure of monogamy and ugliness of motive parallel Bulstrode's history. After Raffles has returned to Middlemarch and begun to blackmail Bulstrode, the latter's past returns to him, "only the pleasures of it seeming to have lost their quality." The scathing commentary on low people in chapter 41 prepares for the sexual suggestion in the description of Bulstrode's terror: memory "smarting like a reopened wound," or "a still quivering part of himself, bringing shudders and bitter flavours and the tinglings of a merited shame." Bulstrode recalls privately "shrinking" from the very business of pawnbroking (ch. 61).[53] If there is a prostitute in Bulstrode's past, however, it is not a frog-faced woman but Bulstrode himself.

George Eliot is now working at a great distance from the initial experience of her own secret, the affair with Lewes and pseudonymous authorship; yet both kinds of secret are present when Raffles appears on the scene in *Middlemarch*. Though it is difficult to speak of shame in any form without recourse to sexual language, it is fair to say that disreputable sexual relations play a distinct part in the small group of characters around Raffles and in the group in Bulstrode's past, and therefore in Ladislaw's ancestry. More evidently the digression on writing in chapter 41, in the inscription in stone "which has been kicked by generations of clowns" but to the eyes of a scholar may "fix the date of invasions and unlock religions," recalls George Eliot's other secret. In the course of the Liggins episode in 1859 Charles

---

53 For George Eliot's revision of these lines in proof, see Jerome Beaty, "The Text of the Novel: A Study of the Proof," in *"Middlemarch": Critical Approaches to the Novel*, ed. Barbara Hardy, pp. 54–55.

Bray had defended C. Holte Bracebridge, the most officious investigator of the novelist's identity, on the ground that, as an archaeologist, Bracebridge was simply acting "in the way of his profession." George Eliot replied with acerbity, in the same letter in which she defended secrets and repudiated "the assumption of entire knowingness," that she was "not yet an 'archäological' subject."[54] The same spirit is apparent in the fine irony that compares the evidence of scholarship to the "bit of ink and paper" of use to a blackmailer. The digression that begins "Who shall tell what may be the effect of writing?" is her introduction of Raffles and his low relations. Insofar as the question is about the experience of writing, it is answered most fully in the chapter that immediately follows, which has nothing to do with Raffles or Bulstrode.

Chapter 42 addresses the nearness of Edward Casaubon's death, from Casaubon's own point of view. In an extended soliloquy, uncharacteristic of *Middlemarch*, he foresees Dorothea's marriage to Ladislaw; and the bitter part of Dorothea in this chapter is to discover the depth of her own resentment of her husband's alienation from her. Yet the background for these dramatic moments is authorship; and the cause of alienation is authorship, for it is Dorothea's opinion of him as a scholar rather than her possible unfaithfulness that Casaubon has come to fear. A fantasy of "triumphant authorship"—he is thinking of Carp and company—modulates toward the indignant prediction of Ladislaw's succession via the "jealousy and vindictiveness" of his situation as a writer. It is not primarily "the autumnal unripeness of his authorship," his failure to complete his work before now, that informs Casaubon's fears and poisons his relation to Dorothea, but an "uneasy susceptibility" inherent in "some kinds of authorship":

> Mr. Casaubon was now brooding over something through which the question of his health and life haunted his silence with a more harassing importunity even than through the autumnal unripeness of his authorship. It is true that this might be called his central ambition; but there are some kinds of authorship in which by far the largest result is the uneasy susceptibility accumulated in the consciousness of the author,—one knows of the river by a few streaks amid a long-gathered deposit of uncom-

54 To Charles Bray, 26 Sept. 1859, *G.E.L.*, III, 163–164 and n8; see chapter 6.

fortable mud. That was the way with Mr. Casaubon's hard, intellectual labours. Their most characteristic result was not the "Key to all Mythologies," but a morbid consciousness that others did not give him the place which he had not demonstrably merited,—a perpetual, suspicious conjecture that the views entertained of him were not to his advantage,—a melancholy absence of passion in his efforts at achievement, and a passionate resistance to the confession that he had achieved nothing.

Clearly such "kinds of authorship" attach to kinds of personality, as the syntax of the last sentence begins to insist. But the necessary condition of this terrible alienation is authorship itself: the distance between writer and readers, the divorce of intellectual effort and result. The subject here is a special form of consciousness, and it is not hard to guess that George Eliot is drawing partly on her own experience. In her following paragraph she translates susceptibility as "no security against wounds" (ch. 42).

Therefore the question addressed to writing when Raffles is first introduced to the novel, the subject of scholarship of the ancient past, and even the indirect allusion to urn-burial have to do also with the experience of Casaubon, he of the "lifeless embalmment of knowledge," whose own death is now rapidly approaching and who will attempt to affect the future through a codicil to his will.[55] Writing and scholarship are closely associated in *Middlemarch* with consciousness itself. Scholars cannot help but be aware of the sometimes tangential bearing of evidence upon the conclusions that they shape in narrative form, which are then published and await uncertain reception. Writers are engaged in a practice that is inherently discontinuous, acutely aware of the distance between inward feeling and the outward result of their being. The silence of the print culture is not pure silence but seething with information, and with attendant anxieties of inference and reputation. Hence the figure for Casaubon's "consciousness of authorship" draws briefly on geology to represent a temporal discontinuity—"one knows of the river by a few streaks amid the long-gathered deposit of uncomfortable mud." Note that the formation of consciousness can only be inferred from the evi-

---

55 The conjunction of Ladislaw's skepticism and Dorothea's knowledge spells disaster for Casaubon. His attempt to keep the two apart is similar in motive to Bulstrode's move against Raffles, and in both cases reputation suffers further from the attempt to save it. For Dorothea, the codicil itself becomes evidence of her husband's unworthiness.

dence, which is as scientific and as chancy as the evidence of inscriptions on stone or of ink on paper. The figure is mischievously oblique. What reader ever supposed that Casaubon's mind resembled a river? One knows there must have been a river, however, because an uncomfortable consciousness remains, just as one knows there have been authors when one finds a lot of print.

It is evident that "consciousness" is of increasing interest to George Eliot—she uses the word itself with increasing frequency in the later novels. By studying the projection and displacements of *Romola*, one can deduce that consciousness requires a degree of doubleness like that which the heroine regrets in Savonarola or contemns in Tito. Consciousness assumes identity of the self over time, yet a life that is in fact single and continuous cannot always see itself very well. Doubleness and discontinuity enable greater consciousness—once the connections have been made. And if consciousness does not develop of itself, shaming may contribute to the process: in *Felix Holt*, because of her secret past, Mrs. Transome has far more consciousness than Harold Transome, but "outside conscience" or shame comes to Harold's assistance. Vivid consciousness is likely to occur when a discontinuous life is revisited—when the life is not strung out year after year, as it were, but doubled back upon itself, year against year. Thus blackmailers may positively enhance consciousness. Of many implicit definitions of "consciousness" in George Eliot's later work, one of the finest—which brilliantly focuses all these considerations—is a striking image for Bulstrode's state of mind after the return of Raffles:

> Into this second life Bulstrode's past had now risen, only the pleasures of it seeming to have lost their quality. Night and day, without interruption save of brief sleep which only wove retrospect and fear into a fantastic present, he felt the scenes of his earlier life coming between him and everything else, as obstinately as when we look through the window from a lighted room, the objects we turn our backs on are still before us, instead of the grass and the trees. The successive events inward and outward were there in one view: though each might be dwelt on in turn, the rest still kept their hold in the consciousness. (ch. 61)

Such consciousness, superimposing "inward and outward" events and occluding a pastoral alternative, results in this case from the experience of being blackmailed.

Blackmail is the stuff of sensation novels, and it is no wonder that students of George Eliot have had difficulty in accommodating the story of Bulstrode to their interpretations of *Middlemarch*, which is nothing like a sensation novel as a whole. The first requirement of such accommodation is to accept Bulstrode's close relation to Lydgate, and by contiguities and partial analogies to other characters in the novel as well. Still, the manifest ambition of the novel to become an epic of society might seem to preclude such crass irony as may be imported by a ruinous bit of information. Like Fielding before her, George Eliot aspired to an epic representation of contemporary life, but her model was finally Dante's epic rather than Homer's. The historical particularity of Dante's characters appealed to her nineteenth-century sense of past and present. The urgency of his dead heroes' longing to establish a link with this world she reinterpreted as a common experience of discontinuity within the world. Her Casaubon identifies himself almost complacently as a ghost: "I feed too much on the inward sources; I live too much with the dead. My mind is something like the ghost of an ancient" (ch. 2). Fame is no less a need for Casaubon than it was for one of Dante's characters, and his apparent complacency turns to anguish as George Eliot enlarges his story and makes it representative of a modern experience of writing in which she shared. But for a character with one life irrevocably fixed in the past and another life in the present, she chose Bulstrode, and arranged things so that the information threatening Bulstrode's career threatened Lydgate's as well.

The Dantean model first inspired Mrs. Transome in *Felix Holt*, a woman whose history actually anticipates Lydgate's modern experience. Like Lydgate, Mrs. Transome "had been thought wonderfully clever and accomplished, and had been rather ambitious of intellectual superiority" in her youth; and she has since experienced "crosses, mortifications, money-cares, conscious blameworthiness" (ch. 1). Yet the promise of her youth is never given a chance to impress the reader, as Lydgate's impresses. It is he whose stature and whose punishment are most Dantean of all—though his life is scarcely as divided as Bulstrode's. The stories of Lydgate and Bulstrode together combine the pursuit of knowledge with the constraint of public opinion, in the one case elaborating the novelist's most careful study of the action of circumstances and in the other melodramatically and metaphorically demonstrating the effect of discontinuity, and of "successive events inward and outward" as they obstinately return from the window of a lighted room.

I 2

Blackmail and Estrangement

In the remarkable novel called *Daniel Deronda* the terror of being known intensifies, just when the wider project of knowledge is purposefully transformed as ideology. The titular hero of the novel, the only fiction by George Eliot besides "The Lifted Veil" expressly set in contemporary times, is the one character involved in all of the actions and themes of knowledge, but he is not consistently the center of dramatic interest. On the contrary, of the three main characters it is Gwendolen Harleth who occupies a center between Daniel Deronda and Henleigh Mallinger Grandcourt. The opening of the novel addresses very clearly this center since the heroine is watched, and to a surprising extent controlled, by Deronda at a crucial pause and departure from her engagement to Grandcourt. It is not finally possible to interpret George Eliot's last novel, equal to *Middlemarch* in its range of interest for the modern reader, by dividing it along fixed lines of plot, character, or style.[1]

The inspiration of Dante is still more evident in *Daniel Deronda* than in the previous two novels, and allusions to *The Divine Comedy*

---

1 In dismissing Deronda's part on all three grounds, F. R. Leavis, *The Great Tradition* (1948; rpt. New York: Anchor, 1954), pp. 101–108, reiterated many early judgments of the novel. In Henry James's *"Daniel Deronda:* A Conversation," which originally appeared in the *Atlantic Monthly* in 1876 and which Leavis reprinted, the speaker Constantius distinguished in the novel "the figures based upon observation and the figures based upon invention." Constantius's judgment obviously weighed against the latter, otherwise called "the Jewish burden of the story" and "the cold half of the book." By renaming the novel "Gwendolen Harleth," Leavis became the boldest detractor of "the bad side," but of course Deronda must remain a principal character even in a novel named for Gwendolen.

support an emphasis on guilt and punishment. For Gwendolen "the process of purgatory" begins in this world (ch. 54); when she is brought to the strand in Genoa, after the death of Grandcourt, it is "as if she had waked up in a world where some judgment was impending, and the beings she saw around her were coming to seize her" (ch. 55). But more pervasively, the novel's veiled and separate lives resemble Dante's worlds of the dead, in which the souls are detached from present time, hidden from normal observation, yet subject to particular passionate intensities. *Daniel Deronda* posits a world of individual histories and of estrangement in the questions with which it opens: "Was she beautiful or not beautiful? and what was the secret of form or expression . . . ? Why was the wish to look again felt as coercion, and not as a longing in which the whole being consents?" The themes of watching, concealment, and coercion pervade the entire novel, to the extent that they finally subsume Deronda's other silent question about Gwendolen, "Was the good or the evil genius dominant . . . ?" (ch. 1). It seems that George Eliot disapproves of her heroine and intends to punish her, partly by making her love Deronda and not allowing her to have him; but the question of good or evil is moot once the inner experience of Gwendolen and the conditions of her life have been decided. These are not conditions of death, as in Dante, but conditions of publicity that result in estrangement.

It is the experience of "coercion" that attests the degree to which individuals are estranged in *Daniel Deronda*. There is also "longing"—the longing of Deronda and of Mirah for lost family, the spiritual longing of Mordecai. But the degree to which power has supplanted love in even the most intimate relations is emphasized throughout. Grandcourt, whose name itself signals the main imposture among the characters, is the epitome of the life devoted to power and not much else. The marvelous little episode with the two dogs, Fluff and Fetch, demonstrates all the reader really needs to know about the personality of the master, and this episode is capped by one of George Eliot's neatest ironic generalizations about the perception of such a man by his public: "Grandcourt kept so many dogs that he was reputed to love them" (ch. 12). That Gwendolen permits herself to become such a dog provides the center of interest for most readers of the novel, but of course Gwendolen herself conceives of most relations in terms of power, lords it over her family, and ironically anticipates "the power to reject" Grandcourt—"there was a pleasure in reckoning up the advantages which would make her rejection splendid" (ch. 11). *Daniel Deronda* has a sharper satirical edge than *Middlemarch*, and it can hardly escape notice that the pairing of the supposed lovers is actually applauded by Gwendolen's uncle, the rector, who sees in the match "increasing power, both of rank and wealth, which may be used for the benefit of others" (ch. 13). In crasser terms George Eliot sketches in the analogous motives of Mirah Lapidoth's father, who literally intended to sell his girl into prostitution after exploiting her on the stage. Even the benign liberal Sir Hugo Mallinger has not been averse to exercising a little power of mystification upon his supposed illegitimate son, Daniel, and the physically and spiritually attractive Daniel has admitted power over both Mirah and Gwendolen. Deronda is very circumspect about this power—for different reasons he is afraid of coercing the feelings of either woman—but it is power nonetheless. One has to remember that the habit of rescuing people in such a world is itself indicative of power. Mirah, driven to London and despair by her nasty father, he fishes up from the Thames; but once Mirah has made her debut at Lady Mallinger's musical party, Deronda's thoughts turn to Gwendolen: "his memory went back, with some penitence for his momentary hardness, over all the signs and confessions that she too needed a rescue, and one much more difficult than that of the wanderer by the river" (ch. 45). Earlier, in one of those confessional episodes, when she has hinted at her feelings of "hatred and anger," it is for Deronda "as if he saw her drowning while his limbs were bound" (ch. 36)—a thought that links Gwendolen to the wanderer by the river and Gwendolen's confessor to the eventual drowning of Grandcourt.[2]

No one in *Daniel Deronda* is entirely immune to the practices of watching and concealment, which are "felt as coercion." No one can fully afford to refrain from these practices or to ignore them. "The beginning of an acquaintance whether with persons or things," according to one of George Eliot's chapter epigraphs, "is to get a definite outline for our ignorance." She subsequently elaborates the point by asking, "who can all at once describe a human being?" and replying, "even when he is presented to us we only begin that knowledge

---

2 Barbara Hardy, *The Novels of George Eliot* (1959; rpt. London: Athlone, 1963), pp. 124–125, relates these rescue operations to "the theme of the lost and the found."

of his appearance which must be completed by innumerable impressions under differing circumstances. We recognize the alphabet; we are not sure of the language" (ch. 11). Her metaphor holds up a meaningless assortment of signs and prescribes a long course of study, in which the initial unfamiliarity can be overcome by mastery of a written language. The very difficulty of the business discourages acquaintance and implies the ease with which acquaintance is balked. The self-regarding individuals of modern times are mysterious to one another, and power consequently accrues to those who can know without being known. Grandcourt, in this sense, is the master of those who know, and who use their power—but he is not alone in this respect, as the opening scene of the novel foretells. Later Gwendolen will think it "futile and irrelevant to try and explain that Deronda too had only been a monitor,—the strongest of all monitors" (ch. 36). Both monitors attain their power over her by watching, while guarding themselves against observation.

Thus it happens that some of the dramatic scenes in the novel consist of the characters watching other characters who are watching them, conscious of being watched and looking for opportunities to communicate unobserved.[3] The long chapters devoted to such maneuvering among Gwendolen, Grandcourt, and Deronda at Topping Abbey (chs. 35 and 36) anticipate the drama of knowing, of penetrating and responding to the thoughts of others, perfected by Henry James. Grandcourt is the star, and undoubtedly the person who most enjoys himself, if any can, by turning countercommunication into a game. "Grandcourt had a delusive mood of observing whatever had an interest for him, which could be surpassed by no sleepy-eyed animal on the watch for prey. . . . an incautious person might have supposed it safe to telegraph secrets in front of him, the common prejudice being that your quick observer is one whose eyes have quick movements." The reference of the metaphor is to the older, vis-

---

3 So much watching of others accounts for the prominence of faces in *Daniel Deronda*, and probably also for the gallery of familiar paintings that George Eliot uses to convey to the reader an idea of the appearance of various characters. Faces and portraits, and mirrors, express but also conceal thought. On faces in the novel see E. S. Shaffer, *"Kubla Khan" and "The Fall of Jerusalem": The Mythological School in Biblical Criticism and Secular Literature, 1770–1880* (Cambridge, England: Cambridge University Press, 1975), pp. 254–255; on the portraits, see Hugh Witemeyer, *George Eliot and the Visual Arts* (New Haven: Yale University Press, 1979), pp. 63–66, 92–104.

ual device of telegraphing rather than the electric, though people do send telegrams by wire in *Daniel Deronda*—a contemporary development that perhaps releases their inhibitions and makes them more wary at the same time. George Eliot's metaphor here is still focused on natural history, with the effects of predacity close at hand. But she does not neglect the quick mental operations of her human species. "If Grandcourt cared to keep any one under his power, he saw them out of the corners of his long narrow eyes, and if they went behind him, he had a constructive process by which he knew what they were doing there. He knew perfectly well where his wife was, and how she was behaving" (ch. 35). He does not regard himself as a jealous husband; he is too confident of knowing, and too content with the equation of knowledge and power, to be alarmed; and he is not much interested in whether or whom his wife loves. Later on, the narrator seems less certain on the score of jealousy, but she stands by her original assessment:

> No movement of Gwendolen in relation to Deronda escaped him. He would have denied that he was jealous; because jealousy would have implied some doubt of his own power to hinder what he had determined against. That his wife should have more inclination to another man's society than to his own would not pain him: what he required was that she be fully aware as she would have been of a locked handcuff, that her inclination was helpless to decide anything in contradiction with his resolve. (ch. 48)

There has been a progress, nevertheless, from the earlier interception of signals at Topping Abbey to this more nearly total absorption with his power. It is now that Grandcourt decides to inform Gwendolen that he knows, not about Deronda, but about her knowledge of Lydia Glasher.

Concealment, the principal defense against observation, is every bit as pressing a need for the characters of *Daniel Deronda* as watchfulness. Of the three main characters, Deronda needs to conceal the least, perhaps, and Gwendolen the most—an inverse measure of the relative power of the three. Deronda is against concealment on principle: embarrassment as a young boy about his own ignorance of his birth has caused him "to regard concealment as a bane of life, and the necessity of concealment as a mark by which lines of action were to be avoided." Yet Deronda is forced to abandon this principle almost as soon as it is set down for him—its pronouncement turns out to be George Eliot's apology for what her hero is about to do. He is committed to making inquiries, into the whereabouts of Mirah's mother and brother, that may involve him in concealment. After meeting the pawnbroking Cohens in London, he finds himself "half inclined to decide that he would not increase his knowledge about that modern Ezra," because he fears the latter may be Mirah's brother of the same name. But this stance (in order to have nothing to conceal, do not inquire) would be entirely unproductive: Deronda's rule against secrets must be compromised. By the end of the chapter he is engaged in a little private espionage at the Cohens; and undecided on the further question whether "to try and determine the best consequences by concealment, or to brave other consequences for the sake of that openness which is the sweet fresh air of our moral life" (ch. 33). Despite the narrator's editorializing on behalf of openness, Deronda's meditation carries him a great distance from the attitude toward openness and concealment implied in *Adam Bede*. By the end of the novel, as Gwendolen's lay confessor, the hero has entered fully into the most dreadful secret of all, her murderous intentions toward her husband. With the best of motives, he will have watched, talked, and pried his way into this secret, much as if he were inventing psychoanalysis in the Vienna of the eighteen-nineties.

When Deronda contemplates achieving "the best consequences by concealment" and approaches the Cohens under false pretenses, he is not engaged in a defensive action or succumbing to a temptation. His purpose is to find out whether the Cohens are related to Mirah before they find out what he wants to know. He has adopted a rational stratagem of investigation. The justification rests with the possibility that they might lie to him for some reason of their own, and in any number of possible deterrents to successful inquiry. Deronda also wants to find out, without their knowing his purpose, whether the Cohens are worthy of Mirah—so that he can protect his client, even against her wishes if necessary. That is less of a rational stratagem, more of an attempt to keep power in his own hands. Where knowledge is power, concealment follows as the night the day. The dynamics of investigation are much the same in the sinister hands of Grandcourt, who watches when he pleases and says little to anyone, and whose character is daringly established by the narrative of his first dialogue with Gwendolen—his first dialogue in the novel, in fact.

The novelist punctuates each one of Gwendolen's remarks with a unique "Pause" in parentheses, together with a phrase indicating *her* thoughts in the interim before Grandcourt replies (ch. 11). The pause, of course, is due to Grandcourt, but his thoughts are not given. From the silences of their first conversation to the silences of their last voyage together, Grandcourt strains every ounce of power from concealment. The sturdiest bit of information he has against Gwendolen is the fact that she knew about his affair with Mrs. Glasher, and this information he saves carefully, as trump for any trick she may try to win. Grandcourt and Deronda may differ in personality and moral character, but the same reserve is necessary to both when it comes to the need and use of information.

Gwendolen is a party to this first concealment. It is not as if either of the Grandcourts had offered to discuss the Glasher affair when they married. Subsequently his knowledge of what she knows becomes the worst possible case for Gwendolen. The letter that she receives with the diamonds, and which she burns on her wedding night, haunts her marriage, and not merely because she has wronged Lydia Glasher and her children. "The definite dread was lest the veil of secrecy should fall between her and Grandcourt, and give him the right to taunt her. With the reading of that letter had begun her husband's empire of fear." Here the narrator thrusts in the appropriate dramatic irony: "And her husband all the while knew it" (ch. 35). But the irony is also poetic justice, because Gwendolen also habitually conceals her thoughts in order to maintain control. In fact, when the woman who proves to be Grandcourt's mistress first addresses her a note, offering to meet her at the Whispering Stones to tell her something that may be of interest to her (and damaging to Grandcourt—a bit of indirect blackmail), Gwendolen is shocked but also pleased, because she does not really wish to marry anyone and because possessing a secret may give her power. "Her mind gathered itself up at once into the resolution that she would manage to go unobserved to the Whispering Stones; and thrusting the letter into her pocket, she turned back to rejoin the company, with that sense of having something to conceal which to her nature had a bracing quality and helped her to be mistress of herself" (ch. 14).

Concealment does not have to be deliberate. Rather, it has become endemic, second-nature to the cultivation of knowledge. A phenomenological survey would easily persuade us that *Daniel Deronda* is a dramatization of knowledge in several respects: the knowing of persons, the perception of relations, the realization of collective aims. The dramatization of such a state of affairs involves the novelist in concealment, even when she seems about to reveal the characters' thoughts: "Now, did he suppose that she had not suspected him of being the person who redeemed her necklace?" (ch. 29). The novel is full of questions of what A knows about B, and how B can know whether A knows—questions often narrated indirectly and never answered. The underlying drama characterizes friendly as well as hostile relations, and some of the lesser participants in the various actions, who seek to communicate and who mean well, find themselves steeped in secrecy of one kind or another. The narrator makes us repeatedly aware of the deceits and reticences by which Mrs. Davilow tries to mediate between her daughter, Gwendolen, and her uncle, half-sisters, and others. Sir Hugo Mallinger is kind and forthcoming, except on the subject of Daniel's birth. The hero eventually learns that "the secrecy" was his mother's wish (ch. 49), but Sir Hugo has played his part so well that "he had learned to hate secrecy about the grand ties and obligations of his life,—to hate it the more because a strong spell of interwoven sensibilities hindered him from breaking such secrecy" (ch. 19). The drama of knowledge and concealment in this action of the novel sorts uneasily with the melodrama of lost heirs. When Deronda meets his mother face to face in Genoa, he is happy to carry away knowledge of the one secret that now matters to him—that he is a Jew; for the Princess Halm-Eberstein, nee Charisi, is the supposed villain of the piece. The actress has concealed her son's Jewishness and lied about him with abandon. When her father's friend Joseph Kalonymos inquired, she told him that her son was dead. To Deronda's partially sincere offer to live near her, she replies, "I have a husband and five children. None of them knows of your existence" (ch. 51). These quite stupendous concealments among members of the same family in the novel are something I shall come back to, but notice that even Mirah Lapidoth hesitates to tell her brother of their father's return and "instinctively" has kept Gwendolen's visit to her a secret from Deronda (ch. 52). In the largest dramatic construction of the novel George Eliot probably intended—though she may not have succeeded in conveying to the reader—a contrast between these private concealments and her new positive vision of knowledge transformed as ideology. Yet even the grand Jewish design of the novel remains more than half mysterious.

Most of this concealment and underlying conflict generates surprisingly little heat, even in the episodes stirred by melodrama. The relative lack of warmth in *Daniel Deronda* can be felt by comparing it to *The Mill on the Floss,* and not necessarily to the early life of Maggie and Tom but to the debate between Maggie and Stephen at the close. Individuals are more isolated in *Daniel Deronda* and the substance of their lives is thinner. The setting is partly urban, and there is little attachment to place.[4] Personal relations are detached, and efforts are bent on testing these relations by study and concealment. But at the same time there seems to be less and less to study or conceal. The loveless contentions of knowing are oddly barren of thought, if thought is meaningful reflection on the world outside the self. The colossal boredom of Grandcourt, closely seconded by Gwendolen's ignorance, is the best evidence of this. The point is made that Grandcourt is utterly uninterested in public affairs, but the person who is interested, Sir Hugo—while not a fool like Mr. Brooke[5]—is primarily a foil for Deronda. A skeptical reader might complain that the young hero is himself bored—has no idea what to do with himself without the visionary role that Mordecai has prepared for him. Deronda's interest in Gwendolen is less than passionate and not altogether compassionate either; it is more nearly a fascination reflecting his own uncertainty and sense of abandonment. In *Daniel Deronda* only two characters are entirely free from the general malaise, and they are Herr Klesmer and his pupil Miss Arrowpoint. The novel makes much of music, and the degree to which characters are susceptible to music is a pretty good measure of their

4 Early in the novel George Eliot explicitly argues the importance of attachment to place as a kind of protection against "the future widening of knowledge": "A human life, I think, should be well rooted in some spot of a native land, where it may get the love of tender kinship for the face of the earth, for the labours men go forth to, for the sounds and accents that haunt it, for whatever will give that early home a familiar unmistakable difference amidst the future widening of knowledge . . . At five years old, mortals are not prepared to be citizens of the world, to be stimulated by abstract nouns, to soar above preference into impartiality . . . The best introduction to astronomy is to think of the nightly heavens as a little lot of stars belonging to one's own homestead." It is as if she were reconstructing her own childhood and the continuity of experience traced in *The Mill on the Floss.* But such experience of place "had been wanting in Gwendolen's life" (ch. 3).

5 U.C. Knoepflmacher, *Religious Humanism and the Victorian Novel* (Princeton: Princeton University Press, 1965), p. 125, notes the resemblance when he calls Sir Hugo "a Mr. Brooke come into power." But Sir Hugo is warmly portrayed and far more sensible than Mr. Brooke in *Middlemarch*—a difference that gives more weight to the criticism of liberal thinking in *Daniel Deronda.*

happiness and even of their authority. Culture mediated by music is a kind of knowledge still unspoiled.[6]

To bring out the sterility of the personal relations involving Gwendolen Harleth the novelist portrays a world of decadent honor. For the chapter in which Grandcourt deliberately fondles his lap dog and kicks (vicariously) his spaniel, she employs as an epigraph Hotspur's lines from *Henry IV*:

> O gentleman, the time of life is short:
> To spend that shortness basely were too long,
> If life did ride upon a dial's point,
> Still ending at the arrival of an hour.

There can hardly be an epigraph in George Eliot's last novels employed more facetiously than this, yet it introduces an important theme. The chapter is the second in which Grandcourt appears, and in it, after he disposes of the dogs, he announces to Lush that he intends to marry Gwendolen—"the other girl," as he says, and not the heiress, Miss Arrowpoint (ch. 12). The idea of the bored Grandcourt as Hotspur is grotesque yet just. His "gratification of mere will" becomes more and more intractable as the action proceeds and is "sublimely independent of definite motive" (ch. 14). He is piqued and challenged by Gwendolen's willfulness, and their courtship is propelled by fruitless contests of pride bolstered by the hope of inflicting humiliation. This is nothing other than a debased struggle of honor, from which love is conventionally excluded. Whereas for Hotspur honor itself was a passion, "Grandcourt's passions were of the intermittent, flickering kind: never flaming out strongly." As George Eliot accommodates the individual to the type, according to her usual humor, the imagery becomes daring even for her:

> a great deal of life goes on without strong passion: myriads of cravats are carefully tied, dinners attended, even speeches made proposing the health of august personages, without the zest arising from a strong desire. And a man may make a good appear-

6 Edgar Rosenberg, *From Shylock to Svengali: Jewish Stereotypes in English Fiction* (Stanford: Stanford University Press, 1960), 171–172, discusses the concentration of musical talent among the Jews, as contrasted with the Gentiles of the novel. He forgets Catherine Arrowpoint, but she of course is both pupil and bride to the musician Klesmer. On the latter, see Gordon S. Haight, "George Eliot's Klesmer," in *Imagined Worlds: Essays on Some English Novels and Novelists in Honour of John Butt*, ed. Maynard Mack and Ian Gregor (London: Methuen, 1968), pp. 205–214.

ance in high social positions,—may be supposed to know the classics, to have his reserves on science, a strong though repressed opinion on politics, and all the sentiments of the English gentleman, at a small expense of vital energy. Also, he may be obstinate or persistent at the same low rate, and may even show sudden impulses which have a false air of dæmonic strength because they seem inexplicable, though perhaps their secret lies merely in the want of regulated channels for the soul to move in,—good and sufficient ducts of habit without which our nature easily turns to mere ooze and mud, and at any pressure yields nothing but a spurt or a puddle. (ch. 15)

In vulgar translation, such a man does his best to piss on others and befouls himself in the process. George Eliot's moralizing of the case inadvertently suggests Grandcourt's base need for shaming others and for degrading life.

At the other extreme, Deronda is supersensitive to the feelings of others, especially women, presumably because of his youthful embarrassment and confusion about his birth. He has also his snobbery and fears about people like the Cohens, however, and is not altogether inhuman. It is Gwendolen who most nearly represents a modern amoral life of pride and fear of humiliation. Because she is inexperienced and a woman, she is the victim of Grandcourt, but the action largely follows from the symbiosis of the two. Gwendolen is not apparently more capable of love than he; her "physical repulsion" to love-making is remarked early (ch. 7), and she is "passionately averse" to Rex Gascoigne. Her "Pray don't make love to me! I hate it" (ch. 8) registers so strong a note that it cannot be excluded from the causes of her hysteria on her wedding night. Like Grandcourt with other men, moreover, "Gwendolen was not a general favourite with her own sex." She is fond of the "homage" of men, but "women did not give her homage" (ch. 11). She is terrified of shame, and the felt "humiliation" of her circumstances (ch. 21) gives Grandcourt his opportunity. Notwithstanding her remorse, of which the narrator makes so much, Gwendolen is above all concerned to escape "indignity" and to avoid making "a spectacle of herself" (ch. 44). Grandcourt could hardly ask for a better match.[7] Even when he is at the

---

7 For comparisons of Gwendolen and Grandcourt, see Jerome Thale, *The Novels of George Eliot* (New York: Columbia University Press, 1959), pp. 127–134; and Judith Wilt, *Ghosts of the Gothic* (Princeton: Princeton University Press, 1980), pp. 213–218.

point of blackmailing her into further submission and is about to inform her that in the case of his death she can live in the house that
Lydia Glasher inhabited, Gwendolen changes her perfume to one
that he likes, for "she liked all disgust to be on her side" (ch. 48). In
the aftermath of Grandcourt's drowning and at the height of her remorse, she desperately asks Deronda, "You will not say that I ought
to tell the world?" (ch. 56) and again, "You will not say that any one
else should know?" (ch.57). Gwendolen is George Eliot's stunning
representation of a peculiarly neutral and unabashed feeling for appearances. She is not the self as encountered in Dante or in Shake-
speare after all, but the self as encountered in Erving Goffman.[8] The
nineteenth-century novelist is not as prepared as the twentieth-
century sociologist to reduce the self entirely to a performance,
but Gwendolen herself has reached this modern accommodation
of the code of honor. Going to church, for example, "was not markedly distinguished in her mind from the other forms of self-presenta-
tion" (ch. 48). No character of George Eliot except Tito Melema so
readily equates self-worth with outward performance. Gwendolen
makes Nicholas Bulstrode seem a highly moral (or immoral) person.

A society of talented performers, each out-guessing the others,
brings rather more pressure to bear on the marriage relation—that is
why the Princess Halm-Eberstein's first marriage broke up, so to
speak. Notice in the first place that the two young heroines of *Daniel
Deronda*, contrasted in so many ways, both make an appearance in
the novel like women on billboards. It is not only Gwendolen Harleth—"really worth some expense," as her uncle says (ch. 3)—who is
seen, gaped at, admired like a race horse and so forth, but also the true
heroine, Mirah Lapidoth. Both young women are striking objects for
the eye and ear, and the latter is a professional performer who has
acted on the stage. According to most precedents of the English
novel, that experience ought to disqualify her as a heroine. George
Eliot labors to establish both her experience and her purity: while
Gwendolen hated men, Mirah hated the theater. But to a surprising
degree both heroines are display pieces, as Hans Meyrick's carica-

---

8 See *The Presentation of the Self in Everyday Life*, rev. ed. (New York: Anchor,
1959). In *Stigma: Notes on the Management of a Spoiled Identity* (Englewood Cliffs,
N.J.: Prentice-Hall, 1963), esp. pp. 75–80, 96–97, and in *Frame Analysis: An Essay on
the Organization of Experience* (New York: Harper, 1974), pp. 109–110n44, Goffman takes up the subject of blackmail from the same general point of view.

tured admiration for both Mirah and Gwendolen—whom he calls "the duchess"—makes clear.[9] Meyrick's superficial feelings (he is not a very good painter) are supposed to set off Deronda's depths, but it is still hard to erase the impression of Mirah as an exhibit: "Deronda felt that he was making acquaintance with something quite new to him in the form of womanhood" (ch. 20). In Gwendolen, similarly, Grandcourt meets something quite new to him. Both men go out of their way to rescue the women they marry from a crisis of humiliation, Deronda with the best will in the world and Grandcourt with the intent to work his will. Each expects to assimilate the sexually attractive object to his own social position. One shuns violence and the other is piqued by it, but both have every reason to anticipate submission. According to Mrs. Meyrick, it is Mirah's nature "to submit" (ch. 20). Gwendolen "did not mean to submit" (ch. 21), but she can be forced. In marriage the men seem to adopt toward these women what is sometimes called the missionary position.

At the end of the novel Deronda marries Mirah Lapidoth and they depart for the East, to see what can be done to bring Mordecai's ideas to fruition. Grandcourt marries Gwendolen Harleth early on and ends his life in the waters of the Mediterranean Sea. I am ignoring the obvious and intended differences of the two marriages and four characters, and exaggerating some initial parallels, in order to emphasize the unprecedented exposure of both heroines in *Daniel Deronda*. Exposure and submission are the elements that reflect most harshly the society depicted in the novel and explain the inward desperation of one of the pairs. While one marriage is relegated to the vague future, the other is pursued to its deadly conclusion. If there is one Victorian plot that openly supports the argument of Sandra Gilbert and Susan Gubar about secret female aggression in the novels of women writers, it is the story of Gwendolen Harleth.[10] The failure of Mirah

9 In "The Decomposition of the Elephants: Double-Reading *Daniel Deronda*," *PMLA*, 93 (1978), 215-227, Cynthia Chase examines the subversive effect of Meyrick's letter to Deronda at the time of the latter's meeting with his mother in Genoa. I cannot agree that "the letter functions as a deconstruction of the novel" (p. 215), but George Eliot obviously employs Meyrick as a light dramatic foil to Deronda, as when he banters about "theology, of course," as the ostensible subject of the hero's conversation with Gwendolen (ch. 45). Chase's analysis shows that the subversion of the hero's position cuts deeper than George Eliot is probably aware, but that is quite common for dramatic writers of powerful intelligence.

10 *The Madwoman in the Attic* (New Haven: Yale University Press, 1979), esp. pp. 495-499. Judith Wilt, *Ghosts of the Gothic*, pp. 191-196, views the murderous marriage as machinery imported from gothic romance.

to murder anyone is startling in its way. She is frightened to death by her father, who is little better than a pimp, but remains kind to him. She has more talent than Deronda, but accepts his protection. Deronda's sensitivity to Mirah's gratitude and reluctance to take advantage of it do not alter the fact that he possesses the advantage. The son deserted by his actress mother is somehow superior to the daughter stolen and put up for sale by her father. Though *Daniel Deronda* is hardly a feminist tract, important feminist arguments can be derived from it.

Only a novelist who was both an intellectual and a woman, perhaps, could appreciate to the fullest extent the pressures modern society was beginning to place on the intimacy of two persons: as an intellectual she experienced the sense of isolation characteristic of communicating through writing, and as a woman she was far more constrained by her relation to George Henry Lewes than he was. In general, modern society has placed immense pressure on the insular family as a refuge and as a substitute for other relations. The life-and-death nature of dyadic relationship was explained, not in sexual but in arithmetical terms, by Georg Simmel at the end of the nineteenth century. A group of three or more persons can survive, as a group, the loss of one; but for the group of two, each is essential to survival. Hence the anxiety of termination is heightened for a partnership of two, and this claim of irreplaceability makes disappointment of either party tantamount to failure of the relationship. It is the "all or nothing" aspect of marriage, concentrated by the attenuation of other human ties, that potentially feeds the fantasy of murder for either sex, whether in retaliation for dependency or merely for disappointment.[11] Women are not different in this regard, but historically more narrowly confined to marriage than men.

Most readers agree that among the most powerful representations in George Eliot's novels are her studies of marital estrangement. F. R. Leavis confirmed this response by arguing that the Grandcourt marriage possessed a moral and psychological depth that eluded Henry James when he came to imitate it in *The Portrait of a Lady*. The derivative novel, according to Leavis, was more taken up with the reve-

11 See *The Sociology of Georg Simmel*, ed. and trans. Kurt H. Wolff (1950; rpt. New York: Free Press, 1964), pp. 122–126. "Dyad" is the translator's equivalent for *Zweierverbindung*. For specific Victorian lore connecting marriage with death, see Alexander Welsh, *The City of Dickens* (Oxford: Clarendon, 1971), pp. 180–212.

lation than with the substance of the estrangement.[12] But this criticism of James may have the effect of calling attention to the sensational element in his source, the process of knowing and concealment, in *Daniel Deronda*. We may say that marriage ought to be a refuge from impersonal society, that even Bulstrode is able to retreat to the compassionate pity of Harriet Bulstrode's care. But it is not always so; the marriage cannot be in and of itself immune to the fear of opinion in the wider culture. Though it ought to be a refuge from fear, fear may be too strong for it. George Eliot took great pains to show the consistency of Gwendolen's fate and of Grandcourt's, and of habits of mind that do not change "precisely at the point of matrimony" (ch. 48). It is by means of their marriage that she demonstrates her understanding of what it is like to be subject to blackmail.

Since marriage affords the opportunity of sharing secrets, and exclusive sharing is one of its chief pleasures, secrets withheld by husband or wife from each other become a focus of estrangement. Consciously withheld knowledge always risks revelation, and the revelation then destroys confidence. "A crisis which suspended affection" occurs in *Silas Marner* when Godfrey Cass decides to tell Nancy that Eppie is his child (ch. 18). Bitter sensations of hurt and disappointment, of violation even, are experienced when Tertius or Rosamond Lydgate acts independently of the other's knowledge in *Middlemarch*. Lydgate receives a cruel rebuff when "his superior knowledge and mental force" were "simply set aside on every practical question" by his wife (ch. 58), who countermands his orders behind his back with a kind of stubborn assumption that she will not be found out. But there is a rather different threat to marriage from secrets that are shared by husband and wife and concealed from everyone else. One of the two may then betray, in reality or imagination, the secret of both; and to threaten this betrayal and to fear it are conditions of blackmail. In *Romola* Tito Melema hides all sorts of activities—sexual, political, and self-aggrandizing—from his wife, and this much concealment itself poses the risk of estrangement. But Tito also fears, more as a danger to himself than as a threat to their relation, Romola's knowing too much. He fears her, in other words, in the same way he fears Baldassare, as one whose real or imagined knowledge is a threat to him. "The terrible resurrection of secret

12 Leavis, *The Great Tradition*, pp. 101-154.

fears, which if Romola had known them would have alientated her from him forever, caused him to feel an alienation already begun between them,—caused him to feel a certain repulsion towards the woman from whose mind he was in danger" (ch. 27). George Eliot clearly understands that the mere supposition about what is going on in the other's mind introduces a feeling of alienation and repulsion. The "danger" inheres in any intimacy that takes a defensive posture toward the world. One need only ask what binds couples together to realize that it is not only the needful pleasures of sharing but the danger of breaching confidence. Close personal attachments are incrementally supported by every confession or shared embarrassment that is dangerous or troublesome to avow publicly. It is obvious whom one should most fear or resent as a blackmailer when such attachments fail: a relatively small variation of trust between two persons plummets them into the unprotected state of society that has increased their need for intimacy in the first place. The failure of confidence within the private relation is a disaster further symptomatic of public conditions with the same tendency.

"The Lifted Veil" is a story of estrangement of this special kind. The narrator, Latimer, potentially knows whatever is hidden, whether in future events or other persons' minds. The exception, at first, is the fair Bertha, "whose present thoughts and emotions were an enigma to me amidst the fatiguing obviousness of the other minds around me," but this ceases to be the case once his passion for her "was completely neutralized by the presence of an absorbing feeling of another kind" associated with the death of his father. As long as Bertha is strange to Latimer, he is "under her power"—the narrative makes no reference to love—but the distraction of his father's death alters this condition. From that time Latimer "saw all round the narrow room of this woman's soul" and scarcely liked what he saw. Bertha in due course begins to suspect his power of reading her thoughts. "She began to be haunted by a terror of me, which alternated every now and then with defiance. She meditated continually how the incubus could be shaken off her life,—how she could be freed from this hateful bond to a being whom she at once despised as an imbecile, and dreaded as an inquisitor" (ch. 2). Over a period of seven years Latimer loses sight of Bertha's thoughts again, but not before learning that she hopes he will commit suicide. Before his death he hears from her dead maid (sic) that Bertha has planned to poison him. Whatever its personal significance for George Eliot (which I cannot fathom), this is a story of intimacy sickened by knowledge, of a marriage that is a casualty of Latimer's special powers of mind. Latimer's initial interest in Bertha, who was his brother's fiancée, is stimulated by curiosity, as Grandcourt is stimulated by curiosity, about what goes on behind the face of a handsome woman. In the end Bertha designs to kill the husband who knows what she knows, as Gwendolen designs to kill.

The justly famous story of this pattern of estrangement is that of the Casaubons in *Middlemarch.* We have already seen how Edward Casaubon's pursuit of knowledge is constrained by opinion, personified by Pike and Carp, and how his identity has been threatened by the conditions of authorship. As early as the wedding journey to Rome it appears that Dorothea Casaubon, instead of being a comfort to a husband whose mind was "weighted with unpublished matter," has become the opposite, "a spy watching everything with a malign power of inference." Her offer to assist him in any way she can, to help write "the book which will make your vast knowledge useful to the world," stirs signs of anger in Casaubon and prompts a little speech on the "mirage of baseless opinion" and "impatient scorn of chatterers." Suddenly "Dorothea was not only his wife: she was a personification of that shallow world which surrounds the ill-appreciated or desponding author." The "close union" of the wedding journey "was more of a subjection than he had been able to imagine," and Casaubon is forced to ask himself, "Instead of getting a soft fence against the cold, shadowy, unapplausive audience of life, had he only given it a more substantial presence?" (ch. 20). For a man so utterly given to the distances of reading and writing, the intimacy of two persons is tantamount to public exposure.

The perceived threat from Dorothea remains a constant of the Casaubons' marriage. While Will Ladislaw—that other "emissary," as he is called by Mr. Hawley—is in the offing at Rome and later at Lowick, Casaubon is not so much jealous of Will as fearful of Dorothea's opinion. Once his illness has occurred, "his intellectual ambition which seemed to others to have absorbed and dried him, was really no security against wounds, least of all against those which came from Dorothea." The language is vaguely sexual (with male penetration reversed) and the claim with respect to jealousy similar to that made about Grandcourt. What Casaubon "was jealous of was her opinion, the sway that might be given to her ardent mind in its judgments, and the future possibilities to which these might lead her" (ch. 42). This self-construed victim of intimate knowledge is not prepared to kill his ostensible blackmailer and thus get free, but his dying wish to contain her knowledge is strong, and he drafts a codicil of his will that inadvertently slanders his wife and himself. To exact an "indefinite promise of devotion to the dead" (ch. 50) is a kind of attempted murder of the living; and the case can also be put the other way around, as Robert Kiely has suggested in arguing that the threat of Dorothea's knowledge is what kills Casaubon.[13] Bulstrode's sudden disgrace, in the same novel, almost seems preferable to Casaubon's "perpetual suspicious conjecture that the views entertained of him were not to his advantage" (ch. 42), yet Bulstrode too might well be wary of a wife who "believed that her husband was one of those men whose memoirs should be written when they died" (ch. 36). Bulstrode, in fact, "was rather afraid of this ingenuous wife." "The loss of high consideration from his wife, as from everyone else who did not clearly hate him out of enmity to the truth, would be as the beginning of death to him" (ch. 61). In the steadily generalizing narrative of *Middlemarch*, discovery threatens everyone. Pride of knowledge is naive, and humiliation common, as of boys and girls shamed into learning at school, or husbands and wives suddenly surprised by one another. "We are all humiliated by the sudden discovery of a fact which has existed very comfortably and perhaps been staring at us in private while we have been making up our world entirely without it" (ch. 35).

Gwendolen, in *Daniel Deronda*, is a woman who has experienced her share of the common humiliations, both those brought on by circumstances and those brought on by pride. But two severe humiliations of discovery are planned for her deliberately by others, the first by Lush operating on his own and the second by Grandcourt with Lush as his instrument. Attempting to forestall a marriage to Grandcourt, Lush prompts Lydia Glasher to confront Gwendolen with the

13 "The marriage to Dorothea . . . exposes Casaubon's closed system to light, curiosity, and life, thereby turning it to ashes and killing the scholar. Marriage, the most obvious of Victorian emblems of concord and exchange, is the 'wreck' of Casaubon's society of one." See "The Limits of Dialogue in *Middlemarch*," in *The Worlds of Victorian Fiction*, ed. Jerome H. Buckley, Harvard English Studies, 6 (Cambridge: Harvard University Press, 1975), p. 111.

knowledge of her prior affair and her four children. Gwendolen ha. instinctively felt an antipathy for Lush, and when she consents to marry Grandcourt despite this knowledge (the subject that is not spoken of between them), her one condition or request is that he get rid of his follower (ch. 27). Symbolically, then, though Gwendolen has not suspected him, Lush stands for "the secrets that made her wretched." When he reappears, she is still ignorant of his role but experiences something "like a disagreeable sensation" that he "knew all about her husband's life." By this time, in effect, she is kept in check by blackmail even though Grandcourt has not made his move: in contrast to Mirah, who submits to duty, "what she submitted to could not take the shape of duty, but was submission to a yoke drawn on her by an action she was ashamed of, and worn with a strength of selfish motives that left no weight for duty to carry" (ch. 45). Her moodiness under this yoke, or fear of exposure for what she has done, inspires her husband to threaten greater humiliation: "he wished Gwendolen to know that before he made her an offer it was no secret to him that she was aware of his relations with Lydia." And for this purpose he resolves to employ Lush on his own behalf, not less because he is aware of Gwendolen's antipathy to his underling. "To Grandcourt it did not even occur that he should, would, or could write to Gwendolen the information in question; and the only medium of communication he could use was Lush, who, to his mind, was as much of an implement as pen and paper" (ch. 48).

Blackmail of wife by husband thus begins in earnest, at an appropriate distance, in chapter 48 of *Daniel Deronda*, and the wife's intention to murder is fixed thereafter. The chapter begins with an ironic summary of Grandcourt's scorn for all the issues of the day— "Schleswig-Holstein, the policy of Bismarck, trade-unions, household suffrage," and the like. "But Grandcourt within his own sphere of interest," we are assured, "showed some of the qualities which have entered into triumphal diplomacy of the widest continental sort." The overkill associated with this domestic Realpolitik he displays in a couple of speeches to Gwendolen after her visit to Mirah. He pretty well sees through the purpose of her visit, and here the narrator compares him to a colonial administrator: "Every slow sentence ... had a terrific mastery in it for Gwendolen's nature. ... If this white-handed man with the perpendicular profile had been sent to govern a difficult colony, he might have won reputation among his ontemporaries. He had certainly ability, would have understood that it was safer to exterminate than to cajole superseded proprietors . . ." George Eliot thus elevates, amid ambiguous company, the husband whose "habitual wont was to put collision out of the question by the quiet massive pressure of his rule" (ch. 48), and then turns over the rest of the diplomatic affair to Lush.

The reader can now for the first time appreciate fully the need for Lush in the novel. He is an inspired creation, the perfect complement to Grandcourt's power and just recognizable as the low type of the blackmailer. Lush has the essential shamelessness for that role, and the shabby pretensions to dignity. He is generally like Raffles but fits into the scene better, notably because he is useful, "as pen and paper," to the secretive Grandcourt. When the two have nothing better to do, which is much of the time, they watch each other. The master has always the comfort "that he might kick Lush if he chose," and their personal familiarity is jaded but mildly erotic. Lush was the younger man's "travelling companion" and "passed for a scholar once" (shades of Baldassarre). Having known Grandcourt for fifteen years and lived off him, he requires not more than "the odour of departed learning" to be useful. Such is the scribe, or "prime minister in all his more personal affairs" (ch. 12), whom Grandcourt commissions to tell Gwendolen that he is aware of what she is aware of, and to summarize the will he has drawn up against his death. Lush does his job:

> "You met a lady in Cardell Chase, if you remember, who spoke to you of her position with regard to Mr. Grandcourt. She had children with her,—one a very fine boy."
> Gwendolen's lips were almost as pale as her cheeks: her passion had no weapons,—words were no better than chips. This man's speech was like a sharp knife-edge drawn across her skin; but even her indignation at the employment of Lush was getting merged in a crowd of other feelings, dim and alarming as a crowd of ghosts.
> "Mr. Grandcourt was aware that you were acquainted with this unfortunate affair beforehand, and he thinks it only right that his position and intentions should be made quite clear to you. . . ." (ch. 48)

The crowd of ghosts recalls the "ghostly army" of opinion that seconds Grandcourt's power (ch. 36). Gwendolen is so terrorized that she can hardly touch or read the paper Lush has drawn up summarizing the will. "She had not prepared herself to hear that her husband knew the silent consciousness, the silently accepted terms on which she had married him" (ch. 48).

Lush for his part "really did not want her to be worse punished." Like a professional blackmailer, his interest is in keeping his clients just short of desperation. "He was glad to think that it was time to go and lunch at the club, where he meant to have a lobster salad" (ch. 48). Just as Hitchcock's blackmailer Tracy is pretty well content with the best cigar in the house, Lush's demands for himself are limited to comforts near at hand—as his name perhaps suggests. After he is first introduced in the novel, the narrator remarks that "if his puddings were rolled towards him in the dust, he took the inside bits and found them relishing," and he goes off in that scene to play "a good hour on the violoncello" in order to soothe his feelings (ch. 12). After doing Grandcourt's dirty work for him, Lush is not heard of in the novel except for a sentence or two: "Lush was not there" on the yacht in the Mediterranean (ch. 54). But he is, of course, merely an instrument that is "useful" to Grandcourt. When he returns from his brief exile at the start of the marriage, George Eliot describes him, in another marvelous figure, *as* the cigar:

> There may come a moment when even an excellent husband who has dropped smoking under more or less of a pledge during courtship, for the first time will introduce his cigar-smoke between himself and his wife, with the tacit understanding that she will have to put up with it. Mr. Lush was, so to speak, a very large cigar. (ch. 45)

13

Murdering Grandcourt

The most studied use of Dante in George Eliot's last novel occurs in the opening of chapter 54, the chapter in which Grandcourt insists on his wife's sailing with him in the bay of Genoa. The allusion is to la Pia, in Canto V of the *Purgatorio*, whose husband, in the novelist's words, "feeling himself injured by her, took her to his castle amid the swampy flats of the Maremma and got rid of her there." In Dante's narrative the soul of la Pia merely asks the poet that she be remembered and states, in effect, that her husband knows what happened to her. George Eliot takes over one of the most beautifully understated histories of *The Divine Comedy* and boldly claims our sympathy for "the better known Gwendolen, who, instead of being delivered from her errors on earth and cleansed from their effect in purgatory, is at the very height of her entanglement in those false meshes which are woven within more closely than without, and often make the inward torture disproportionate to what is discernible as outward cause." The poet's commentators, as it happens, have been unable to identify la Pia with any certainty—hence "the better known" heroine whom the novelist has presented. George Eliot egregiously stretches the resemblance between her married couple and Dante's by reversing the roles of male and female in the presumed murder; yet the reversal is not such a gross distortion as it might appear to less sensitive readers than she. Dante grants la Pia six lines of speech and no narrative introduction or explanation: the wife's reticence apparently absolves the husband and preserves their marriage, or renders it indifferent who killed whom. As the novelist remarks in her commentary, "we may infer with some confidence that the husband had never been a very delightful companion," and "in relieving himself of her he could not avoid making the relief mutual" (ch. 54). The positions of Grandcourt and his wife are similarly interchangeable in *Daniel Deronda* as a whole. By insisting upon Gwendolen's feelings of guilt, George Eliot comes close to absolving Grandcourt of blame; yet murdering Grandcourt, as is generally the case with murdering a blackmailer, would seem to most readers partially justified.

The character of Gwendolen Harleth evolves from earlier characters of George Eliot. In her mirror-glimpsed importance, her excessive will and imperfect understanding, her cold beauty and inability to love, and her estrangement from her husband, she is a woman something like Rosamond Vincy—if one can imagine a Rosamond with a sense of humor and outward daring. In her relation to Deronda she is more like Esther Lyon, overawed by a hero whom the novelist seems to take more seriously than many of her readers can. A sense of something or someone missing from her life, she shares with the superficially very different Romola. Her vanity and capacity for murder are at least as developed as the same qualities in Hetty Sorrel; and still further back, she resembles another young person with a concealed dagger in her possession, Caterina Sarti of "Mr. Gilfil's Love Story," whose abortive attempt at murder proves that aggression in heroines was not exactly a new possibility for George Eliot. But in interpreting the canon of such a novelist it is not safe to draw dividing lines according to sex. The too handsome Tito Melema lies somewhere behind Gwendolen Harleth, the sensations of a Casaubon being watched and questioned by his spouse are familiar to her, and most important, her main action in *Daniel Deronda* recalls that of Bulstrode in *Middlemarch*.[1] Like Bulstrode praying for Raffles's death, Gwendolen the unbeliever longs for the death of her tormentor: "If it had been any use, I should have prayed—I should have prayed that something might befall him. I should have prayed that he might sink out of my sight and leave me alone." Like Bulstrode, moreover, she thinks so hard on the desired event that she succeeds in her wish. "That was in my mind—he would come back. But he was gone down again, and I had the rope in my hand—no, there he was again—his face above the water—and he cried again—and I held my

---

1 Leslie Stephen, *George Eliot* (London: Macmillan, 1902), p. 186, saw the resemblance of Gwendolen to Bulstrode as well as to Caterina.

hand, and my heart said, 'Die!'—and he sank" (ch. 56). That Grand-court suffers a drawn-out, willed death similar to that of Raffles is evident; that he is a blackmailer, more insidious than Raffles, needs to be spelled out a little more fully. In *Daniel Deronda* the fear of opin-ion penetrates the marriage relation and stirs a violent response; in a hidden part of the heroine's mind, the estrangement is total; and an-other sort of fear, or guilt, must be nurtured to counter the fear of opinion.

Bulstrode is not as subject to guilt as Gwendolen, for he has his special idea of Providence and is not so alone as she. Just before the drowning, Gwendolen "was afraid of her own wishes . . . was afraid of her own hatred." The thought of Deronda, a kind of substitute for God, might "save her from acting out the evil within. And yet quick, quick, came images, plans of evil that would come again and seize her in the night, like furies preparing the deed that they would straight-way avenge" (ch. 54). The narrator's language for plans of murder, immediately before the boating accident that concludes the marriage, echoes the unusual language employed to describe Gwendolen's real-ization that Grandcourt intends to propose to her, after she has learned of his affair with Lydia Glasher: "Here came the terror. Quick, quick, like pictures in a book beaten open with a sense of hurry, came back vividly, yet in fragments, all that she had gone through in relation to Grandcourt," and that she wished she "had never known" (ch. 26). In this famous simile terror takes the quality of rapidly reviewed information from a book, though one would con-ventionally suppose that pictures in books were a slow and safe means of communication. For the fear of approaching violence the narrator further alludes to the Furies of classical myth, and this allu-sion echoes her summary of the "hysterical violence" of the Grand-courts' wedding night, when Gwendolen received the diamonds and accusing letter from Mrs. Glasher: "in some form or other the Furies had crossed his threshold" (ch. 31). These Furies were doubly am-biguous, for "some form or other" might be either woman in Grand-court's life or both, and it is "his" threshold they have passed, even though Gwendolen takes their punishment more to heart. At Genoa, apparently, the Furies are still pursuing both parties to this marriage of concealment and of threatened revelation, "preparing the deed that they would straightway avenge." Both consummations of the mar-riage, the sexual act and the violent end, are tactfully elided in the narrative, though the second is later recounted by Gwendolen to Deronda. Whereas Nicholas Bulstrode could find refuge in his marriage, Gwendolen Harleth is punished by hers from the start, and by guilt thereafter.

The possibility of an "infelonious murder" was apparent from Gwendolen's strangling of a canary in her childhood (ch. 3), but the reader is only gradually allowed to become aware of the full extent of violence in her thoughts. At Topping Abbey she tells Deronda that she is frightened of herself and alludes generally to feelings of "hatred and anger" (ch. 36). Before their next encounter in London the narrator writes more freely of "moments of secret hatred" (ch. 44), and Gwendolen's inward opposition to Grandcourt becomes the major line of suspense in *Daniel Deronda*—more so than the question of Deronda's birthright, in fact, because Gwendolen's thoughts are persistently narrated and at the same time concealed. Once Lush has conveyed Grandcourt's message about what he knows, in chapter 48, these thoughts become far more explicit. "What release, but death? Not her own death. . . . It seemed more possible that Grandcourt should die,—and yet not likely. The power of tyranny in him seemed a power of living in the presence of any wish that he should die." Despite the power of tyranny, Grandcourt does die—whether from accident or Gwendolen's desire. That his danger from the latter is suddenly made real by his decision to inform his wife of what he knows is evident from the narrator's repeated insistence that he is making a mistake: the method that he chooses to exact further submission from his wife is "less ably calculated" than his speeches; some experience of the depth of Gwendolen's remorse "could have saved him from mistake." The narrator further remarks the "stupidity" that results from "want of sympathy," and quips that "Mephistopheles thrown upon real life, and obliged to manage his own plots, would inevitably make blunders" (ch. 48). If Grandcourt blunders, it is hard to see how, unless it is by driving his wife to the point where she is certain she wants him to die. The chapter closes upon his announcement that he is taking her yachting in the Mediterranean.

Not counting the intervening chapters in which Deronda meets his mother by appointment in Genoa, Grandcourt has only one more chapter to live—to live in "do-nothing absolutism" on the yacht. And "had Grandcourt the least conception of what was going on in the breast of this wife?" The narrator replies generally in the negative

283

and uses the occasion to reveal to the reader more of Gwendolen's thoughts than hitherto.

> Some unhappy wives are soothed by the possibility that they may become mothers; but Gwendolen felt that to desire a child for herself would have been consenting to the completion of the injury she had been guilty of. She was reduced to dread lest she should become a mother. It was not the image of a new sweetly budding life that came as a vision of deliverance from the monotony of distaste: it was an image of another sort. In the irritable, fluctuating stages of despair, gleams of hope came in the form of some possible accident. To dwell on the benignity of accident was a refuge from worse temptation.

The narrative is still ominously indefinite, but the rare allusion to child-bearing triggers the now unmistakable suggestion of murder. In the paragraph that immediately follows, the desire is said to be rooted in fear rather than aggression:

> the intensest form of hatred is that rooted in fear, which compels to silence and drives vehemence into a constructive vindictiveness, an imaginary annihilation of the detested object, something like the hidden rites of vengeance with which the persecuted have made a dark vent for their rage, and soothed their suffering into dumbness. Such hidden rites were in the secrecy of Gwendolen's mind, but not with soothing effect,—rather with the effect of a struggling terror. Side by side with the dread of her husband had grown the self-dread which urged her to flee from the pursuing images wrought by her pent-up impulse. The vision of her past wrong-doing, and what it had brought on her, came with a pale ghastly illumination over every imagined deed that was a rash effort at freedom, such as she had made in her marriage.

Censuring "a rash effort at freedom" would seem to mirror the moral world of *The Mill on the Floss*, in which rebellion had to be contained and ended, except that here the imagined means include murder. The long indirect meditation returns to murder and recalls the scene of gothic terror early in the novel, in which the paneling at Offendene sprang open and revealed the painting of a dead face and fleeing figure:

> her vision of what she had to dread took more decidedly than ever the form of some fiercely impulsive deed, committed as in a

dream that she would instantaneously awake from to find the effects real though the images had been false: to find death under
her hands, but instead of darkness, daylight; instead of satisfied
hatred, the dismay of guilt; instead of freedom, the palsy of a
new terror,—a white dead face from which she was forever trying to flee and forever held back. (ch. 54)

Without question her escape is to take the form of murder, and not
some lesser dash for freedom of the kind that might make Gwendolen
appear ridiculous or a loser. Two obvious considerations, however—
that the death when it comes is at least partly accidental, and that
Gwendolen has apparently experienced "dismay of guilt" since the
days before she met Grandcourt—argue that this whole line of suspense in the novel has more to do with psychological guilt than with
the kind that would land the heroine in an Italian jail.

There is a significant imbalance to the moral valuation of estrangement and death in *Daniel Deronda*. The focus on Gwendolen's state
of mind—with omissions largely dictated by suspense—helps the
reader to side with her against Grandcourt, who acts without warning either his wife or the reader. Grandcourt is cold and deceptive, a
disaster in store for any woman, but in weighing Gwendolen's consciousness and studying the management of guilt, George Eliot
scarcely brings the evil of Grandcourt back into the equation. No
matter how hatefully he behaves—and he is a thoroughly convincing
villain—his behavior apparently does not weigh against, or justify,
Gwendolen's desire to kill him. The reader would be pleased to hold
his head under water for any length of time, but the author never
ventures to say that this is what he deserves. She demonstrates
Grandcourt's ruthlessness but does not judge him as she judges
Gwendolen, because she wishes to concentrate and not dilute her
study of the heroine's fear of shame and discovery of guilt. This is the
action of *Daniel Deronda* much celebrated by Leavis and many other
critics since the time it was first published; but as Calvin Bedient has
protested, George Eliot plays down the injury Gwendolen has done
to herself in marrying Grandcourt, exaggerates the injury she has
done to Lydia Glasher, and in assessing blame tends to forget her
own explicit commitment in *The Mill on the Floss* to "the special circumstances that mark the individual lot."[2] Put another way, it might
be said that the novelist takes Grandcourt's and Glasher's wickedness

2 *Architects of the Self* (Berkeley: University of California Press, 1972), pp. 63–66.

for granted but insists far more on Gwendolen's wickedness, by elaborating only her state of mind. Then, to redress the balance of poetic justice, she kills the eminently deserving Grandcourt herself.

A second way of explaining the imbalance in this narrative is to see Grandcourt, despite—or because of—his magnificent characterization as an inhuman person, a typed character destined for ritual killing as a blackmailer. "Such hidden rites were in the secrecy of Gwendolen's mind," the narrator tells us of terror and vengeance. George Eliot's main interest, and that of the reader, is in Gwendolen's mind. Grandcourt is secondary, and can be described from the outside. But Grandcourt's particularly insidious knowledge is now lodged in the mind to be studied and makes its difference there. Killing the one who put it there is like killing the undesirable truth, killing her mistake, killing the past. There is no actual murder, after all—if we can trust Gwendolen's account of the drowning, told after the fact to Deronda. Yet the suspense is concentrated on the drowning; more is finally made of the murderous wish than the wrong to Lydia Glasher; and far more is made of both than of the wrong Gwendolen has done to herself by marrying Grandcourt. For all her contrition and need to confess, Gwendolen gives Deronda only the sketchiest representation of her encounter with the mother of Grandcourt's children (ch. 57). In marked contrast, she spells out in detail the near experience of murder (chs. 56 and 57), and even beforehand she has hinted more often to him of her murderous wish than of the wrong she has done. In brief, the ritual of killing Grandcourt predominates in the narrative because it has the power of representing and disposing of these other wrongs.

One has to try to understand this ritual and why, in George Orwell's terms, murdering a blackmailer "doesn't count" as other murders count.[3] In the first place, killing a blackmailer has the undoubted virtue of shutting his mouth or halting his pen for good. It is a practical way to bring relief from impending shame, when shame is unbearable, as it is for Gwendolen. Even if he has not and may never tell anyone the secret, the blackmailer himself knows, as Grandcourt knows and Lush knows. If he has boasted that he is the only person who knows (and a professional blackmailer needs to claim this just to go into business), the practical usefulness of getting rid of him is so

3 See chapter 1, note 13.

much more obvious. In addition, since the blackmailer has threatened his victim, her anger and resentment can be satisfied by attacking him in return. This thought inspires more fear, and even justifies the blackmailer killing the blackmailed, as in a regular feud. The thought of Grandcourt's death "would not subsist" for Gwendolen: "it turned as with a dream-change into the terror that she should die with his throttling fingers on her neck avenging that thought" (ch. 48). The nightmare of reciprocation, and the means of death spontaneously imagined by Gwendolen, recall the fatal embrace of Tito and Baldassare in *Romola*. Such deaths do not count as other murders count because the blackmailer has threatened the reputation and moral being of his victim, and because by the time the ritual has run its imagined course, the two are as one person.

Symbolically, another range of motives comes into play. Killing the blackmailer is like expunging information, undoing the past, reversing wrongdoing, expressing disdain instead of fearing it. Some excellent reasons for killing a blackmailer, both practical and symbolic, apply equally to the death of informers, who also rely upon a "ghostly"—and not so ghostly—army of public condemnation of their victims. But strictly speaking an informer does not threaten to inform—he is either about to do so or may already have done so. More subtle reasons apply to the death of blackmailers, in whose true interest it lies *not* to inform on anyone but only to be in a position to do so. The blackmailer forgoes even that unpleasant moral advantage boasted of by informers, because he does not align himself unequivocally with public condemnation. He holds out hope of preventing, or at least postponing, condemnation by concealing his client's case from public knowledge. In return he proposes to institutionalize a shared personal knowledge from which he can profit, in the form of a gain in property, sexual advantage, or increased submission to him. Killing the blackmailer has the practical motive, then, of stopping payment and also the social motive, not applicable to killing informers, of attacking someone who professes neither private nor public loyalty to anyone. Additional symbolic motives follow from the exclusive personal confidence into which the blackmailer, uninvited, has entered. By a number of inconsistent projections, such as most people are capable of, the secret sharer can secretly be used to represent and to punish an undesired self—so that it is possible to imagine being blackmailed and to project one's unease on the blackmailer. As a portent of public condemnation, the blackmailer is like a bad conscience; killing him is getting rid of the bad conscience. As a tolerator of wrong and an encourager of concealment, the blackmailer is like a weak conscience, and killing him is a way of coping with weakness. Neither Grandcourt nor Lush intends to inform against Gwendolen or to destroy her reputation. To bring her to heel it is enough to let her know that Grandcourt shares her secret. The blackmail is a "mistake" on Grandcourt's part, because it determines his wife to hope for his death. It would be too lucky if he should simply die on his own, she feels, and hence she begins to intend his death. But Grandcourt's death would importantly bring a "double deliverance," from his tyranny and her injuring of Lydia Glasher. "The thought that his death was the only possible deliverance for her was one with the thought that deliverance would never come,—the double deliverance from the injury with which other beings might reproach her and from the yoke she had brought on her own neck" (ch. 48).

The relationship of Gwendolen and Grandcourt and the death of the latter pose a solution to the moral problem of the continuity of the self over time. George Eliot has never believed in deliverance from injuries done to others: "it can never be altered," as Gwendolen says of the drowning itself in *Daniel Deronda* (ch. 56). But in probing more urgently what the equally skeptical Herbert Spencer called "a Moral Therapeutics,"[4] she began to make bolder use of the blackmail relation that had teased her imagination since the invention of "Brother Jacob." Though she has not surrendered the doctrine of moral consequences, she now seriously wishes to describe what it is like to survive the infliction of wrong upon others. The result is an imaginative shifting of responsibility to the thoroughly expendable blackmailer. When Maggie Tulliver prayed for "patience and strength" to live out her life at the end of *The Mill on the Floss* (bk. VII, ch. 5), her prayers were answered by the flood and the drowning of herself and Tom. Gwendolen longs for the "double deliverance" of Grandcourt's death and intends personally to survive. As Joan Bennett comments on the drowning in *Daniel Deronda*, " 'It can never be altered'—that is a theme that runs through all George

4 *Social Statics* (1850; rpt. New York: Schalkenbach Foundation, 1954), p. 54. For this and other Victorian attitudes on the impossibility of mending wrongs, see Alexander Welsh, *The City of Dickens* (Oxford: Clarendon, 1971), pp. 101–117.

Eliot's novels, 'what's done cannot be undone,' but nowhere else has she raised the problem of responsibility in this deeply perplexing form."[5]

Still a third reason why the wickedness of Gwendolen looms so much larger in the narrative than the wrongs done to her is the role George Eliot conceives for Deronda. Grandcourt's acts do not score against him as they ought, and his ritual killing comes to signify more than his life signifies, because Deronda is to count most of all. The plot demands the substitution of one kind of "monitor" for the other, of a therapist who comes to be worshiped for a husband secretly hated and drowned, and of the act of confession for the fear of blackmail. Both Grandcourt and Deronda have carefully designed roles to play, and if the one character seems more successfully drawn than the other, it is partly because he is drawn from the outside, partly because villainy is easier to put down than goodness is to build up, and partly because of the originality of what George Eliot was trying to do with Deronda. Like Gwendolen herself, Deronda has forebears, in such characters as Philip Wakem, Felix Holt, and others in the earlier novels.[6] But his role in *Daniel Deronda* grows from the same deep conception as Grandcourt's, the general pattern of watchfulness and concealment, the power of concentration on another person's mind. That his relation to Gwendolen resembles that of a psychotherapist is very apparent to twentieth-century readers. It is not surprising to us that Gwendolen thinks, "I wish he could know everything about me without my telling him" (ch. 35), or that a transference of affection leads her to love the man from whom she seeks direction. Nor does it surprise us that a perceptive and sympathetic person should listen patiently to so many inchoate confessions, or calm her with assurances that she has not murdered anyone (chs. 56 and 57). What may be surprising is that this modern role parallels and rivals the role of the blackmailer in *Daniel Deronda*.

Gwendolen is the study of both Grandcourt and Deronda. They both might be said to penetrate her "keen remorse" (ch. 36), though

5 *George Eliot: Her Mind and Her Art* (1948; rpt. Cambridge, England: Cambridge University Press, 1962), p. 194.

6 Cf. Barbara Hardy, *The Novels of George Eliot* (1959; rpt. London: Athlone, 1963), p. 57: "The hero as mentor recurs throughout the novels, beginning with Tryan, in *Janet's Repentance*, and ending with Daniel Deronda."

the purpose of one is to subdue her and the wish of the other is to
help her. In this novel suffused with relations of knowing and concealment, and with power exercised by these means, the heroine has
dreaded Deronda's knowledge even before she has learned to dread
Grandcourt's. Though it was not the former's intent to respond in
kind to the "coercion" he felt in her glance at Leubronn (ch. 1),
nothing could be better calculated to take advantage of her embarrassment than his anonymous return of the necklace she has pawned.
By the time she meets him again, after her engagement to Grandcourt, "her anger towards Deronda had changed into a superstitious
dread,—due, perhaps, to the coercion he had exercised over her
thought." "And superstitions," the narrator puts in, "carry consequences which often verify their hope or their foreboding" (ch. 29).
Hope comes to predominate in Gwendolen's moves toward Deronda
in the course of the novel, but the hope is propelled by fear. To fear is
Gwendolen's nature, and when she comes to dread not only her husband but her growing impulse to kill him, she deliberately tries to
think of Deronda: "she had learned to see all her acts through the impression they would make on Deronda. . . . He seemed to her a terri-
ble-browed angel from whom she could not think of concealing any
deed so as to win an ignorant regard from him" (ch. 54). Afterward
she fears that he will abandon her unless she tells him "the exact
truth" at last (ch. 56).

When Grandcourt blackmails his wife in chapter 48, Deronda
plays his part. The long chapter describes several encounters and is
narrated from a constantly shifting point of view (even paragraphs of
Daniel Deronda have sometimes this quality of rapid movement, as if
straining to bring all the lines of action and of consciousness together). Gwendolen visits Mirah Lapidoth in order to assure herself
that the singer is not Deronda's mistress, as Grandcourt has implied.
The hero is there in the next room, reading Hebrew with Mordecai,
and the women leave him undisturbed; but the visit precipitates
Grandcourt's terrific speech and his move against Gwendolen by
means of Lush. The success of that move depends on the wife's not
breaking out of the marriage and braving the scandal that the husband implicitly threatens. The power of Deronda, both the image
of their relation if she were separated from her husband and his
judgment of her, works in conjunction with Grandcourt's blackmail:

And always among the images that drove her back to submission
was Deronda. The idea of herself separated from her husband
gave Deronda a changed, perturbing, painful place in her consciousness: instinctively she felt that the separation would be
from him too, and in the prospective vision of herself as a soli-
tary, dubiously regarded woman, she felt some tingling bashful-
ness at the remembrance of her behaviour towards him. The
association of Deronda with a dubious position for herself was
intolerable. And what would he say if he knew everything?

Before the end of the chapter she is determined to meet with Deronda
again, and for the first time makes an appointment with him to call at
her own house in London. She wants to ask him, without making her
meaning too clear, what she can do to prevent herself from getting
"worse." It is the therapist's opportunity, in effect, to prevent murder: "the feeling Deronda endured in these moments he afterwards
called horrible. . . . How could he grasp the long-growing process of
this young creature's wretchedness?—how arrest and change it with
a sentence?" The advice that he is about to give her—"Confess
everything to your husband; leave nothing concealed" (ch. 48)—is so
hopelessly wrong that it could only drive Gwendolen to greater desperation. But before Deronda can utter these words, Grandcourt has
deliberately returned to the house.

It goes without saying that Grandcourt's influence is malevolent
and Deronda's benevolent: Gwendolen is blackmailed by one and
goes to confession to the other. But it is instructive to see that the two
relations are functionally similar, much as the roles of blackmailer
and detective tend to converge in Hitchcock's *Blackmail.* Blackmailers and confessors offer to help manage secrets and to shield the
secrets from wider human knowledge. The blackmailer performs this
service for his own advantage, but not exclusively so, since it may be
worthwhile for his victim to pay him something. The confessor seeks
to benefit his client, but again not exclusively, for in these secular
times he usually receives a fee for his services or receives psychic
payment—just as Deronda "liked being near" Gwendolen (ch. 48).
Blackmailers and confessors nevertheless represent more general
opinion than their own, else they would have no purchase on the
minds of those they hope to influence. Toward the end of *Daniel
Deronda*, but before the hero painfully breaks the "transference" (as
well as the "countertransference") with Gwendolen by informing

her that he is engaged to marry Mirah, George Eliot generalizes from the specific case to the importance of confession in a secular society:

> Would her remorse have maintained its power within her, or would she have felt absolved by secrecy, if it had not been for that outer conscience which was made for her by Deronda? It is hard to say how much we could forgive ourselves if we were secure from judgment by another whose opinion is the breathing-medium of all our joy,—who brings to us with close pressure and immediate sequence that judgment of the Invisible and Universal which self-flattery and the world's tolerance would easily melt and disperse. In this way our brother may be in the stead of God to us, and his opinion, which has pierced even to the joints and marrow, may be our virtue in the making. (ch. 65)

This statement touches on important differences between confession and blackmail. The "judgment of the Invisible and Universal" significantly differs from that of public opinion, the force of which is here denied altogether by equating it with "the world's tolerance." It matters what the person chosen as confessor thinks and believes: he or she should not be a mere window for public opinion. Nonetheless, that person becomes, as a blackmailer insists on becoming, a sort of exclusive bargaining agent for "outer conscience."[7] Throughout her sessions with Deronda after the drowning of Grandcourt, Gwendolen has pleaded with him for secrecy. "You will not say that I ought to tell the world? . . . I must tell you; but you will not say that any one else should know" (ch. 56). Deronda has implicitly accepted this condition all along, he has reassured her about it several times, and he now solemnly confirms their agreement for the last time: "We agreed at Genoa that the burthen on your conscience is what no one ought to be admitted to the knowledge of. The future beneficence of your life will be best furthered by your saving all others from the pain of that knowledge" (ch. 65).

It might be charged that Gwendolen has not learned a thing. Her anxious desire for concealment is as strong, or stronger, after her experience as before. The husband who made her suffer for it is dead, and the man before whom "her proud secrecy was disenthroned" (ch. 65) has absolved her. And to some extent George Eliot wants us to believe that Gwendolen lacks understanding and is merely in love

7 As "outside conscience," the phrase occurs in *Felix Holt* (ch. 36). Raffles, too, might be said to become the outer conscience of Bulstrode.

with Deronda.[8] " 'A *Jew!*' Gwendolen exclaimed, in a low tone of amazement, with an utterly frustrated look, as if some confusing potion were creeping through her system." Deronda's aspirations of restoring a Jewish nation provide Gwendolen "a shock which went deeper than personal jealousy," but only his marriage persuades her that they are really parting (ch. 69). *Daniel Deronda* will not be reduced to a detective novel or to a successful case history in psychoanalysis. To allow Gwendolen to go free, with charges dismissed or cured of guilt, is quite the opposite to George Eliot's intentions, as many allusions to "remorse" and the singular reference to "the Invisible and Universal" attest.

Whereas Grandcourt preys on Gwendolen's fear of being found out, Deronda tries to cultivate in her a sense of guilt. The distinction is sometimes hard to discern, since Gwendolen's "fear" is prevalent throughout; but the fear that is natural to her is fear of shame or exposure, and her sense of guilt has to be enlarged. The whole thrust of Deronda's program for Gwendolen is hard for us to appreciate, since psychoanalysis has led to a popular view of guilt as a dangerous overloading of the psyche.[9] But Deronda and George Eliot believe that guilt may be cultivated to a purpose, and that persons "who would be comparatively uninteresting beforehand," as Gwendolen supposedly is to begin with, "may become worthier of sympathy when they do something that awakens in them a keen remorse." In successive interviews, or snatches of conversation at Topping Abbey, the application of this rule is to Gwendolen's "wrong-doing," which Deronda intuits. Wrongdoing is a "yoke" to bear, but "one who has committed irremediable errors may be scourged by that consciousness into a higher course than is common." Gwendolen's questions and repeated assertions that she is "frightened at everything . . . frightened at myself" bring Deronda to the urgent speech that she will recall—without any specific effect—immediately before her husband's drowning:

8 E. S. Shaffer has brought the most interesting external evidence to bear on the sexual attraction of Gwendolen and Deronda, by comparing the latter to the Jesus of Ernest Renan. See her *"Kubla Khan" and "The Fall of Jerusalem"* (Cambridge, England: Cambridge University Press, 1975), pp. 265–276. Renan's *La Vie de Jésus* appeared in 1863.

9 Hence Jerome Thale, *The Novels of George Eliot* (New York: Columbia University Press, 1959), pp. 135–136, calls Deronda "a lay analyst, and a poor one," presumably because the latter places so much stress on the value of Gwendolen's continuing to feel guilty.

Turn your fear into a safeguard. Keep your dread fixed on the idea of increasing that remorse which is so bitter to you. Fixed meditation may do a great deal towards defining our longing or dread. We are not always in a state of strong emotion, and when we are calm we can use our memories and gradually change the bias of our fear, as we do our tastes. Take your fear as a safeguard. It is like quickness of hearing. It may make consequences passionately present to you. Try to take hold of your sensibility, and use it as if it were a faculty, like vision. (ch. 36)

Deronda seems to be arguing that a generalized guilt, trained by habit into a reflex, can prevent one from falling into crime or thoughts of crime. At the same time, far more than he knows, Gwendolen's wrongdoing has been brought about by her pride and fear of humiliation. Therefore to "turn" her fear is to shift its object from shame to guilt.

The one character whom George Eliot had previously portrayed as terrified of shame but ignorant of a higher form of dread was Tito Melema. Numerous actions and asides in *Romola* testify to Tito's cowardice and susceptibility to shame, but one passage in particular speaks to the absence of guilt and affords a classical source for the idea:

His mind was destitute of that dread which has been erroneously decried as if it were nothing higher than a man's animal care for his own skin: that awe of the Divine Nemesis which was felt by religious pagans, and, though it took a more positive form under Christianity, is still felt by the mass of mankind simply as a fear at anything which is called wrong-doing. Such terror of the unseen is so far above mere sensual cowardice that it will annihilate that cowardice; it is the initial recognition of a moral law restraining desire, and checks the hard bold scrutiny of imperfect thought into obligations which can never be proved to have any sanctity in the absence of feeling. "It is good," sing the old Eumenides, in Æschylus, "that fear should sit as the guardian of the soul, forcing it into wisdom,—good that men should carry a threatening shadow in their hearts under the full sunshine; else, how should they learn to revere the right?" That guardianship may become needless; but only when all outward law has become needless,—only when duty and love have united in one stream and made a common force. (ch. 11)

George Eliot here shows herself prepared to refute a Hobbesian reduction of social relations to brute force, which would not distinguish between cowardice and dread, as well as the liberal extension of force as "the hard bold scrutiny of imperfect thought into obligations which can never be proved . . ." But she stops short of announcing the arrival, at the other extreme, of the Religion of Humanity and opts generally for an evolutionary and anthropological proof of the terror of the unseen, backed by the same Furies that cross Grandcourt's threshold in *Daniel Deronda*.

George Eliot is still committed to a naturalistic ethics, but she has a more confident idea of its scientific basis than when she was writing *The Mill on the Floss*. The serious evolutionary significance of her account of fear as "the initial recognition of a moral law" in *Romola* may be compared with her statement in a review of W. E. H. Lecky's history, *Rationalism in Europe*, written two years later:

> Fear is earlier born than hope, lays a stronger grasp on man's system than any other passion, and remains master of a larger group of involuntary actions. A chief aspect of man's moral development is the slow subduing of fear by the gradual growth of intelligence, and its suppression as a motive by the presence of impulses less animally selfish; so that in relation to invisible Power, fear at last ceases to exist, save in that interfusion with higher faculties which we call awe.[10]

By "man's moral development" George Eliot almost certainly refers both to the course of civilization and to individual growth. She and Lewes were acquainted with the work of Ernst Haeckel in biology at this time: it was Haeckel who derived the principle that ontogeny recapitulates phylogeny, and who markedly influenced Freud's explanations of the stages of individual growth as repeating human biological and social evolution.[11] The authority of Darwin enhanced all such theories, and it is understandable that *Daniel Deronda* would not only trace the moral development of its hero but bring him to realize "the effect of brooding, passionate thoughts in many ancestors" (ch. 63). George Eliot also quite typically appeals to the evidence of various cultures rather than to speculation about the nature of "the

10 "The Influence of Rationalism," *Fortnightly Review*, I (1865); Pinney, p. 403.
11 See Lewes's letter to Darwin, 12 Nov. 1868, *G.E.L.*, VIII, 436; also V, 150n5. For Haeckel and Freud, see Stephen Jay Gould, *Ontogeny and Phylogeny* (Cambridge: Harvard University Press, 1977), esp. pp. 76–85, 155–164; and Frank J. Sulloway, *Freud, Biologist of the Mind: Beyond the Psychoanalytic Legend* (New York: Basic Books, 1979), esp. pp. 199–204, 259–264.

unseen." What is "still felt by the mass of mankind" is the issue, and not the existence of Divine Nemesis in *Romola* or of the Invisible and Universal in *Daniel Deronda*.[12]

Tito Melema is scarcely as complicated a character as Gwendolen Harleth. The experience of higher dread is simply closed to him, and the fear of shame is the only check on his behavior. In my judgment he is at best half a character, a projection of the Romola in hiding. But Gwendolen experiences sharp premonitions, terrors that she cannot quite identify or explain, that accompany and mix with her persistent fear of exposure even before she has met Deronda. Her playfulness and daring, willfulness and incaution, are merely the other side of her susceptibility to shame and failure, and this entire constellation of feelings is posed in the novel against an archaic moral dread, as in this early dialogue with her mother:

> "Oh, mamma, you are so dreadfully prosaic! As if all the great poetic criminals were not women! I think men are poor cautious creatures."
> "Well, dear, and you—who are afraid to be alone in the night—I don't think you would be very bold in crime, thank God."

Habits such as sleeping in her mother's room and symptoms such as sensitivity to changes in light when she is alone are in themselves indeterminant, but the promise of Gwendolen's development tends to lie in her liability to such irrational fears, her capacity for a dread that is at once greater and more mysterious than shame. Thus "solitude in any wide scene impressed her with an undefined feeling of immeasurable existence aloof from her," though she is unable to make anything of this at the time (ch. 6). The important turning toward a consciousness of guilt occurs when she engages herself to marry despite her knowledge of Mrs. Glasher and her children. Immediately before Gwendolen accepts Grandcourt, the narrator allows that, "even apart from shame, her feeling would have made her place any deliberate injury of another in the region of guilt" (ch. 27), though in the moment of decision, pride and circumstances prove stronger still.

---

12 Gillian Beer studies the influence of Darwin on George Eliot's last novel in *Darwin's Plots* (London: Routledge, 1983), pp. 181–209, 221–235.

Thereafter Gwendolen "was appalled by the idea that she was going to do what she once had started away from with repugnance. It was new to her that a question of right or wrong in her conduct should rouse her terror." Now she returns to "the darkness and loneliness of her little bed" with a sense of "calamity," and "all the infiltrated influences of disregarded religious teaching, as well as the deeper impressions of something awful and inexorable enveloping her, seemed to concentrate themselves in the vague conception of avenging power" (ch. 28). This "vague conception" corresponds to the "vague fear" named in *Romola*. Gwendolen is blessed with it, however, and Tito is not.

As far as the "right or wrong in her conduct" is concerned, Gwendolen's part in *Daniel Deronda* is played out swiftly. She does not repent sufficiently of her conduct to break with Grandcourt a second time; they marry, and her terror can no longer be vague to her after her wedding night. Her recognition of wrong is as amply represented by her marriage as the right and happiness of countless other novel heroines are certified by theirs. The main portion of Gwendolen's story, which is yet to come, can have only to do with the problem of living with guilt. As a further lesson in conduct that story is unnecessary and even regressive. The "avenging power" that she immediately encounters is Grandcourt, and not the "judgment of the Invisible and Universal"; her wrongdoing and experience of a higher dread are translated back into a contest of pride and shaming after all, and thence to intended murder rather than to the higher moral understanding that Deronda teaches. Gwendolen need never have wanted to murder Grandcourt in order to experience the guilt she feels in supplanting Lydia Glasher, and whether—at the crucial moment in the bay of Genoa—she successfully employed fear as a safeguard or effectively killed her husband by failing to throw the rope remains in doubt. Though the anguish of her parting from Deronda is convincing, the nature of her final recognition is also obscure. Gwendolen exits from the novel as if she were renouncing death— just as her rival Mirah entered contemplating suicide. Deronda kneels at her feet, almost in parody of a marriage proposal, and receives her promise to live—"I shall live. I mean to live" (ch. 69). For all her own and Deronda's intellectual efforts, Gwendolen is still sensitive chiefly to publicity, and stopping blackmail has been for her an exercise in modern survival tactics. All George Eliot finally cedes to her is survival, whereas to Mirah she grants the conventionally unexamined marriage of novel endings.[13]

The main story of Gwendolen is not of conduct, however, but of the "process of purgatory ... on the green earth" (ch. 54), a purgatory imaged in her relation to Grandcourt and Deronda both. This inward process makes use of blackmail, intended murder, and confession for the fictional mending of Gwendolen's soul—her personal identity over time. Hers were sins of pride and of ignorance to begin with. She subsequently wrongs another woman and makes a terrible mistake in regard to her own well-being. Her relatively slight (though sternly insisted upon) wrong to Mrs. Glasher and her much greater (though generally overlooked) wrong to herself are then subsumed by the desire to kill the one who has knowledge of both wrongs and threatens to humiliate her. This inward response on her part is criminal and therefore serves to amplify her guilt. Accordingly, it is allowed to warp the narrative, and to grow disproportionately to the enacted wrongs of the earlier part of the story. At the same time, the amplified guilt can now be located precisely and dealt with. Murdering a blackmailer, as we have seen, is a "double deliverance" from guilt and coercion. Moreover, murderous thoughts can be purged by confession. This, in sum, is George Eliot's experiment in narrative repair of moral wrong and mistake.

As we also have seen, blackmail, intended murder, and confession enhance the part Daniel Deronda has to play in the novel. As "images that drove her back to submission," among other things, Deronda and Grandcourt are closely matched in Gwendolen's story, and if the novel were a game of chess Deronda would have to be identified as the white mailer. His involvement with Gwendolen in some ways recapitulates his own story. His efforts to persuade her of the virtues of a higher form of dread, instead of a Tito-like fear of shame, apparently answer to his own emotional needs; embarrassment from supposed illegitimacy motivates his Romola-like determination to adhere to family and seek out obligation. "It was the habit of his mind to connect dread with unknown parentage" (ch. 19). But it hardly

13 George Eliot obviously drew partly upon her own history of living with Lewes. Once their affair commenced, she insisted upon regarding it as a marriage and treated his children as her own. Thus no further problem of conduct confronted her, but rather the residual problems of living with her decision, her violation of accepted morality, and the wrong (however justified) to Agnes Lewes and the children.

seems to matter whether dread of shame or of guilt is meant in this case, since Deronda instinctively converts dread to duty. He requires no instruction in moral matters and suffers no moral recognition, though his story turns out to be less ordinary—and more romantic— than mere boyish embarrassment: he was abandoned by his mother and forcibly excluded from the faith of his fathers, and he thereupon embraces that faith more strenuously. One psychoanalytic explanation of an excessive sense of shame, in fact, is that it is a response to abandonment rather than punishment as a child.[14]

The chapter that follows will show how the public and private themes of *Daniel Deronda* coincide in something like abandonment. The novel begins, it might be said, with abandonment—of Deronda by his mother, of Gwendolen by the death of her father and remarriage of her mother, and most blatantly of Mirah by the wretched Cohen-Lapidoth. The novel that thus begins with abandonment and shame, and portrays characters watching and concealing themselves from one another, then proceeds toward the cultivation of guilt and the celebration of Hebraism. The argument of *Daniel Deronda* reaches to the wider abandonment of close ties in the information culture of the nineteenth century and to the importation of ideology as an answer. George Eliot linked public opinion directly to shame and remotely to blackmail in *Felix Holt,* and the pursuit of knowledge to the troubles of being known in *Middlemarch.* Knowledge touches the life of one individual still more deeply in *Daniel Deronda*, and his case of "unknown parentage" provides a commentary on the positive aims of ideology.

14 Cf. Gerhart Piers and Milton B. Singer, *Shame and Guilt: A Psychoanalytic and a Cultural Study* (1953; rpt. New York: Norton, 1971), pp. 23–30; and Helen Merrell Lynd, *On Shame and the Search for Identity* (New York: Harcourt, 1958), pp. 64–71. For an essay that links shame to abandonment in Dickens's writings, see Robert Newsom, "The Hero's Shame," *Dickens Studies Annual,* 11 (1983), 1–24.

14

Ideology in *Daniel Deronda*

In her last novel George Eliot continues the critique of knowledge established in *Middlemarch*. She renders this critique subjective and takes it in a new, positive direction. Transformed as ideology, in fact, knowledge can be valued once more for its emotive power. Hence *Daniel Deronda* also tenders a mild satire of native ignorance, with the English propertied classes bearing the brunt of it—though even among the working-class "Philosophers" who convene at the Hand and Banner in London only three are unmistakably English and the others Jewish, Scottish, Celtic, or German. In the country and the West End, the composer Klesmer—German, Slav, and Jew—provides a persistent reminder of English cultural impoverishment among the classes who can afford better. Herr Klesmer has occasion to remind Gwendolen Harleth in person of her ignorance: the chapter that introduces her abortive plans for a career in the theater commences with a heavy epigraph, or short discourse, on "the power of Ignorance."[1] Later Gwendolen's ignorance appears less debilitating than her reading of Descartes, Bacon, Locke, Butler, Burke, and Guizot is futile. Significantly, she receives more "mental enlargement" from paying unaccustomed attention to her family than from "dashes into difficult authors" (ch. 44).

The main critique of knowledge is presented subjectively in the

1 "It is a common sentence that Knowledge is power; but who hath duly considered or set forth the power of Ignorance?" the epigraph begins (ch. 21). The answer must be a good many people, for the figure was a Victorian commonplace: see *The Speeches of Charles Dickens*, ed. K. J. Fielding (Oxford: Clarendon, 1960), p. 82; Samuel Smiles, *Thrift* (London: Murray, 1880), pp. 57–59; and *Felix Holt*, ch. 30.

narrative of Daniel Deronda's upbringing, then positively through the influence of Mordecai and the discovery of Deronda's Jewishness. Instead of displaying the limitations of knowledge in terms of the constraints of reputation, as in *Middlemarch*, George Eliot implants in her hero an early discontent with some customary ways of carving a career from knowledge in England. The intellectual model to be avoided, apparently, is that of Deronda's presumed father, Sir Hugo Mallinger, who writes and takes an active role in politics. "Deronda set himself against authorship"—whether in reaction to Sir Hugo or from wider motives is obscured by a narrator's aside equating authorship with "a vocation . . . understood to turn foolish thinking into funds." The difficulty of choosing a vocation George Eliot represents as "common in the young men of our day." She qualifies that observation by limiting it to "young men in whom the unproductive labour of questioning is sustained by three or five per cent on capital," but this is one of several respects in which *Daniel Deronda* strikes us as still more modern than she knew, since the number of middle-class youths in the same predicament today far exceeds those living on capital in this narrow sense. Deronda is occupied in his early twenties "chiefly with uncertainties about his own course," uncertainties that for him have "wide-sweeping connections with all life and history" and take the shape of strong antipathies, at least, to "that routine of the world which makes men apologize for all its wrong-doing, and take opinions as mere professional equipment" (ch. 17). Thus he faces both the problem of finding a use for himself and the problem of his world, in which study and opinion are divorced from purpose and moral judgment. Opinions as such have no compelling interest; they are so many storable and exchangeable sets of information, with commodity value and nothing else. Later Deronda will tell Sir Hugo, "I cannot persuade myself to look at politics as a profession," and "I don't want to make a living out of opinions." Sir Hugo claims there can be no other choice in the matter: "the business of the country must be done." Rather cannily he anticipates and rejects Deronda's unspoken need of "prophecy" or "inspired vocation" (ch. 33).

George Eliot frames this discussion with a contrast between the heroic imagination of an earlier day and the commonplaces of the modern, between "a prophetic vision of knowledge" and "newspaper placards, staring at you from a bridge beyond the cornfields" (ch. 33). When Sir Hugo and his ward speak of "opinions," they mean the stuff of journalism and parliamentary debate, of newspapers and advertisements, and reports of all kinds. Behind the discussion lies the profound liberal faith of the best Victorian minds, which can be summarized in some such terms as the following: from the exchange and competition of ideas something called public opinion arises and performs the business of the world merely by defining and representing it; the reporting of conditions precedes and may even preclude legislation, for when everyone more or less understands what the arrangement of things should be, things will arrange themselves; a few rules of noninterference keep thought free to form opinion, from which thought must be free to create a new consensus, and so on— successively and peacefully into an undisturbed future. As the treatment of public opinion in *Felix Holt* suggests, George Eliot both approved and began to question this way of conducting the business of the world. It can be wearisome and even oppressive, as is evident from the sheer work of exchanging information, the enormous patience required in arriving at consensus without forgoing truth, and the acute distress experienced when members of the society become themselves the object of opinions. Even if progress on this basis should not be oppressive, it is bound to be a little uninspiring. The sorting and weighing of ideas, most of which are to be discarded, has no very immediate motive or purpose to seize upon. Nor does the collective enterprise of establishing truths through debate and over time provide truths with readily identifiable authority. Reports are not the same thing as commands, and generally are not responded to with alacrity. When Mill, in *On Liberty*, proposes to restore the liveliness of belief, it is because he is confronting such modern problems as these. Whether infusions of more study, more exchange of ideas, more freedom can resolve problems they partially help to create, is a problem for liberalism itself.

In *Daniel Deronda* George Eliot challenges the liberal exchange of ideas and liberal progress.[2] But more than this, in the history of Deronda's development she questions her own steady faith in sympathetic understanding, the humane equivalent of liberal persuasion that has hitherto enabled her to weigh all sides—to balance Maggie

2 Robert Preyer, "Beyond the Liberal Imagination: Vision and Unreality in *Daniel Deronda*," *Victorian Studies*, 4 (1960), 33–54, makes the general point. George Eliot was reacting to the "numbing" complexity of "the vast, tangled spectacle of society" (p. 39).

Tulliver's yearnings with Tom's felt constraint, or Dorothea's bewilderment with Casaubon's pained anxiety—the suspensions of judgment, in short, that have made her fictive analyses of humanity liberal classics of a very high order. As many of her astute readers from Edward Dowden to U. C. Knoepflmacher have observed, the world represented in *Daniel Deronda* differs broadly from the world represented in *Middlemarch*.[3] The difference of representation corresponds to a fresh argument by George Eliot on how the world of men and women ought to be understood. Through Deronda, off exploring the Judengasse in Frankfurt, she now ponders a particular weakness in her previous liberal stance: namely, the tendency of sympathetic understanding or suspension of judgment "to hinder any persistent course of action." It is precisely Deronda's sensitivity and mental ability, not unlike the author's own, that threaten to "neutralize" sympathy by drenching it with understanding.

> His early-wakened sensibility and reflectiveness had developed into a many-sided sympathy, which threatened to hinder any persistent course of action: as soon as he took up any antagonism, though only in thought, he seemed to himself like the Sabine warriors in the memorable story,—with nothing to meet his spear but flesh of his flesh, and objects that he loved. His imagination had so wrought itself to the habit of seeing things as they probably appeared to others, that a strong partisanship, unless it were against an immediate oppression, had become an insincerity for him. His plenteous, flexible sympathy had ended by falling into one current with that reflective analysis which tends to neutralize sympathy. (ch. 32)

Only George Eliot, it may be thought, has earned the right to such a comparison as this of the Sabine warriors, a comparison that enlists the pain and frustration of broken marriages to express the bewilderment of liberal debate in its most generous form. The partisan opposition of opinions may be hostile; but the deliberate opposition of opinions, in a program for arriving at truth, is paradoxically both hostile and interested. Love may be too strong an expression of this

---

3 Dowden argued that in *Middlemarch* "the facts are taken more in the gross," whereas in *Daniel Deronda* "there is a passionate selection of those facts" (*Contemporary Review*, 29 [1877]; Carroll, p. 441). Knoepflmacher writes, "The world of *Middlemarch* is one of infinite gradations: *Daniel Deronda* offers only a choice between black and white" (*Religious Humanism and the Victorian Novel* [Princeton: Princeton University Press, 1965], p. 122).

interest for any but a Deronda, but the possibility of "insincerity" goes to the heart of liberal debate.[4]

The indirect meditation in the Judengasse continues, with Deronda's sense of history disturbing his liberal habit of "innate balance." The chief danger of the latter is that of paralysis and inaction, and this line of thinking about sympathy leads to a bitter denunciation of knowledge in the abstract:

> A too reflective and diffusive sympathy was in danger of paralyzing in him that indignation against wrong and that selectness of fellowship which are the conditions of moral force; and in the last few years of confirmed manhood he had become so keenly aware of this that what he most longed for was either some external event, or some inward light, that would urge him into a definite line of action, and compress his wandering energy. He was ceasing to care for knowledge,—he had no ambition for practice,—unless they could both be gathered up into one current with his emotions; and he dreaded, as if it were a dwelling place of lost souls, that dead anatomy of culture which turns the universe into a mere ceaseless answer to queries, and knows, not everything, but everything else about everything,—as if one should be ignorant of nothing concerning the scent of violets except the scent itself for which one had no nostril. (ch. 32)

So if Gwendolen in this novel finds herself in purgatory, Deronda is initially in limbo, the limbo of dead culture and knowledge about "everything else about everything." George Eliot's impatient syntax speaks wonderously of knowledge divorced from feeling and an age that has turned "the universe itself into a mere ceaseless answer to queries," as if both habitat and habitants were enclosed in some crossword puzzle or detective novel, a research project or case study.

---

4 Walter E. Anderson has persuaded me of the almost certain influence of Mill's *Autobiography* upon the conception of *Daniel Deronda*. We think of the famous "crisis" in Mill's life as taking place forty years earlier, but of course his account of this crisis was written at the end of his life. Mill himself thus provided a fresh perspective on "the habit of analysis," the inhibitions of a career of writing, the importance of music, and other Deronda-like concerns. "I am now convinced," he wrote, "that no great improvements in the lot of mankind are possible, until a great change takes place in the fundamental constitution of their modes of thought. . . . until a renovation has been effected in the basis of their belief, leading to the evolution of some faith, whether religious or merely human, which they can really believe" (*C.W.*, I, 245–247). George Eliot read Mill's *Autobiography* in November 1873 and especially approved "the presentation of his Father": see *G.E.L.*, V, 458, 461.

A way out of this limbo is already being prepared unconsciously, by remarking the absence of a "selectness of fellowship" that would provide a nonrational ground to stand upon.

Deronda clearly longs to escape from the culture of ceaseless questions and answers, and unlike the frustrated female protagonists of George Eliot's earlier novels, he is destined to find his way. Up to this point in the action of *Daniel Deronda*, however, the way is still restricted by questioning:

> He wanted some way of keeping emotion and its progeny of sentiments,—which make the savours of life,—substantial and strong in the face of a reflectiveness that threatened to nullify all differences. To pound the objects of sentiment into small dust, yet keep sentiment alive and active, was something like the famous recipe for making cannon,—to first take a round hole and then enclose it with iron; whatever you do, keeping fast hold of your round hole. Yet how distinguish what our will may wisely save in its completeness, from the heaping of cat-mummies and the expensive cult of enshrined putrefactions? (ch. 32)

The long paragraph of indirect meditation thus concludes with a weak joke and a strong backlash of rationalism. Making cannon is an activity redolent of the nationalism that was the nineteenth century's chief recourse for "selectness of fellowship," and which becomes the salient point of Deronda's mission as a Jew. Yet the joke expresses, if anything, the hopelessness of deriving moral force from intellectual analysis. Then follows the question about "cat-mummies" and "enshrined putrefactions"—which I take to be evidence of the foolish or stupid cults of mankind's past. Rationalism thus far persists in asking, in surely contemptuous tones, how can one prefer one cult to another, and how can one transcend the comparative anatomy of culture, however dead or alive the bodies may be, once anatomizing— culture rather than cult—has become the intellectual way of life.

The earliest influences on Deronda's mental development are not ideas such as can be picked up in the classroom but the peculiar embarrassments of the supposed illegitimate child. He imagines himself as object of others' knowledge before he embarks on his quest. "If his father had done any wrong, he wished it might never be spoken of to him: it was already a cutting thought that such knowledge might be in other minds. . . . Daniel fancied, as older people do, that every one else's consciousness was as active as his own on a matter which was vital to him." It is as if Deronda were experiencing at the beginning of his life what Casaubon, Lydgate, and Bulstrode experience at the end. George Eliot makes the point that unspoken feelings are his real education: "It is in such experiences of boy or girlhood, while elders are debating whether most education lies in science or literature, that the main lines of character are often laid down." Though Deronda is critical of the ordinary pursuit of knowledge at school or university, he has a very able mind. "He found the inward bent towards comprehension and thoroughness diverging more and more from the track marked out by the standards of examination: he felt a heightening discontent with the wearing futility and enfeebling strain of a demand for excessive retention and dexterity without any insight into the principles which form the vital connections of knowledge." Fortunately, his friendship for Hans Meyrick and "his boyish love of universal history" encourage him to leave Cambridge for study abroad (ch. 16).

A number of George Eliot's heroes and heroines, from Maggie Tulliver on, have the qualities of intellectuals. Lydgate is an intellectual of the specialized kind, a medical scientist. But the first intellectual free of specialization and European in outlook, alien to politics and yet desiring to lead others, is Deronda. For such an intellectual to play a decisive role, knowledge is essential, but it must be knowledge fused with feeling and purpose. As Deronda instructs Gwendolen, "for us who have to struggle for our wisdom, the higher life must be a region in which the affections are clad with knowledge." It is true that in the previous sentence he has linked in apposition "the higher, the religious life" (ch. 36), but this is before the discovery of his own Jewishness, and even after that discovery his mission is more national and historical than religious. His role as confessor to Gwendolen is still more obviously a secular one. The fusion of knowledge with feeling, something that George Eliot has always advised in moral relations, has now become programmatic and an alternative to the commonplace and threatening exchange of information. The increased reference to consciousness in *Daniel Deronda*, and the increased depth and range of consciousness, makes room for a finer mixture of impulses than those attributed traditionally to head and heart, or in the modern world to information and profit. The theory of scientific hypotheses shared by George Eliot and George Henry Lewes further authenticated a quest of mind beyond empiricism or mere mastery of facts.[5] In *Daniel Deronda* analogies to scientific method lend credence to actions that in the earlier novels would remain unauthenticated coincidence. When Mordecai, for example, both expects and succeeds in meeting Deronda at Blackfriars Bridge, the narrator remarks that "his exultation was not widely different from that of the experimenter, bending over the first stirrings of change that correspond to what in the fervour of concentrated prevision his thought has foreshadowed" (ch. 40). At first Deronda is cautious in entertaining Mordecai's invitation to kinship, wondering whether the consumptive Jew retains "that wise estimate of consequences which is the only safeguard from fatal error." But he senses the quality of "passionate belief which determines the consequences it believes in," and again the narrator associates vision with science: "even strictly measuring science could hardly have got on without that forecasting ardour which feels the agitations of discovery beforehand, and has a faith in its preconception that surmounts many failures of experiment." The weight of the argument begins to shift, always against knowledge divorced from feeling and toward a new accommodation of "what will be." It is George Eliot's continuation and reply to her own critique of knowledge in *Middlemarch*. Some formal truths are merely fictions, and some visions are true:

> The driest argument has its hallucinations, too hastily concluding that its net will now at last be large enough to hold the universe. Men may dream in demonstrations, and cut out an illusory world in the shape of axioms, definitions, and propositions, with a final exclusion of fact signed Q.E.D. No formulas for thinking will save us mortals from mistake in our imperfect apprehension of the matter to be thought about. And since the unemotional intellect may carry us into a mathematical dreamland where nothing is but what is not, perhaps an emotional intellect may have absorbed into its passionate view of possibilities some truth of what will be,—the more comprehensive massive life feeding theory with new materials, as the sensibility of the artist seizes combinations which science explains and justifies. (ch. 41)

One has only to grasp that the "wise estimate of consequences" is no longer the final consideration to see how far George Eliot has come since the writing of *Adam Bede*. Now it is a matter of effecting some

5 See George Levine, "George Eliot's Hypothesis of Reality," *Nineteenth-Century Fiction*, 35 (1980), 17–28.

consequences rather than avoiding them, and the most promising means (perhaps the only means) is "an emotional intellect" akin to the outreach of art and methods of science. Hence the next move by Mordecai is to escort Deronda to the Hand and Banner, where a discussion is in progress among the Philosophers on "the causes of social change." The discussion is complicated by the modern craftsmen's awareness of society as an aggregation of parts that possibly can only be interpreted statistically. Statistics do not even express an opinion; their abstract power of description—as the early advocates of statistics boasted—is strictly neutral as to the conditions represented. One of the Philosophers, a copying-clerk, has been arguing that "in relation to society numbers are qualities," yet the numbers "give us no instruction." Another, a seller of secondhand books, has countered with "the power of ideas" as "the main transforming cause." Still another, a wood-inlayer, believes that ideas present too general an approach to social change, because "all actions men put a bit of thought into are ideas." The argument to which Deronda attends in the Hand and Banner thus moves from the haplessness of information to this possible role for ideas. A Jewish watchmaker then cynically raises "the idea of nationalities" and gives Mordecai his opening: "Unless nationality is a feeling," the latter asks, "what force can it have as an idea?" The watchmaker protests that "the whole current of progress" is against nationalism in the nineteenth century, and another Jew, an optical instrument maker, speaks up for assimilation and "making our expectations rational." But Mordecai does not consider his position irrational:

> I too claim to be a rational Jew. But what is it to be rational,— what is it to feel the light of the divine reason growing stronger within and without? It is to see more and more of the hidden bonds that bind and consecrate change as a dependent growth,—yea, consecrate it with kinship: the past becomes my parent, and the future stretches towards me the appealing arms of children.

Mordecai scorns any intellectual Jew who, though capable and learned, treats his inherited culture not as "memories that bind him to action" but "as mere stuff for a professorship." But significantly he argues the point not in the synagogue but among determinedly rational proletarians in a tavern. His expressive figures and his "yea" number him with the prophets, yet he is only barely a theist. "I praise no superstition," he says; "I praise the living foundations of enlarging belief" (ch. 42).

Eventually Deronda will announce to his former friends, "I have taken up some of Mordecai's ideas, and I mean to try and carry them out" (ch. 67). It is no violation of George Eliot's intentions to say that Mordecai's ideas, especially as they are embraced by Daniel Deronda, constitute an ideology and are advocated as such. I do not mean to play down the Jewishness of the ideas—it would be foolish and misleading to argue that George Eliot is merely using the Zionist idea to illustrate, within a tradition involving the future with the past, the fusion of knowlege and feeling. As E. S. Shaffer has ably demonstrated, the Jewish content and the intensely European cast of thought in *Daniel Deronda* are no accident.[6] It is an emphatic part of George Eliot's design that Deronda should have a Jewish mother, and a Jewish grandfather, Daniel Charisi, who bore a personal resemblance to his namesake and possessed a faith like Mordecai's: "Ah, you argue and you look forward," Joseph Kalonymos tells Deronda—"you are Daniel Charisi's grandson" (ch. 60). It is equally a part of Geoge Eliot's design that her hero should marry Mordecai's sister, Mirah, whose "religion was of one fibre with her affections, and had never presented itself to her as a set of propositions" (ch. 32). Still, to argue and to look forward in the nineteenth century is to be an ideologue. Mordecai's ideas are repeatedly characterized as rational and deeply studied.[7] His most hopeful visions are warranted to be something like the "concentrated prevision" and "preconception" of advances in science. It is possible and necessary for him to debate his ideas, including the question of whether ideas have power, with rationalists who are distinctly modern in their independence of patronage or religion. Finally, Deronda must be able rationally to fol-

6 *"Kubla Khan" and "The Fall of Jerusalem"* (Cambridge, England: Cambridge University Press, 1975), pp. 225–291. My own effort is to show how this Jewish and European bias complements George Eliot's representation of her own society, in *Daniel Deronda* and the earlier novels. Graham Martin, *"Daniel Deronda:* George Eliot and Political Change," in *Critical Essays on George Eliot,* ed. Barbara Hardy (London: Routledge, 1970), pp. 147–150, contends that Deronda's program is so thoroughly contrasted with the English political scene that it finally "has no evident bearing on English life."

7 On the rationality of Mordecai's vision, see Sara M. Putzell-Korab, "The Role of the Prophet: The Rationality of Daniel Deronda's Idealistic Mission," *Nineteenth-Century Fiction,* 37 (1982), 170–187.

low Mordecai's teachings, however much his likings and inherited instincts may prompt him and however much "emotional intellect" is an article of belief. Such a consciousness distinguishes an ideology from a religious faith that is not experienced as a rational choice. Even the commitment that follows from it is urged on the grounds of a need for commitment.

Even when "ideology" is used descriptively, as here, the word is in danger of conveying a contentious charge of falsehood. Destutt de Tracy, the first writer to use the term, urged the positive need for a science of ideas, for the purpose of enhancing the role of thought in public affairs; but Condillac, one of Destutt's authorities, had already cited Bacon's Idols as model arguments for the reformation of thinking.[8] Napoleon's contempt for the ideologues of the French Institute and Marx's critique of the "German ideology" long ago fixed the negative connotations of the term, which subsequent arguments for the need for revolutionary ideologies have generally failed to overcome. It was only when beliefs began to change very rapidly at the end of the eighteenth century that ideology could be perceived.[9] Here I wish to draw back from the heat of left-wing theorizing and from the strict sociological premise that ideas are the products of the conditions of life, in order to contemplate the twofold significance of ideology in *Daniel Deronda*, as an object of study and as the translation of study into action—the skeptical debate of the Philosophers of the Hand and Banner about "the power of ideas" and the privileged carrying out of "Mordecai's ideas." The latter can hardly be supposed to be free of the limitations and liability to error of other ideologies, but before the false consciousness of the novel can be laid bare, more needs to be said about George Eliot's positive representations.

Mordecai's ideas exhibit some common features of ideologies. For one thing, the ideas are explicit. The reader of *Daniel Deronda* may not see or hear very many of them, but it is understood that they are connected ideas, written down and available for interpretation, to be used by Deronda and those he can interest in their furtherance. Sec-

8 George Lichtheim, *The Concept of Ideology and Other Essays* (New York: Vintage, 1967), pp. 3–11. See also Emmet Kennedy, *A Philosophe in the Age of Revolution: Destutt de Tracy and the Origins of "Ideology,"* Memoirs of the American Philosophical Society, 129 (Philadelphia, 1978), pp. 44–74, 334–346.

9 Karl Mannheim, *Ideology and Utopia: An Introduction to the Sociology of Knowledge*, trans. Louis Wirth and Edward Shils (New York: Harcourt, 1936) p. 75.

ond, the ideas are designed for particular adherents and not for dissemination far and wide, at least not at present (one reason they are not very generously supplied to the reader). There have to be adherents and nonadherents for an ideology to take hold, to gather energy from the choosing of sides. The scenario is entirely different from the constant exchange and adjustment of opinion at large assumed by Mill in *On Liberty*. Third, the ideas are not those of the establishment. On the contrary, they are purposely opposed to established institutions and assumptions, if only in their imputation of certain qualities of experience and commitment missing from society at large. Fourth, the ideas have a strong emotional hold, so as to give thought and action direction. Fifth, they have the general intent of "sacralizing" individual and social lives that have become meaningless.[10] Moreover, the adherents and especially the leaders of the movement are conscious of all such features of the ideology, which strike them as advantageous. George Eliot is conscious of the same features and, with the tentativeness appropriate to a work of fiction, also approves them.

Prominent among the tenets of Mordecai that are shared with the reader are his hopes of founding a Jewish state.[11] It is this project that will eventually take Deronda to the East and which is described in some detail to the skeptical audience at the Hand and Banner:

There is a store of wisdom among us to found a new Jewish polity, grand, simple, just, like the old,—a republic where there is equality of protection, an equality which shone like a star on the forehead of our ancient community, and gave it more than the

10 Each of these characteristics is associated with ideology by Edward Shils, *The Constitution of Society* (Chicago: University of Chicago Press, 1982), pp. 203-223—an article originally written for the *International Encyclopaedia of the Social Sciences* (1968). Shils claims that "an intellectualized religion provides the precondition for the emergence of ideology" (p. 211); he differs from George Eliot in opposing science to ideology.

11 The same emphasis on nationalism is evident in George Eliot's "The Modern Hep! Hep! Hep!" in *Impressions of Theophrastus Such*, Illustrated Cabinet Edition (New York: Merrill and Baker, n.d.), pp. 184-213. "That the preservation of national memories is an element and a means of national greatness; that their revival is a sign of reviving nationality; that every heroic defender, every patriotic restorer, has been inspired by such memories and has made them his watchword . . . these are the glorious commonplaces of historic teaching at our public schools and universities, being happily ingrained in Greek and Latin classics. They have also been impressed on the world by conspicuous modern instances" (p. 185).

brightness of Western freedom amid the despotisms of the East. Then our race shall have an organic centre, a heart and brain to watch and guide and execute; the outraged Jew shall have a defense in the court of nations, as the outraged Englishman or American. And the world will gain as Israel gains. . . . (ch. 42)

This plan will give Jews advantages that other peoples enjoy but also some benefits—peace and community—notably lacking in the West. Mordecai's vision is more national and practical than religious, and for Deronda it provides a radical alternative to his accustomed way of life. Deronda supports Mordecai in the argument, in fact, by invoking the recent unification of Italy. Alvin W. Gouldner has written suggestively on the broad difference between such nineteenth-century outlooks—more colorfully represented in the novel by Mirah's repeated singing of Leopardi's *O patria mia*—and the tragic vision of unchanging fate, to which individuals are subject and must perforce be reconciled. In the ideological as opposed to the tragic vision, "the word and the ideal are seen as having the power practically to change What Is, here in this world, and it intimates that this world is all there is . . . Although grounded ultimately in the Judaic-Christian tradition, ideology always secularizes transcendence."[12]

It is not my purpose to insist on the secular grounds of Mordecai's ideas or to go into the merits of founding a Jewish state, in the nineteenth or the twentieth century. Rather, I wish to show how the adventure of *Daniel Deronda* complements George Eliot's study of her secular society, which is in so many respects continuous with our own.[13] Gouldner is particularly helpful because he writes about ide-

---

12 *The Dialectic of Ideology and Technology* (New York: Seabury, 1976), p. 87. Lewis S. Feuer, *Ideology and the Ideologists* (Oxford: Blackwell, 1975), contends that ideologies generally enlist a Mosaic or Jacobic myth (pp. 1–16) but also that anti-Semitism inheres in virtually all ideologies of the left or right (pp. 138–151), which he opposes to science and condemns as immature.

13 One of the saddest consequences of the bent toward nationalism in George Eliot's last novel is the apparent acceptance of warfare as a test of true belief. Thus she describes the impact of Deronda's announced mission on "Gwendolen's small life" by means of the following awesome analogy: "There comes a terrible moment to many souls when the great movements of the world, the larger destinies of mankind, which have lain aloof in newspapers and other neglected reading, enter like an earthquake into their own lives,—when the slow urgency of growing generations turns into the tread of an invading army or the dire clash of civil war, and gray fathers know nothing to seek for but the corpses of their blooming sons, and girls forget all vanity to make lint and bandages which may serve for the shattered limbs of their betrothed hus-

ology as a response to the growth of information and communication in modern times. "The proliferation of ideologies," he believes, "was one fundamental response to the new communications revolution; it was, in part, an effort to supply meaning where the overall supply of information was greater than ever." One may question the implications of his metaphor, "the increased market for meaning," because at least in its original impulse an ideology is an attempt to get out of the market and back to a shared community of ideas; but undoubtedly "the sheer increase in *bits* of information that the communication revolution spread in every direction" was a condition of the rise of ideologies.[14] An ideology can respond to the indiscriminate massing of information by privileging certain ideas, whether by attaching them to a strong personality (Mordecai's ideas), invoking a sacred tradition (such as Zionism), borrowing from the prestige of science (as in Marxism and Positivism), or segregating undemocratically (by nation, race, or class). Ideology addresses the motivelessness of the exchange of information by rejoining affect and purpose to opinion. The threat of exposure in modern society no longer need be faced alone, and personal accountability can be fixed and diverted to a group. While the incremental progress of public opinion is painfully slow and beyond anyone's control, leadership has become conceivable again and some goals are attainable within a lifetime. "Since I began to read and know," Deronda confides to Mordecai (and reading and knowing are a significant beginning), "I have always longed for some ideal task, in which I might feel myself the heart and brain of a multitude,—some social captainship, which would come to me as a duty, and not be striven for as a personal prize" (ch. 63).

Identification with a group is one of the obvious advantages of adhering to an ideology, through which some semblance of manageable community can be restored.[15] But at the same time, few ideologies are

---

bands. . . . Then it is that the submission of the soul to the Highest is tested, and even in the eyes of frivolity life looks out from the scene of human struggle with the awful face of duty, and a religion shows itself which is something else than a private consolation" (ch. 69). One can take in good part the need to exchange "newspapers and other neglected reading" for immediate experience without cheering a sense of "duty" and "religion" that would seem to lead directly into World War I.

14 Gouldner, *The Dialectic of Ideology and Technology*, p. 93.

15 George Eliot offers a similar defense of separateness as a ground for community in "The Modern Hep! Hep! Hep!" in *Impressions of Theophrastus Such*, pp. 200–202.

without some pretension to universal significance, a pretension nurtured by the group. In *Daniel Deronda* Mordecai mostly speaks of national aspirations for his people, but he also refers to "the divine Unity" that is "the chief devotional exercise of the Hebrew" and "made our religion the fundamental religion for the whole world." He further deduces from this ancient principle of Judaism that "the divine Unity embraced as its consequence the ultimate unity of mankind," and remarks the irony that Jews have nevertheless been "scoffed at" because of their "separateness" (ch. 61). Mordecai does not spell out the contradiction, but overrides it in favor of the eventual unity of all peoples.[16] The somewhat less tolerant Daniel Charisi, in an earlier generation, is reported to have insisted "that the strength and wealth of mankind depended on the balance of separateness and communication, and he was bitterly against [the Jews] losing themselves among the Gentiles." Deronda, in promising to call himself a Jew, does not promise "to believe exactly as my fathers have believed," but he too imagines he "can maintain my grandfather's notion of separateness with communication" (ch. 60). George Eliot's thoughtful contemplation of her hero's Jewishness thereby enables her—with a single stroke, as it were—to accommodate a special sense of direction and purpose within a world of opinion that is increasingly homogenized, sifted into a mere heap of thought, by modern means and frequency of communication. Separateness can at once resist communication in that sense and eventually provide a model for a wider community.

Every ideology is "Jewish" in that it reinvents sectarian faith and restores a hierarchy of some kind, if only a hierarchy of interpretation. Gouldner characterizes ideology as "both a bridge and a moat; it both separates believers from nonbelievers and, also, connects them." The inner community of adherents is protected by this means. "When optimally constructed according to its own inner logic (or fantasy), ideology allows the believer to influence, *but not to be influenced reciprocally* by the nonbeliever. It thus constructs a boundary with a special, one-way permeability."[17] Even in the frank discussion at the Hand and Banner, George Eliot does not permit a

16 Cf. George Lichtheim's conclusion in *The Concept of Ideology* that "it remains the task of the critical intellect to evolve modes of thought which will enable men to recognize the common purpose underlying their divergencies" (p. 44). This liberal-Marxist essay affords the best concise history of ideology.

17 Gouldner, *The Dialectic of Ideology and Technology*, pp. 81–82.

full examination of Mordecai's ideas. She further insulates the ideas through the personal relation with Deronda, a kind of discipleship common to religion and to ideology. She devotes some care to the narrative of the friendship of Deronda and Mordecai, but not to their *mutual* interaction. The one is the student of the other; the "strong man whose gaze was sustainedly calm and his finger-nails pink with health, who was exercised in all questioning, and accused of excessive mental independence, still felt a subduing influence over him in the tenacious certitude of the fragile creature before him . . ." (ch. 40). The mild irony here is at the expense of Deronda, but not at all against the fact of submission. The luminous ideas of the consumptive teacher are self-evidently prior to those of his pupil. Deronda and others must learn as they can; there is no leveling, competitive exchange in which ideas and participants are all at risk. The advantage to acolytes is that the ideas are not shaken, doubted, or withdrawn before they can be studied and embraced.

Sectarianism and voluntary submission are remedies prescribed by ideology for the discontinuity of experience and knowledge at a distance of modern society. It is just because *Daniel Deronda* is George Eliot's most searching study of shame and personal estrangement that it offers her most radical alternative, the deliberate acceptance of separation and deliberate submission to the knowledge of another. Ideology confronts the power of public opinion in its stultifying aspect, the shaming force that George Eliot tentatively celebrated in *Felix Holt* and decisively criticized in *Middlemarch*, by welcoming separateness and supplanting the ceaseless comparison of ideas. Ideology declares that individuals shall not stand alone, exposed on every side, and need not search for wisdom among all possible truths. At the same time the rescue from exposure and the commitment to explicit ideas are thought to serve as a bridge to all humankind. One can see similar strategies operating in Gwendolen Harleth's relation to Deronda: a linking to another person and submission to his thought, a defense against shame in the higher reaches of guilt. To embrace an ideology or to welcome a confessor is not an act of uncontrolled rebellion, but of separation and submission. The power of the extended public to indict at random has been evaded, but new standards have been chosen and approval concentrated in an exceptional teacher or hierarchy of interpretation.

By concentrating the power of opinion in a kind of priesthood of Derondas and Mordecais, one can ignore the random threat of facts and opinion personified by a Raffles. The recourse to ideology actually restores a partial opening for heroism among the leadership. Deronda has before him the heroic possibilities of success or failure—"failure will not be ignoble, but it would be ignoble for me not to try," as he says (ch. 63). The novel then closes with the death of Mordecai, with four verses spoken by Manoa at the end of *Samson Agonistes* for an epitaph:

> Nothing is here for tears, nothing to wail
> Or knock the breast; no weakness, no contempt,
> Dispraise, or blame; nothing but well and fair,
> And what may quiet us in a death so noble.

In previous novels George Eliot celebrated—sometimes against the tendency of her own representations—the incremental achievement of "unhistoric acts," to use the phrase from her finale to *Middlemarch*. The important thing was to do one's small part, in one's own necessarily limited path. She does not now forgo this typically Victorian conception of duty, but she proposes a more conspicuous heroism as well. Thus Deronda's estimate of Mordecai's greatness, which she narrates indirectly, includes both homelike virtues and the far-reaching "march of human destinies":

> this consumptive Jewish workman in threadbare clothing, lodged by charity, delivering himself to hearers who took his thoughts without attaching more consequences to them than the Flemings to the ethereal chimes ringing above their market-places,—had the chief elements of greatness: a mind consciously, energetically moving with the larger march of human destinies, but not the less full of conscience and tender heart for the footsteps that tread near and need a leaning-place; capable of conceiving and choosing a life's task with far-off issues, yet capable of the unapplauded heroism which turns off the road of achievement at the call of the nearer duty . . . (ch. 43)

There is no one quite like Mordecai in George Eliot's earlier work. But as Shaffer has argued, Deronda himself resembles Renan's Jesus.[18]

---

18 See chapter 13, note 8. That George Eliot writes of "footsteps that . . . need a leaning-place" may suggest that she is rather mindlessly repeating Victorian commonplaces.

A long dramatic poem that George Eliot began before writing *Felix Holt* and completed in 1868, *The Spanish Gypsy,* prefigures the treatment of race, nation, and homeland in *Daniel Deronda.* Some notes found among the author's papers make it certain that she intended this poem about "hereditary conditions in the largest sense" as a tragedy, defined as an "irreparable collision between the individual and the general." Fedalma, the heroine, accepts her hereditary lot by adhering to her father Zarca, leader of the Gypsies, and forgoing marriage to Don Silva, a Christian nobleman. The latter attempts to join the tribe and reunite himself with Fedalma, but in a paroxysm of shame he finally kills Zarca (Silva, if anyone, is the bewildered Gwendolen of the poem). Fedalma is deprived of her marriage and of her father, but stands morally in the clear. "It is the individual with whom we sympathize," according to George Eliot's notes, "and the general of which we recognize the irresistible power." She even goes so far as to state that "what we call duty is entirely made up of such [hereditary] conditions; for even in cases of just antagonism to the narrow view of hereditary claims, the whole background of the particular struggle is made up of our inherited nature."[19] In more ways than one, the poem that looks forward to *Daniel Deronda* also harks back to *The Mill on the Floss.* Maggie Tulliver when a child wished to become Queen of the Gypsies—it is ironic that Fedalma, the one heroine of George Eliot to occupy high office in her own name, and by this very title, should do so at her father's severe behest and sail off to the promised homeland bearing his coffin. "But," in Fedalma's own words, "faithfulness can feed on suffering, / And knows no disappointment" (bk. 3).

Though the action of the poem points to the future, though the future envisioned is that of independent nationhood, and though Zarca jealously guides the separate interests of his people and rigorously insists on submission to his point of view, *The Spanish Gypsy* contains scarcely a hint of ideology.[20] The principle of the Gypsies, on the contrary, is direct personal loyalty from one Gypsy to another. In

19 "Notes on the Spanish Gypsy and Tragedy in General," in J. W. Cross, *George Eliot's Life as Related in Her Letters and Journals,* 3 vols. (New York: Merrill and Baker, n.d.), III, 31–37.

20 Leslie Stephen, *George Eliot* (London: Macmillan, 1902), pp. 165–166, calls it a *reductio ad absurdum* of the positivists' doctrine of the social organism and mocks the principle of "descent" evoked by the poem.

contesting verbally with Silva, Zarca scorns Christian belief as something merely learned. For him, truth is simply equivalent to being true:

> Our people's faith
> Is faithfulness; not the rote-learned belief
> That we are heaven's highest favourites,
> But the resolve that, being most forsaken
> Among the sons of men, we will be true
> Each to the other, and our common lot. (bk. 3)

The poem's dramatic personae also include a Jew, appropriately named Sephardo, who is a trustworthy person and highly respected for his science and prophecy. Sephardo has one noteworthy speech on the twin guides of Reason and Memory, but he too concludes that "over all belief is faithfulness, / Which fulfils vision with obedience" (bk. 2). Thus the note of faithfulness is persistently struck—Zarca and Sephardo are not allies. *The Spanish Gypsy* is a tragedy of clashing loyalties, and its "vision" can be summed up as "obedience" without recourse to ideology. Zarca scarcely introduces himself to Fedalma, who was stolen from him as a child, before she exclaims, "Father! yes. / I will eat dust before I will deny / The flesh I spring from" (bk. 1). The first book of the poem concludes in a perfect orgy of obedience to the father, who cuts down, one after another, Fedalma's perfectly reasonable arguments in favor of her engagement to Silva.[21] A similar mind-set in heroines was much more subtly elaborated in *Romola* and *The Mill on the Floss*. Similar insistence on inherited family loyalty and strict obedience to fathers is evident in *Daniel Deronda* as well—but only very oddly so. It seems that in *Daniel Deronda* very few parents and children bear the same family name, and with one egregious exception, the key fathers are simply missing from the novel. It is this special configuration of the family that helps to make clear the role of ideology. The novel is not, as George Eliot suggests of her dramatic poem, beholden to the *Ores-*

---

21 "The flesh I spring from" as applied to her father suggests that Fedalma is not very mindful of her deceased mother, whom Zarca at least mentions. Donald Stone, *The Romantic Impulse in Victorian Fiction* (Cambridge: Harvard University Press, 1980), pp. 230–234, gives an acerbic interpretation of the poem as George Eliot's projection of her own "heroic" role in life. Such an autobiographical interpretation places still greater weight on the family fantasy, since unlike Fedalma the author did not have her father's sanction for her career.

teia, but to the *Purgatorio,* and ideology has superseded tragedy.

Parents and children bear different names in *Daniel Deronda* because the various actions arise from discontinuities of family life. The experiences of the protagonists do not afford concrete memories of place or identity, and these have to be somehow substituted for amid the incoherence of society. Gwendolen Harleth is the only Harleth there is; her father is hardly referred to in the novel, and the mother signs herself, in her letter to Gwendolen, "Fanny Davilow" (ch. 2). (Davilow we do hear of—it is he who has fathered the four step-sisters and disposed of Fanny's jewels.) Gwendolen has never had a "spot of native land" with which to identify, no home that would offer "a familiar unmistakable difference amidst the future widening of knowledge" (ch. 3). A name and a home are advantages that Mary Ann Evans enjoyed, but her *Daniel Deronda* begins from the state of dispossession. Behind Mrs. Davilow, after the loss of her small independence, are "the sad faces of the four superfluous girls," now likened to "those other many thousand sisters of us all" (ch. 21). Though the novel frustrates every practical feminist concern,[22] George Eliot makes symbolic use of superfluous sisters and children throughout, as the sex and age group most representative of a population without name or function: there are the three brotherless daughters of Lady Mallinger, who regard Deronda as their "cousin"; the three fatherless daughters of Mrs. Meyrick, who at least have distinct personalities; the two girls and two boys of Mrs. Glasher, one boy very handsome; the five other children of unspecified sex of the Princess Halm-Eberstein.

Will Deronda's children bear the name "Deronda"? Gwendolen, we know, "was reduced to dread lest she should become a mother" (ch. 54), but this is supposedly because her children would disinherit Mrs. Glasher's all over again. The novel gives no hint whether

22 The narrator calls Gwendolen's abortive interest in an acting career a "higher crisis of her woman's fate" than marriage to any man, but this question of "whether she could not achieve substantiality for herself, and know gratified ambition without bondage" (ch. 23), is first answered for her in the negative by Klesmer and then simply forgotten. The more suitable talents, training, and personalities of both Mirah Lapidoth and Catherine Arrowpoint are used to show up Gwendolen, but these women are also reduced to marriage, without any qualms on George Eliot's part. The notorious Alcharisi, Deronda's mother, is the only woman in any of the novels who pursues a career after marriage. For an essay taking off from "superfluous girls," see Nancy Pell, "The Fathers' Daughters in *Daniel Deronda,*" *Nineteenth-Century Fiction,* 36 (1982), 424–451.

Deronda will have children or whether he will remain content with the name his mother purposely gave him in order to conceal his identity. His own father, Charisi, is only slightly more prominent among deceased persons than the father Harleth. But Daniel Deronda has longed from infancy to break through the secrecy that surrounds his identity. Like Romola earlier, he wants to keep up all connections, even those he knows nothing about—though unlike Romola he is superficially one who has been wronged by his parents rather than one who fears to wrong them. Though he hardly seems obliged to any parents other than Sir Hugo, he is searching for a sense of obligation, on the principle enunciated in George Eliot's notes to *The Spanish Gypsy* that "what we call duty is entirely made up of such conditions." So far, after meeeting Mordecai, "he had not the Jewish consciousness, but he had a yearning, grown the stronger for the denial which had been his grievance, after the obligation of avowed filial and social ties" (ch. 43). The social obligation, like the filial, operates through an acceptance of guilt, though Deronda has never consciously done anything wrong. When he encounters his mother at last—who "willed to annihilate" him, not the other way around—and is informed of his Jewishness, he can lecture her spontaneously on the principles she has violated:

> "I see no other way to get any clearness than by being truthful,—not by keeping back facts which may—which should carry obligation with them,—which should make the only guidance towards duty. No wonder if such facts come to reveal themselves in spite of concealments. The effects prepared by generations are likely to triumph over a contrivance which would bend them all to the satisfaction of self. Your will was strong, but my grandfather's trust which you accepted and did not fulfil—what you call his yoke—is the expression of something stronger, with deeper, farther-spreading roots, knit into the foundations of sacredness for all men. You renounced me—you still banish me—as a son,"—there was an involuntary movement of indignation in Deronda's voice,—"but that stronger Something has determined that I shall be all the more the grandson whom also you willed to annihilate." (ch. 53)

This turning of the other cheek is so pronounced as to be childish. It suggests that a strong fantasy underlies Deronda's counseling of Gwendolen along the same lines. The hated concealments of shame resulted from the child's abandonment—like the abandonment at large of "those other many thousand sisters of us all." But the child refuses to abandon the parent, even though he would like to and she deserves it. There is "involuntary" anger in him, and guilt—or a sense of obligation—that he would cultivate as his safeguard. His father he never encounters at all.

George Eliot overrides Deronda's hostile feelings, if any, while she makes Gwendolen's the main interest of suspense. But it is testimony to her gifts as a novelist and to her qualified truthfulness that she has signaled all along the ambivalence of Deronda's search for his family. Gwendolen's "dread" and its transformation are given much greater play, but Deronda's does not go unregistered: "it was the habit of his mind to connect dread with unknown parentage." Where this dread explicitly emerges is in his acquaintance with Mirah Lapidoth, still another person whose name differs from that of her family, and one who has had to run away from her father. She does not mention the father to Deronda, after he has saved her from suicide, and he instinctively conveys her to a home—the Meyricks'—where there is none. Mirah has come all the way from Prague in search of her mother and brother, however, and it is incumbent upon Deronda to help her. His alarm at her unguarded and unhesitating quest prompts the full consciousness, or nearly full consciousness, of his own fears: "the desire to know his own mother, or to know about her, was constantly haunted with dread; and in imagining what might befall Mirah it quickly occurred to him that finding the mother and brother from whom she had been parted when she was a little one might turn out to be a calamity" (ch. 19). The ambivalence here is played out dramatically in Deronda's anxiety lest the Cohens whom he encounters in London (and who it turns out have "lost" a daughter in the conventional Victorian sense) prove to be Mirah's family, and above all in the eventual arrival on the scene of Mirah's actual wretched father.

Deronda's ambivalence—or his author's—shows up in his own case through the working out of the plot. His mother summons him to Genoa to meet her, thus demonstrating that he is right about "Something" stronger than her own will; but conveniently, she summons him only to banish him again, refusing his offer to remain in her vicinity and abbreviating their lifetime acquaintance to two brief interviews. The secret of unknown parentage has, after all, lent a certain glamour to Deronda's life—as he tells his mother in the first interview, "I have always been rebelling against the secrecy that looked like shame" (ch. 51). But like all secrets, it rapidly loses its interest in the revelation, and at the end of the second interview Deronda is pretty much free of the so-called "tragic experience which must forever solemnize his life and deepen the significance of the acts by which he bound himself to others" (ch. 53). By these same terms, of course, his story is not a tragedy, but a purgatory only less well defined than Gwendolen's. The search for Deronda's parents is successful—brilliantly successful—precisely in the degree that it is ambivalent. Despite the steadfast inclusion of "nearer duty" in the definition of greatness and despite the avid insistence on restoring the continuity of the family, it seems that Deronda's father scarcely existed and that his mother means to hold him to no obligations or acquaintance whatever. Deronda is not going to have to put up with any parents after all, and an unintended moral of *Daniel Deronda* is that the only good father is a dead grandfather, the only good mother one who ceases to interfere with her son. George Eliot's fictions are strewn with deceased fathers, some of them—Tulliver, Bardo, Baldassare, Zarca—more significantly dead than others. In *Daniel Deronda* the deceased Harleth and Charisi hardly signify. The history of humankind, it might be said, is a history of dead fathers; the history of modern society is a history of missing fathers.

Instead of an immediate family, respected parents with whom to quarrel and live from day to day, Deronda discovers to his greater satisfaction his Jewishness and an idea to live by. When he reports to Mordecai that he is a Jew, the latter responds in Hebrew with "the liturgical words which express the religious bond: 'Our God, and the God of our fathers' " (ch. 63). In that case the liturgical fathers have taken the place of ordinary fathers, as Mordecai well ought to know from his own unhappy experience of the latter. It is also the general result of migration, the labor market, and the reorganization of society by information in the nineteenth century, that the authority of real-life fathers is waning. Authority must be created, instead, from the knowledge that is available. One of the finest ironies of *Daniel Deronda* is that the hero's desire to repossess his family should eventually be satisfied by papers that once belonged to his grandfather Charisi and have been carefully preserved by Joseph Kalonymos in Mainz. Thus Deronda's mother can waive details of his history by referring him to these papers, and so also can Deronda discover his life's direction by conducting research, with Mordecai's help, into papers in Spanish, Italian, Hebrew, Arabic, and Latin. Deronda has sought assurances from his mother (ch. 51) and from Kalonymos that his grandfather's "knowledge was not narrow" (ch. 60); now the knowledge can be put to use, the nature of which will require study (ch. 63). As Gouldner suggests, true ideologues show their belief in the potency of ideas "by the very act of communicating them emphatically through writing, by the importance they attribute to writing, by the sheer amount of time and energy they devote to writing. Not to speak of reading."[23] To be sure, this emphasis on writing is mine and Gouldner's, but a brief recollection of the different attention George Eliot pays to writing in *Middlemarch* will suggest how knowledge has been restored to authority in *Daniel Deronda*.

The writings that Deronda will study preserve something of the mystery about his life that the interviews with his mother have tended to disperse. That adept at "sincere acting" is herself aware of the attraction of mystery and has confidently advised her son, if "you are glad to have been born a Jew . . . that is because you have not been brought up as a Jew" (ch. 51). Similarly, when he tells her of Mirah, she ventures that Mirah is loyal to "the Judaism she knows nothing of" (ch. 53). Discount the Alcharisi's hatred of her own Jewishness, she still has a point and exhibits the kind of understanding that parents often possess. The mother's perspective reflects a larger criticism, that ideology as well as religion thrives on studies not yet complete of tendencies not wholly clear. When Mordecai enters the discussion of the power of ideas, at the Hand and Banner, he defends the use of reason "to see more and more of the hidden bonds that bind and consecrate change as a dependent growth" (ch. 42). It is precisely the "hidden" object that distinguishes this from Enlightenment rationality. The known bonds, including those of family, that unite men and women into communities have either failed or been superseded by reports and public opinion; hidden bonds and tendencies must now be sought to take their place. The appeal to mystery is generically very close to that of numerous real or imagined secret societies of the nineteenth century, which fended against the open debate implicit in democracy and the collapse of traditional commu-

23 Gouldner, *The Dialectic of Ideology and Technology*, p. 80.

nities by instilling selectness and club secrets. There is a Jewish plot in *Daniel Deronda* in both senses of the word. The movement to be enacted from "Mordecai's ideas" may very well lose its personal appeal if—as his mother hints—Deronda should become used to being a Jew. Events are often less inspiring than plans to alter them, and an accepted identity is less intriguing than a secret one. It is such considerations, no doubt, that cause many readers to lose interest in the plot of the novel once Grandcourt has been drowned and Gwendolen left to her guilt.

Further mysteries, unspoken and unresolved, are produced in *Daniel Deronda* by implicit comparisons between the Alcharisi and Gwendolen, and between Deronda and Grandcourt. George Eliot divided the novel into eight books and named the book in which two lines of suspense are resolved, "The Mother and the Son" (chs. 50-57). The letter from Leonora Halm-Eberstein "to my son, Daniel Deronda," the two interviews in Genoa, and their parting are the substance promised by this title and constitute the only appearance of the mother in the entire novel. But the same book ensconces the gathering intensity of Gwendolen's murderous wishes, the ominous putting about of the boat (the drowning of Grandcourt occurs between chapters), and *her* confession to Deronda. The title says nothing of these events, nor of "that new terrible life lying on the other side of the deed which fulfils a criminal desire" (ch. 57); the Princess Halm-Eberstein comes and goes, reveals that which Deronda has wanted to hear, and renews his personal banishment from her presence. Readers are still entitled to judge from this brief appearance that the mother bears a certain resemblance to Gwendolen Harleth, the "princess in exile" of Offendene (chs. 3 and 4) and "Princess Eboli" of Mirah's comparison (ch. 52), who has hoped to exploit her beauty on the stage.[24] The Alcharisi is a successful Gwendolen Harleth, also incapable of love and enjoying her power over men. "I am not a loving

24 The Princess Eboli is the odd woman out in Schiller's *Don Carlos*—and since Mirah is a singer, in comparing Mrs. Grandcourt to Eboli she probably has in mind Verdi's opera of 1867. The somewhat venomous comparison is just because of Eboli's beauty and penitence. She is secretly in love with the hero and virtually declares herself to him, but the love is not returned. Don Carlos is in love with his stepmother, the queen; in a crucial scene, he encounters Eboli when he expects his stepmother; and the princess subsequently takes the latter's place by bedding with Don Carlos's father, the king. Thus the interchange of the two women seems especially prescient of similar interchanges in the seventh book of *Daniel Deronda*.

woman," she matter-of-factly boasts. "I was never willingly subject to any man. Men have been subject to me" (ch. 53). When she first receives her son, she is draped loosely in black lace from head to foot (ch. 51); when he has last seen Gwendolen in London, she was wearing her black dress—the one she wore to receive Grandcourt's proposal of marriage—with a square of black lace concealing her hair and neck (ch. 48). Jean Sudrann has suggested that the resemblance of the two goes deeper, to the "dread" that inspires Gwendolen and the "great horror" (ch. 51) that has caused the princess to summon Deronda.[25]

A number of fantasies may contribute to this resemblance of Deronda's favorite patient to his mother. There is the round-about possibility that Grandcourt stands for more than one of the missing fathers in the novel,[26] and that his drowning satisfies Deronda's wishes as well as Gwendolen's. Some caution is necessary, however, in attributing the turn of the action to Oedipal motives—if only because George Eliot was a woman. Though *Daniel Deronda* owes more to projection and displacement than either *Felix Holt* or *Middlemarch*, it does not have the egocentric form of *Romola*. Rather, the unspoken connections among the characters are multiple and shifting, and the action in this part of the novel displays one correspondence and then another. Each of the characters achieves some kind of release in "The Mother and the Son," after which, in "Fruit and Seed," the novel comes to an end. The Princess Halm-Eberstein has discharged, after her own fashion, an obligation to her son and to her father. Gwendolen, most obviously, is free of Grandcourt and also free to marry again (though that possibility is not even hinted as yet). Deronda is now free of both women. His mother's revelations about her own role—her aggressive concealments and personal abandonment of her son—tend to cancel any moral obligation to her. More subtly, Gwendolen's "deed which fulfils a criminal desire" (and the narrator slips a little in admitting it a "deed") releases Deronda in some degree from obligation to her. Meanwhile Grandcourt has been painlessly released from Gwendolen and his life in this world. The model for the shifting significance of the actions in "The Mother and the Son" is undoubtedly the novelist's commentary on

25 *"Daniel Deronda* and the Landscape of Exile," *ELH*, 37 (1970), 450–451.

26 Cf. Dianne F. Sadoff, *Monsters of Affection* (Baltimore: Johns Hopkins University Press, 1982), pp. 99–101.

the fate of la Pia in the *Purgatorio*—"in relieving himself of her he could not avoid making the relief mutual" (ch. 54). George Eliot's casual reversal of the sexes in Dante's story seems to license the cross-purposes of this part of her novel.

Some Oedipal pattern would seem inevitable in a book entitled "The Mother and the Son," and confirmed in the outcome of the novel. Deronda assuredly finds release in the drowning, even if he does not suffer the guilt; Grandcourt meets violent death, and Deronda at least survives him. But any indirect evidence of a lineal or generational rivalry between these two can be matched by more evidence of their collateral standing in the novel—as rival heirs (so it is thought) to Sir Hugo Mallinger's estates, as husband and potential lover to Gwendolen, and above all as her two "monitors." Though one is spurred by ill will and the other by good, Grandcourt and Deronda have been rivals in watchfulness and concealment and "coercion" throughout.[27] In a passage of thoughtful Victorian reticence, George Eliot even admits that the young Deronda could become, like Grandcourt, a father of illegitimate children. When the hero first encounters the beautiful Mirah Lapidoth, that is, he experiences "an anxiety stronger than any motive he could give for it" that his actions be open and above suspicion. Because of the secrecy concerning his birth, "Deronda had made a vow to himself that—since the truths which disgrace mortals are not all of their own making—the truth should never be made to disgrace another by his act. He was not without terror lest he should break this vow ..." (ch. 19). Deronda seems to vow that he will never blackmail or tell on anyone, but the context shows the prohibition to be the fathering of illegitimate children and his hidden thought, therefore, the seduction of Mirah. O Daniel! Turn your fear into a safeguard, one is tempted to retort—if that were necessary.

What does it mean for Deronda to be released from Grandcourt as well as from his mother and Gwendolen in "The Mother and the Son"? As in almost any novel, it means the triumph of good over wickedness and the commencement of the future. In the complex overlay of characters of *Daniel Deronda*, it means release from family obligations and from the guilt attached to ending them: Deronda never has to deal directly with his father or with Grandcourt, and

27 See chapter 12.

after he makes the right filial gestures, his mother discharges him. Throughout the novel he has been implicitly compared and contrasted with Grandcourt, and when we recall that Daniel is a male being "not without terror" lest he father an illegitimate child, the riddance of Grandcourt makes sense as a comment on the wrong kind of fathering. The interesting thing about the reticence of the earlier narrative of Deronda's temptation is the way in which, in a novel bent on ideology, the language equates mere biological fathering with "truths" and "the truth." These are "truths which disgrace mortals" but nonetheless truths. Will it be any less true that Deronda, or any man, may one day father a legitimate child? The truth referred to in this carefully abstract way is the hidden truth of all fathering—an inference rather than an observed fact. There is no need to speak of "the truth" of mothering, because the connection of mothers with children can be observed directly; mothers bear their children, give birth to them, and nurse them. Fathering is almost a myth, and yet "the truth" that serves to link one generation with the next.

Being rid of Grandcourt means, among other things, the prospect of marriage for Deronda and the fathering of a proper family. George Eliot does not approve of illegitimate fathers and vigorously defends their illegitimate children against them. She has gone out of her way earlier to exculpate her supposed bastard hero by comparing him to notorious Shakespearean types and to defend his better instincts with one of her most scathing attacks upon unfeeling knowledge, including outdated scientific knowledge:

> He was the reverse of that type painted for us in Faulconbridge and Edmund of Gloster, whose coarse ambition for personal success is inflamed by a defiance of accidental disadvantages. To Daniel the words Father and Mother had the altar-fire in them; and the thought of all closest relations of our nature held still something of the mystic power which had made his neck and ears burn in boyhood. The average man may regard this sensibility on the question of birth as preposterous and hardly credible; but with the utmost respect for his knowledge as the rock from which all other knowledge is hewn, it must be admitted that many well-proved facts are dark to the average man, even concerning the action of his own heart and the structure of his own retina. A century ago he and all his forefathers had not had the slightest notion of that electric discharge by means of which they all wagged their tongues mistakenly; any more than they were

awake to the secluded anguish of exceptional sensitiveness into which many a carelessly begotten child of man is born. (ch. 37)

The stridency and involution of this attack on careless begetting, the sudden scorn for the average man and "all his forefathers," may be partly explained by the unease of potential contradiction. The narrator is wandering rather far from the case of Deronda, who was abandoned by his mother but is nevertheless the legitimate son of a Charisi. Moreover, the plot of the novel moves silently to throw over fathers and mothers, "and the thought of all closest relations of our nature," in favor of ancestry and liturgy and ultimately ideology. An implied contrast of Deronda and Grandcourt *as* fathers and a passage such as this argue that there are but two kinds of fathering, legitimate and illegitimate, whereas all fathering (as opposed to mothering) is hidden and subject to interpretation. In *Daniel Deronda* "the truths" of biological fathering at once merge with and are subsumed by the "hidden bonds" of Mordecai's teaching. At best, legitimate and illegitimate fathers are shadows of true and false ideology.

The general substitution of ideology for fathers in *Daniel Deronda* answers a personal need of the novelist.[28] George Eliot was not fully aware, perhaps, of the emotion she brought to bear on the narrow truth in question, the link between a particular child and father. But she is more than aware, and ready to argue, that ideology may supply the social need of an abandoned generation. In the absence of actual fathers for Deronda and Gwendolen in the novel, she labors to give ideology a biological and evolutionary basis identical to "the truths" of fathering. It is her grand purpose to repair the discontinuity of modern lives by invoking the continuity of generations over time. The "stronger Something" that Deronda asserts against his mother's will has its hereditary basis "in my grandfather's trust" (ch. 52). "It is you," Deronda tells Mordecai, "who have given shape to what, I believe, was an inherited yearning,—the effect of brooding, passionate thoughts in many ancestors,—thoughts that seem to have been intensely present in my grandfather" (ch. 63). Such truths, however,

28 Just before the death of her father, Mary Ann Evans wrote, "What shall I be without my Father? It will seem as if a part of my moral nature were gone. I had a horrid vision of myself last night becoming earthly sensual and devilish for want of that purifying restraining influence" (letter to Mr. and Mrs. Charles Bray, 30 May 1849, *G.E.L.*, I, 284). None of George Eliot's biographers fails to stress the influence of Robert Evans upon her life.

and Mordecai's hidden bonds are not scientifically any different from "the truths which disgrace mortals." Therein lies the difficulty: biology has as yet no means of distinguishing truths that honor from truths that disgrace.[29] George Eliot is conscious of the difficulty and does not push the hereditary thesis very hard as biology. Instead she permits it to invade her novel as an element of romance and mystery surrounding the improbable life of Deronda. She can be more clear and forthright about the uses of ideology than she can about actual fathers, and perhaps unfortunately for her thesis, she does admit to her novel a good many actual mothers—most important, besides Mrs. Glasher and Mrs. Meyrick, the timorous but far from insensible Fanny Davilow and the sincerely acting Leonora Halm-Eberstein. During her too brief engagement, the last of these mothers speaks a number of strong lines that grate against her son's yearnings, against fathering, and against ideology: "I relieved you from the bondage of having been born a Jew," and "I delivered you from the pelting contempt that pursues Jewish separateness" (ch. 51). The force of these lines, subversive of the hereditary thesis in its most ambitious form, is in the mother's "I delivered you." For every child is delivered so, free of ideology and of metaphorical fathering at least, if constrained in some respects by heredity.

George Eliot is genuinely troubled by the freedom into which men and women are born, the absence of authority and direction in a secular society. Deliverance into the modern society of information and opinion is like a general abandonment of boys and superfluous girls, and "those other many thousand sisters of us all"—a deliverance that is also into shame and easy blackmail. *Daniel Deronda* is her last, marvelous effort to discover instead, in consciousness itself, some authority for individual behavior. She dwells repeatedly on the consciousness of this character or that; she enlarges consciousness to make room for command and obedience, and for a saving sense of guilt. Still, questions as to the nature of this consciousness persist. Neither a subjective nor an objective account of the authority vested in consciousness can be satisfactory: if it is subjective, then it is to a

29 Darwin agreed that "virtuous tendencies" might be inherited, but he conceded that "senseless customs, superstitions, and tastes . . . ought on the same principle to be transmitted." On the first point he cited Spencer, "our great philosopher." See *The Descent of Man, and Selection in Relation to Sex*, 2nd ed. (London: Murray, 1875), pp. 123–124.

certain extent arbitrary; and if it is objective, it is a form of knowledge and subject to error. In *Daniel Deronda* George Eliot experiments with a subjective authority and does her best to rid it of arbitrary or immediate influences. She discounts the influence of actual fathers and speculates on an inherited sense of direction, associated with a healthy terror of wrongdoing. For objective authority she employs an ideology, not one that she has invented but one suffused with ancient tradition. This ideology can be objectively learned, brought into consciousness—not of course from a mere exchange of information, but through committed study. In such case, however, the forms that consciousness takes are the forms of knowledge rather than instinct, and the possibility of false consciousness arises.

According to Feuerbach, in George Eliot's translation of *The Essence of Christianity*, "the religious mind does not distinguish between subjective and objective,—it has no doubts; it has the faculty, not of discerning other things than itself, but of seeing its own conceptions out of itself as distinct beings." In concluding that "the secret of theology is nothing else than anthropology," Feuerbach argued that seeming "facts" are simply beliefs that are not acknowledged as such:

> A fact, I repeat, is a conception about the truth of which there is no doubt, because it is no object of theory, but of feeling, which desires that what it wishes, what it believes, should be true. A fact is that, the denial of which is forbidden, if not by an external law, yet by an internal one. A fact is every possibility which passes for a reality, every conception which, for the age wherein it is held to be a fact, expresses a want, and is for that reason an impassable limit of the mind.[30]

But the "secret" of theology, unknown to the religious mind, is known to Feuerbach. For him, for his translator, and for his readers there can be no escaping the difference between a subjective and an objective view; a fact, they know, is that "which passes for a reality." Hence a consciousness of possible falsehood has been admitted. No matter how eagerly one urges the desirability of a fusion of thought and feeling, the conception of truth may be false, the fact fiction.

The same specter of falsehood must haunt any ideology that is embraced in the hope of achieving some social end, unless it is embraced

30 *The Essence of Christianity*, trans. George Eliot (1854; rpt. New York: Harper, 1957), pp. 204–207.

as fact by a religious mind. In *Daniel Deronda* Mordecai's ideas are finally accepted by Deronda as true, but Deronda has not by any means a religious mind. There is some evidence that, before he is aware of his Jewish birth, he is attracted to Mordecai because of his interest in false beliefs. "Deronda's sensitiveness was not the less responsive because he could not but believe that this strangely disclosed relation was founded on an illusion." He gives himself over to Mordecai's strong feelings and reflects, "Great heaven! what relation has proved itself more potent in the world than faith even when mistaken,—than expectation even when perpetually disappointed?" (ch. 40). This is all very much a deliberate act of belief, and almost a deliberate subordination of truth to chance. Later, in Mainz, Deronda learns that his grandfather possessed some of the same spirit, a determination toward belief so strong that error can be tolerated. Kalonymos tells him that "Daniel Charisi used to say, 'Better a wrong will than a wavering; better a steadfast enemy than an uncertain friend; better a false belief than no belief at all' " (ch. 60). Though these words were supposedly uttered two generations earlier, they too are not the expression of a religious mind in Feuerbach's sense. Rather, they are the expression of a post-Enlightenment recuperation of belief, voiced by an ideologue who is prepared to gamble on the truth rather than debate it.

These scattered statements are George Eliot's frank admission of the possibility of false consciousness in her representation of ideology. More effective challenges to Mordecai's ideas are the brief opposition of the Princess Halm-Eberstein, the whimsical deflections of Hans Meyrick, and even the forbidding presence of Henleigh Mallinger Grandcourt. *Daniel Deronda* is not a tract but a large, irregular novel by a writer of dramatic flair and unsurpassed intelligence. The most devastating self-criticism of all lurks in the odd humor of the final chapters, in which the most notorious missing father of the novel makes a long-threatened appearance—his first and last appearance, something like Deronda's mother's—and wreaks his own kind of vengeance on ideology, on the family, and on all excessive guilt. The gambling quality of Deronda's and Charisi's commitments to strong belief is suddenly cast in a new light by the antics of this compulsive gambler, a despiser of his own Jewishness, and the nearest character besides Lush to the type of the blackmailer. In the seriocomic return of Cohen-Lapidoth, George Eliot provides a dramatic inversion of what Ernest Gellner has called the "offensiveness" of ideology, and by placing this episode in the denouement of the novel she gives her reader lasting pause. In Gellner's view "all belief systems are offensive . . . and hence all are tension-generating, simply because men can never have the evidence adequate for a viable system of ideas." But his comments are particularly directed at ideologies, as these are derivative from religion. An "offence-generating property is *inherent*" in ideologies, since they supply "contentions which are inherently fear- and hope-inspiring and are meant to be such":

> Ideologies contain hypotheses, but they are not simply hypotheses. They are hypotheses full of both menace and sex-appeal. They threaten and they promise; they demand assent with menaces; they re-classify the moral identity of the believer and sceptic; they generate a somewhat new world. The world is different according to whether one looks at it from within or without a given ideology.[31]

Gellner, obviously, is resisting ideology throughout these reflections. He describes what he dislikes, and deliberately he reduces the attraction and coercion of "offensiveness," a concept borrowed from Kierkegaard's theology, to sex-appeal on the one hand and criminal behavior on the other: a "demand with menaces" is a statutory definition of robbery in England, and specifically a definition of modern blackmail.[32] Something in George Eliot also resists ideology, for it is she who invents the blackmailing Lapidoth and allows him to steal the scene at the end of her novel. The latter's scheme mocks the grand theme of ideology and even produces its sexual effect. Nor is it absolutely clear that this is the last Deronda will hear of his father-in-law.

Whereas metaphorical fathering in *Daniel Deronda* stands for the authority sadly missing from the modern world, on the very day in

31 "Notes towards a Theory of Ideology," in *Spectacles and Predicaments: Essays in Social Theory* (Cambridge, England: Cambridge University Press, 1979), pp. 118–119. Kierkegaard uses "offensiveness" to characterize the demands placed on the believer by Christianity—the individual feels almost mocked or insulted by the extraordinary privilege placed before him. See Kierkegaard, *The Sickness unto Death*, trans. with *Fear and Trembling* by Walter Lowrie (Princeton: Princeton University Press, 1968), pp. 214–218.

32 Section 21 of the Theft Act of 1968 reads, "A person is guilty of blackmail if, with a view to gain for himself or another or with intent to cause loss to another, he makes any unwarranted demand with menaces . . ." See J. C. Smith, *The Law of Theft*, 4th ed. (London: Butterworth, 1979), p. 244.

which Deronda returns to London to tell Mordecai and Mirah of his Jewishness, the "embodied presentiment" of a father seizes his daughter's wrist in the street and pronounces her name "with a persuasive curl of accent" (ch. 62). Mrs. Meyrick prudently warns Mirah not to have any dealings in secret with her father, for he is an inveterate extortionist as well as gambler. The latter sizes up the situation, however, and—himself being a source of disgrace—hits upon a plan to have Deronda "advance a considerable sum for the sake of getting rid of him." As it happens, the plan is aborted, because Lapidoth is tempted by an easier crime and hies himself off. In the strange episode that follows, Deronda removes his "memorable ring" and lays it on the table; Lapidoth lays his hat over the ring and then absconds with it, never to return (presumably) and face prosecution. The riddance is even more fortunate than Deronda's mother's refusal of his acquaintance. Moreover, in the humiliation of Mirah, the hero finds his opportunity. "In this moment of grief and shame" he proposes, "giving her the highest tribute man can give to woman" (ch. 68).

Supporting this denouement are sturdy conventions of comedy—of fathers gracelessly giving ground to lovers—which no doubt have some basis in life. As Edgar Rosenberg has suggested, the business also harks back, through Scott's Isaac of York to Shylock and the Jew of Malta, to a stereotyping of irrascible Jews with attractive daughters.[33] Yet it is curious after so much raising of consciousness to guilt that the novel should offer one final testimony to the power of shame. More pointedly, Lapidoth is a personification of the shamefulness of being Jewish—he is both ashamed of himself as a Jew and the cause of shame in others. Though Deronda has been anxious from the beginning lest Mirah's people turn out to be vulgar Jews—and her father is something worse than that—the narrative has had only positive things to say about his personal feelings in confirming his own Jewishness. Surely Deronda also commits himself to this shame of being Jewish, voluntarily becoming what most of his acquaintances think of as a pariah in order to assert his mastery over childhood feelings of being unwanted. His early sensation of others knowing something about him that he did not know can be thwarted

---

33 *From Shylock to Svengali* (Stanford: Stanford University Press, 1960), pp. 168–170. See also Judith Wilt, *Ghosts of the Gothic* (Princeton: Princeton University Press, 1980), pp. 225–226, on the subversive effect of Lapidoth's return.

and reversed by announcing a connection unknown to nearly all, and a connection for which all too many persons in history have been blackmailed or persecuted outright. The sectarian identity shields against diffuse possibilities of blackmail in modern society, and a deliberate return to separateness prefers, in principle, a collective difference from others to indifferent exposure on all sides. But still there is the poetic justice of spontaneous comedy in the return of the blackmailing Lapidoth. The ring he makes off with is the symbol of Daniel Deronda's solemn pact with his fathers.

V

A Psychopathology of Information

Breuer heard of the case, the patient was sent to me and I endeavoured to cure her tendency to paranoia by trying to reinstate the memory of the scene. I failed in this. . . . In reply to my searching enquiries as to whether something "embarrassing" had not happened all the same, I was met with the most decided negative, and—saw her no more. She sent me a message to say that it upset her too much. Defence! That was obvious. . . .

She was sparing herself something; something was repressed. We can guess what it was. She had probably really been excited by what she had seen and by its memory. So what she was sparing herself was the reproach of being a "bad woman." Afterwards she came to hear the same reproach from outside. Thus *the subject-matter remained unaffected;* what was altered was something in the *placing* of the whole thing.

—Freud to Wilhelm Fliess, 24 January 1895

15

Blackmail and
the Unconscious

The weakening of faith in divine sanctions for behavior, the absence of fixed political authority and its replacement by representation, the fluctuation of belief and the breakdown of community, the substitution of information for precept—the absconding of fathers, to borrow a scandalous metaphor from *Daniel Deronda*—were all reasons to turn for guidance, in the later nineteenth century, to the study of individual consciousness. The widening and deepening exploration of consciousness in successive novels by George Eliot can be thought of as a European phenomenon, as the following credo, or *non credo*, of Benedetto Croce attests:

> We no longer believe . . . like the Greeks, in happiness of life on earth; we no longer believe, like the Christians, in happiness in an other-worldly life; we no longer believe, like the optimistic philosophers of the last century, in a happy future for the human race. . . . We no longer believe in anything of that, and *what we have alone retained is the consciousness of ourselves, and the need to make that consciousness ever clearer and more evident*, a need for whose satisfaction we turn to science and to art.[1]

Croce's consciousness, upon which science and art rather than religion and politics are brought to bear, corresponds to the "emotional intellect" associated in *Daniel Deronda* with an ideology, the vision

---

1 Quoted by H. Stuart Hughes, *Consciousness and Society: The Reorientation of European Social Thought, 1890–1930*, rev. ed. (New York: Vintage, 1977), pp. 428–429.

of "some truth of what will be,—the more comprehensive massive life feeding theory with new material, as the sensibility of the artist seizes combinations which science explains and justifies" (ch. 41). Just as Croce addresses both mental and social life, the syntax of George Eliot's argument hovers uncertainly between mental and social activity: the terms of "more comprehensive massive life" are collective, yet the context and the apposition of the singular artist indicate that the activity in question is that of individual consciousness. The association between consciousness and ideology ("raising one's consciousness," in the latest idiom) is a natural one for modern times. "More comprehensive massive life" *is* collective in a certain sense, though the words strictly denote individual life that provides "more" than "unemotional intellect." George Eliot in this passage addresses "human thinking, whether in its sum total or in the separate minds that have made the sum."

The need for ideology arises from the same accumulation of knowledge as the faith in public opinion. While ideology professes the same hope as public opinion for the advance of society and the prevention of backsliding, it seeks to enhance the power of society to set a course, by narrowing the focus of opinion and repairing the indiscriminate threat of publicity. Ideology is historically and logically the later development, an outgrowth of the realization that a hegemony of public opinion is a mixed blessing. Without the effects of shame on the one hand or proselytizing on the other, the widening knowledge of humankind would not be sufficient to regulate conduct. Similarly with the interest in consciousness: whatever the individual knows, and enlarges upon through art and science, must have an edge and a purpose. As a condition to be counted on and cultivated, consciousness is just as surely an historical phenomenon and a product of information as ideology.[2] Consciousness in this sense—the ample consciousness that Croce and George Eliot rely upon—is acquired. It is the completion of the work of literacy and a replication inside of information outside the mind, a historical concomitant of the rapid rise of information in the nineteenth century.[3] Literacy itself is an exclusively

2 Cf. George Levine, *The Realistic Imagination* (Chicago: University of Chicago Press, 1981), p. 255: "The relation of consciousness to matter and to other consciousnesses is the subtext of many late-nineteenth-century works."

3 I am not concerned here, obviously, with the ancient discovery of writing but with the suffusion of commerce and industry and government with information, the

verbal or numerical capacity for experience, a distancing of the world, other beings, and the self from the self. Writing and reading preserve this distance over time, sharpening the comparison between past and present that is part of what we mean by consciousness. In his *Confessions* Rousseau wrote, "I don't know how I learned to read; I only remember my first readings and their effect on me: it is from that time that I date without interruption my consciousness of myself."[4] Mass literacy and the rise of information are surely the primary cause of the modern historical phenomenon described as consciousness. Consciousness is not that inner force celebrated by Puritans as "conscience," but the inward awareness of the outward forces of information. "Usually," according to Nietzsche, "one takes consciousness itself as the general sensorium and supreme court; nonetheless, it is only a means of communication: it is evolved through social intercourse and with a view to the interests of social intercourse."[5] And like the power of public opinion or the rallying call of ideology, the effective strength of consciousness depends upon a generalized avoidance of shame.

The modern imputation of *un*consciousness in every mind also follows from the rapidly expanding role of information. Just as information is latent knowledge and its application, or discrete revelation, a continual reminder of the quantity that remains hidden, so there may be stored secrets as well as conscious thoughts affecting the interchanges within the mind. The unconscious is commonly, and quite properly, said to be the discovery of Freud, who labored for a lifetime to match the art of psychoanalysis with explanations of science. Freud had predecessors in a number of fields, however, and his investigations would not have been conceivable before geology and evolutionary biology had persuaded scientists and others of the explanatory power in fragmentary and disjunctive narratives of the

---

exponential growth of science and learning, the universalization of literacy and success of inexpensive communications in Europe. On the ancient Greek experience, which is also relevant, see Bruno Snell, *The Discovery of the Mind: The Greek Origins of European Thought*, trans. T. G. Rosenmeyer (1953; rpt. New York: Harper, 1960); and Eric A. Havelock, *Preface to Plato* (1963; rpt. Cambridge: Harvard University Press, 1982).

4 Quoted by Robert Darnton, "The Origins of Modern Reading," *New Republic*, 190 (27 Feb. 1984), 27.

5 *The Will to Power*, trans. Walter Kaufmann and R. J. Hollingdale (New York: Vintage, 1968), pp. 283–286. Cf. also pp. 265–266.

past. Nor can the scientific precedents be isolated from general developments in the use of information, since the evidence of hidden actions and the deployment of the evidence in narrative were also the study of crime prevention and of a great deal of imaginative literature in the nineteenth century. In the words of Paul Ricoeur, "facts in psychoanalysis are in no way facts of observable behavior. They are 'reports.' "[6] One can go further and argue that the depersonalized relations of the information society—an era for which the condition of being "the observed of all observers" was no longer a compliment, as it was intended for Hamlet, but a threat of exposure—supplied an essential model for the concealment and estrangement of one part of the mind from another.

Quite obviously attempts to describe and explain activities of mind will enlist the forms and vocabulary of outward experience. Neither an art nor a science of consciousness—or unconsciousness—can thrive without metaphor. Freud could not conceive of a patient sparing or judging herself, being excited or frightened by her memories, or reproaching herself as a "bad woman" without restaging a drama that is ordinarily understood as taking place among separate persons. The unfamiliar has to be imagined in terms of the familiar, and some such drama is certain to be imported whenever thought is directed to the dynamics of consciousness. In a lecture tracing the desynonymization of "conscience" and "conscious" from Greek and Latin to English usage, C. S. Lewis called attention to the transposition from collective to psychological meanings at every stage in the history of the words:

> Hobbes . . . gives English *conscious* exactly the classical meaning of *conscius:* "When two or more men know of one and the same fact [i.e., deed] they are said to be conscious of it one to another."
>
> Since secrets often are, and are always suspected of being, guilty secrets, the normal implications of *conscius* and *conscientia* are bad. My *conscius,* the man who is *conscius mihi,* who shares my secret, who can give evidence about something I have done, is usually the fellow-conspirator; therefore the possible

6 "The Question of Proof in Freud's Psychoanalytic Writings," *Journal of the American Psychoanalytic Association,* 25 (1977), 837. In this influential article, Ricoeur examines the data, narratives, and interpretive procedures of psychoanalysis in order to show in what senses the theory can be verified.

witness against me, the possible blackmailer, or at least the man who can taunt me with my deed and make me ashamed.

In the twentieth century Lewis naturally reaches for the figure of the blackmailer as a threatener of secrets. In turning from consciousness as "external witness" to consciousness as "internal witness," he follows through with a second personification of the same: "a person . . . is privy to his own acts, is his own *conscius* or accomplice. And of course this shadowy inner accomplice has all the same properties as an external one; he too is a witness against you, a potential blackmailer, one who inflicts shame and fear."[7] We ought to ask to what degree such metaphors from the modern social experience may actually have shaped the modern understanding of the mind, including theories with scientific pretension such as Freud's. If our understanding of conscious agency in the mind depends on metaphor, then unconscious agency will be a hypothesis invoking additional dramatic personification.

Neither Freud nor C. S. Lewis is the authority who has immediately persuaded me of the close association between publicity in the modern world and construction of what takes place in the mind, but rather George Eliot in her last two novels.[8] In *Middlemarch* she introduced Bulstrode—in tandem with Lydgate—and confronted him with a melodramatic return of the past in the form of Raffles. The blackmailer of Bulstrode brings before him "the scenes of his earlier life," which happen to be tinged with disagreeable sexuality, and this return of the past is like "a loathsome dream." Not surprisingly some interpreters of the novel read Raffles as a "double" for Bulstrode or personification of "unpleasant facts" rather than as a character in his own right. Silencing Raffles is a crude means of suppressing the past, a self-cure for Bulstrode of the kind that George Eliot explores much more thoroughly, though still indirectly, in the representation of Gwendolen Grandcourt's motives for killing her husband. In *Daniel*

7 "Conscience and Conscious," *Studies in Words*, 2nd ed. (Cambridge, England: Cambridge University Press, 1967), pp. 185–187.

8 Freud read and admired both novels in the 1880s, to what effect we do not know. Ernest Jones tells us only that *Middlemarch* "appealed to him very much, and he found it illuminated important aspects of his relations" with his future wife, and that *Daniel Deronda* "amazed him by its knowledge of Jewish intimate ways that 'we speak of only among ourselves.'" See *The Life and Work of Sigmund Freud*, 3 vols. (New York: Basic Books, 1953–1957), I, 174.

Deronda, not only is the psychology much finer, but Grandcourt's secret knowledge of the past is carefully matched with Gwendolen's—it is the *same* knowledge, of the communication between the heroine and Lydia Glasher and all that the passive reception of that communication implies. There is no need for Grandcourt to threaten to expose his wife, only to let her know that he knows. The situation between them, including the curious role of Lush, more nearly resembles an interior exchange of information than the relation of Raffles and Bulstrode. The pair have to live together, for one thing, like the Latimers and Casaubons before them. The death of the husband therefore more nearly resembles a killing of the self that knows, a stopping of payment to the past and putting an end to a kind of self-torture. Similar constructions may be placed upon Lady Dedlock's excellent motives for killing Tulkinghorn in *Bleak House*—the more so because she does not kill him—or upon the outward actions of many sensation novels of the Victorian era, with their intricacies of legal and mental cases. Imagined relations of information and coercion, of threatened shame and embarrassment, are introjected as guilt and interior struggle. Not surprisingly, one of the chapters of *Lady Audley's Secret* is called "Retrograde Investigation," as if in anticipation of the investigations of psychoanalysis, and the narrator remarks that "physicians and lawyers are the confessors of this prosaic nineteenth century."[9] Merely to name those two professions in conjunction with confession exemplifies the point I am making about the translation of social experience to a speculative account of the mind.

A strong case for this translation, or the apparent repetition of modern social conditions within the inmost recesses of mind, is made by the persistent psychological reference of *Daniel Deronda* as a whole. The same novel that effectively represents observation and concealment, the power and felt coercion of knowing among the characters, makes repeated reference to the dynamics of consciousness and unconsciousness within characters. Especially in the case of Gwendolen Harleth, George Eliot provides both explicit comment on this inner dynamics and, more impressively, numerous casual allusions in the narrative. In reporting "something vague and yet mastering" in Gwendolen's feelings, for example, the narrator comments

9 Mary Elizabeth Braddon, *Lady Audley's Secret* (New York: Dover, 1974), chs. 25 and 36.

that "there is a great deal of unmapped country within us which would have to be taken into account in an explanation of our gusts and storms" (ch. 24). Such cartographic and meteorological metaphors at least conceivably bring the unconscious within reach of scientific "explanation," and in the most elaborate of such assertions in the novel, an epigraph to the history of Deronda's childhood, George Eliot underlines the scientific possibilities of research in this area by extravagant comparison with astronomy:

> Men, like planets, have both a visible and an invisible history. The astronomer threads the darkness with strict deduction, accounting so for every visible arc in the wanderer's orbit; and the narrator of human actions, if he did his work with the same completeness, would have to thread the hidden pathways of feeling and thought which lead up to every moment of action, and to those moments of intense suffering which take the quality of action . . . (ch. 16)

The darkness here is the most general metaphor for what is concealed in the mind, though in *Daniel Deronda* words such as "hidden" and "secret," which usually apply to the concealments from others' knowledge, apply also to that which is concealed from the self by the self, as in "the secret windings and recesses" of feeling (ch. 35). "Fantasies moved within [Gwendolen] like ghosts, making no break in her more acknowledged consciousness and finding no obstruction in it: dark rays doing their work invisibly in the broad light" (ch. 48). A certain amount of information apparently manages to flow from the dark to light places. It may be that "in the dark seed-growths of consciousness a new wish was forming itself" (ch. 26); or that a motive can be felt without being recognized, and thus remain "a mystery of which she had a faint wondering consciousness" (ch. 11).

George Eliot was not writing according to any fixed topography of the mind. Her attention is on the possible or partial awareness of what is still hidden, and the passage from unconscious to conscious thought. She once uses the term "under-consciousness" (ch. 31) and several times "undercurrent," in something like the sense of Freud's "preconscious." "Something like this was the common undercurrent in Deronda's mind" (ch. 32); and "all the while there was a busy undercurrent in [Gwendolen], like the thought of a man who keeps up a dialogue while he is considering how he can slip away" (ch. 26).

The fine simile likens the half-conscious activity of mind directly to the partial concealment of one individual from another in conversation, which is instanced in the pauses of Grandcourt and elsewhere in the novel. The general comparison to refused speech recurs when the subject happens to be, not Gwendolen or Grandcourt, but Mirah Lapidoth: "she was pressed upon by a crowd of thoughts thrusting themselves forward as interpreters of that consciousness which still remained unuttered to herself." The representation of conscious and unconscious thought in the novel is not limited to the principal characters. In fact Mirah, as the "true" heroine, conventionally ought to repress more thoughts than her rival: "what notion, what vain reliance could it be that had lain darkly within her and was now burning itself into sight as disappointment and jealousy?" (ch. 61). In writing of Mirah's awakening to love, George Eliot generalizes about "the busy constructions that go on within us, not only without effort but even against it," but she reserves the word "unconscious" for old-fashioned innocence: "the disturbance of Mirah's unconsciousness" comes from outside (ch. 52).

Like George Eliot's last contribution to the art of the novel, Freud's contributions to psychoanalysis have persistently to do with information that is either accessible or inaccessible to consciousness. The focus upon exchanges of information that may or may not take place, upon threatening information or frustrating concealments, is the aspect of psychoanalysis that most concerns us here and one that clearly attaches it to a particular historical moment.[10] The object of study is not primarily human instinct or behavior in the ordinary sense but the state of self-knowledge, for which psychoanalysis posits more or less constant concealment and indirect revelation. The study of conscious and unconscious thought stops short of resulting moral

10 Of the many recent efforts to describe the historical context of Freud's thought, two of the most comprehensive are Henri Ellenberger, *The Discovery of the Unconscious: The History and Evolution of Dynamic Psychiatry* (New York: Basic Books, 1970), which traces sources in literature and psychology, and Frank J. Sulloway, *Freud, Biologist of the Mind: Beyond the Psychoanalytic Legend* (New York: Basic Books, 1979), which brilliantly covers the scientific ground. In the first volume of *The Bourgeois Experience: Victoria to Freud, Education of the Senses* (New York: Oxford University Press, 1984), Peter Gay supplies another context from social history. By "psychoanalysis" in the following pages, I mean the movement of thought represented by the writings of Freud, not necessarily psychoanalysis as it is practiced today.

actions. Psychoanalysis is not interested in murder, nor in the guilt of murderers, but in thoughts of murder—such as those entertained by Gwendolen Grandcourt of her husband—and guilt feelings. Just so, it is not interested in wish-fulfillment but in the representation of wish-fulfillment in dreams or jokes or stories of all kinds. In *Civilization and Its Discontents* Freud professes that he would "not be surprised if a reader were to exclaim angrily: 'So it makes no difference whether one kills one's father or not—one gets a feeling of guilt in either case!' " He goes on to distinguish carefully psychological guilt from the "remorse" of one who has done wrong.[11] A mischievous passage near the beginning of *Daniel Deronda* plays on a similar distinction, as George Eliot writes of the simultaneous presence of conflicting impulses in her heroine's mind (ch. 4). The novelist appeals, in fact, to *Macbeth*, a favorite study of guilt with psychoanalysts precisely because it is a story.[12]

The object of study for psychoanalysis is neither action nor desire but internalized information, ostensibly words or figures that are stored or transmitted within the mind. The secondary nature of the investigations of psychoanalysis has sometimes been characterized as a linguistic, a scientific, or a narrative stance toward its data. For Jacques Lacan, psychoanalysis is essentially an extension of linguistics, since its object is language. "One out of every three pages in the complete works of Freud is devoted to philological references, one out of two pages to logical inferences, and everywhere the apprehension of experience is dialectical, with the proportion of linguistic analysis increasing just insofar as the unconscious is directly concerned." The *un*conscious, note—it is Lacan's contention that the dreamwork described in *The Interpretation of Dreams* corresponds point by point to the functions of language as described by Ferdinand de Saussure.[13] For Philip Rieff, the degree of abstraction in psychoanal-

---

11 *Civilization and Its Discontents* (1930), S.E., XXI, 131–132.

12 E.g., Oscar Pfister, *Christianity and Fear: A Study in History and in the Psychology and Hygiene of Religion*, trans. W. H. Johnston (New York: Macmillan, 1948), pp. 74–78. Angus Fletcher has suggested to me that Pfister may be seen as mediating between George Eliot's interest in fear and psychoanalysis.

13 See "The Insistence of the Letter in the Unconscious," trans. Jan Miel, in *Structuralism*, ed. Jacques Ehrmann (1966; rpt. New York: Anchor, 1970), pp. 117–120. Lacan's argument is very suggestive, though it sacrifices the distinction between report and experience. As against his welding of Freudian analysis to language, I would urge that it is linked to the final advance of literacy.

ysis is due to the influence of modern science. "It is characteristic of modern science that nature, the object of knowledge, is seen as withdrawn and definitely unlike the way we experience it—this in contrast to ancient and medieval science, which presumed no disjunction between experience and the truth of nature." Rieff takes this fundamental principle and shows, in effect, that as modern science is inherently skeptical and prepared to "decode" the data it collects, so Freud approaches the hidden and possibly deceptive operations of the mind.[14] For Roy Schafer, finally, psychoanalysis is essentially a narrative art that critically depends on the metaphors it employs to describe the mind. This position is also persuasive, and in my view is supported historically by the narrative achievements of nineteenth-century novelists—though in the process of reforming the metaphors in order to improve the art, Schafer tends to erase the original associations of psychoanalysis with science and information.[15]

The notion of an exchange of information in the mind can be traced to the earliest days of psychoanalysis. In the theoretical portion of *Studies on Hysteria*, published jointly with Freud in 1895, Joseph Breuer did his best to defend the anomaly of attributing "ideas" to the unconscious. There was, he wrote, a threshold of consciousness through which ideas might pass if they increased in intensity. The theory postulated an "ideational substratum" and posed the problem of "how an idea can be sufficiently intense to provoke a lively motor act, for instance, and at the same time not intense enough to become conscious."[16] Despite this theoretical difficulty, psychoanalysis persisted in focusing on conscious and unconscious ideas, wishes, or representations in the mind. The awareness or ignorance of such is

14 *Freud: The Mind of the Moralist* (1959; rpt. New York: Anchor, 1961), pp. 73–76. I am indebted to Rieff for calling attention to the texts discussed in the next two paragraphs. Earlier he suggests that, "by focusing so exclusively on the human subject in a state of recovering its capacity for decision, Freud breaks the bonds between psychology and natural science. . . . It is as a *social* science that Freudian psychology must be dealt with" (p. 18).

15 See "Narration in the Psychoanalytic Dialogue," *Critical Inquiry*, 7 (1980), 29–53; and *A New Language for Psychoanalysis* (New Haven: Yale University Press, 1976), esp. pp. 155–178.

16 *Studies on Hysteria*, S.E., II, 223–225. Where there has seemed any question about the inferences to be drawn from the language of these passages, I have checked the *Standard Edition* against the German of the *Gesammelte Werke*, ed. Anna Freud, Marie Bonaparte, et al., 18 vols. (London: Imago, 1940–1952, and Frankfurt: Fischer, 1968).

always the issue, the cause of neurosis and the key to its cure. The theory invites and sustains an investigation of the unconscious by the conscious mind. Consciousness itself is limited and transient, but as by analogy to science, the object of its investigation is limitless and somehow permanent. In the theoretical chapter of *The Interpretation of Dreams*, Freud concludes that the unconscious is *"as much unknown to us as the reality of the external world, and it is as incompletely presented by the data of consciousness as is the external world by the communications of our sense organs."*[17] By invoking "the reality of the external world," Freud indeed brings to mind the researches of science, as Rieff suggests, though strictly speaking the analogy is between consciousness and the perceptual system.

The subsequent development of the theory preserves at least this much distance between consciousness and unconsciousness. There is always the distance implied by perception, and usually the distance implied by full-dress investigations of science or of psychoanalysis itself. Bringing to consciousness is never compared to an experience of pleasure or pain, of fear, hunger, thirst, or sexual desire, but rather to the comprehension of the evidence or statement of feeling. In his metapsychological paper "The Unconscious," Freud asserts:

> I am in fact of the opinion that the antithesis of conscious and unconscious is not applicable to instincts. An instinct can never become an object of consciousness—only the idea that represents the instinct can. Even in the unconscious, moreover, an instinct cannot be represented other than by an idea. If the instinct did not attach itself to an idea or manifest itself as an affective state, we could know nothing about it. When we nevertheless speak of an unconscious instinctual impulse or of a repressed instinctual impulse, the looseness of the phraseology is a harmless one. We can only mean an instinctual impulse the ideational representative of which is unconscious, for nothing else comes into consideration.[18]

The overriding analogy here is still to science or other investigative proceeding that assimilates information—facts that can be impersonally sorted and exchanged by anyone precisely because they are not, "even in the unconscious," directly accessible as experience. The

17 *The Interpretation of Dreams* (1900), *S.E.*, V, 613.
18 "The Unconscious" (1915), *S.E.*, XIV, 177.

providing of access to normally inaccessible information, then, and the recombining of the information with that which is already known are the main tasks of psychoanalysis.

The effect of information depends on its revelation, and the moment of revelation can be controlled to a great extent by narrative. Because classic psychoanalytic therapy "works by transforming what is unconscious into what is conscious,"[19] it relies very much on a narrative for the effective timing of revelations about the self, a timing that may be as important as the information revealed. Freud seems to have stumbled upon the significance of narrative for his art by reflecting on his own early case studies. In a well-known passage in *Studies on Hysteria* he observed that narrative, "such as we are accustomed to find in the works of imaginative writers," helped to explain as well as to describe the disorders of his patients.[20] When he subsequently decided that many or most of the sufferers from hysteria whom he treated had invented, rather than experienced, episodes of seduction in their childhood, he began to countenance the production of fictions that were, he believed, as useful as fact in getting at the truth. Freud thus conferred upon his patients a certain right to construct stories and indirectly confirmed the usefulness of psychoanalysis for the criticism of imaginative literature.[21] In the mature technique of analysis he combined his own formidable storytelling ability with that of the patient to achieve the desired results. According to *An Outline of Psychoanalysis,* published posthumously in 1940, the patient's knowledge must be his own, but by anticipating the full story the analyst can assure the effectiveness of this knowledge:

> We avoid telling him at once things that we have often discovered at an early stage, and we avoid telling him the whole of what we think we have discovered. We reflect carefully over when we shall impart the knowledge of one of our constructions to him ... As a rule we put off telling him of a construction or explanation till he himself has so nearly arrived at it that only a single step remains to be taken, though that step is in fact the decisive synthesis. If we proceeded in another way and over-

19 *Introductory Lectures on Psycho-Analysis* (1916–1917), S.E., XVI, 280; see also *Five Lectures on Psycho-Analysis* (1910), XI, 9–20.

20 *Studies on Hysteria,* S.E., II, 160–161.

21 See Jones, *The Life and Work of Sigmund Freud,* I, 262–267; and Sulloway, *Freud, Biologist of the Mind,* pp. 204–207, 312–315.

whelmed him with our interpretations before he was prepared for them, our information would either produce no effect or it would arouse a violent outbreak of *resistance* . . .

The "construction" of a forgotten past has thus become as complicated for psychoanalysis as for a novel. The plot is like that of a detective or sensation novel and concludes with a satisfying explanation of all the facts. "If we have prepared everything properly," Freud continues, "it often happens that the patient will at once confirm our construction and himself recollect the internal or external event which he had forgotten. . . . On that particular matter *our* knowledge will then have become *his* knowledge as well."[22] The timing of the revelation, or handling of the suspense, is important because the patient must share in the discovery, much as the reader of a well-constructed novel shares in the discovery. But an action of sheer knowledge will not be especially moving, perhaps, unless the knowledge is somewhat scandalous—unexpected and disapproved of, as the possible "violent outbreak of *resistance*" implies in Freud's summary of psychoanalysis or the past of Bulstrode proves in George Eliot's novel.[23]

Freud's division of the mind, with its potential for suspenseful narrative, may be contrasted to Plato's conception of the division of the soul. The one psychology belongs to an age of information and public opinion and the other obviously does not—though it is Plato, interestingly enough, who more openly states the social basis of his scheme. Book IV of the *Republic* introduces the tripartite arrangement of the soul as frankly analogous to the deliberative, executive, and productive roles of individuals in the state. The claim is made that it is easier to understand the social distribution of roles than the mental, and then to see the necessary connection of the two. As with Freud, the interest really lies in the conflict between one part of the soul and another, but there are important differences.[24] In the first place, in Plato the rational part of the soul opposes directly the appetite. Reason is not baffled by any shortage of information about the desires of the body; it does not seek or receive any indirect reports of

22 *An Outline of Psycho-Analysis*, S.E., XXIII, 178.

23 For an argument that psychoanalysis may virtually be equated with the construction of fictions, see Donald P. Spence, *Narrative Truth and Historical Truth: Meaning and Interpretation in Psychoanalysis* (New York: Norton, 1982).

24 Cf. Rieff, *Freud: The Mind of the Moralist*, pp. 62–63.

desire. Reason both knows and commands the appetite, and should reason be overcome, unchecked appetite will take its own course. Unlike Freud's conception of the mind, Plato's is hierarchical. There is a healthy subordination of the whole to reason, which is opposed by appetite but served by spirit. Reason appreciates the proportionate value of each part, and in the just soul, as in the just state, each has its proper place. The division of the mind by psychoanalysis, even after the introduction of the superego, is strictly neutral; each division is characterized by a certain state of information, by what is known or unknown. Instead of a potential for insubordination, there is a potential for a kind of scandal. Two concomitants of information, indirection and concealment, are what make the Freudian scheme unmistakably modern.

Universal literacy and the rise of information are very much implicated in this difference. The silence of the print culture has contributed to increased private consciousness, and increased consciousness to the impression of a silencing within. Most of what is out there is unknown to the senses or unread, and by analogy most of what is inside is unknown and unread. The hidden information need not be thought of as mysterious or prohibited to us, like the knowledge of God, but as information that can be properly—and professionally—unearthed when needed by men and women of sufficient determination. A favorite tenet of information science is that knowledge, unlike matter, accumulates without limit: "the further we advance from the origin of our knowledge," in the words of Charles Babbage, "the larger it becomes."[25] The past, from this point of view, exists with a comprehensiveness all out of proportion to present experience. This is also the view of psychoanalysis, "that in mental life nothing which has once been formed can perish—that everything is somehow preserved and that in suitable circumstances . . . it can once more be brought to light."[26] Far more information is stored than is in use, and if we turn from nineteenth-century proponents of knowledge like Babbage to sensation novelists like Wilkie Collins, the indestructibility of all this information becomes all the more significant. In the "unintelligible world," according to Collins, "the trivial and the terrible walk hand in hand."[27] Similarly, in the theory and practice of

25 See chapter 3, note 29.
26 *Civilization and Its Discontents*, S.E., XXI, 69.
27 See chapter 5, note 34.

psychoanalysis no detail in the vast store of the unconscious is without its potentially unsettling revelation. A way was prepared for the peculiarly unsettling potential of information, in novels and psychoanalysis, not by science so much as by the movement of crime prevention and the well-advertised virtues of circumstantial evidence for the determination of criminal intent. What was secret to the criminal, or to the person happily deterred from crime, could be made known; hence what was secret and unconscious could be made conscious.[28]

Freud's informational model of the mind takes for granted a general pacification of humanity. Contrary to Plato's view of the matter, the nineteenth century could think of appetite as largely satisfied or repressed, and the need for physical subordination of one person to another as far less apparent than the need for information. For Nietzsche, indeed, immurement "within the walls of society and of peace" was the primary reason for the evolution of consciousness. Through the process of civilization, humans "were reduced to thinking, inferring, reckoning, co-ordinating cause and effect, these unfortunate creatures; they were reduced to their 'consciousness,' their weakest and most fallible organ!" Nietzsche attributed to civilization an "internalization" of aggression and also associated guilt with repression, much as Freud would later.[29] But the general assumption of repression was shared much more widely by conservative thinkers who scarcely dreamed of calling attention to its adverse effects. That a general pacification of humanity was possible and desirable—that it had in fact been achieved—was the conclusion of every contract theory of society and of virtually every novel after Scott, and it was taken up by the new study of sociology—in the decided superiority of industrial over militant societies celebrated by Herbert Spencer, for example.[30] In some ways the mainstream thinking on this score is more revealing than its radical criticism.

The effects of repression that Freud would eventually complain of in *Civilization and Its Discontents* were nearly all implicit in the

28 In "Psycho-Analysis and the Establishment of the Facts in Legal Proceeding" (1906), *S.E.*, IX, 103–114, Freud likened the evidence for "a carefully guarded secret" in cases of hysteria to the evidence in criminal trials. Cf. Bentham on "facts of the psychological kind" necessary to prove intention in a criminal case (chapter 5, note 17, above).

29 *On the Genealogy of Morals*, ed. and trans. Walter Kaufmann (1967; rpt. New York: Vintage, 1969), pp. 84–85.

30 *The Principles of Sociology*, 3 vols. (New York: Appleton, 1896), II, 568–640.

thinking of Mill, whom Freud never cites in his collected writings but whom he translated and reacted to as a young man.[31] For Mill, it is clear, a majority have long been reduced to pacific—but potentially scarifying—exchanges of information. "The fitting adjustment between individual independence and social control," may be said to be his principal subject, and his working assumption that the independence and control in question are more mental than physical. "All that makes existence valuable to any one, depends on the enforcement of restraints upon the actions of other people"; at the same time, "the likings and dislikings of society, or of some powerful portion of it, are ... the main thing which has practically determined the rules laid down for general observance, under the penalties of law or opinion." The tendency to social repression of some ideas is obvious, and Mill replies to it by condemning "the peculiar evil of silencing" and "all silencing of discussion." His argument assumes that virtually all conflicts that matter to the modern world reflect differences in knowledge.[32] It is the liberal protest against social repression of thought that Freud internalized in describing exchanges between conscious and unconscious ideas. His discoveries depend as much on widespread assumptions of the importance of information as on the nature of language or contemporary science; and if it were not that modern society functions by means of threatening as well as saving information, it is unlikely that Freud would have conceived of the mind in the

31 In 1880 Freud translated vol. 12 in the German edition of Mill by Theodor Gomperz. The two important works in this volume were *The Subjection of Women* and Mill's long essay on Plato, originally a review of George Grote's *Plato and the Companions of Sokrates* (1866; *C.W.*, XII, 375–440). We know how Freud responded to the former, because of a letter to Martha Bernays contending against the equality of women; and Ernest Jones suggests that Freud may have learned his Plato from Mill's essay: see *The Life and Work of Sigmund Freud*, I, 55–56, 175–177.

32 *On Liberty*, *C.W.*, XVIII, 220, 222, 229. Again, the counterarguments of James Fitzjames Stephen may be needed to throw Mill's modern position into relief. For Stephen "the essence of life is force," and an infringement of liberty occurs when one force overcomes another. His is the archaic position, associated with feudal or military—and instinctual—responses that are pretty much unthinkable to Mill and Freud. Stephen believes that an oppressive society might be attacked with "sword in hand," but that "no man has a right to give the signal for such a battle by blowing the horn, unless he has first drawn the sword and knows how to make his hands guard his head with it." He does not seem to feel that this situation is likely to occur in Victorian England, however, and the defensive gesture of warding off blows to the head gives his idea of the probable result if it did. *Liberty, Equality, Fraternity*, ed. R. J. White (Cambridge, England: Cambridge University Press, 1967), pp. 103–104, 118.

terms that he did. A social pathology preceded the psychopathology of everyday life.

Social and political developments are intrinsic to Freud's theory. Carl E. Schorske has shown, in particular, how the concept of "the censorship" in psychoanalysis arises from the political, professional, and religious situation of Freud's early life.[33] This metaphor for the treatment of information has unmistakable political origins, and the Austrian regime under which Freud labored for professional advancement was undoubtedly more oppressive than that of Victorian England. But as the use of the metaphor is extended, to characterize the prohibiting but pervious border between consciousness and the unconscious, it becomes obvious that the vehicle of Freud's metaphor is approximately the same as the tenor of Mill's, when the latter inveighs against "a hostile and dreaded censorship."[34] What is finally meant in each case is social rather than political restraint. The reference extends to the entire range of behavior and expression prohibited by custom or majority opinion in a given society, though "censorship" casually reinterprets this as information of concern to the state. The concept is all important to *The Interpretation of Dreams*, and scarcely less so to Freud's later writings, but he typically illustrates rather than defines the censorship. For reasons that I shall hazard in a moment, the concept never won a firm place in the metapsychology. When the illustrations of censorship are examined, they show Freud regularly taking for granted that consciousness entertains such thoughts as might be spoken of freely with others and refuses those that cannot be—chiefly sexual thoughts but also such ideas as personal ambition, aggressive intentions, or negative judgments of others. Again and again in *The Interpretation of Dreams* Freud assumes that the discourse of the mind with itself suffers roughly the same inhibitions as social discourse.

Though the notion of censorship arose naturally in a work that asserted Freud's independence as a thinker and writer, it was not the happiest metaphor for his purposes. His general approach to the mind is that of pathology, the study of disease or of systems not

---

33 *Fin-de-Siècle Vienna: Politics and Culture* (New York: Vintage, 1981), pp. 181–207. See *The Interpretation of Dreams*, S.E., IV, 106–121, 136–145; and also Erik H. Erikson, "The Dream Specimen of Psychoanalysis," *Journal of the American Psychoanalytic Association*, 2 (1954), 5–56.

34 *On Liberty*, C.W., XVIII, 264.

functioning properly. Censorship is a human institution that exercises some freedom or selectivity, perhaps, but does not necessarily behave erratically and certainly has no motive for hinting or leaking the very information that it is bound to suppress. The censorship is not the same as the general mechanism of repression (an operation difficult enough of itself to conceive). Precisely because Freud is studying the slight exceptions or failures of repression, he needs to imagine an agency with the human or bureaucratic liability to error. But a censor still has no motive for slipping up, far less for dragging up secrets from the unconscious. One main reason that Freud appeals to the metaphor, obviously, is that he conceives of the unconscious as constantly longing to be free. "I consider that these unconscious wishes are always on the alert, ready at any time to find their way to expression when an opportunity arises for allying themselves with an impulse from the conscious and for transferring their own great intensity on to the latter's lesser one."[35] This important feature of Freud's model he would later refer to in quotation marks as the "upward drive" of the unconscious, and there are political undertones to this metaphor as well.[36] The quotation marks may be a reminder that there is no actual "up" or "down" in the mind, or a sign that Freud acknowledges the tenuousness of the very existence of the upward drive. One problem with the concept is that it allows for no relaxed or natural forgetfulness.

A different metaphor for the agency that negotiates between consciousness and the unconscious would express directly the threat of information and render unnecessary the concept of an upward drive. Something like Nietzschean forgetfulness would take the place of a constant struggle of the unconscious with the ego, and the full range of possible scandals in social life would fill out the narrower set of offenses against government implied by the censorship. Such a metaphor is blackmail, and it would have the further advantage of many

35 *The Interpretation of Dreams*, S.E., V, 553. Note that greater "intensity" is now attributed to unconscious wishes, though only a few years earlier Breuer (above, note 16) took it for granted that a conscious idea must be more "intense."

36 "[The unconscious] has a natural 'upward drive' and desires nothing better than to press forward across its settled frontiers into the ego and so to consciousness" (*An Outline of Psycho-Analysis*, S.E., XXIII, 179). Freud sometimes seems to identify the unconscious with a democratic force against which the ego is rather helpless; but in another late work he proposes that the ego, through something like control of "the press," can manage to manipulate the pleasure principle, here compared to "public opinion." See *Inhibitions, Symptoms and Anxiety* (1926), S.E., XX, 92.

pre-Freudian elaborations in imaginative literature. Surely the actions of censorship in late nineteenth-century novels are exceeded in number and subtlety by the actions of blackmail—evidence in themselves that people tend to forget what they have experienced as shameful or subjecting them to punishment, though they may sometimes be forced to remember.[37] In a number of ways, apart from the reversal of the upward drive, the figure of a blackmailer would suit Freud's theory of neuroses better than a censor. One or the other figure is needed to explain the selectivity of the neurosis, in contrast with the general effects of repression, and a blackmailer is precisely one who hopes to exact payment of some kind by his threats. His purpose as an active agency of mind would be to instill and also to maintain, if he could, a certain level of suffering in the ego; he would have the motive and the economy of action that the censorship lacks. A blackmailer is capable of the enterprise, the intimacy, and even the humor that are impossible for a bureaucracy; and yet the substitution of blackmail for censorship in the model would in no way interfere with classic psychoanalytic therapy. The ego has only to stop making partial payment and face the threatening information openly; or, after long acquaintance, the blackmailer himself may be blamed for the trouble and dismissed. Such routines are common in the literature of blackmail.

From a liberal viewpoint, blackmail and censorship are perverse institutions of information—the one conniving at secrecy and the other enforcing it. They are institutions antithetical to the faith of Mill and of Freud but nevertheless endemic in Mill's conception of society and Freud's conception of the mind. In many ways the novelists of the nineteenth century are the best expositors of this paradox, since they registered both the abstraction of the information society and the unease that it generated. Because a spirit of rebellion inhabits Freud's early work, as Schorske has shown, it would be possible to make some extensive comparisons of his discoveries to radical novels written in England at the end of the eighteenth century.[38] But I

37 I believe this is true even for the novels of Dostoevsky, who was very well acquainted with political censorship. His fine blackmail novel is *The Adolescent* (1874).

38 William Godwin's *Caleb Williams*, published in 1794 with the cryptic title *Things as They Are*, is perhaps the best example. Not only is Godwin's novel a study of repressive law and induced guilt, with an incessant play on secrets and threatened disclosure, but the rivalry of Falkland and Caleb is like that of father and son; it is both a political and a psychological fiction.

would prefer to instance a conservative novel by Scott, for the reason that Scott directly influenced the direction of the novel, European and American as well as British, for several generations. His treatment of the difference between modern and archaic culture is well illustrated by *Rob Roy*. The hero of civil society, Francis Osbaldistone, still resists a commercial calling but is pointedly contrasted with Rob Roy, the outlaw and representative of the clans. The contrast can be exemplified by a clash between Osbaldistone, who narrates the novel, and the proud highlander who introduces himself only as "a man."

> "A man!" I repeated;—"that is a very brief description."
> "It will serve for one who has no other to give," said the stranger. "He that is without name, without friends, without coin, without country, is still at least a man; and he that has all these is no more."
> "Yet this is still too general an account of yourself, to say the least of it, to establish your credit with a stranger."
> "It is all I mean to give, howsoe'er; you may choose to follow me, or to remain without the information I desire to afford you."
> "Can you not give me that information here?" I demanded.
> "You must receive it from your eyes, not from my tongue— you must follow me, or remain in ignorance of the information which I have to give you."[39]

This refusal of the outlaw to give "an account" of himself, to establish his "credit," or to impart "information" at second hand actually results in the civilized hero's being led to the repressive institution of society, the Glasgow prison. Scott is firmly on the side of the law, and his eschewal of violence is as certain as Mill's or Freud's. Yet the Glasgow chapters of the novel repeatedly portray the anxiety, and even the guilt feelings, of the well-behaved hero.

A famous expression of the opposition to force in *Rob Roy*—famous at least to those historians who still appreciate the importance of Scott to the nineteenth century—comes from the lips of Bailie Nicol Jarvie, who boasts of the triumph of credit over honor:

> I maun hear naething about honour—we kan naething here but about credit. Honour is a homicide and a bloodspiller, that gangs about making frays in the street; but Credit is a decent honest man, that sits at hame and makes the pat play. (ch. 26)

39 *Rob Roy* (Edinburgh: Black, 1886), ch. 21.

The humor of the bailie cuts both ways. The obvious reduction of honor to street brawls has a subtle parallel in the ironic play on pacific and profitable "Credit." Credit, as we can see from Osbaldistone's use of the word in the sense of credentials, imports far more than the system of financial transactions in modern society. It includes the demand for abstract identification and information that the hero addresses in vain to Rob Roy, and the broad assumption of personal accountability that inhabits the social contract. It flatly denies that the best things in life are free. At the same time credit carries the personal significance of honor, with its terrific possibility of shame, into the modern world. If one no longer need defend one's honor by toppling enemies in the street, how shall one support one's credit against the chances of indiscriminate information? The bailie's humor just touches on the nature of modern reputation, safe from bloodspilling but vulnerable all the same. The incipient pathology of credit in due course also became a subject for novel-writing, and with the bailie's general disarming of honor in *Rob Roy* can be compared the specific disarming of Baldassare in *Romola:*

> He could search into every secret of Tito's life now; he knew some of the secrets already, and the failure of the broken dagger, which seemed like frustration, had been the beginning of achievement. (ch. 38)

Though these words may demonstrate that pathology is seldom as memorable as wit, the same contrast between violence and pacific achievement is apparent here, clothed in the humor of the indirect style. George Eliot cannot really mean "achievement"; this is a mock of Baldassare. Yet the substitution of information for daggers might be agreed, by Scott and George Eliot and others, to be the course of civilization.

According to Nietzsche and Freud, civilization itself is a sort of blackmail, exacting payment within the self while it takes its own course without. But novelists also imagined this internalization of social life. As the principle of social control shifts from the quick penetration of bodies to the slow penetration of secrets, an implausible Baldassare comes to figure as the inward representation of potential scandal. He begins to make sense as a psychological projection of Romola, especially useful against another projection called Tito. The ambiguity of the blackmailer in nineteenth-century fiction can resemble that of neurotic states of mind, in which some still unconscious idea at once causes great suffering and holds a grain of truth. Such a figure of the mind plays opposite to the therapist, when a therapist is available. If in George Eliot's fiction Baldassare is a precursor of Lush and Lapidoth, then he is a vicarious opposite to Daniel Deronda as well. And like the blackmailer, a therapist is an expendable character, or ought to be, once a heroine has come safely through a blackmail action. Both blackmail and counterblackmail are possible, as the exactions of destructive and constructive information.

16

From Chillingworth to Freud

In the constructive management of scandal, Freud keeps faith with the great novelists of the nineteenth century. A novel did not have to be "a sensation novel" to dwell on real or imagined embarrassment, the potential revelation of secrets or the chances of information. As we have seen in some detail in the case of George Eliot, from "The Sad Fortunes of the Reverend Amos Barton" onward, scandal is a wonderfully persistent theme. It would be equally possible to instance pleasing and instructive novels by Dickens, Thackeray, Trollope, Meredith, Hardy, and James—to say nothing of Stendhal and Balzac, Tolstoy and Dostoevsky—novels that delineate quite sharply the constraints of publicity and its snares, as well as test the protagonists' responses to endless small discoveries. Blackmail stories are only a special type, in which projection and displacement are facilitated, in which discovery may be concentrated in particularly damaging information, and in which the credit or identity of a character can be tested over time. The blackmail action, or explicit threat of information, permits the negotiation of scandal in the plot as a whole. The blackmailers in George Eliot's fictions of discontinuity, beginning with *Silas Marner*, sometimes pose as enemies yet perform in the narrative as friends, for the projection and disposal of guilt or shame. In the completed narrative, instead of paying the blackmailer, the protagonist—like the patient in the art of psychoanalysis—may learn from the threatening information and make amends with the past at the blackmailer's expense. Full knowledge is knowledge of the entire story of transgression and accommodation, and if there were not blackmailers at hand, they could be invented. So important is a completed action or full knowledge that sometimes a single character, often a fallen woman, as Nina Auerbach has shown, may represent allegorically both scandal and the recouping of scandal.[1]

An American work, *The Scarlet Letter*, is the classic nineteenth-century narrative of this kind. The management of and even triumphant recovery from scandal in Hawthorne's novel—or romance, as he called it—were by no means confined to social relations of knowing other persons but probed as well the hidden, personal knowledge of guilt. *The Scarlet Letter* was the depressive author's marvelous and witty story of repression—"We must not always talk in the market-place of what happens to us in the forest," as Hester Prynne tries to explain to the irrepressible Pearl.[2] The story offers a nearly systematic comparison of the knowledge of guilt with the fear of shame; it introduces the best-advertised and proudest of all fallen women, with the sign upon her breast; and in a devilish action of blackmail it locates the kind of inner suffering that Freud would attempt to relieve a half-century later. The relation of Roger Chillingworth to Arthur Dimmesdale most concerns us here. Instead of behaving as the wronged husband trying to put an end to the relation between his wife and her lover, Chillingworth at once investigates and uses his knowledge against Dimmesdale. He is not exactly the cuckold in this adventure of adultery, since his identity remains hidden from all but Hester while he successfully works on the guilt of his rival. Hawthorne carefully delineates an action that is just plausible as between blackmailer and victim but of which the main impact is psychological.[3]

The key ambiguity of *The Scarlet Letter* is the way in which Chillingworth is drawn to Dimmesdale in the first place. Once he has

---

1 *Woman and the Demon: The Life of a Victorian Myth* (Cambridge: Harvard University Press, 1982). For Hester Prynne, see pp. 166–167.

2 *The Scarlet Letter*, ed. Seymour Gross et al., 2nd ed. (New York: Norton, 1978), ch. 22.

3 Cf. Nina Baym, *The Shape of Hawthorne's Career* (Ithaca: Cornell University Press, 1976), p. 138: "Chillingworth can be interpreted as Dimmesdale's 'superego.' That he is intended as a part of Dimmesdale's personality is made clear not only by the magical ways in which he appears on the scene and disappears from it, and his unrealistic fixation (for a cuckolded husband) on the guilty *man*, but also by the spatial disposition of the two in a single dwelling."

become the latter's physician and hit upon the truth, he becomes "not a spectator only, but a chief actor, in the poor minister's interior world," and Dimmesdale's real suffering begins (ch. 11). Hawthorne does not explain how Chillingworth uses his knowledge or conveys it to the sufferer; Dimmesdale is aware of his guilt, but unaware that he is being tortured on this account by the physician. The narrative is vague about what is taking place between the two men, and Hester belatedly conjectures that her sometime husband has seized "bad opportunities" with her sometime lover, by means of which "the sufferer's conscience had been kept in an irritated state" such as can lead to "insanity" or "madness" (ch. 17). The only healer with good intentions in this romance, Hester then intervenes by telling Dimmesdale who Chillingworth is, but this partial information results in a kind of stalemate in the analysis. Now Dimmesdale knows that Chillingworth knows that he is guilty, and Chillingworth knows that he knows. The moment is like that in which Lush informs Gwendolen Grandcourt that her husband knows what she knew at the time she married him. Hawthorne's comment, in fact, returns questions about Dimmesdale's mental state to the social relation once more:

> The physician knew, then, that, in the minister's regard, he was no longer a trusted friend, but his bitterest enemy. So much being known, it would appear natural that a part of it should be expressed. It is singular, however, how long a time often passes before words embody things; and with what security two persons, who choose to avoid a certain subject, may approach to its very verge, and retire without disturbing it.

Dimmesdale has emerged from the forest meeting with Hester "wiser," with a "knowledge of hidden mysteries" that might be wholesome (ch. 20). But Hester is not finally able to save him, in part because she herself is not, or ought not to be, free of the past. *The Scarlet Letter* concludes not with the drowning of a blackmailer but in disclosure and something like suicide.

The narrative nevertheless relieves the minister from blame by making a villain of the physician. Chillingworth's sin consists in little more than knowing and hinting about the adultery, yet the reader is likely to agree with Dimmesdale that "that old man's revenge has been blacker than my sin" (ch. 17). In the course of the action Chillingworth comes to represent Dimmesdale's secret sin; he *is* the sickness that pursues the minister and promises to afflict him even at sea, if he should join Hester on the piratelike ship that awaits in the harbor. At the same time, Chillingworth's "delving," "prying," and "probing" bring on the crisis. The devil in this physician both threatens his victim and promises to keep the secret, and the only way to stop paying and be rid of him is to make the secret worthless by betraying it—ridding oneself of the sickness at the same time. Chillingworth tries at last to prevent the confession that he has made so imperative, but the good doctor in him has helped to point the way: "there was no place so secret,—no high place nor lowly place, where thou couldst have escaped me,—save on this very scaffold!" (ch. 23). Dimmesdale does find a cure at last, though his victory is of the kind anyone might win over a physician, by dying on him.

Though *The Scarlet Letter* is a good deal less modern than *Daniel Deronda* in its insistence on merciful death for the sinner, in its projection of the threatening past upon a "blacker" character it adumbrates a solution to the consciousness of guilt not unlike George Eliot's. Hawthorne's romance as a whole is a tale of the past. Its hints of supernatural influences are appropriate to seventeenth-century Salem but demand some sophisticated translation from nineteenth- and twentieth-century readers. Its frequent recourse to the notion of demonic possession would not have bothered Freud, who was quite curious about the devil,[4] but does jar with the claims of this book about novels and the information revolution. The Salem that Hawthorne describes, after all, is a close community rather than an impersonal modern society. When he writes of "the propensity of human nature to tell the very worst of itself, when embodied in the person of another" (ch. 13), he is referring to the projections of gossip rather than a threat from information. His blackmailer is not a disinterested third party but a party to the original marriage and "old" enough to be the father. He is a seeker of "knowledge" in general, a man of "intellectual gifts" (ch. 4), and so is Dimmesdale, famed for his studies at Oxford; but the smoldering air of "these two learned persons" (ch. 9) is more Faustian than modern. At the same time, the author strikes none too subtly at the seeming community, summarizing its institutions as "the clerical band, the judicial robe,

4 For Freud's interest in the devil, see David Bakan, *Sigmund Freud and the Jewish Mystical Tradition* (1958; rpt. New York: Schocken, 1965), pp. 187–237.

the pillory, the gallows, the fireside, or the church." Hawthorne sees Salem with both a satiric and a sociological eye, as a "social system" with "its regulations, its principles, and even its prejudices" (ch. 18). Most important, he makes conscious use of his historical perspective. He has read his Scott attentively, and he deliberately resorts to the past for its contrasts with the present. He calls attention to the different grounds of authority, "the quality of reverence" then as opposed to "what we call talent" now, and "natural authority" as opposed to "activity of intellect" in the present (ch. 22). Such terms for past and present were common in the early nineteenth century. It is the absence of reverence and authority in his own times, or their presence only in troubled consciousness, that prompts Hawthorne to imagine a community once led by "military men and civil fathers" (ch. 23), a community that then becomes a testing ground for present internal knowledge of guilt or fear of shame.

The occasion for writing *The Scarlet Letter* was at once impersonal and personal, a true nineteenth-century affair. From 1846 Hawthorne held the post of surveyor in the Customhouse of Salem, the town in which he had grown up and to which he had returned once before, after his college years. This post, which only occupied him mornings, was attained for him by his friends as a means of supporting his young family. He nevertheless was able to write very little at the time—until he was discharged from the surveyorship by the Whig administration that came to power in 1849. Under the spoils system no reason was needed for firing Hawthorne, though there were also precedents for allowing a person of literary merits to continue in office regardless of party. It was when the writer's friends came to his defense that the Whigs, in order to justify themselves, publicly attacked Hawthorne's qualifications and performance in office.[5] So it happened that the then unproductive writer but reasonably faithful federal servant found himself slandered in the public press. As Hawthorne tells us in his preface, he never could have written *The Scarlet Letter* in the Customhouse had he "remained there through ten Presidencies to come"; and indeed he now wrote three novels in rapid succession, in easily the most productive years

5 For a summary of the facts, see Arlin Turner, *Nathaniel Hawthorne: A Biography* (New York: Oxford University Press, 1980), pp. 177–187. The recent biographies, however, do not make as much of the known facts of Hawthorne's early life as they might: see my "Lives of Hawthorne," *Yale Review*, 70 (1981), 421–430.

of his life. It is extremely unnerving, no matter how sure one is of one's ground, to be attacked in print, especially if one wishes to make a living through print. Hawthorne's defense was at once wry and soul-searching, angry and conciliatory. The minor aggression against his person he returned to the public in major writings that are both satire and confession. In very brief compass Hawthorne experienced feelings similar to those which, in more diffuse form, would shortly thereafter inspire George Eliot's designs upon the reading public—or at the end of the century, the professional ambitions that prompted Freud to write books both personal and impersonal, artful and scientific.[6]

Hawthorne's brilliant preface, "The Custom-House," both names the occasion for writing and discourses on one individual's response to public opinion—for "the press has taken up my affair." It combines certain conventions of novel prefaces, such as the discovery of an old manuscript, with disarming confession and adroit description of the atmosphere and inhabitants of the Customhouse. The author frankly tells his reader that he was unable to write during his sojourn in that place and attributes his inability to being on the dole, so to speak, from Uncle Sam. But the preface bristles with a new reason for writing, which is to recoup the nearly inadvertent injury to his reputation. "It is a strange experience, to a man of pride and sensibility, to know that his interests are within the control of individuals who neither love nor understand him, and by whom"—Hawthorne's sentence now takes the mental turn that *The Scarlet Letter* completes—"since one or the other must needs happen, he would rather be injured than obliged." The writer's tactic is to convert publicity to an affair of honor, to admit the injury and recover his dignity through quiet scorn.[7] Accordingly, the tale that follows will be set in ancient times, for it is "nearly two centuries and a quarter" since the first Hawthorne set foot in Salem. "The Custom-House" tells the

6 Though Hawthorne seems far less committed to science than either George Eliot or Freud, his responses to science have often been the object of close study. See especially Frank Kermode, *The Classic: Literary Images of Permanence and Change* (1975; rpt. Cambridge: Harvard University Press, 1983), pp. 90–114.

7 The expressed moral of *The Scarlet Letter*, "Be true! Be true! Be true!" (ch. 24), is not a celebration of truthfulness in some absolute sense. The words that follow— "Show freely to the world, if not your worst, yet some trait whereby the worst may be inferred"—suggest an insurance policy against being caught by surprise, a policy of anticipating revelations about oneself and thereby precluding blackmail.

reader where to look for the writer in *The Scarlet Letter*. He is in each of the three principal characters, and not least in Hester Prynne, whose scarlet letter of shame he first holds to his own breast and receives there a burning sensation—"the reader may smile, but must not doubt my word." No wonder Hester wears her letter like a badge of honor and makes "a pride" of her punishment (ch. 2), from her first appearance in the door of her prison to her grave among "monuments carved with armorial bearings" (ch. 24). The writer is equally in the guilty-guiltless Arthur Dimmesdale, whose despairing progress is toward suicide. In the preface Hawthorne quips that his experience "resembled that of a person who should entertain an idea of committing suicide, and, altogether beyond his hopes, meet with the good hap to be murdered." In the novel suicide is intermingled with moral murder, and the murderer goes under the name of Roger Chillingworth.[8]

Hawthorne's projection of his case in more than one character, his pillorying and investigation of himself, are what give the romance its depth psychology. The writer would appear again under several guises in *The House of the Seven Gables* and, less confidently, in *The Blithedale Romance*. Yet the most egocentric of the three romances, and the one set in the remote past, is perhaps the most modern. To see this, one has to peer beneath the scandal of adultery and bedevilment in colonial times and read *The Scarlet Letter* as the management of a more general condition of social life in Hawthorne's time. Hester Prynne is a projection of the author's pride and intellect and also the person most different from himself, a woman.[9] The concentration of the fiction is such that Hester is virtually the only woman of Salem except for Mistress Hibbins, the governor's sister and a witch. She is unusually sexual in her being in that she is not a man. A person need not be an adulteress to experience "a thousand unrelenting eyes, all fastened upon her, and concentrated at her bosom" (ch. 2): that is where men gaze, and whence they are persuaded that the creature is sexual. Indeed, the defiance with which Hester wears her

8 For the importance of "The Custom-House" to the interpretation of *The Scarlet Letter*, see especially Baym, *The Shape of Hawthorne's Career*, pp. 123–151.

9 "It is remarkable, that persons who speculate the most boldly often conform with the most perfect quietude to the external regulations of society. The thought suffices them, without investing itself in the flesh and blood of action" (ch. 13). These words about Hester describe Hawthorne's intellect rather than hers and hardly do justice to her active role in the novel.

embroidered "A" has become something of a commonplace in a later stage of the information revolution, when messages are routinely displayed over breasts on T-shirts. The sexuality of women has long been obvious to men, and male preconceptions about their dress and behavior in *The Scarlet Letter* are not very distant from the preconceptions about women that Freud brought to the late nineteenth-century consulting room. The sexuality of men is both more taken for granted and less evident, much less evident in reproduction. Little Pearl, the most prominent sign in the romance besides the prejudicial "A" on Hester's breast, is notably "this child of its father's guilt and its mother's shame" (ch. 8).

"Its father's guilt and its mother's shame"—the minister himself, the unacknowledged father of Pearl, speaks these words to the governor of the colony. The main line of suspense in *The Scarlet Letter* concerns just this famous secret. If we put to one side the question of adultery and concentrate on the suspense, we are left with something like the admitted sexuality of women and the secret of fatherhood once again. Hawthorne was a legitimate and acknowledged father who copied, in the antics of Pearl, the antics of his own daughter Una, and at this level of invention the story and the mystery are those of fatherhood. Little Pearl wonders if a scarlet letter will not "come of its own accord, when I am a woman grown?" Her mother does not answer directly but replies, "Run away, child . . . and catch the sunshine! It will soon be gone"—the sunshine that Pearl has just said "is afraid of something on your bosom" (ch. 16). The social relation thus obliquely referred to is far more general than adultery, though a kind of scandal still inheres in it. On a later occasion Pearl exclaims, "Mistress Hibbins says my father is the Prince of the Air!" (ch. 22). A secret fatherhood lies at the heart of the romance, the heart that the minister keeps covering with his hand—but Hibbins is a witch and may be teasing all little girls and their parents. In *The Scarlet Letter* Hawthorne creates a sharp contrast between the questionable fathering of Pearl and the implacable fathers of the Puritans much as Freud would contrast the inherited guilt of sons with the strong rule of a primal father.[10]

Hawthorne may have been mildly surprised at his fathering of Una and his other children, while being somewhat struck by the absence

10 *Totem and Taboo* (1912–1913), S.E., XIII, 156–161.

of authority over his own life (his own father died at sea before he was old enough to remember). He needed a place in the Custom-house because he had to support a family; after his discharge, in "The Custom-House," he wondered what his ancestors would have thought of him. " 'What is he?' murmurs one gray shadow of my forefathers to the other. 'A writer of story-books! What kind of a business in life,—what mode of glorifying God, or being serviceable to mankind in his day and generation,—may that be? Why, the degenerate fellow might as well have been a fiddler!' " Accordingly, in *The Scarlet Letter* Hawthorne represented the guilt of a son, of a person not quite a father in his own right, as well as the shame of a discharged surveyor. Dimmesdale has no credentials as a father except for the threatened accusations of Chillingworth, the legitimate husband old enough to be his or Hester's father. In addition to the personal burden of guilt centered upon Dimmesdale, he bears the author's problem of addressing the "business of life" and "being serviceable" in the nineteenth century. The people of Salem are mistaken in the respect, and the sexual admiration on the part of some women, that they pay to their young minister. His authority as a father is pitiful—think of Pearl!—as against "the train of venerable and majestic fathers" of that town (ch. 23). Those fathers are very much of an era.

The Scarlet Letter made its own marked contribution to the series of nineteenth-century fictions that elaborated a myth of the American past, and as such it merits comparison with the myths of the prehistory of society that Freud began to elaborate at the end of his life. As a psychological narrative or a divine comedy, as a story of threatening information that would be satisfying in its completeness, the romance lacks one very important character—an opponent for the blackmailing Chillingworth. Hawthorne has not conceived, at the mid-century, of the dramatic intervention of a neutral character of the highest motives to counteract the vague destructive nagging of a secret.[11] "A man burdened with a secret," he writes of Dimmesdale, "should especially avoid the intimacy of his physician" (ch. 9). The warning is appropriate in its context but opposite to the conventional wisdom

---

11 He comes closer to doing so in the multiple projections of *The House of the Seven Gables*, and *The Blithedale Romance*, since the authorial figures Holgrave and Coverdale, though hardly disinterested, provide some counterpoise to the other characters.

of a later generation. The narratives of Freud are hardly ever complete without the inclusion of a physician who, whether he sides with the ego or, now and then, with the unconscious, is diametrically opposed to such an agency as Chillingworth's. "Our therapy," writes Freud, "works by transforming what is unconscious into what is conscious, and it works only in so far as it is in a position to effect that transformation." To place himself in the right position, the physician assumes a role in the narrative. He can then point out that the patient is being blackmailed, in effect, by some shadowy perceiver with partial knowledge of his or her own being. When certain information is brought to the fore, with the encouragement of the physician, the narrative assumes a satisfying completeness. "Our thesis that the symptoms vanish when their sense is known remains true . . . All we have to add is that the knowledge must rest on an internal change in the patient such as can only be brought about by a piece of psychical work with a particular aim."[12] Hawthorne can dispense with this second expert in secrets because he is constructing what is openly a fiction and remains a fiction, with a strong cautionary ending that would be less satisfying in real life. The scaffold and death are not for patients who can benefit from help, and even Chillingworth resents the unfortunate resolution of Dimmesdale's case. Hawthorne and his readers were not fully prepared to view guilt as needless and divorced from deeds—though when Dimmesdale contends that "that old man's revenge has been blacker than my sin," this seems an argument for canceling out some degree of guilt, and in this argument readers are likely to concur. The so-called revenge amounts to Chillingworth's mere presence and secret knowledge of the past, but this presence makes a large difference in our sympathy for the minister.

Other novels do employ a character who is opposed to the blackmail action and prepared to help bring it under control. Such a character is the hero of *Daniel Deronda*, and we have seen what new possibilities the use of Deronda discloses—that guilt, in the degree that it is not purely a moral result, may be rationally understood and abided. A novel in a different mode, but one that also tells of the fear of shame transformed by aggression into guilt, is *Bleak House*. That famous mystery, which has blackmail at the heart of its personal narrative, employed a detective to counter this action and thus became

12 *Introductory Lectures on Psycho-Analysis*, S.E., XVI, 280–281.

the prototype of many popular novels. The scandal of private life in *Bleak House* turns on Esther Summerson's illegitimacy and Lady Dedlock's sexual affair. The necessary clues to the past have been seized upon by Tulkinghorn, a master blackmailer whose "calling is the acquisition of secrets, and the holding possession of such power as they give him, with no sharer or opponent in it."[13] Early in the novel Dickens designs a relation of intense watching and knowing such as George Eliot and Henry James were to elaborate in their social narratives of consciousness. His Tulkinghorn and Lady Dedlock "appear to take as little notice of one another, as any two people, enclosed within the same walls, could. But whether each evermore watches and suspects the other . . . what each would give to know how much the other knows—all this is hidden" (ch. 12). The arrangement later permits the murder of Tulkinghorn to become the appropriate psychological response in the present action of *Bleak House* to the secret knowledge of the past. That shameful past has been concentrated in the figure of the blackmailer, who is now to be struck down. Lady Dedlock does not herself perform the act that answers to her wishes, but her wishes are as certain as Gwendolen Grandcourt's and similarly justified. Not only has she often wished Tulkinghorn dead but she experiences the death, in a passage of typical Dickensian psychology, as if "she really were the murderess" (ch. 56). She is therefore rightly suspected of murder, and so for that matter is Esther, the true affective center of the novel, implicated in the crime. The deed is done by the French maid in Lady Dedlock's clothing, but Dickens and his readers are far more interested in the "innocent" guilt of the principal characters than in the fate of the maid, and the role of the famous Inspector Bucket is to establish their material innocence. The murder of Tulkinghorn (in this admittedly schematic view of the novel) has indirectly put an end to the shame of Esther's birth, and through Bucket's work the guilt belonging to this action is explained away.

Bucket is a professional detective and has a role more narrowly circumscribed than that of Deronda in Gwendolen's life. Of the two, Deronda is easily more like a psychoanalyst, and he is also a major character in his own right. For the story of Lady Dedlock and her il-

---

13 *Bleak House*, ed. George Ford and Sylvère Monod (New York: Norton, 1977), ch. 36.

legitimate daughter, nevertheless, Bucket is the counterpart of the lawyer Tulkinghorn, the possessor of threatening secrets. It is also Bucket's job to cope with the petty blackmailers in *Bleak House*— Mr. Smallweed, Mr. and Mrs. Chadband, and Mrs. Snagsby—who threaten to reveal what they know of the story.[14] Bucket knows "so much about so many characters, high and low, that a piece of information more or less" cannot surprise or corrupt him (ch. 54), and thus he is adept at countering threats of this kind. There are characters with similar roles in the sensation novels of the period. In *The Woman in White* Walter Hartright—a healer of sorts, as his name suggests—opposes his knowledge and that of Marian Halcombe to the distortions of Sir Percival Glyde and Count Fosco; and Robert Audley, through considerable effort, resolves and relieves the strained family situation in *Lady Audley's Secret.* The tendency of these Victorian fictions, carefully noted by Henry James,[15] is toward a neutralization of threatened scandal and of guilt, and this tendency will be still more evident in a fiction like that of Alfred Hitchcock's *Blackmail.* As we have seen, the camera in Hitchcock's film avoids the actual stabbing as the narrative of George Eliot avoids the actual drowning of Grandcourt. Still, Alice White does kill her would-be seducer and finally admits to her detective that she has done so. The prevention of shame and management of guilt in the film depend on the death of the unsympathetic blackmailer and the consent of the sympathetic detective—who is not merely a detective in this case but also, by a kind of transference built into the plot, the heroine's boyfriend.

The implication of *Blackmail,* particularly the outcome of the film, would seem to be that the state of information, a precise measure of the concealment or discovery of the facts, has finally supplanted considerations of justice, of guilt or innocence, and even of conscience. The only reminder of moral consequences is Hitchcock's irony at the end. The last appearance of the painted jester on the screen and the heroine and her boyfriend's dissolving into nervous laughter suggest that the viewers of the film, like the characters within it, still expect a

14 Chadband's is perhaps the most marvelously worded, though idiosyncratic, of all blackmail threats: "Air we in possession of a sinful secret, and doe we require corn, and wine, and oil—or, what is much the same thing, money—for the keeping thereof? Probably so, my friends" (ch. 54).

15 See chapter 5, note 39.

tale of rewards and punishment. Yet the amorality of the film has also been prepared for in Victorian thinking. At about the time of writing *Daniel Deronda* George Eliot entered in a notebook, under the caption "Science subordinate as experience," four sentences about the past and personal identity so teasing that one suspects her of deliberately casting them in the form of an enigma. Should they be read as one more prescription of moral consequences, or as the factual report—"we are actually punished"—of the sort of guilt that Freud made his study?

> As if the rod & cone structure of the retina were more important than the fact of using my eyes to see with! As if the question whether personal identity can be proved were more weighty than my experience that what my past self felt & did is affecting my present self! The old pre-occupation was, "Is it just that I should be punished for my past?" The supremely important point is, that we are actually punished for our past both individual & collective, & that we are determining in our measure the amount of punishment to be suffered by those who are to come.[16]

Even the historical romance of the nineteenth century can be seen to anticipate the neutral stance of psychoanalysis. In *The Scarlet Letter*, it is the physician who believes that "the powers of nature call so earnestly for the confession of sin," and who nags his patient to death with the pain of "unspoken crime." The liberal minister believes that sin is more a private matter and that the heart may conceal certain secrets until the day of judgment. The outcome of the story reproves Dimmesdale's confidence in his own strength of mind, to be sure, but Hawthorne nevertheless endows him with a very modern view of the final judgment. That eventual "disclosure" of all secrets will not have the purpose of "retribution"; on the contrary, it will "promote the intellectual satisfaction of all intelligent beings, who will stand waiting, on that day, to see the dark problem of this life made plain." In moderate tones that perhaps conceal his own despair, Dimmesdale adds, "A knowledge of men's hearts will be needful to the completest solution of that problem" (ch. 10).

While refusing to consider the ethical significance of wishes and

16 In Thomas Pinney, "More Leaves from George Eliot's Notebook," *Huntington Library Quarterly*, 29 (1966), 370–371.

dreams, at the close of *The Interpretation of Dreams*, Freud gradually drew a sharper distinction between mental and physical phenomena than his original scientific intentions called for. "If we look at unconscious wishes reduced to their most fundamental and truest shape," he wrote in later editions of the book, "we shall have to conclude, no doubt, that *psychical* reality is a particular form of existence not to be confused wih *material* reality."[17] By thus segregating psychical from material reality, he was making a move similar to George Eliot's insistence on experience and freeing psychoanalysis for the exploration of what Hawthorne called the dark problem of life. The stress on psychical reality meant that psychoanalysis would continue to be concerned with narrative, whether stories based in private introspection or designed for public consumption as literature. For interpreting most forms of expression and narrative, true or fictitious, the methods of psychoanalysis have now been widely adopted. The reading of George Eliot's or Hawthorne's works today usually takes for granted the basic rules of the Freudian dream-work. As Meredith Anne Skura has ably argued, the technique is invaluable for literary criticism, "provided that we use *all* the resources of the psychoanalytic process—with its attention to the different aspects of the text; its distrust of literal reference; its lack of tact and its openness to counterintuitive meanings; and its self-consciousness about the process of interpretation."[18]

The service of psychoanalysis to literature is mutual, for the novels of the nineteenth century display some of the general and specific grounds for belief in psychoanalysis. When both imaginative literature and the movement that Freud founded are placed in a social historical frame, the reciprocal relation of the two is all the more apparent. But if the threat of blackmail in social life has declined since the first two or three decades of this century, so have the traditional novel and psychoanalysis been affected by change. The success of both would seem to depend on revelations controlled by the narrative and on the general conditions for scandal: a belief that much pertinent information that is unknown may become known, and rather strict agreement about what can or cannot be spoken openly to

17 *The Interpretation of Dreams*, S.E., V, 620 and n. The sentence was added in 1909 and modified in 1914 and 1919.

18 *The Literary Use of the Psychoanalytic Process* (New Haven: Yale University Press, 1981), p. 243.

others. Not only is it doubtful whether these conditions any longer prevail, but the success of the psychoanalytic movement must gradually tend to defeat itself. If patients are not genuinely surprised and a little shocked by their secret thoughts, they may not benefit as dramatically from analysis as in the past. I am not in a position to judge in this matter, except to suggest that psychoanalysis arose from a strong emphasis on the demarcation of conscious and unconscious thoughts, and that this emphasis in turn derived from a social consciousness of information and concealment in the nineteenth century. It is still true that information suddenly acquires and then loses value in the revelation, but the way in which revelations occur may be more or less dramatic; recent information theory speaks of the mere opening and closing of minute circuits, as in a computer.[19] Also, at least as much as the Victorian novel, psychoanalysis has assumed a strong sense of personal identity over time and the need for a continuous narrative. Though what we have thought or done in the past always bears on the present, the past may not return for us today with quite the force that it had for Nicholas Bulstrode. Personal identity still does matter, but perhaps not with the urgent sense of accountability that prevailed a hundred years ago. People may become used to the discontinuities of the information revolution and indifferent to blackmail.

As soon as Freud had both gained and lost followers, he began to place his art and science at the service of a movement, of which he claimed—with appropriate recognition of certain philosophers—to be the founder. After the breaks with Alfred Adler and Carl G. Jung, his turn to ideology is unmistakable. Freud's paper "On the History of the Psychoanalytic Movement" portrayed him as a martyr to the cause and sounded a rallying call to ideology: "Men are strong so long as they represent a strong idea; they become powerless when they oppose it."[20] Though Freud's own ties to biology were real enough, virtually every ideology makes some claim to science, and psychoanalysis was no exception in this regard. The movement made other typical claims as well—claims of a tradition, of membership, of the training of acolytes, and most obviously claims of what did or did not

19 Freudian dream theory is now being challenged accordingly. See especially Robert W. McCarley and J. Allan Hobson, "The Neurobiological Origins of Psychoanalytic Dream Theory," *American Journal of Psychiatry*, 134 (1977), 1211–221.
20 "On the History of the Psycho-Analytic Movement" (1914), *S.E.*, XIV, 66.

constitute psychoanalysis. To protect their position, Freud and his loyal followers even resorted in 1912 to a secret society known as the Committee. Ernest Jones explains that the Committee was his idea, but he also records his leader's response. Freud praised the idea of "a secret council composed of the best and most trustworthy among our men to take care of the further development of psycho-analysis and defend the cause against personalities and accidents when I am no more" and enjoined that it "be *strictly secret* in its existence and in its actions."[21] The main assurance to be gained by this means was that there would be no more surprises, no scandalous defections or revelations of differences. To use an expression that Freud would shortly employ in another connection, psychoanalysis would be master in its own house.

Despite his formal disapproval of using analysis for polemical purposes, Freud in this period began to attribute almost any disagreement with his theories to "resistance," like the resistance of a patient to unconscious thoughts and to the analyst. By so representing their disagreement, of course, Freud implicitly threatened his opponents with his knowledge of their inward fears, and in this role he became more like a master blackmailer on the intellectual scene than a physician helping his patients throw off their own psychical blackmailers. Such a polemic was akin to the "demand with menaces" or "offensiveness" that Ernest Gellner finds characteristic of ideologies generally.[22] Freud's argument about resistance to psychoanalysis, made repeatedly at this time, indirectly confirmed that the truths of psychoanalysis were the scandalous, objectionable truths of the unconscious or of sexuality. Freud rightly took pride in facing these truths, but at the same time he would not allow his public to forget that they were objectionable. In his boldest account of the resistance to psychoanalysis, he likened it to the resistance to the Copernican and Darwinian revolutions in science. Drawing upon his theory of narcissism, in a popular article of 1917, he proposed "to describe how the universal narcissism of men, their self-love, has up to the present suffered three severe blows from the researches of science." The first

21 *The Life and Work of Sigmund Freud,* 3 vols. (New York: Basic Books, 1953–1957), II, 152–167.
22 "Notes towards a Theory of Ideology," in *Spectacles and Predicaments: Essays in Social Theory* (Cambridge, England: Cambridge University Press, 1979), 117–132.

blow was the cosmological discovery, associated with the name of Copernicus, that humans were not at the center of the universe. The second blow was the biological discovery, associated with Darwin, that humans were fellow-creatures of the animals. The third and "probably the most wounding" blow is psychological. Freud modestly did not claim that he personally had struck the third blow but credited "famous philosophers," notably Schopenhauer, for the idea of the unconscious and psychoanalysis for its demonstration.

That this trilogy is patently a construction of ideology need not detract from its historical validity. In bringing the argument of this book to a close, I merely wish to call attention to the language in which the third, and most wounding, blow is presented. First, Freud describes the normal functioning of the mind in terms of "reports" and "news of all the important occurrences in the mind's workings." Then he describes a condition of disease or unease in which "thoughts emerge suddenly without one's knowing where they come from." And finally, so habitual to Freud is a narrative in which the analyst can participate that he has a personification of "psychoanalysis" transmit two long paragraphs directly to the "ego" of humanity. This lecture to the ego concerns the limitations of its knowledge, and the lecture too is couched in terms of news and information. One may be reminded of George Eliot's phrase, in *The Mill on the Floss*, about "people who hear some news that will require them to readjust their conceptions of the past" (bk. V, ch. 4):

> You feel sure that you are informed of all that goes on in your mind if it is of any importance at all, because in that case, you believe, your consciousness gives you news of it. And if you have had no information of something in your mind you confidently assume that it does not exist there. Indeed, you go so far as to regard what is "mental" as identical with what is "conscious"— that is, with what is known to you—in spite of the most obvious evidence that a great deal more must constantly be going on in your mind than can be known to your consciousness. ... In every case, however, the news that reaches your consciousness is incomplete and often not to be relied on ... Even if you are not ill, who can tell all that is stirring in your mind of which you know nothing or are falsely informed?

When Freud resumes his own voice at the conclusion of the article, he explains that the third blow to the self-love of humanity really consists of two discoveries: "that the life of our sexual instincts"—now first mentioned—"cannot be wholly tamed, and that mental processes are in themselves unconscious." And "these two discoveries amount to a statement that *the ego is not master in its own house.*"[23]

If we can be guided by Freud's choice of language in this article, the successive blows to the self-love of humanity are the Copernican, the Darwinian, and the information revolutions, the last internalized and viewed pathologically by psychoanalysis. The pride that is threatened by information—or by the voice of "the people" in the political extension of the metaphor—is still personified as the master of the house, and if it were not understood in these archaic terms, there would not be the same threat. Freud is at once modern in his perception of the threat and conservative in his conception of what is threatened. When he recites the same trilogy of blows in the *Introductory Lectures*, again in explanation of the resistance to psychoanalysis, he writes as follows: "human megalomania will have suffered its third and most wounding blow from the psychological research of the present time which seeks to prove to the ego that it is not even master in its own house, but must content itself with scanty information of what is going on unconsciously in its mind."[24] In this version also, a modern commonplace—the lack of sufficient information—makes horns at patriarchal power and dignity. It was the historical coincidence of two forces, traditional authority and encroaching information, that created the opportunity for psychoanalysis, as for blackmail.

What cunning inspired Hawthorne to make his cuckold, blackmailer, and physician one and the same person? In their different ways, Hawthorne and George Eliot reserved judgment about the master of the house. Possibilities were open to them as "writers of story-books"—possibilities rife with irony—that were not available to a doctor or leader of a movement, no matter how gifted in the art of narrative. George Eliot's personal need for authority was strong, and in *Daniel Deronda* she argued impressively for the adoption of an ideology. But she provided dramatic counterpoise to her argument, and she could tease a little Deronda's solemn pact with his fathers by

23 "A Difficulty in the Path of Psycho-Analysis" (1917), *S.E.*, XVII, 141–143.

24 *Introductory Lectures on Psycho-Analysis, S.E.*, XVI, 285. For a more hopeful interpretation of this passage, see Roy Schafer, *A New Language for Psychoanalysis* (New Haven: Yale University Press, 1976), pp. 152–154.

bringing on his scandalous father-in-law at the end. As novelists, both she and Hawthorne intuitively understood that the absence of strong fathers in the modern world would entail the waning of the very ideologies that were to take their place.

Index

Index

Leopardi, Giacomo, 312
Levin, Harry, 81
Levine, George, 143n, 173, 174n, 188n, 201n, 224, 237, 248n, 307n, 338n
Lewes, George Henry, 27, 67, 113–118, 123–124, 126–129, 133–134, 226–227, 228, 237–238, 298n, 306; *Physiology of Common Life*, 218n; *Problems of Life and Mind*, 224, 227n
Lewins, William, 53–58
Lewis, C. S., 340–341
Lewis, Helen B., 156n
Libel Act (1843), 6
Liberalism, 302–304, 355
Lichtheim, George, 310n, 314n
"Lifted Veil," 130, 259, 274–275
Liggins, Joseph, 128–131, 254–255
Literacy, 37–38, 78–79, 118–120, 338–339, 345n, 350
Lukács, Georg, 195
Lynd, Helen Merrell, 299n

Macaulay, Thomas Babington, 5, 53
Machlup, Fritz, 33–34
Mack, Eric, 6n
Mackay, Robert William, *Progress of the Intellect*, 121, 186
Mackensie, Manfred, 82n
Mannheim, Karl, 310n
Mansel, Henry, 102–104, 106
Marcus, Steven, 136
Marotta, Kenny, 139n
Marriage, 170–172, 179–181, 196, 235, 271, 272–279, 280–285
Martin, Graham, 229n, 309n
Martineau, Harriet, 117n, 128n
Marx, Karl, 310
Mason, Michael York, 224n
Maxwell, James Clerk, 42n
Maxwell, Richard, 104n
Mayne, Richard, 92
Mayr, Ernst, 134n
McCarley, Robert W., 373n

McCulloch, J. R., 42, 43
McGowan, John P., 225n
McLuhan, Marshall, 37n
Meliorism, 213–215
Memory. *See* Forgetfulness
Meredith, George, 359
Merz, John Theodore, 42n
Metropolitan Police Act (1829), 85
Meunier, Jean Joseph, 65
Middlemarch, 3, 10, 12n, 14, 15, 20, 40, 50, 80, 86, 92, 96, 101, 129, 159, 162–163, 187, 191, 195–200, 204–205, 211–214, 216–258, 259, 261, 273, 275–276, 281–282, 299, 300–301, 303, 307, 315–316, 325, 341
Mill, John Stuart, 67–71, 76, 78–80, 93n, 200, 355–356; *Autobiography*, 304n; "Civilization," 67; *On Liberty*, 68–71, 79, 208–210, 302, 311, 352–353; *Subjection of Women*, 252n; *System of Logic*, 97n
Miller, D. A., 26n, 102n, 104n
Miller, J. Hillis, 80, 224–225
Mill on the Floss, 3, 28, 79–80, 118–121, 133, 134, 138n, 141–153, 159–160, 168, 170–172, 180, 185n, 189–190, 195–196, 239, 267, 284, 288, 295, 317, 318, 375
Milton, John: *Paradise Lost*, 251–252; *Samson Agonistes*, 316
Mintz, Alan, 242–243
Mitchell, B. R., 38n, 51–52n, 53n
Moers, Ellen, 28n
Molesworth, W. N., 202
Morrison, Philip and Emily, 39n
Mothers, 319–329, 366
Mouat, Frederic J., 42
"Mr. Gilfil's Love Story," 126, 281
Murphy, Jeffrie G., 6n
Myers, F. W. H., 87
Myrdal, Gunnar, 72n

Nadel, Ira Bruce, 26n
Napoleon Bonaparte, 65, 310

Index

Index

Woolf, Virginia, 196n
"Worldliness and Other-Worldliness: The Poet Young," 122–123
Writing, 44, 47, 55–56, 113–117, 125, 126–127, 186–187, 233, 249–257, 275, 322–323

Yeats, William Butler, 173
Yeazell, Ruth Bernard, 152n
Young, Edward, 122–123

Zionism, 308–309, 311–312